The Poet's Craft

Richard Eberhart

Karl Shapiro

Allen Ginsberg

Erica Jong

Amiri Baraka

Robert Penn Warren

James Dickey

The
POET'S CRAFT

INTERVIEWS FROM *THE NEW YORK QUARTERLY*

Edited by William Packard

 PARAGON HOUSE PUBLISHERS
New York

Published in the United States by
Paragon House Publishers
2 Hammarskjöld Plaza
New York, New York 10017

Library of Congress Cataloging-in-Publication Data

The Poet's Craft

 Rev. ed. of: The Craft of Poetry. 1st ed. 1974.
  1. Poets, American—20th century—Interviews.
2. Poetics. I. Packard, William. II. New York
Quarterly. III. Craft of poetry.
PS135.P3 1986 811'.5409 86-22643
ISBN 0-913729-30-2
ISBN 0-913729-55-8 (pbk.)

Interviews

Foreword

William Packard's earlier version of this book, THE CRAFT OF POETRY, was published by Doubleday in 1974. The book, featuring seventeen poets, proved valuable to a broad public of general readers, established poets, and fledgling writers. No other collection of interviews focused similarly on the actual craft of writing. It has long been out of print.

Packard's new collection includes thirteen poets from the earlier book plus twelve additional poets, all featured in issues of THE NEW YORK QUARTERLY. In general the editor opts for poets with large reputations. Most of the new voices included here belong to highly visible poets—Gary Snyder, Karl Shapiro, Robert Penn Warren, Amiri Baraka, W.D. Snodgrass, Charles Bukowski, Richard Eberhart, and May Swenson. Less well-known are Leo Connellan, Helen Adam, and Michael Moriarity. This is a varied stable—traditional, ethnic, projective verse, streetwise, and academic poets. There's a premium on maturity—Eberhart, Warren, Shapiro, and Adam are well on in years. Moriarity is the youngster of the lot.

The editor's intent is clearly to present the state of poetry now, as practiced by a baker's two-dozen of our best known writers. Including no unknown writers, he's not adventuresome and seems uninterested in experimental writers, or in any of the so-called language poets. This is not, in other words, a book for shaping taste; rather, it is a record of where we have been and where we are. It provides views of the Parnassian peaks for that host of poets, critics, and readers clustered on the lower slopes. Packard and his assistants have done their homework; they have read the poets' works and have set the trap with the right bait to generate excellent responses. Little time is wasted. Since these are writers with reputations, there is no need to provide much background. There is no idle chatter, pettiness, arrogance, stupidity, or prima donna turns. Nor do the interviewers use the occasion for self-advertisement or showing off. No poet sounds ill-at-ease or bored. All seem enthusiastic, desiring to give their best to the interviewers' questions. Bukowski alone seems curmudgeonly. Of the interviews, he says, "I haven't learned anything . . . except that the poets were studious, trained, self-assured and obnoxiously self-important. I don't think that I was ever able to finish an interview; the print began to blur and the trained seals vanished below the surface."

Work habits are described—few poets appear to have a fixed writing schedule. This should cheer young poets anxiously displeased with their own dilatoriness. Most poets revise much—and if this book is adopted in writing workshops (as it deserves to be), it should do much to demolish the idea, common to apprentice poets, that first drafts are "inspired" and hence, must not be changed. Here is Anne Sexton on the matter: "How do I write? Expand, expand, cut, cut, expand, expand, cut, cut. Do not trust spontaneous first drafts. You can always write more fully. The beautiful feeling after writing a poem is on the whole better even than after sex, and that's saying a lot." Ginsberg is one of the exceptions; he uses "as little revision as possible. The craft, the art consists in paying attention to the actual movie of the mind. Writing it down is like a by-product of that. If you can actually keep track of your own head movie, then the writing it down is just like a secretarial job, and who gets crafty about that?"

Attitudes towards formal poetry vary—most of Packard's poets respect the great formalist tradition of English (and American) verse. They feel that any professional must know rules in order to depart from them. Most insist that poets must read, and read, and read, not only their contemporaries, but writers from the past. The quasi-trance appears to be an ideal state for "receiving" poems. Although the writer is rare who will own up to a traditional belief in the supernatural, most believe in "mystery" and "dictation." Few see hallucinogenics or booze as useless for writing. For most, social commitments are logical extensions of their poet roles. Some, like Ginsberg, Levertov, Snyder, and Baraka, have devoted much creative energy to world issues. One of the dissenting views is James Dickey's. He blasts Robert Bly and Allen Ginsberg for using poetry as "an occasion for making Bohemian speeches." He continues: "If you go to a reading by Ginsberg . . . you hear all this applause, say, where he works in material about Bobby Seale and the Chicago trial and the political conventions and that sort of business—and the audience applauds wildly—they're applauding themselves for holding the currently fashionable social and political opinions that this guy gets up and tells 'em about. That has nothing to do with poetry."

Many poets talk frankly about their states of mind. Galway Kinnell and Muriel Rukeyser are the frankest of all. Kinnell suffers immobiliz- ing periods of depression. Rukeyser endured "terrible" depressions. During these times she tried to keep writing—if none of her own work came she turned to translation. Paul Blackburn, too, found translation helpful whenever his own reservoir was dry. Richard Wilbur is reassuring: "One advantage of getting older is that you have been through it before and before and before: though it doesn't do very much good, you can tell yourself that you will come out of it, that you will write again, and therefore you can stay somewhat this side of despair."

In addition to all the helpful conversations on the creative process itself, there are valuable insights into specific works by these poets. With his usual verve and intelligence Ginsberg details key influences on HOWL and other poems. Kinnell discusses his use of motifs from nature, as they appear in his best work. Ashbery is fascinated by music and philosophy and provides hints for reading THE SKATERS. Dickey analyzes images from THE LIFEGUARD and THE MOVEMENT OF FISH.

Most of these writers have been or still are teachers. While they may express a jaundiced view of writing workshops, most find contact with young poets stimulating, a means of keeping in touch with younger ideas. Diane Wakoski, who has visited numerous colleges as Writer in Residence, and who is on the permanent faculty of Michigan State University, has thought more deeply than most teaching poets about teaching. Here is her advice on reading as it relates to learning one's craft: "I think the way you learn craft is the same way you learn criticism. And that is by reading everything that you can find. I don't think you learn any kind of discrimination if you only read masterpieces . . . it's not until you read about a hundred more pieces that are nothing like masterpieces. . . .[When] you suddenly recognize how badly written they are, you have already learned some craft." W.D. Snodgrass, an enthusiastic mentor of writing workshops, and himself a product of Iowa's famous writing program, wonders whether the craft of poetry can be "taught." At Syracuse where he teaches, he values much reading aloud of both student and traditional poems. He says that you can teach somebody to write, but not anybody: "Again, there are people who will get it without being taught, or will teach themselves, or will find different methods of instruction. . . . One way or another you learn your art from your predecessors, from other people, usually slightly older people working in your art form."

This is exactly what the THE CRAFT OF POETRY provides, an atmosphere in which our leading poets expatiate on their art, providing that rare commingling possible only within the covers of a book—a true community of poets. The feast is substantial, and all poets, young and old, will find much to excite them here. William Packard has done much to redeem that much abused genre, the literary interview.

Robert Peters
Huntington Beach, California

Introduction

We live in the age of the interview. Moderators interview celebrities on TV talk shows, newsmen interview presidents at press conferences, and young people interview each other to see if they want to sleep together. Everywhere one turns, everyone is busy interviewing everyone else. There has never been such a passion to verbalize the world around us: there are panel discussions, encounter groups, workshops, seminars, symposiums, committee meetings and public hearings. All this talk talk talk talk talk must come from some very deep insecurity at the source of things. And of course, there is the danger that charisma may take the place of character, and chatter may take the place of matter.

So it is no wonder if the practising poet, caught up in an unreal world of words, may seek to keep his own counsel. For he alone knows that whatever is deeply intuitive cannot really be revealed except in rhythms and images. He may even feel that talking itself is a distraction from true communication. As Thoreau wrote in WALDEN: "Speech is for the convenience of the hard of hearing." And so the poet may choose to retreat from a Babel of tongues, and obey THE SERMON ON THE MOUNT, when it says very simply:

But let your communication be, Yea, yea; Nay, nay: for whatsoever is more than these cometh of evil.

Even so: there will always be a good deal of legitimate curiosity about poetry, and the poet will always be asked certain questions by readers who are eager to learn more about the art. It seems inevitable, then, that the poet should submit himself to be interviewed, along with everyone else in our universe.

Very well, then, but what kind of interview? There are interviews, and there are interviews.

James Joyce in ULYSSES said that Shakespeare is the happy hunting ground for all minds that have lost their balance, and we can well imagine the sort of interviews which Shakespeare would be subjected to, if he were to return among us today. Because there are certain classic approaches might manifest themselves in relation to Master William Shakespeare.

First, there would be the "Professorial Interview." This approach would try to clear up a lot of pesky questions about subtexts and footnotes in the various works. For example:

What is the correct spelling of your name? Why did you spell it differently on different documents? Or are you really Francis Bacon? In that case, did you hide a biliteral cipher in any of your plays? If so, what is the secret key to reading it?

You have Hamlet say: "O that this too too solid flesh would melt". Instead of "solid flesh", what do you think of the variant quarto reading "sullied flesh"? Or what about the German critic Himmelbummer who suggested "soiled fish"? How about the 1807 edition reading of "salad flash"? Would you believe "smelly flush"?

Who was the third murderer in MACBETH? Why did you drop Donalbain from the plot? And whatever happens to Fleance? And why did you never dispose of the three weird sisters? Were you saving these characters for another play? Is this a lost manuscript?

Here we can imagine Shakespeare might smile, shrug, and give a few mechanical answers. These questions would not be of any great concern to him, any more than they would be to most of his readers.

Then, there would be the "Opinionated Interview." This line of questioning would focus attention on the subject's political, religious, and socio-economic attitudes. For example:

Introduction

Shakespeare, do you believe in God? Or would you characterize yourself as a skeptic? A freethinker maybe? An agnostic? An atheist? Did you belong to the Church of England? If not, why not?

What were your feelings about Queen Elizabeth? King James? What did you feel about the Essex uprising? What about his beheading? Were you sympathetic with the notion of civil disobedience, when it is warranted?

Are you in favor of constitutional monarchy? What do you feel about the concept of republican democracy? Christian socialism? Marxist communism? Freudian psychoanalysis?

Here we can imagine Shakespeare telling the interviewer that, for heaven's sakes, he had gone to some considerable pains during his lifetime to try and stay away from the various political and social arenas of his day, so he could remain relatively anonymous and try to practise his art with as much autonomy as possible. Wasn't that enough?

And then, there would be the "Gossipy Interview". This line of questioning would dwell on Shakespeare's personality and his extra-poetic activities. For example:

What was Anne Hathaway like in bed? Did you recite poetry to her when the lights were out? And what did she do with herself back there in Stratford while you were off working in London?

Who was the Dark Lady of Sonnets? Who was the young man? Did you ever have any homosexual experiences? If not, why not? If so, did you enjoy them?

What did you and Ben Jonson talk about in the Mermaid Tavern? What did you drink? Could you both hold your malt? Who picked up the tab?

Here, we can imagine Shakespeare might simply scowl and tell the interviewer to go to hell.

Finally, there would be the "Craft Interview". This line of questioning would try to discuss the circumstances of an artist's work, and not the work itself. And it would try to restrict its questions to those which might occur to a practising writer. For example:

Your rate of writing comes to about 2 plays a year, and that means that in some years you wrote plays like HAMLET and THE MERRY WIVES OF WINDSOR both in the same year. Did you ever feel any special problem in switching over from one type of play to another? Did you prefer doing one type of play, so far as the actual writing was concerned? Did your work habits vary, from comedy to tragedy to history?

Was Ben Jonson right when he said you never blotted out a single word? Was there no revision? How much work did you do in your head before you began setting it all down?

Keats tried to imagine the physical situation of your writing. Did you always sit at a desk, or could you sometimes compose lying down, or walking late at night through the streets of London?

Here, we can imagine Shakespeare giving matter-of-fact answers to the questions, because they are, after all, the sort of specific things which would concern him as a practising poet.

And these are, in fact, the sort of questions we try to pursue in our NYQ Craft Interviews. With a profound respect for the innate privacy of a poet's own intuition, we try to approach the matter with as much tact and practicality as possible.

Granted, the poets we choose to interview will sometimes try to inundate us with their own opinions, professorial tidbits, footnotes, socio-economic theories, or plain gossip about themselves. But not as a rule. Usually they are grateful that we are that interested in their true identities as craftsmen poets.

Following are guidelines we have been using for NYQ Craft Interviews since the very first issue:

In approaching a craft interview, of course there is no substitute for a solid grounding in the work of the poet being interviewed, a familiarity with his own poems and his stated views on poetry, etc. The interview itself will reflect this familiarity if there are specific citations of sections of the work of the poet, which can serve as a basis for discussion between interviewer and poet. Ideally this discussion should be more in the form of an intercourse than a "question and answer" approach which sometimes feels more like a game of ping pong. The questions below, then, are meant more as general suggestions of areas that might be covered with specific reference to the poet's own work, rather than as prescribed "questions" which must be asked at each and every interview:

Introduction

1. Would you describe the physical conditions of writing your poetry? Are you always at a desk? Do you do first drafts on typewriter or with pencil or with pen? On what kind of paper? As poems progress, what do you do with worksheets that you no longer need?

2. When you are away from your desk or writing area, do you carry a notebook with you? What do you do with thoughts or impulses that come to you when you are unable to record them easily?

3. What would you say about revision? Is it a creative act with you? Have you written anything that did not need extensive revision? Do you have any special procedure for revising a poem?

4. What do you feel is the value of the poetry workshop for a young poet? Did you take any when you were beginning to write poetry? What do you feel about student criticism of each other's work?

5. Do you ever experience a dry period in writing, and if so what do you do about it?

6. Do you ever play games with the craft of poetry, prosody, for the fun of it, or for what it might lead to? Anagrams, palindromes, etc?

7. What do you feel about the need for isolation in the life of a writer? How does it affect personal relationships? Professional activities such as teaching?

8. Have you ever received lines of poetry which you were unable to incorporate into a poem? What would you do with them, as a rule?

9. If a poet is about to fall asleep and suddenly thinks of an interesting poem or some interesting lines for a poem, what should he do?

10. What reference books do you feel are useful for a young poet to have on his desk, for consultation?

11. Do you feel we live in a particularly permissive age so far as education and discipline in craft are concerned, and if so, what

effect is this having on the present state of poetry being written today?

12. What poet do you feel would be a good model for a young writer to begin learning about poetry?

—William Packard

1

W.H. Auden

Q: *What poets influenced the craft and form of your early work?*

A: I have always been a formalist. Now that I look back on it, I suppose the first poet I admired was Thomas Hardy. Then I went on to Edward Thomas. I read Frost before many others knew him.

Q: *What poets influence your work now?*

A: I'm reading a lot of medieval stuff. Like everybody, one has one's pets. Mine are Thomas Campian and William Barnes—both are minor poets but I adore them. Obviously, one doesn't need to mention the greats. I tend not to read much contemporary work. I am now on a Horace jag.

Q: *What musicians or composers do you admire?*

A: I was brought up on Bach. Later, I developed a love for Wagner and Schumann. You go through composers as people you will love in the same way you do poets. But one can't be influenced as a poet by a composer because they are two different arts.

Q: *Have you ever played a musical instrument?*

A: I play the piano very badly, not for other people to hear.

Q: *Have you ever been in a workshop situation, and what are your feelings about workshops?*

A: No, I've never been in a workshop. This is something quite peculiar to America. At Oxford, naturally one knew other people who wrote, and we used to read to each other. When I was there it was quite a small place—only four thousand including the girls. In a big city I suppose you have to plan these things.

Q: *How much teaching have you done? Do you think teaching helps or hinders one's own creative work?*

A: I have taught all ages, from seven to seventy. I spent three years at Swarthmore. To earn my living, I started teaching boys from seven to fourteen, which is the age I prefer to teach because you can do something then, can give them standards and a sense of their own capabilities. When they are older, twenty or so, they have to do it for themselves. By that age, one should be able to say, "This book will interest you."
Obviously one needs help with Chaucer or Milton, but I am always surprised when students want to have courses in modern literature. In England we read these for ourselves—the whole fun was in discovering for oneself. I have always refused to teach modern literature. It does affect my writing. Contemporary literature comes too near what one does.

Q: *What about poetry readings?*

A: I like doing it if one gets into it; it is something quite different. The thing you have to be careful about is not to try and think of a style of writing that is too declamatory. There are 500 people out there in the audience, but they are thinking of you as speaking to one person.

Q: *Do you find, after you've written criticism, that your own poems may break some of the rules you've set down?*

A: No, I stick by whatever my principles are. I make it a rule only to review books that I basically like. In negative reviews, there is a certain malice. Reviewing books one doesn't like especially may be witty, but it isn't very useful. If one is right about a book, time will take care of it. If one is wrong, one will look a fool later. Bad art is bad in a particular way that is characteristic of the times.

Q: *Which critics do you find most useful for their craft principles?*

A: There are certain critics I owe a great deal to—Auerbach, Spitzer, C. S. Lewis, Valéry. They are good critics. And then, of course, Chesterton. Nobody reads him, now. I'm doing a selection of his non-fiction prose.

Q: *Do you feel in your own work there is a major area of strength? The visual, the aural, or the conceptual?*

A: I don't know whether these areas are separable. All I know is the way I work, and I imagine others do the same. I have two things working—some kind of theme, and certain formal problems —metrical structure, diction. The language looks for the subject, and the subject finds the language.

Q: *Do you ever play games with craft, write poems in specific forms more for the joy of writing than for the content?*

A: Anyone interested in form has to do this in a way. Everybody knows if you play a game you have to have rules. I would find it ghastly dull not to have some kind of formal thing. The fun of games is always present, but you have to have something to say as well.

Q: *Do you revise much?*

A: I do an enormous amount of revising. I think of that quote from Valéry, "A poem is never finished, only abandoned." Some people feel revisions have idealogical significance. I revise if I feel the language is prolix or obscure. Your first idea is not always your best.

Q: *Do you ever revise published poetry?*

A: Constantly. In my COLLECTED POEMS, a lot of the poems have been radically revised.

Q: *In SEPTEMBER 1, 1939, you revised one line ("We must love one another or die"), and then omitted the entire stanza in which this line occurs.*

A: I have scrapped the whole poem. I took out that section, then I decided the whole thing had to go. I will put it this way: I don't think a writer can decide how good or bad something he writes is. What he can tell, though, is whether the poem is authentic, really written in his own hand. I decided this poem is unauthentic as far as I am concerned. It may have certain merits but I should not have written it.

Q: *By rejecting entire poems outright, you must be arriving at a definition of your own style.*

A: You can see in the COLLECTED SHORT POEMS what I have removed. It is different from revising poems. When one revises, one

3

is not revising emotions, but reworking the language. But the poems I decided were unauthentic went out. There was something false about them. The others which I have revised a great deal had more a question of language.

Q: *In* SEPTEMBER 1, 1939 *there is the line, "Find what occurred at Linz"—which raises the question of specific reference, whether the reader should be expected to know that Linz was where Hitler spent his childhood years.*

A: There is a terrible problem with proper names. Poets in older times had half the work done for them. Proper names were in poetry. Everyone knew them. Where I have used them, editors have glossed them. In one extreme case in a poem written, I suppose, in 1934, I referred to Garbo, and I was sure that everyone knew who she was. But an editor glossed the name, dropped a footnote. I thought everyone knew it, you see. I never was tempted to add a gloss to anything I've done. If a person does know it, the gloss looks rather superior: "You poor thing, you wouldn't know it."

Q: *A poet like Marianne Moore footnotes her work scrupulously.*

A: It is a sort of joke with her. I don't know when she does it, it really helps you to understand the poem. She is scrupulously honest. She will quote an idea from someone, then gloss it; it is a matter of literary honesty.

Q: *Can you work with music in the room?*

A: No. I must have silence. I work in my study upstairs. I cannot work when people I know are about, but I can work in a cafeteria, if there's no music and no one I know, and it's quiet. The people there might be cows or trees.

Q: *Do you like to show unpublished work to friends?*

A: Yes, to people whose judgment I value, who can see something is uncertain. They have to be poets because other people's comments wouldn't be useful. They wouldn't be able to put their finger on what was wrong.

Q: *Do you ever write with a specific person or type of person in mind?*

A: One writes an occasional poem for a specific audience. One can only say one writes a poem for people who read it. One hopes for someone who will like it.

4

Q: *Do you feel that translating affects the technique and content of your poems?*

A: I happen to enjoy doing it. Theoretically, it is impossible. One has to try. But apart from the fun of doing it, I do feel that translating is good to do. You always find out something about your own language. For example, you get into the habit of asking what does it mean? It causes us to notice the decline in the preciseness of language. I was six when I started Latin, and nine when I started Greek.

Q: *What do you do with single lines that you haven't been able to use in a poem?*

A: I jot down lines which I intend to use at some time or other. They are more apt to be words than lines.

Q: *Do you keep a journal?*

A: No, I don't keep a diary. That's more for novelists. All one puts down are things about the weather, or what happened in the garden, or when the first snow peas arrived. The lives of writers are not very interesting. The relationship between life and art is so obvious that nothing need be said and so complicated that nothing can be said. When Catullus wrote a love poem to whatever-her-name-was, no doubt you can see what is going on, but you can't find out why he wrote that particular poem. Investigations about the poem itself are necessary to tell me why that poem is any good. What I object to is simply keyhole peeping which is then called scholarship. About two years ago, there was a biography of Lytton Strachey. Some of the letters in this work were his private business. Why should anyone see them?

Q: *Do you ever need periods of isolation to work on your poems?*

A: Some of the day one must be alone. I am a lot of the time by myself. I don't go out much. But I don't seek this.

Q: *What about extended periods, periods of withdrawal from other activities?*

A: No. The need for isolation isn't a problem.

Q: *In your work, have you established a pattern of writing, a time and a place which are most conducive to productivity?*

A: I like to work in the mornings, also between tea and cocktails. I never work after dinner. Obviously, it's difficult to work if you are moving around. Most of my work I do in the summer, in Austria. There is no phone and it is nice.

Q: *Does a foreign environment influence the kind of poems you write?*

A: How can I tell? You are away from your native language. I share the house with a friend and we talk English. I happen to be fond of German as a language.

Q: *Living now in New York, do you find yourself getting images specifically related to the city?*

A: Yes, one picks up images. That obviously one does.

Q: *What sort of work are you engaged in now, and what are you planning for the future?*

A: My own view is that you never talk about what you are doing—what you have done, but not what you are up to. I'm very superstitious.

Q: *What books of craft would you recommend that poets keep on their shelves?*

A: Saintsbury's A HISTORY OF ENGLISH PROSODY. All thirteen volumes of the OXFORD ENGLISH DICTIONARY. I have two sets, one in Austria and one here.

Q: *What advice do you have for young poets?*

A: You have to see their work, really. I have no advice in general for these people except to read fairly widely. It is necessary for a young writer to find his own models, the kind of language that may go through any period. On the whole, I am not in favor of one's reading very much criticism. When one is starting out it is not good.

Q: *Can you tell us something of the origin of* THE RAKE'S PROGRESS?

A: I can tell you about that quite clearly. I got a message from Stravinsky that he wanted to write an opera on the subject of THE RAKE'S PROGRESS. I went to see him and wanted to find out about it. He was looking at the Hogarth engravings, one of them a figure of a

6

blind fiddler playing on one string, another of them in a brothel. The difficulty is that if you take Hogarth's engravings, what he gives you is the picture of low life in eighteenth century London, and the only central figure is the Rake, and he has no story. We had to work to invent a story, and keep certain things intact, and everything else had to be changed. There was a problem in doing a character of a young man who always yields to temptation, who is a passive character, who still has speeches. So we gave him a sort of Mephisto, who would suggest things. Then we made him into a manic depressive so that he had a kind of emotional range.

Q: *What are your feelings about the level of technical competence today?*

A: There is a reaction against competence. And there is a lack of interest in the past which seems to be growing. But what one wonders at, at present, is that with all these young people, one cannot be distinguished from another.

Q: *There seems to be a reaction today against form. Now, your work had a tremendous influence on the technical competence of the forties and fifties—*

A: Did it? I wouldn't know about that. But there is a reaction now against form, and I wonder if there is any virtue in the reaction. We shall see. It may be I am getting old and can't get used to new things.

Q: *The two elegies that you wrote, on Freud and Yeats, seem to be more general as elegies than, say, elegies like* LYCIDAS *or* ADONAIS.

A: Those elegies of mine are not poems of grief. Freud I never met, and Yeats I only met casually and didn't particularly like him. Sometimes a man stands for certain things, which is quite different from what one feels in personal grief.

Q: *To what extent do you feel a poet ought to be engaged in social or philosophical or political issues?*

A: One must be engaged. All I see is that poetry can do nothing about it. I do not think that writing poems will change anything. I think Dr. Johnson was right when he said the aim of writing is to enable readers a little better to enjoy life or a little better to endure it. Would it really have been any different if all those great artists had never lived—Dante, Shakespeare, Mozart, Goethe, Beethoven? Simply talking in terms of social, political, or historical things, I don't think I would say it would. There are exceptional places—in a country like Russia, where they have never had a free press. Sometimes a

7

writer can say something within a political framework, and you don't hear it from anyone else.

Q: *Would you tell us something about the "shorts" you have given us to publish in* THE NEW YORK QUARTERLY?

A: They are accentual elegaic couplets. It is a recent interest of mine, I have never done it before.

Q: *In closing, we'd like you to comment on the fact that we're not planning to run any book reviews in our new magazine. Perhaps an occasional review of a technical prosody book, but no reviews of poetry books as such.*

A: I find that interesting because my only complaint when I am reviewed is the critic's lack of knowledge. The one thing I am vain about is my knowledge of meters. I do think a reviewer should know his job. I look to see how a poem is made before I think what it says. Then I begin to read it.

2

Paul Blackburn

Q: *What poets have influenced your work?*

A: W. H. Auden was an early influence. My mother sent me a copy of his COLLECTED POEMS when I was in the Army. When I was nineteen, I could write a pretty good Auden poem, and I feel that I picked up a formal sense of musical structure from him. In college I began to read Ezra Pound. His PERSONAE, not to mention the CANTOS, was an incredible revelation to me as to what you could do in terms of making music with different line lengths, and how rhythm could be so rich and varied. I think I learned a lot of my ear from reading Pound. At the same time I was studying Pound, I was picking up influences from my contemporaries—Robert Creeley, Charles Olson, and Cid Corman. I was learning to strip my style of as much as I could and get down to very simple statements, while still keeping it reasonably musical. I think a lot of the William Carlos Williams influence came to me, not through Williams so much as through Williams' influence on Creeley. In a review of my first book, the critic blamed both Creeley and me on Williams. I thought, "Oh, wow! I've got to read Williams!" So I got hold of PATERSON, and what was then his COLLECTED POEMS. I wanted to find out where my influences were coming from. I wanted to find out who my father was.

Q: *Those contemporaries you mentioned—Creeley, Olson, Corman —didn't you all form the Black Mountain School of poetry?*

9

A: Black Mountain doesn't do it at all as a label, because presumably it should apply to the people who either studied or taught at Black Mountain College, and it doesn't. Robert Duncan taught at the college and contributed to THE BLACK MOUNTAIN REVIEW, but he really can't be considered to be Black Mountain. He's much more musical than many of the Black Mountain people. And he doesn't necessarily work from speech rhythms—he's more formal. Mostly what this Black Mountain thing is all about is what we were all working at—speech rhythm, composition by field, or something from that set of ideas. By 1951, Olson had tied a lot of it together in that "Projective Verse" essay. So we even had a set of principles to keep in our heads. But this is not to say that we were developing similar styles. Does Creeley write like Olson; does Olson write like Denise Levertov? In the end, every poet is an individual, and if you can group them it's because they drink together once in a while.

Q: *You said that you "learned a lot of your ear from reading Pound." Your ear must play a great part in the writing of your poetry.*

A: Certainly the ear is a prime judge of what I've accomplished or have not accomplished. I wouldn't even know whether a poem was finished or not unless my ear told me. I think music must be in the poem somewhere. Poetry is traditionally a musical structure. Now that forms are as open as they are, each poem has to find its own form. It has to do with the technique of juxtaposition and reading from the breath line and normal speech raised to its highest point. But that's abstracting a principle. When you're writing, these things are at the back of it. It's almost as though your technique is in your wrists and you're sitting at a typewriter instead of at a piano. As far as I'm concerned, people who don't hear the poems are missing a good deal, and a poet who doesn't hear his own poems is missing everything. He's got to hear his own voice saying it. It's got to come off the page in a way that concrete poetry cannot.

Q: *What do you feel about concrete poetry?*

A: Concrete poems are not written to be read aloud, they're written as objects. In other words, they have to stay on the page. It has to do with the arrangement of sounds and words, of their interpolations or their extrapolations, how they mix or cross. I mean, it's there on the page, whatever the joke is. And basically it is a game.

It can be a particularly beautiful game or a fairly dull one, depending on who's playing it.

Q: *Do you play that kind of game?*

A: No, I've never been able to stand crossword puzzles, anagrams, that kind of thing.

Q: *What purpose does punctuation and indentation serve in your poetry?*

A: Punctuation serves much the way that spacing does—that is, to indicate the length of a pause. For example, if there is a space between the last letter of a word and the period, the pause is longer than it would be if the period were right beside the last letter. If there is a period, the pause is longer than it would be if there were no punctuation and you moved over to the left margin to pick up the next line. There is a longer pause between the end of the line and the left margin than there is between the end of the line and the succeeding line picking up in the middle or three-quarters of the way through the line. And certainly even less of a pause (because this is the way the eye runs) if it moves to the end of the line and simply drops off and continues on the next line. So you're using the common way of reading to control the speed of the words as read.

Q: *What importance does form have in your work?*

A: Strict form is by no means a necessity. Quite the opposite, each poem must find its own music, its own form. It's much harder to do that than to write quatrains all the time.

Q: *How do you respond to criticism?*

A: It depends on who's doing the criticizing. If it's someone like Cid Corman, I'll listen, I'll consider it seriously, even if I think he's dead wrong. But there aren't many editors or critics who are in his category. He's a solid man. You wouldn't dare send him anything but your best work.

Q: *Have you published any criticism?*

A: I've written two articles for KULCHUR. One was an analysis of the whole Black Mountain thing, the other was about Robert Kelly. I consider Kelly to be a great poet. As a matter of fact, I considered him to be a great poet before he was thirty, and there aren't many people

11

who are willing to make that kind of statement about a man who is under thirty. But I'm an amateur, I'm no professional critic. Anyway, I hate writing prose—I've never taken any pleasure in writing it.

Q: *Do you feel that poetry workshops are useful?*

A: It depends on the student and what he's ready for. Certainly, to be in a group of people working together is often a very valuable experience for a young person. Not only what he may get in the way of advice from his instructor, but also the reactions of his contemporaries. However, it can be completely useless if a writer not only feels cut off, but wants to feel cut off, and insists on cutting himself off. He'll have a miserable time in the workshop because part of the learning process does depend not only upon his easy relationship to his instructor (and presumably the instructor has something to say that will be of use), but also upon his not building his defenses so great that he can't move past where he is. If he's already got his head set and he doesn't want to break it—if he wants to stand there and prove how good he is to everybody then he's liable to get nowhere in the workshop. With such people it's sometimes useful just to blow their minds, to open them up and see what happens. So that's one value of a workshop—the opening up. Another value is giving the person a built-in audience. A young writer doesn't get a set of intelligent mirrors very often. Friends are something else. They may be helpful if they are themselves writers. Otherwise, they're liable to act as a dear reassurance which, God knows, is a necessity sometimes. But a workshop situation gives, at best, a fair cross section of a potential audience, lets you know if you're coming across—and how, and why.

Q: *Where do you write?*

A: Anywhere, anytime, when it hits me I write. I don't ask any questions. It can be dead silence, the kid (his six-month-old son, Carlos) can be screaming, I can be sitting on the subway during rush hour. You write when you have to write, when it comes to you. Some people need a formal circumstance around them in order to write. I don't. Neither do I schedule myself when I'm writing poetry. However, I do schedule my translating. Translation requires a steadier concentration. But getting back to the question, what happens when you're being dictated to and you don't know where the dictation is coming from? All you know is you have to sit down and write it and you may not know what the damn thing means when you're done. And somehow, later on, you find out where the piece belongs—either in a long poem, or as a separate piece.

Q: *Tell us something about your translations.*

A: I don't become the author when I'm translating his prose or poetry, but I'm certainly getting my talents into his hang-ups. Another person's preoccupations are occupying me. They literally own me for that time. You see, it's not just a matter of reading the language and understanding it and putting it into English. It's understanding something that makes the man do it, where he's going. And it's not an entirely objective process. It must be partially subjective; there has to be some kind of projection. How do you know which word to choose when a word may have four or five possible meanings in English? It's not just understanding the text. In a way you live it each time, I mean, *you're there*. Otherwise, you're not holding the poem.

Q: *How do you feel about writing in a travel situation?*

A: I think travel is an ideal situation in which to write. In a way there's a kind of spiritual and sensory vacuum present. Take the subway, for instance. People blank out, you see the dullest faces there. What are they thinking, what are they doing? They're going from here to there and nothing's happening to them. They'd be lucky to have their pockets picked, at least that would be something. So you see, the demands on you as to movement or thought or even personal contact are minimal. And I have an idea that a lot of things come to the surface in such a situation that might not otherwise get there. The only thing left to come into this vacuum is whatever is in your head at that particular moment. And although the subway is moving, you're stationary; you're always looking at the same thing. Then there's the sound, trolley cars, trains, wheels on the tracks, will set rhythms going in your head, a kind of ground-rhythm against which your own ear works, can turn you on, turn your voice into that emptiness. Buses also, especially on wet pavement. I always feel very sensual on buses, never so on planes; there's too much formality, all those chicks serving you drinks and food. I'd rather read or sleep or stare out the window at cloud formations. One is really stationary in a plane; you're being boxed or shipped, and the sound is a constant roar—no rhythm to it, and muted besides. Ginsberg wrote his Wichita Vortex Sutra on a plane, though, so we can't eliminate the possibility of that working for some people. Allen has a panvision of the world

13

anyway. John Keys has a couple of poems from an aircraft point of view. ". . . the clouds like a parking lot/sort of hump hump hump, if you see what I mean." It would be different on a boat because you could get up and walk around, vomit on the deck or something. At least there's a kind of personal movement on a boat which cannot be found on most other types of conveyances. It's not the boat that makes the waves, but where we are right now, as they say, the motion of the ocean. To come back to the city, though, the subway is an incredible place for girl-watching. You find one face or a good pair of legs—you can look at them for hours. You think, "Oh god, I hope she doesn't get off at 34th Street."

Q: *What do you do when you have a dry period, when you can't write?*

A: I don't get upset about it. As a matter of fact, I'm happy when I'm not writing. When I'm writing, I've got to work. Not that writing isn't a joy—it is at times, but there are great periods when I simply don't write anything, or very little. In a very real way I use translations to fill in that time, because I do enjoy translating, getting into other people's heads.

3
Anne Sexton

A: I have a terrible memory—it's all a mystery to me, it all just happens.

Q: *Do you revise much?*

A: Yes, I've revised as much as three hundred times on one lyric poem. The title of that poem was THE TRUTH THE DEAD KNOW. I showed it to Robert Lowell after I'd rewritten it fifty times. He said the ending wasn't right. I don't remember—I ended it with the dead saying something. He said the dead don't speak. The more I thought about it the more I agreed with him, and that's when I turned them into stone.

Q: *How long did you work on that poem?*

A: I don't remember how many months it took—maybe two. The poem, FLEA ON YOUR DONKEY—I rewrote that for four years. I hung onto it and revised it every six months. Everyone said it was a useless poem; even my best friend said, "It embarrasses me," and Cal Lowell said it was better to be a short story. I fussed with it and I played with it and I worked with it.

Q: *What physical conditions do you find best for revision?*

A: I think that would depend on the physical conditions of the

15

first writing. My play was written to music by Villa Lobos, and I put it on tape so I could play it all the while I was writing.

When the kids were young, I would turn on a symphony to make a constant noise to drown them out so I could work. I wrote the poem VISION APART TO SWAN LAKE. I often write in silence, too. I can't just have the radio on. Any talking distracts me. I like quiet. Once I tried to write a poem a day. I wrote for eighteen days. The kids would walk by my room and say, "Shhh, Mommy's writing a poem!"

Q: *What do you think is valuable about poetry workshops?*

A: They were very valuable to me. It's where I started. All you need is one friend to tell you to write a poem a day. It's not the criticism—it's the stimulation, the countered interest. It's a time to grow. My first workshop was with John Holmes in Boston, with George Starbuck and Maxine Kumin. If I'd gone to a real poetry workshop I'd have been scared. As it was, this was a friendly group. You'd always have enough ego to bring two poems. We all met once a month. We missed it very much when it ended.

Q: *Then you went on to study with Robert Lowell. Was this the beginning of your confessional poetry?*

A: At that time Lowell had not revealed what he was doing. He was very stern. He went line by line. Sometimes he would spend five minutes on a first line. It was line dissection. What was inspiring was that he would take a poem by a great poet and relate it to the workshop poem.

Q: *That must have been stimulation in an advanced sense.*

A: It was. Lowell introduced me to Lawrence, and to his own poetry. I came there at just the right time. I had TO BEDLAM AND PART WAY BACK almost finished, and he helped me to hold it down.

Q: *Why did you choose to write poetry?*

A: I haven't got the slightest idea. When I was eighteen or nineteen I wrote for half a year. One time I tried painting, but I wasn't good. When I was twenty-eight, I saw I. A. Richards on television. He was talking about the form of the sonnet, its images, and I thought, I can do that. I would like to be a photographer if the camera could work the way fingers work. I like to capture an instant. A picture is a one second thing—it's a fragile moment in time. I try to do it with words.

Q: *Do you ever play craft games with your poetry?*

A: I always call it tricks, not craft.

Craft is a trick you make up to let you write the poem. The only game I ever played was with the word Star. I did everything I could with the arrangement of S-T-A-R. Conrad Aiken once saw a palindrome on the side of a barn: Rats Live On No Evil Star (and I want that to be on my gravestone, because I see myself as a rat, but I live on no evil star). Rats and Star: I wrote a list of all the words I could make out of those letters. Then I sat down with the words and made up a poem. The game I do play is I say to myself, This poem is too hard to write. It is impossible for me, I can't do it. Then I start fooling around with some stanzas, running a syllable count. I use syllabics and rhyme. I get a good beginning to the poem. Then I say to myself, But I can't do the poem, it's too hard. I use this as a kind of super-ego. Then I proceed to do the poem. I make up the game, and then I don't follow it too carefully.

Games don't get me involved. It's always the content that gets me involved. I make up the game to go along with the content. I start every poem with a powerful emotion. I write in the morning. I use yellow paper, sometimes lined school paper. I write at the typewriter and make extensive corrections. I sit at a desk, my feet up on a bookcase. I have cigarettes, naturally, burned down to one long grey ash.

How do I write? Expand, expand, cut, cut, expand, expand, cut, cut. Do not trust spontaneous first drafts. You can always write more fully. The beautiful feeling after writing a poem is on the whole better even than after sex, and that's saying a lot.

Q: *How would you define confessional poetry?*

A: How would *you* define confessional poetry?

Q: *We'd probably say it was autobiographical—associated with a certain purgation, and sometimes classified as therapy.*

A: Was Thomas Wolfe confessional, or not? Any poem is therapy. The art of writing is therapy. You don't solve problems in writing. They're still there. I've heard psychiatrists say, "See, you've forgiven

17

your father. There it is in your poem." But I haven't forgiven my father. I just wrote that I did.

Q: *Do you feel a tension between the narrative impulse and the lyric impulse?*

A: I'm too rhythmic. You fight what you've got. I can't bear to be too rhythmical if I'm going to be confessional. I'm very fond of rhymes. I don't feel that off rhymes have the slam-it-home feeling of an on rhyme. Once in a while I use an off rhyme. I like double rhyme. Driving once into Boston, I suddenly thought that "cancer" rhymes with "answer." And so I wrote some lines. They are macabre, and yet it's an honest way of saying it. It makes it more real.

Q: *What do you do with lines that you can't use?*

A: I put them all on paper, and then I put them in my rejection drawer. It's usually a set of lines, not just one.

Q: *Does anything keep you away from poetry?*

A: Talking. Talking keeps you away from poetry. Not teaching, teaching keeps you close. I think I teach by instinct. I'm getting more vulgar in my old age. Now, what do I mean by "vulgar?" Not tasteless. Of the people. Common, is that it? Vernacular. A little less effete. Writing in the vulgate, but that sounds effete. We are being influenced now by South American poets, Spanish poets, French poets. We are much more image-driven as a result. Neruda is the great image-maker. The greatest colorist. Rilke is marvelous, but Neruda springs me loose, also Roethke. Images are the heart of poetry. And this is not tricks. Images come from the unconscious. Imagination and the unconscious are one and the same. You're not a poet without imagery.

Q: *To get images out of yourself you have to have a good relationship with yourself.*

A: Yes—no, look at Hart Crane. He didn't have a very good relationship with himself, but look at his images. That's why I say you have to start with Neruda. Literal translation is best. When I am translated I want just the images, never mind the syllables and the rhymes. I'm proud of them, of my images.

Q: *Since, for you, images are the most vital part of poetry, what painters do you feel closest to?*

Anne Sexton

A: I suppose Van Gogh, although that's sentimental to say—all the impressionists. Who was that wonderful man who painted all the jungle scenes? Rousseau.

Q: *How do you feel about concrete poetry?*

A: What is concrete poetry?

Q: *Poems that are reduced to basic elements, as letters, letters as pictorial symbols.*

A: A poem is spoken. A poem has to be spoken. I like it on the page, I like to see the stops of the lines.

Q: *How do you feel about public readings?*

A: I care very much about my audiences. They are very dear to me, but I hate giving readings. I feel I've revealed so much of myself anyway, in the language. People always say, "You do it all so gracefully," and so forth. I can just see myself retreating, wearing a big hat and hiding behind dark glasses.

4

Stanley Kunitz

Q: *A few years ago, many of our poets were also serious critics. Today there doesn't seem to be the same interest in critical theory that there was when Mr. Ransom, Mr. Winters, Mr. Brooks, and Mr. Warren—*

A: Oh well, it's part of the revolt against the establishment, which is also a revolt against conventions and standards, including critical standards.

Q: *And it seems also as if some poets are their own aestheticians, such as Mr. Olson. Now, does this take part of a poet's energy, part of what used to be given to him?*

A: Yes, but on the other hand it means that the possibilities are more open; that nobody is required to write in the prevailing style or in the voice of the master. The danger, of course, is in thinking that anything goes in the new dispensation.

Q: *Perhaps there will be a swing back; perhaps there will be new criticism after this period is over.*

A: I suspect there will be. These are energetic and confusing times. There will have to be an evaluation of the work of a whole generation. In fact, it is already happening—look at the spate of freshly minted anthologies. I note, by the way, that reputations are being shuffled faster than ever.

Stanley Kunitz

Q: *This must be one of the freest periods of your whole career, in terms of what can be done.*

A: Freer than ever—but tied to the same old carcass! Incidentally, I can't think of it as a career. To me it's a life.

Q: *Mr. Auden has complained about the abuses of this period, that there seems to be a lack of interest in history on the part of some young poets, a lack of interest in meter, in craft, in prosody. He was very concerned, distressed.*

A: Who will be left to admire his great craft? When I first began to teach, in the late 40s, it seemed quite obvious that instruction in prosody was part of a workshop discipline. Today the young are mostly indifferent to such matters; not only indifferent but even strongly antipathetic. They praise novelty, spontaneity, and ease, and they resist the very concept of form, which they relate to mechanism and chains. Few understand that, for a poet, even breathing comes under the heading of prosody.

Q: *You once said that the originality of any poetry consists to a large degree in the poet's finding his own key images, those that go back to his roots and traumas. Can a poet talk about these images?*

A: Not unless he's very sick, or very foolish. Some poets are both. One oughtn't to try to explain everything away, even if one could. It's enough to reconcile oneself to the existence of an image from which one never gets very far. No matter how one turns or where one travels in the mind, there inescapably it is, sending out vibrations —and you know it's waiting, waiting to be seized again.

Q: *Several years ago, you said that certain themes—those of the quest, the night journey, and death and rebirth—preoccupied you.*

A: I must have been reading Jung then. Those are archetypes built into the structure of the mind.

Q: *In discussing* FATHER AND SON *in the Ostroff book (*THE CONTEMPORARY POET AS ARTIST AND CRITIC*), you referred to your sister, and to the big house on the hill, and you said, "They belong to that part of my life which I keep trying to rework into legend." What does that mean?*

A: What the alchemists meant when they spoke of converting dross into gold.

Q: *The voice in the poem you call simply* POEM *is intensely personal, and at the same time the events described have a sense of universal myth behind them.*

A: When I wrote that poem I was young and ignorant. But even then, as now, I wanted to get below the floor of consciousness, to wipe off the smudge of the day. The poems I like best, I suppose, are the ones that are steeped in "the taste of self"—Hopkins' phrase. Such poems are hard fought for.

Q: *What do you feel about improvisations, about randomness as a prime creative principle?*

A: My advice to myself is, Trust in your luck, but don't trust in it absolutely. I recall that after a couple of excruciating experiences as an amateur mycologist, John Cage saw that though the principle of chance operations was good enough for his music, it could not be extended to his mushroom-hunting without killing him. Was he aware of the irony implicit in that revelation? Maybe he didn't pursue his insight far enough.

Q: *So far, THE NEW YORK QUARTERLY is more or less dependent on the quality of the poems that are submitted to us. What do you feel about the level of the poems that are appearing in the Quarterly, and what should we do to improve the quality? We're always looking for that one poem that will be "below the floor of consciousness," as you have said.*

A: Standards were easier to maintain in an aristocratic society. Emerson said somewhere that democracy descends to meet. All the modern arts are being threatened by the cult of the amateur. And being nourished, too. You have to know the difference between naiveté and simplicity, novelty and originality, rhetoric and passion. The most insidious enemy of the good is not so much the bad as it is the second-best. I mean particularly, in this context, the inferior productions of first-rate reputations. Anyone can see that we have plenty of talent around—what civilization had more? The trouble is that our gifts are not being used well. On the face of it, our literature reflects a mediocre or silly age, sometimes an angry one. When are we going to wake up to the fact that it's tragic?

Q: *Have you had any experience with editing, with magazines?*

A: The only magazine I ever edited, after the Classical High School, ARGUS (Worcester, Mass.), was a library periodical. But last year I became editor of the YALE SERIES OF YOUNGER POETS, succeeding the late Dudley Fitts. That means reading some 500 book-length manuscripts a year. Nobody believes me, but I actually make an effort to read every one of them, though not necessarily every page. It's a responsibility I refuse to unload on others, because—who knows? —the most miraculous, most original work of all might get weeded out in the first round, as sometimes happens in competitions of this kind. At least half the submissions can be put aside at once as hopelessly inept or maudlin—usually both. It isn't asking much of a manuscript that it prove reasonably competent and tolerably readable, but I've learned that no more than 100 out of the 500 can be expected to pass that test. Eventually it becomes clear that there are only three or four manuscripts, maybe, in the lot from which any sort of fire breaks each time you turn to them. As far as I am concerned, these finalists are all winners, and I wish the rules of the game didn't require me to make an arbitrary choice. I have always hated the business of ranking poets. What was it Blake said? "I cannot think that Real Poets have any competition. None are greatest in the Kingdom of Heaven."

Q: *You have said that you used to play technical games, and do craft exercises. Have any of your poems come out of one of those games?*

A: Not that I can recall. But, of course, there is a game element in all poetry. In the very act of writing a poem one is playing with language, playing with the capacities of the mind to hold together its most disparate elements. The object of the game is to fuse as many of one's contradictions and possibilities as one can.

Q: *Before we began to record our interview, you said that most of your poems have begun with something that was "given" to you, a very strong opening voice. Doesn't, then, the challenge of realizing the poem require a great understanding of craft in extending the impulse through to the end? So many poems by mediocre poets seem to start beautifully and then are not brought off.*

A: Practically all my poems start with something given to me, that is, a line or a phrase, or a set of lines, that take me by surprise. When that happens, the challenge is to accept the blessing and go along with it. Only in the process of writing the poem do you discover why the gift was bestowed on you and where it will lead you. Craft is there to sustain and fortify the original impulse, and to preserve the momentum, now by letting go, now by pulling back. Sometimes you find in the end you have to throw out the very lines that gave the poem its start, because they have become embodied in the whole act of the poem and are no longer necessary. Sometimes they require modification, because they may not have come to you perfect. For

23

example, in END OF SUMMER, the opening lines, as they announced themselves to me, were *"The* agitation of the air,/ *The* perturbation of the light."* At a certain point in the revision my ear told me that the four definite articles thickened the lines unpleasantly. I changed them to *"An* agitation of the air,/ *A* perturbation of the light"*—much more open, airy, fluid.

Q: *Now surely this process of rewriting and trying to fulfill the intention of the given lines must require a full understanding of verse and prosody. This is the whole reason for craft.*

A: As I indicated earlier, prosody isn't just metrics. It's closer to biology than to mechanics. It involves everything that has to do with the making of a poem, the way it moves, the way it sounds, the way it lives from word to word, the way it breathes.

Q: *It is interesting to hear that the beginnings of your poems often consist of "inspired" material, because so much attention has been paid to the way you have ended your poems—particularly those that turn at the end in a line or two in a way that seems both to come out of the poem and to be something new. Do you ever begin the writing of a poem with the ending?*

A: Occasionally I am astonished to find, through all the devious windings of a poem, that my destination is something I've written six months or a year or two years before, and that is what the poem's been seeking out. The mind's stuff is wonderfully patient.

Q: *This process of retention, of being able to carry these lines for years and years, requires a tremendous memory. Is there ever any confusion with lines that have been written by other poets? Do you ever find yourself not sure if you wrote a line?*

A: In the beginning, sometimes, I would say to myself, I wonder —is this line really mine? And I discovered quite soon that if I questioned it, the only thing to do was to forget it, because the mind has its own conscience, which has to be trusted. A little doubt is all you need to know.

Q: *You keep a notebook of quotations that mean something to you. Has an entry from that notebook ever inspired a poem of yours? Or, do you ever incorporate other people's words into the body of a poem?*

A: The mind is a prolix gut. That's a phrase I suspect I stole from Woodrow Wilson, of all people, though I can't be sure. All poets are thieves—or magpies, if you want me to be euphemistic. The imagination keeps looking for information to digest, and digestion is a process of reconstitution. I don't really care much for paste-and-scissors jobs.

Q: *Do you consciously try to control the speed of lines in your poems? In* BENEDICTION, *the line "God drive them whistling out" has speed and force, and in the same poem the line "No shy, soft, tigrish fear" is suspended and slow.*

A: The variable pulse of a poem shows that it is alive. Too regular a beat is soporific. I like to hear a poem arguing with itself. Even before it is ready to change into language a poem may begin to assert its buried life in the mind with wordless surges of rhythm and counterrhythm. Gradually the rhythms attach themselves to objects and feelings. At this relatively advanced stage, the movement of a poem is from the known to the unknown, even to the unknowable. Once you have left familiar things behind, you swim through levels of darkness toward some kind of light, uncertain where you will surface.

Q: *It's improbable, isn't it, that this kind of experience would ever be given in sum to a poet, without the long struggle, without the long process of—*

A: I wish it were easier. How I envy prolific poets!

Q: *To go back to your underwater metaphor for the creative process, what is the sensation at the point of surfacing?*

A: Joy. As though a burden had been removed. One is freer than before.

Q: *Then a false ending to a poem would be an attempt to create this result without actually achieving it.*

A: If you fake it, your rhetoric betrays you.

Q: *Have you always written in the way you have just described?*

A: I think so. Even the earliest poems. FOR THE WORD IS FLESH, for example.

Q: *How young were you when you began to write poetry?*

A: Even in grade school I was rhyming—doggerel, mainly. But I enjoyed that. And I was reading all the bad poets, along with some good ones, and loving them equally. Words always fascinated me, regardless of whether I knew what they meant. In fourth grade, I recall, I began a composition on the Father of Our Country with the sentence: "George Washington was a tall, petite, handsome man."

Q: *Which of the poets you read as a young person had the most influence on the development of your own writing? Did reading Tennyson affect the development of your ear?*

A: During my high school years I admired Keats and Tennyson for their music. One day my English teacher read Herrick in class. Later, a neighbor gave me Wordsworth's collected poems. Those were red-letter days. At Harvard I discovered the metaphysicals and Hopkins, and they shook me up. Afterwards, in the thirties, the later Yeats became important to me, and I began my long friendship with Roethke.

Q: *Would you say something about your feelings concerning faith and religion? This process you describe of struggling with the given lines of a poem might almost be an Old Testament wrestling with the Dark Angel in order to find God through intuition rather than through outside revelation.*

A: I suppose I am a religious person without a religion. Maybe because I have no faith, I need it more than others. And the wrestling is damn good exercise.

Q: *Do you often change words in poems after they have been printed? There are two versions of* DECIDUOUS BRANCH *in print—the first says "Passion" where the later one has "Summer."*

A: "Summer" made the metaphor harder and cleaner. I can't usually bear to read my early poems, but once in a while I am tempted to see whether I can make some small improvements in the ones I want to keep. I haven't the slightest interest in rewriting them *en todo*, even if I could, nor do I propose to make major changes.

Q: *This brings up the matter of a poet's going back and revising, or even disclaiming, early poems which the public has already come to know. How can he blot them out? Should a poet keep trying to bring his work up to date, or should he let the record stand?*

A: A poet tends to be a perfectionist. I see no reason why he should be disqualified from trying to improve his own work, published or unpublished. As long as he's alive, it's his property. After his death, posterity will have the privilege of determining which versions of his poems, if any, it chooses to remember.

Stanley Kunitz

Q: *What prompted you to edit those massive collections of literary biographies,* TWENTIETH CENTURY AUTHORS, EUROPEAN AUTHORS, *and the rest?*

A: Simply that I had to earn a living. After college I went to work for a publisher in New York and soon discovered that I wasn't geared for an office existence. So I fled to a farm in Connecticut, where I produced a crop of herbs, flowers and reference books. And, perennially, poems.

Q: *Now you seem to be spending a good part of your time on Cape Cod, in Provincetown.*

A: I'm truly happier there. I have a great world of friends in New York, but the city depletes me. I need to grow things and to breathe clean air. Then, I have my involvement with the Fine Arts Work Center in Provincetown. A few of us have banded together, with the help of some foundation money, including a grant from the National Endowment for the Arts, to invite a selected group of young writers and artists each year to join a productive winter community up there by the sea. We give what help we can. Alan Dugan and I are the ones most concerned with the poets. And we bring in all sorts of brilliant people from the outside for weekly seminars.

Q: *That sounds like an exciting program. How does one find out more about it?*

A: By writing to the Fine Arts Work Center, Box 565, Provincetown, Mass., 02657.

Q: *Poetry seems to be the orphan child of the arts—it is always difficult to find public support for projects involving poetry. Do you see any sign of improvement? Will a person who wants to become a poet always have to look forward to a lifetime of struggling, and working at vocations he doesn't really enjoy in order to support his art?*

A: Hasn't that usually been true? I'm not sure that a poet should expect to be rewarded for his voluntary choice of a vocation. If he has any sense at all, he should realize that he's going to have a hard time surviving, particularly in a society whose main drives are exactly opposite to his. If he chooses, against the odds, to be a poet, he ought to be tough enough, cunning enough, to take advantage of the system in order to survive. And if he doesn't, it's sad, but the world is full of the most terrible kinds of sadness.

27

Q: *What do you think of the way in which poetry and literature have been presented to elementary school children through our present educational system?*

A: Almost anybody would have to agree that the American system of education has been a dismal failure. Certainly one of the areas in which it has most significantly failed is in teaching students how to cope with poetry. The failure begins at the grade school level. But there are some promising signs—first of all, a general recognition of the failure. The new young educators, clearly, know the essential truth about the injury done to the imagination of the child, and there are many signs of revolt against the educational system, just as there is a revolt against the political system.

Q: *Many high school and college students feel that poetry has no importance for them, in their lives.*

A: So many of the young today doubt that classroom instruction in general and the reading of poetry in particular is what they need most. I can understand their negativism. They fail to see that the work of the imagination is precisely what has to be achieved if we are going to save our civilization from disaster. And that a poem, regardless of its theme, can embody for us a principle of the free mind engaged in a free action.

Q: *Wasn't* THE MOUND BUILDERS *written out of a political situation?*

A: Many of my poems are, but in an oblique way. By its nature poetry is hostile to opinions, and the opinions of a poet on public affairs are, in any case, of no special interest. The poems that attract me most, out of the contemporary dilemma, are the peripheral ones that are yet obviously the product of a mind engaged with history. THE MOUND BUILDERS, I can recall, came out of the resumption of nuclear testing by President Kennedy in 1962, when I was traveling through the South, and looking at the archeological traces of a civilization that flourished in this country between 900 and 1100 A.D., the greatest civilization of the Eastern seaboard, and maybe the greatest civilization north of Mexico, of which nothing now remains except a few shards. There in Georgia the inscription reads, "Macon is the seventh layer of civilization on this spot." Macon, one of the seats of racist injustice in this country. So all these elements entered into the making of the poem, including the fact that I was traveling, and reading my work, and talking to college students in the South.

28

Stanley Kunitz

But most readers would say, not without justification, "It's a poem about mound builders."

Q: *Are you writing dramatic monologues now?*

A: My new book has several poems that are basically dramatic in their structure. They're not quite dramatic monologues—I don't know really what to call them—but in each case there is a dramatic action incorporated in the poem, sometimes appearing and sometimes disappearing. The very last poem I wrote for the book is called AROUND PASTOR BONHEOFFER. Bonhoeffer, you know, was the Lutheran pastor in Germany who, after a great struggle with his conscience, joined the plot to kill Hitler. The plot failed, and he was exterminated. The conflict between his Christian principle of nonviolence and the political necessity for action seems to me a parable for our times. I myself am a nonviolent man with radical feelings about the way things are.

Q: *When will that book be published?*

A: Next March.

Q: *And it's called* THE TESTING-TREE?

A: With a hyphen.

5
Allen Ginsberg

Q: *You have talked about this before, but would you begin this interview by describing the early influences on your work, or the influences on your early work?*

A: Emily Dickinson. Poe's BELLS—"Hear the sledges with the bells—Silver Bells! . . ." Milton's long line breath in PARADISE LOST—

> Him the almighty power
> Hurled headlong flaming from the ethereal sky
> With hideous ruin and combustion down
> To bottomless perdition, there to dwell
> In adamantine chains and penal fire,
> Who durst defy the omnipotent to arms.

Shelley's EPIPSYCHIDION—"one life, one death,/ One Heaven, one Hell, one immortality,/ And one annihilation. Woe is me! . . ." The end of Shelley's ADONAIS; and Shelley's ODE TO THE WEST WIND exhibits continuous breath leading to ecstatic climax.
Wordsworth's INTIMATIONS OF IMMORTALITY—

> Our birth is but a sleep and a forgetting:
> The soul that rises with us, our life's Star,
> Hath had elsewhere its setting,

—also Wordsworth's TINTERN ABBEY exhortation, or whatever you call it:

> a sense sublime
> Of something far more deeply interfused,
> Whose dwelling is the light of setting suns,
> And the round ocean and the living air,
> And the blue sky, and in the mind of man;

That kind of poetry influenced me: a long breath poetry that has a sort of ecstatic climax.

Q: *What about Whitman?*

A: No, I replied very specifically. You asked me about my *first* poetry. Whitman and Blake, yes, but in terms of the *early* poems I replied specifically. When I began writing I was writing rhymed verse, stanzaic forms that I derived from my father's practice. As I progressed into that I got more involved with Andrew Marvell.

Q: *Did you used to go to the POETRY SOCIETY OF AMERICA meetings?*

A: Yes, I used to go with my father. It was a horrifying experience —mostly old ladies and second-rate poets.

Q: *Would you elaborate?*

A: That's the PSA I'm talking about. At the time it was mainly people who were enemies of, and denounced, William Carlos Williams and Ezra Pound and T. S. Eliot.

Q: *How long did it take you to realise they were enemies?*

A: Oh, I knew right away. I meant enemies of poetry, very specifically. Or enemies of that poetry which now by hindsight is considered sincere poetry of the time. *Their* highwater mark was, I guess, Edwin Arlington Robinson; EROS TYRRANOS was considered, I guess, the great highwater mark of twentieth century poetry.

Q: *Where did you first hear long lines in momentum?*

A: The texts I was citing were things my father taught me when I was prepubescent.

Q: *Did he teach them to you as beautiful words, or as the craft of poetry?*

A: I don't think people used that word "craft" in those days. It's

31

sort of like a word that has only come into use in the last few decades. There were texts of great poetry around the house, and he would recite from memory. He never sat down and said now I am going to teach you: Capital C-R-A-F-T. Actually I don't like the use of the word craft applied to poetry, because generally along with it comes a defense of stressed iambic prosody, which I find uncraftsmanly and pedantical in its use. There are very few people in whose mouths that word makes any sense. I think Marianne Moore may have used it a few times. Pound has used it a couple of times in very specific circumstances—more often as a verb than as a general noun: "This or that poet has crafted a sestina."

Q: *Would you talk about later influences on your work? William Blake? Walt Whitman?*

A: Later on for open verse I was interested in Kerouac's poetry. I think that turned me on more than anyone else. I think he is a very great poet and much underrated. He hadn't been read yet by poets.

Q: *Most people associate Kerouac with prose, with* ON THE ROAD, *and not so much with* MEXICO CITY BLUES. *Or maybe they differentiate too strictly between prose and poetry.*

A: I think it's because people are so preoccupied with the use of the word craft and its meaning that they can't see poetry in front of them on the page. Kerouac's poetry looks like the most "uncrafted stuff" in the world. He's got a different idea of craft from most people who use the word "craft." I would say Kerouac's poetry is the craftiest of all. And as far as having the most craft of anyone, though those who talk about craft have not yet discovered it, his craft is spontaneity; his craft is having the instantaneous recall of the unconscious; his craft is the perfect executive conjunction of archetypal memorial images articulating present observation of detail and childhood epiphany fact.

Q: *In* HOWL, *at the end of Section One, you came close to a definition of poetry, when you wrote:*

> *Who dreamt and made incarnate gaps in Time &*
> *Space through images juxtaposed, and trapped*
> *the archangel of the soul between 2 visual*
> *images and joined the elemental verbs and set*
> *the noun and dash of consciousness together*

> *jumping with sensation of Pater Omnipotens*
> *Aeterne Deus*

A: I reparaphrased that when I was talking about Kerouac. If you heard the structure of the sentence I was composing, it was about putting present observed detail into epiphany, or catching the archangel of the soul between two visual images. I was thinking then about what Kerouac and I thought about haiku—two visual images, opposite poles, which are connected by a lightning in the mind. In other words "Today's been a good day; let another fly come on the rice." Two disparate images, unconnected, which the mind connects.

Q: *Chinese poets do that. Is that what you are talking about?*

A: This is characteristic of Chinese poetry as Ezra Pound pointed out in his essay "The Chinese Written Character as a Medium for Poetry" nearly fifty years ago. Do you know that work? Well, 'way back when, Ezra Pound proposed Chinese hieroglyphic language as more fit for poetry, considering that it was primarily visual, than generalized language-abstraction English, with visionless words like Truth, Beauty, Craft, etc. Pound then translated some Chinese poetry and translated (from Professor Fenellossa's papers) this philosophic essay pointing to Chinese language as pictorial. There is no concrete in English, and poets could learn from Chinese to present image-detail: and out of that Pound heiroglyph rose the whole practice of imagism, the school which is referred to as "Imagism." So what you are referring to is an *old* history in twentieth century poetry. My own thing about two visual images is just from that tradition, actually drawing from Pound's discovery and interpretation of Chinese as later practiced by Williams and everybody who studied with Pound or who understood Pound. What I'm trying to point out is that this tradition in American poetry in the twentieth century is not something *just* discovered. It was done by Pound and Williams, precisely the people that are anathema to the PSA mediocrities who were attacking Pound and Williams for not having "craft".

Q: *In that same section of* HOWL, *in the next line, you wrote:*

> *to recreate the syntax and measure of poor human*
> *prose and stand before you speechless and intel-*
> *ligent and shaking with shame, rejected yet confess-*
> *ing out the soul to conform to the rhythm of*
> *thought in his naked and endless head.*

A: Description of aesthetic method. Key phrases that I picked up around that time and was using when I wrote the book. I meant again that if you place two visual images side by side and let the mind connect them, the gap between the two images, the lightning in the mind illuminates. It's the *sunyata* (Buddhist term for blissful empty void) which can only be known by living creatures. So, the emptiness to which the Zen finger classically points—the ellipse—is the unspoken hair-raising awareness in between two mental visual images. I should try to make my answers a little more succinct.

Q: *Despite your feeling about craft, poets have developed an attitude towards your work, they have discovered certain principles of breath division in your lines—*

A: Primary fact of my writing is that I don't have any craft and don't know what I'm doing. There is absolutely no art involved, in the context of the general use of the words "art" and "craft". Such craft or art as there is, is in illuminating mental formations, and trying to observe the naked activity of my own mind. Then transcribing that activity down on paper. So the craft is being shrewd at flash lighting mental activity. Trapping the archangel of the soul, by accident, so to speak. The subject matter is the action of my mind. To put it on the most vulgar level, like on the psychoanalyst's couch is supposed to be. Now if you are thinking of "form" or even the "well made poem" or a sonnet when you're lying on the couch, you'll never say what you have on your mind. You'd be babbling about corset styles or something *else* all the time instead of saying, "I want to fuck my mother," or whatever it is you want. So my problem is to get down the fact that I want to fuck my mother or whatever. I'm taking the most hideous image possible, so there will be no misunderstanding about what area of mind you are dealing with: what is socially unspoken, what is prophetic from the unconscious, what is universal to all men, what's the main subject of poetry, what's underneath, *inside* the mind. So, how do you get that out on the page? You observe your own mind during the time of composition and write down whatever goes through the ticker tape of mentality, or whatever you hear in the echo of your inner ear, or what flashes in picture on the eyeball while you're writing. So the subject is constantly interrupting because the mind is constantly going on vagaries—so whenever it changes I have a dash. The dashes are a function of this method of transcription of unconscious data. Now you can't write down *everything* that you've got going on—half-conscious data. You can't write down everything, you can only write down what the hand can carry. Your hand can't carry more than a twentieth of what the mind flashes, and the very fact of writing interrupts the mind's flashes and redirects attention to writing. So that the observation (for writing) impedes the function of the mind. You might say "Observation impedes Function." I get down as much as I can of genuine material, interrupting the flow of material as I get it down and when I look, I turn to the center of my brain to see the next thought, but it's probably about thirty thoughts later. So I make a dash to indicate a break, sometimes a dash plus dots. Am I making sense?—

Saying "I want to fuck my mother"—that's too heavy. Wave a red flag in front of understanding so we don't have to use that as the archetypal thought. Like "I want to go to heaven" may be the archetypal thought, instead of "I want to fuck my mother." I just wanted to get it down to some place that everybody knows where it is. If I say "I want to go to heaven" you might think it's a philosophic conception.

Q: *How much do you revise your work?*

A: As little revision as possible. The craft, the art consists in paying attention on the actual movie of the mind. Writing it down is like a byproduct of that. If you can actually keep track of your own head movie, then the writing it down is just like a secretarial job, and who gets crafty about that? Use dashes instead of semicolons. Knowing the difference between a dash—and a hyphen -. Long lines are useful at certain times, and short lines at other times. But a big notebook with lines is a helpful thing, and three pens—you have to be shrewd about that. The actual materials are important. A book at the nightstand is important—a light you can get at—or a flashlight, as Kerouac had a brakeman's lantern. That's the craft. Having the brakeman's lantern and knowing where to use the ampersand "&" for swiftness in writing. If your attention is focused all the time—as my attention was in writing SUNFLOWER SUTRA, TV BABY poem later, (WICHITA VORTEX SUTRA later, in a book called PLANET NEWS)—when attention is focused, there is no likelihood there will be much need for blue penciling revision because there'll be a sensuous continuum in the composition. So when I look over something that I've written down, I find that if my attention has lapsed from the subject, I begin to talk about myself writing about the subject or talking about my irrelevant left foot itch instead of about the giant smog factory I'm observing in Linden, New Jersey. Then I'll have to do some blue penciling, excising whatever is irrelevant: whatever I inserted self-consciously, instead of conscious of the Subject.

Where self-consciousness intervenes on attention, blue pencil excision means getting rid of the dross of self-consciousness. Since the subject matter is really the operation of the mind, as in Gertrude Stein, anything that the mind passes through is proper and shouldn't be revised out, almost anything that passes through mind, anything with the exception of self-consciousness. Anything that occurs to the mind is the proper subject. So if you are making a graph of the movements of the mind, there is no point in revising it. Because then you would obliterate the actual markings of the graph. So if you're interested in writing as a form of meditation or introspective yoga, which I am, then there's no revision possible.

Q: *Your poem about the sunflower shows remarkable powers of concentration.*

A: SUNFLOWER SUTRA, the original manuscript in pencil's somewhere at Columbia University Library. In examining it you will see the published poem deviates maybe five or ten words from the original penciled text, written in twenty minutes, Kerouac at the door, waiting for me to go off to a party, and I said "Wait a minute, I got to write myself a note." I had the Idea Vision and I wanted to write it down before I went off to the party, so I wouldn't forget.

Q: *Did it dictate the sense, or did you just do it for yourself?*

A: Observing the flashings on the mind. As somebody said, the craft is observing the mind. Formerly the "Craft" used to be an idea of rearranging your package, rearranging. Using the sonnet is like a crystal ball to pull out more and more things from the subconscious (to pack into the sonnet like you pack an ice cream box). Fresher method of getting at that material is to watch mind flow instantaneously, to realize that all that is, is there in the storehouse of the mind within the instant any moment: that's the Proust of eternal recall, remember, the entire *REMEMBRANCE OF THINGS PAST* came to him just as he was dunking that little bit of madeleine cake into his tea. You know, the whole content of that one instant: that epiphanous instant, working with that instant—the mind then and there. That method I learned from Kerouac and I am interested in. That method is related to other "classical" methods of art composition and meditation like Zen Buddhist calligraphic painting, haiku composition also a spontaneous art, *supposed* to be spontaneous. People don't sit around revising haikus. They are supposed to be sitting around drinking saki, near a little hibachi (charcoal stove) with fireflies and fans and half moons through the window. And in the summertime you are supposed to say, "Ah, the firefly has just disappeared into the moon . . ." Make it up then and there. It's got to come from the perception of the moment. You can't go home the next day and send your friend the haiku and say "I thought of a funny one: the firefly just . . ." That wouldn't be real.

Q: *Do you see time used as a unit of structure, as well as a point of view?*

A: Time of composition is the structure of the poem. That is the subject. What is going on in the mind during that moment is the subject. "Time is of the essence," said Kerouac in a very great little essay on writing poetry, a one page set of advice, "Essentials of Spontaneous Prose."* I learned my theory from Kerouac. The preoccupations I have are Hindu, Buddhist, Hassidic—I spend one hour every morning sitting cross-legged, eyes closed, back straight, observing my consciousness and quieting my consciousness, watching processions of mental imagery. Someone who isn't into that kind of meditation might find it an unknown territory to go into, chaos, and see it as much too chaotic to get involved with.

Q: *You once wrote, I won't write my poem until I'm in my right mind.*

A: Yes. Of course, *that* poem is like a series of one-line jokes, so to speak. At the expense of the body politic, at the expense of the mass media, Hallucination of Being entertained by the middle class.

Q: *Does this refer to an attitude of yours about state of mind?*

A: I'm referring to a nervously comical attitude toward America. It ends "I'm putting my queer shoulder to the wheel." What I'm saying is, my poetry—this particular poem—my poetry in general —shows as such drivel because the United States is in such a state of apocalyptic drivelhood, that we're destroying the world, actually, and we're really destroying ourselves, and so I won't write my poem until I'm in my right mind. Until America gets out of its silly mood.

Q: *Would you discuss travel? When you're in different places do you find yourself affected by the prosody of the place?*

A: I try to learn what I can. I got involved with mantra chanting when I was in India and brought it back to America. I do a lot of mantra chanting here. Just because I was interested in it and it had something to do with poetics, I thought. It also had to do with

---

* *Evergreen Review* #5, Summer, 1958. Grove Press. N.Y., 1958.

vocalization in that it did relate to preoccupations that I was familiar with in Pound's dictum "Pay attention to the tone leading of vowels." Sanskrit prosody has great ancient rules involving vowels and a great consciousness of vowels or a consciousness of quantitative versification. Like Pound is conscious of that too, tried to bring that to the awareness of poets in the twentieth century, tried to make people more conscious of the tone leading of vowels and shift away from hyper-attention to accentual rhythm. Pound said that he thought the future America prosody would be "an approximation of classical quantity," he thought *that* would be formal substitute for iambic count, stress count. The whole poetic movement of the century, climaxed in what was known as Beat of San Francisco or Hippie or whatever Renaissance movement, was finally a realization of a new form of prosody, a new basis for the prosody.

Actually I've written a great deal about the subject. I don't know if you're familiar with much of it, but some poetics is covered in a Paris Review interview [PARIS REVIEW #37, Spring, 1966]. The relationship between Poetics and Mantra is gossiped on in a Playboy interview [April, 1969]. A closer analysis of stress prosody, that kind of craft, sits in a preface to my father's book*—where I referred (as in answer to an earlier question) to one of the books that influenced me when I was young, called AMERICAN POETRY, edited with Introduction, Notes, Questions, and Biographical Sketches by A. B. De Mille, Simmons College, Boston, Secretary of the New England Association of Teachers of English, Boston, Allyn and Bacon, 1923, Academy Classic Series. It was, like, the high school anthology, for most older high school teachers who teach now, their education. It was the standard anthology of the early twenties and used around the schools. I read Dickinson and Poe and Archibald Rutledge and Whittier and Longfellow and Thoreau and Emerson and John Hay Whitney, all the bearded poets of the nineteenth century, in that book. This book described accentual prosody as "particularly well adapted to the needs of English poetry . . . definite rules, which have been carefully observed by all great poets from Homer to Tennyson and Longfellow." They gave as an example of accentual prosody in this book for teachers and students:

Thŏu tóo/ săil ón,/ Ŏ Shíp/ ŏf Státe.

Remember that line? They had it marked, as above. As you notice,

---

* Louis Ginsberg: *Morning in Spring.* Morrow, N.Y., 1970.

they had an unaccented mark for O and then an accented mark for Ship. When you read it you will realize that O is an exclamation, and, by definition, you *can't* have an unaccented mark for that and an accented mark for Ship. Which means that by the time 1923 had come about, teachers of English prosody had so perverted their own ears and everybody else's ears that they could actually write down O, as unaccented. See, it was done like that. Well, what it means is that nobody could pronounce the line right. They were teaching people to mispronounce things. It would have to be: "Thóu tóo/sáil ón,/Ó Shíp/ŏf Státe," many long vowels. But when you got up on the elementary or high school lecture platform, they used to say: "Thŏu tóo/săil ón,/Ŏ Shíp/ŏf Státe." Hear? Another example they had in there was:

Whose héart/ -strĭngs aŕe/ ă luŕe.

when it quite obviously is "heárt-strĭngs." So, in other words, that's where "craft" degenerated. That's why I'm talking about how do we get out from under that. Because that was the POETRY SOCIETY OF AMERICA's standard of poetics. And that's what Pound was fighting against. And replacing with a much more clear ear. And of course that's what Williams was working on, and that's what Creeley, Olsen and Kerouac have always been compensating for. That's why I'm so mean about the use of the word "craft." Because I really wanted to make it clear that whatever people think craft is supposed to be, that what they've been taught at school, it's *not* that at all. One had better burn the word than abuse it as it has been abused, to confuse everybody.

Q: *How does your own teaching affect your work?*

A: I don't teach too much; I go around and give poetry readings. When I go around to a college generally I'll teach a course in, like, talk. It ranges oddly from abnormal psychology courses to psychology courses, whether I'm discussing drugs or consciousness. But that also leads into a discussion of letters because that also concerns consciousness. Sometimes drugs. Sometimes if there's a course in Blake I'll teach that, mainly by singing Blake's SONGS OF INNOCENCE AND OF EXPERIENCE which I've been putting to music. ("Blake's SONGS OF INNOCENCE AND OF EXPERIENCE Tuned by ALLEN GINSBERG" MGM/Verve FTS 3083 O.P.) Learning music and examining the prosody in Blake syllable by syllable tonally, making them tunes. I lectured last week at Columbia Law School, mainly about research that I've been doing that implicates the CIA in opium traffic in Indo

39

China. And I'll be lecturing next week at the NYU Medical School for the New York Medical Committee on Human Rights, on the rights of junkies being persecuted by police, by narcotics agents who themselves are peddling dope. A lot of teaching or lecturing but it's scattered all over and up and down and it's not all poetry.

Q: *You have been giving readings with your father.*

A: We've done about four a year since 1965. We started at the PSA. But we don't do it often, it would get to be too much of an "act". Generally we do it when there's some sentimental or aesthetically interesting occasion. Like at the PSA, that was interesting aesthetically. At the Y the other night, that was interesting because it is the traditional place for "distinguished poets" to read. I do it because, partly, to live with my father, because he's not going to be here forever. Nor am I. As a poet I'm interested in living in the same universe with him, and working in the same universe with him. We both learn something from it, get a little bit into each other's souls, the world soul. A father can learn a son's soul and a son can learn a father's soul; it's pretty much knowing God's soul, finally. It's like a confrontation with my own soul which is sometimes difficult. But it usually winds up pleasurable. Sometimes I have to see things in myself or face things in my father that are quite hideous, confront them. So far this has turned out to reconcile us more and more.

Q: *Do you think things are getting easier?*

A: As the world slowly draws to its doomy dead ocean conclusion in the 2000th year, it gets harder and harder. You know THE NEW YORK TIMES editorial said that the oceans will be dead as Lake Erie in the year 2000. It was in the paper today. "Reputable scientific evidence" say that given the present rate of waste, the world's oceans where Leviathan has already been extincted will be dead as Lake Erie. Which is what I was thinking when I was coming here. The poetic precedent for this situation is like Ezekiel and Jeremiah and the Hebrew prophets in the Bible who were warning Babylon against its downfall. Like Eldridge Cleaver presently using the Poetics of Jonah. They were talking about the fall of a city, like Babylon, or the fall of a tribe, or cursing out the sins of a nation. But no poets have ever had to confront the *destruction of the entire world* like we have to. No poet has ever had to confront an editorial in THE NEW YORK TIMES that says the oceans will be dead as Lake Erie in the year 2000. It's so incredible as a subject that you can't even go back to the biblical prophets for a model to say "Well, I think I'll write a poem like

40

Allen Ginsberg

Jeremiah now, or I'll tell these people at the NEW YORK QUARTERLY
I'm working in the tradition of Jeremiah." But really, no, because not
even Jeremiah had to confront a subject as immense as what I and you
have to deal with, which is the end of the habitable human world. It is
a possibility. Or the millenial salvation of the human world. If we
make it past 2000. Talking in terms of craft, the easy way would be to,
say, let us model . . . I think I'll come on with a big con . . ."I'm
modeling my recent work after Jeremiah." I'll go back and read the
Bible and model all my latest, a whole bunch of electronic poetry
about the oceans being polluted. I'd just make a lot of images. You
know: "Woe on thee, New York." But the whole thing is so serious
and vast that you can't go back because it didn't work. Jeremiah didn't
save Babylon or wherever he was trying to save, I forgot. This is a life
and death matter for the entire world. So the old craft, the old images
and the old examples, even as deep and profound as the Bible, don't
provide the model that we can faithfully copy or project from in order
to save our souls and our skin now. The poet is now confronted with
all human history to date, the accumulation, the ecological chain
reaction of all human history from the Magdalenian cave painting
forty thousand years ago to the end of this century. All the bad vibes
and good vibes put together. All human consciousness now totaled
up in the libraries and on microfilm and on tape available, all the
paintings ever done available in museums, music, all ever written
down and available on tape machines, cassettes, hi fi systems, all
human conceptual consciousness that could have been formulated
available in the British museum and the New York library. And
simultaneously, apparently, the end of the world approaching, not as
a politic image, but as an absolute fact reported in the newspapers. So
I think that actually comes to affect one's sense of poetics. For
instance, I begin to wonder what's the point of writing poems down
on paper and printing them, when neither paper nor print nor
electricity nor machines nor newspapers nor magazines will survive
the next thirty or forty years. Wouldn't it be best if one were
interested in what would survive; wouldn't it be best just if one were
to deal only in those forms which are memorizable and singable and
which could survive beyond the printing press, if one were interested
in "immortality." If one were interested in art which is perennial,
endurable, that is useful in caves, if people have to live in caves, from
that point of view, for that reason, there would be only music, lyrics.

Q: *Did you ever study music? Take up an instrument?*

A: No, I began doing repetitive mantra chanting and studying

Indian music, and developed out of that, together with the Blake work. Mantra chanting involved just one chord. Hare krishna, Hare krishna, Krishna, Krishna, Hare, Hare, etc. all done in a C chord, C major. Then I got to some variations. I've put most of Blake's Songs to music now; I think I've got thirty-five out of the forty. There's a record out of half of them. I'll finish that up someday; it's quite a project, a huge project.

Q: *Have you ever taught the poetry of Blake?*

A: Well, I teach him by singing him. Because Blake sang, you know, that's why they're called Songs of Innocence and of Experience. He was a literal poet.

Q: *What was his own music for the songs like?*

A: Nobody knows. They are not written down. There were some scholar musicians according to biographers who heard him but didn't notate. Probably similar to what I'm doing, so I'm told by Foster Damon, who was a great Blake scholar, and who was a musician too. What I'm doing is sort of in the style of the hymns of Isaac Watts and people of that time.

Q: *Why do you suppose you feel a kinship for Blake, for exalted works?*

A: I think I mentioned earlier Intimations of Immortality, Tintern Abbey, that pantheistic nature, the specific line I quoted:

> a sense sublime
> Of something far more deeply interfused,
> Whose dwelling is the light of setting suns,
> And the round ocean and the living air,
> And the blue sky, and in the mind of man;
> A motion and a spirit, that impels
> All thinking things, all objects of all thought,
> And rolls through all things.

So I quote that as a psychedelic statement, "mind-manifesting," fit for classical meditators and modern dope fiends.

Q: *Was Pantheism behind your starting your own farm?*

A: As reflected in a poem called Wales "Visitation" in Planet News book, which is a poem written on LSD. When I get onto LSD or psylocybin Mexican mushrooms now, the vision trips I get on are mostly like Wordsworthian common daylight, connected with the symmetry of the thistle or the emptiness inside the lamb's eye. So the last time I took LSD it was in Wales, when I wrote that poem, and that turned me on to the possibility of actually altering my immediate environment and living in that world permanently. Which I do now.

Q: *Did you find yourself?*

A: It helped. I don't do it too much because I'm on a commune. A couple of acres with organic gardening and we have our own cow for milk and we get our own eggs from our chickens and there's a pet pig. Have a vegetarian table, have a horse, goat milk, and goats, ducks. Lots of dogs and cats. Anywhere between 7 and 20 people. It's ecologically inadvisable to be eating meat from here on out, meat is wasteful of the acreage.

Q: *What do you do with the pigs then?*

A: We're having spiritual communion with the pigs, discovering the personality and the emotions of the pigs. Pigs are the smartest of the barnyard animals; they are also extremely emotional. Ducks are pretty dumb. They keep sitting on rotten eggs all the time.

Q: *You read the* WALES VISITATION *poem on the Buckley interview?*

A: Yes—WALES VISITATION.

Q: *Is this your favorite poem?*

A: Of my most recent poems, this is, like an imitation of a perfect nature poem, and also it's a poem written on LSD which makes it exemplary for that particular modality of consciousness. It's probably useful to people as a guidance, as a mental guideline for people having bum trips because if they'll check through the poem they'll see an area which is a good trip. An ecologically attuned pantheistic nature trip. Also it's an example of the fact that art work can be done with the much maligned celebrated psychedelic substances.

Q: *Didn't T. S. Eliot say that he didn't believe in that?*

A: Yeah. But Eliot was not a very experienced writer. He didn't write very much. He didn't write much poetry. Anyhow there's a tremendous amount of evidence that good work can be done in all states of consciousness including drugs. Not that drugs are necessary. It's just that it's part of the *police* mythology that nothing can be done, that LSD leads only to confusion and chaos. That's nonsense.

Q: *In non-drug states, do you ever work half-asleep?*

43

A: Yes, as I said, I keep a notebook at my bedside for half-conscious, preconscious, quasi-sleep notations. And I have a book out now called INDIAN JOURNALS which has such writing in it, including poems emerged out of dreams and remembered in half waking, long prose-poetry paragraphs, using double talk from a half-sleep state.

Q: *That seems a very relaxed and vulnerable kind of writing, as opposed to what you spoke of before, where you tried to get everything into the mind.*

A: They're both related to consciousness study. Take it as part of a tradition going back to Gertrude Stein who was a student of William James at Harvard, whose subjects were varieties of religious experience and alterations of consciousness. That was James' big subject —the pragmatic study of consciousness—the modalities of consciousness. Stein applied her Jamesian studies and her medical studies to the practice of composition and saw composition as an extension of her investigations into consciousness. That's the tradition that I would like to classify myself within, and I think that's a main legit tradition of poetics—the articulation of different modalities of consciousness, almost, you can't say *scientific,* but the *artful* investigation or articulation of extraordinary states of consciousness. All that rises out of my own preoccupation with higher states of consciousness on account of, as I said over and over, when I was young, 24 or so, some poems of Blake like AH SUN-FLOWER, THE SICK ROSE and the LITTLE GIRL LOST catalyzed in me an extraordinary state of mystical consciousness as well as auditory hallucinations of Blake's voice. I heard Blake's voice and also *saw* epiphanous illuminative visions of the rooftops of New York. While hearing Blake's voice. While reading the text of AH SUN-FLOWER, THE SICK ROSE and THE LITTLE GIRL LOST. This was described at great lengths in other occasions. But I want to go back to that just to reiterate that I see the function of poetry as a catalyst to visionary states of being and I use the word visionary only in these times of base materialistic media consciousness when we are so totally cut off from our own nature and nature around us that anything that teaches nature seems visionary.

Q: *Don't you feel that is changing?*

A: No, I feel it's getting worse and worse. We are getting more and more enraptured in our robot consciousness. Robot consciousness itself is beginning to break down, so there may be a change in the sense that the young people are aware that something has gone wrong with human nature, in America at any rate. We don't know. It says in the TIMES that we have until the year 2000 when the oceans will be dead as Lake Erie. That's a sense of doom. I mean no generation can change that.

Q: *The* TIMES *may not be right.*

A: Well, underground papers for years have been saying that the ecological catastrophe is a world-wide thing that's coming soon, and scientists have been saying it for years. Finally it's gotten around even to the newspapers even though the TIMES isn't necessarily right. So it's something that has to be taken seriously, someone has to start believing it. It is really certainly going to be right. Unless people accept that that *is* the state of things, nobody is going to have the energy or the decision to change it. If everybody merely accepted the fact that we had till the year 2000 there would *have* to be changes. They would have to be instantaneous. Every single air conditioning unit would have to be turned off beginning this month, December 1970. It means every single automobile has got to be stopped. Every new highway has to be stopped. It means people have to instantly boycott every nonreturnable bottle.

Q: *But maybe people would rather die.*

A: Apparently people would rather die. "To be or not to be, that is the question."

Q: *What do you feel about a poet's duty to protest, his responsibility to speak out?*

A: I'm hoping to save my own skin. I was hoping to live to the year 2000. I'm going to be seventy-four in that year and the oceans are going to stink like the garbage heap of the Passaic River. I've already given up the idea of having any children. I don't want to have children, definitely not, into this situation. That old poem of Dylan's you know? "You're hurled the worst curse that could ever be hurled afraid to bring children into the world." I won't have children but I'*m* going to have to suffer through this. We'll have to face whatever apocalypse there is with our own bodies. We'll all have to. Everybody who expects to be living another twenty years is going to face the Great Squeeze.

Q: *But people who should be reading protest poems, don't read them. What then?*

A: Try to maintain the same prophetic consciousness, which isn't very hard to maintain, all you have to do is read the editorial in the

NEW YORK TIMES, they say the oceans will be dead in our lifetime. And at the same time try to find some medium for penetrating ordinary human consciousness with that awareness, which is what I'm doing. As the ship sinks. But the young people already know. There's a latent inclination toward apolcalyptic awareness in young people, which is why their behavior is so amazing. It's mostly the older people that don't begin to account the consequences of their own deeds. Which is partly why I read with my father, to try to communicate with older people, too. It's a desperate situation. Also, I think the game is lost anyway. It's a question of preparing others how to die, how to enjoy the apocalypse, how to go through it without too much panic. Ride out the bum trip. The other side is like the great white void. I just don't think it would be a good idea if everybody died painfully, resentfully, kicking and screaming. So if people can learn to die properly they might learn to live.

Q: *What do you mean, learn it quickly?*

A: Well, we've got about 20 years. It's amazing how much people have learned. The generation changes are so vast, just from the point of hair style—could you imagine long hair with beards ten years ago? It would be unthinkable, the things that people are putting up with now, as normal change. Things like legalizing grass, just about on the verge of that now, reducing punishment for possession. Because these are such minor tiny things, it doesn't really amount to very much. I don't think anything will happen until the NEW YORK TIMES and television and everybody gets panicked. Looking to save their skins.

Q: *Could you comment on very specific details of your writing patterns?*

A: Like?

Q: *Do you ever write with music on in the background?*

A: Musical background imposes a rhythm, has its own rhythm. And I am sort of articulating my own body rhythm, body mind pulsations. So I don't consciously turn on, like Hart Crane, to a jazz record before I write. Kerouac used to do a lot of writing with St. Matthew's Passion in the back. His B minor Mass.

Q: *You once said you were a worry wart. Yet you have such a sense of joy and freedom, in reading, and in writing, too.*

A: Ideally, the ambition, my childhood desire is to write during a prophetic illuminative seizure. That's the idea: to be in a state of such complete blissful consciousness that any language emanating from that state will strike a responsive chord of blissful consciousness from any other body into which the words enter and vibrate. So I try to write during those "naked moments" of epiphany the illumination that comes a little bit every day. Some moment every day, in the bathroom, in bed, in the middle of sex, in the middle of walking down the street, in my head, or not at all. So if it doesn't come at all, then that's the illumination. So then I try to write in that too. So that's like a rabbinical Jewish Hassidic trick that way. So I try to *pay attention all the time*. The writing itself, the sacred act of writing, when you do anything of this nature, is like prayer. The act of writing being done sacramentally is pursued over a few minutes, it becomes like a meditation exercise which brings on a recall of detailed consciousness that is an approximation of high consciousness. High epiphanous mind. So, in other words, writing is a yoga that invokes Lord mind. And if you get into a writing thing that will take you all day, you get deeper and deeper into your own central consciousness.

Q: *And does this lead you to a greater reality?*

A: A greater attention? Not attention, more *feeling* emerging out of that. So you walk down the city streets in New York for a few blocks, you get this gargantuan feeling of buildings. You walk all day you'll be at the verge of tears. More detail, more attention to the significance of all that robotic detail that impinges on the mind and you realize through your own body's fears that you are surrounded by a giant robot machine which is crushing and separating people, removing them from nature and removing them from living and dying. But it takes walking around all day to get into that state. What I mean is if you write all day you will get into it, into your body into your feelings, into your consciousness. I don't write enough, actually, in that way. HOWL, KADDISH and other things were written in that way. All-day-long attention. My writing now—I don't spend enough time writing. Partly I'm spending my energy, my time on other things. One thing is learning music, so I find I spend more time composing music and working at the Blake than I do in composing my own poetry. I also find that answering letters from people—there being maybe twenty letters a day—diverts me from what I should be doing, so I wish people would stop writing me letters: I try to answer and every letter I answer takes me away from my own poetry. I'm also involved in a project for the P.E.N.* Club—I'm a member of their

---

* *Unamerican Activities*. P.E.N. American Center Report: The Campaign Against the Underground Press, Geoffrey Rips, City Lights Books, S.F, 1981.

Executive Board and Freedom to Read Committee, in which I'm surveying the government's attack on what amounts to 60% of the underground newspapers: bombings of their offices—arrests of vendors of the underground papers—narcotics arrests in which drugs are planted in the offices—obscenity accusations and prosecutions —FBI visits to printers and distributors warning them off. So I'm compiling files several feet thick for a "White Paper" that they're putting together. I'm also involved in a research project investigating dope peddling by the Narcotics Bureau and the CIA involvement with traffic of opium in Indochina, and I am working on documentation of that now.* So I got my attention split into too many areas to be very effective as a poet. So I'm going to withdraw from it, and hereby as a signal I'm making an appeal for people to stop writing me letters.

Q: *Maybe you could delegate these things.*

A: I just do it because there's nobody doing it. Sixty per cent of the underground papers have been busted and there is nobody in the middle class that has taken on this situation. Certainly the TIMES doesn't do it. The P.E.N. Club didn't do it. Authors' Guild didn't do it. Libraries didn't do it. The little magazines didn't do it. It's a responsibility.

Q: *Everybody is trying to stay away.*

A: Everybody's busy. A total proliferation of signals in every direction, and photographs. Nobody can read or keep track of everything any more. At one point I found that Mafia people had gotten involved with one of the larger defense contractors, and I thought that was, like, a Big Headline type story for the WASHINGTON POST. I talked with a POST reporter named Nick Von Hoffman. He said yeah, he knows about that particular story "but there's so much shit going down in Washington" that it's just one of many ripples as the entire world collapses. What difference does it make, one little problem about little magazines or if the CIA is peddling dope or the oceans are being poisoned and the atmosphere is poisoned and the overpopulation is outleaping itself, and every newspaper that reports it is a further drain on the tree life and using all these batteries to discuss it is a drain on the electric power, and every time you switch on a recording machine the flowers burn, and every time you pick up an issue of THE NEW YORK TIMES to denounce pollution, 60 thousand

* *Alan Verbatim: Lectures on Poetry, Politics and Consciousness.* Ed., Gordon Ball, McGraw Hill, N.Y. 1974. Political opium, pps. 39-97.

trees go down and pollute the waterways. So maybe every time I open my mouth it's polluting the environment. It's hard to know what to do.

Q: *You can always write poetry.*

A: Only way out is grow your own food, and compose in an art form which doesn't require material consumption. In other words compose in a poetry which is memorizable, that might be the way out—bypass both print and television and radio—if somebody could come up with an interpersonal art form that would completely eliminate the power of the mass media electricity-consuming network.

Q: *That's the oral tradition all over again.*

A: Right, back to Neolithic, which is what Gary Snyder has been suggesting all along: An art just requiring our bodies. Everybody's practicing that except middle class Americans. In any indigenous scene where you don't have the giant electric media to divert our consciousness into electronic simulacra there are still interpersonal, "primitive," shamanistic, religious, communal art forms.

Q: *Perhaps children could be made aware of this.*

A: Right now I just came from Paterson, New Jersey and the kids around there were raking up leaves to burn. I'm told that in China at the age of two, kids are propagandized to plant trees: "Plant trees, plant trees, plant trees."

(The phone rings in NYQ office)

The same problem. I have that same problem. How do you do something which requires attention if the phone rings all the time? I answer it. Lately I've been sitting every day for an hour in the morning, so I've just been sitting through and letting it ring. It's disturbing to think that other people are beginning to lose hope in the possibility of a connection. Finally lose hope. It's terrible to be involved in the collapse of a network, an overextended network, all those failed hopes. Salesmen dying.

Q: *Would you talk about the concept of the catalog, in poetry?*

A: Catalog serves a lot of different functions, one function is to simply log all the processions of thoughts in the mind, one way of *linking together* the mind's thoughts. This was done by Christopher Smart in his catalogues: REJOICE IN THE LAMB (JUBILATE AGNO). Just a method of free association, and a method of freeing associations. For associational *processions*, just like a mnemonic trick. Loosening the

49

mind, associating. For catalogs, the "who" catalog in HOWL seems to me to exhaust that form. And so in SUNFLOWER SUTRA I moved on to get a rhythmic pulsation going through the entire poem that would not depend on cataloging. Nor depend on "who" at the beginning of each line, SUNFLOWER SUTRA is an example of trying to get beyond the catalog: syntactically balanced, a giant sentence which will include the whole associational mobile. Also the catalog has another function which is the old Bardic lyric instrumental pulsation at the beginning of each line as you stroke the lyre and say: Blom—Leif went forth merrily into the ocean and then, Blom—Naiads came up out of the rocks and waved to him. Blom—And then old Neptune showed his horned hair above the grey water, and Blam—The porpoises danced about the ship. When you have a catalog and you say "and" or "who" or "for" as Smart did, you have that lyric tone like the chord struck by the finger. It sets up a rhythmic pulsation. Religions use the same technique, the litany form, church uses the same technique, really an articulation of body movement. Religious forms like litany exploit the same physiological body potentialities that Christopher Smart's litany did.

Q: *Do you think that long lists within a single line are trying to get past something?*

A: Getting past something but also including everything that you've been thinking about. Try to include everything and come to a conclusion. Include everything that you thought of all day long, so you list them all within a line, a litany, any way you can put them down, and say, all right, now what does all this mean?

Q: *Is there no sense in eliminating things?*

A: If it was something I really wanted to eliminate, I just wouldn't include it. If it were that boring or that insignificant . . .

Q: *What about the Old Testament writers, is it the same reason, the natural breath line?*

A: Yes. Because I don't know Hebrew, so I don't know what . . . Or Aramaic, so I don't know what their literal motifs might have been. You know, all that stuff might have been rhymed. So, God knows. But we know the English thing, and the English version seems to satisfy the needs of present prophetic versification, or got near to it anyway, or be a basis on which to begin that form, including litany. So getting back to our original splenetic denunciation of the use of the word "craft" is that the problems confronted in attempting to graph the operations of the mind in language and the problems confronted historically at this apocalyptic-end-of-history-time are so complex and so new and previously unexperienced by any culture that we have within memory—(this might all have gone before but all recollection was destroyed with the apocalypse, last time) the forms are so new as far as human history is concerned that no previous models of speech forms are sufficient, and we have to invent our own, just as no previous models of life style within memory are sufficient, and we're going to have to invent our own out of our own native genius, out of our own imagination, as Blake and Whitman proposed. The old poetic task is that we have to invent our own lives, make our own miracles. Which is the beauty of our situation, as well as its misery: the fearful aspect but it's also the most beautiful aspect. Whatever survival, if we survive, is going to come because we decided to survive. If we're magnanimous enough to continue, to wish to continue to work with each other to survive. And if we find a poetry adequate to that, it's just that we will have taken a realistic estimate of our bodies, of our breath, and of our machinery and our history, and imagined it—a beautiful enough prophecy with such exquisitely penetrant prosody that the hardest hat will vibrate with delight.

December, 1970

6

Denise Levertov

Q: *What stories or poems from your childhood reading do you remember particularly? Which ones do you think may have had an influence on your development as a poet?*

A: Well, it's always difficult to know what did and what didn't affect your work later. My mother read aloud to me a great deal when I was a child, even after I was reading to myself. She read Beatrix Potter, whom I consider a great stylist, the Andrew Lang fairy books, Hans Anderson. She read aloud very well, and she read not only to me, but to the assembled family, consisting of my sister, my father, and myself—all of Dickens, all of Jane Austen, and most of George Eliot, most of the nineteenth century classics. It was a somewhat nineteenth century household, I think, in that in the evenings we would sit around listening to reading out loud.

Q: *Your name is often linked with the names of the Black Mountain poets, with William Carlos Williams, Ezra Pound, and H.D. Who are some of the other poets, early or contemporary, whose work has significantly affected your own?*

A: As a child, when I started reading poetry, I read Keats and Tennyson and Wordsworth. Then I also read the younger poets, the kind of avant garde ones in England during my childhood—Auden and Spender and Eliot. I read lots of Elizabethan poetry as a child—lots. When I was growing up, people in England were really very ignorant of American poetry. I really did not know many writers, and the ones I did know were not reading Pound. I did not read him until about a year before I came to America. Williams was totally unknown to me until that time. H.D.—of course, one always saw the Imagists' stuff, but I didn't know the latest. There is a lot of H.D. which was published in England which has never been published here. Stevens I began to read in Paris, the year before I came to America. I read, you know, the English people who were just a little older than I was, and who were being published in England when I was first publishing. And well, I'd read some French poetry at that time—a little Rimbaud and Baudelaire, nothing much else, really.

Q: *The words "dance," and "dancing" appear regularly in your poetry, but only in your most recent collection,* RELEARNING THE ALPHABET, *is there a poem about the experience of dancing itself. Are there ways, perhaps in the area of rhythm, where your having been a dancer is reflected in your work?*

A: I have come to feel that there definitely are. You see, I studied very strict ballet when I was intending to become a dancer. I was sort of pushed into that by my sister, and when I quit I had a revulsion against it and didn't even like to think about it for a number of years. Then I danced again, just for pleasure. I did some modern dance in New York with a friend, Midi Garth, who is a very fine dancer; and when we lived in Mexico I found a ballet class which I went to a couple of times a week for a year, and I got quite good again, and began to enjoy the dancing for itself. I had looked on it as something with such a rigid technique, as something that did not seem to connect at all with what I became interested in—in writing and the other arts. But I came to feel that my experience dancing had definitely given me some sense of internal rhythm, and of gesture as it translates itself into language, of pace, of energy, of things like that, which possibly I wouldn't have felt if I'd never danced. So it was a rather obscure influence . . .

Q: *What about the kind of self-discipline a dancer has to learn? Do you discipline yourself in your writing—write at certain regular times, in a particular place?*

A: No. I don't really believe in anything that rigid and that imposed from without. I feel that classic ballet with its rigid discipline is a very very narrow medium—it doesn't have a wide or deep range of expressiveness. It can be very beautiful, I enjoy seeing it, but I think of it as decorative and relatively superficial, among the art forms.

Q: *Do you feel differently about modern dance?*

A: Well, theoretically. Actually, I have very rarely seen modern dance that seemed to reach the kind of depth and subtlety and have the range of language arts or music. The dancer I spoke of, Midi Garth—I've seen some performances of her solo works, her own choreography, that did seem to me to be very high art, but I've rarely seen modern dance that deeply satisfied me.

Q: *You encourage your students to keep writing notebooks. Do you do that yourself?*

A: Yes, I do.

Q: *What is the relationship between the look of your notebooks, and the collection of material in your* Notebook *poem?*

A: It's really something of a misnomer. That was just a sort of handle, to refer to the poem by. The part that you've seen, in Relearning the Alphabet, has been augmented, and it will be part of a book called Staying Alive.

Q: *When will that be published?*

A: There's a slim chance that it may be out in the fall, if we have a lot of luck in getting it together and get a printer to do it in time, but otherwise it will be out next spring. New Directions doesn't have a winter list. I'd like very much to have this book out in the fall, if it's humanly possible, because I have a certain sense of urgency about it—both because of its nature, and because one feels urgent anyway, at this time. Everyone feels somewhat apocalyptic, I suppose, one feels in a hurry to get things done and to speak to one's brothers and sisters while there's still time.

Q: *The new book continues the revolution theme?*

A: Yes.

Q: *What effect has your teaching had on your writing?*

A: I think it's had a mixed effect. Often it definitely takes time and energy away from writing. On the other hand, it's had a profound effect on my life in bringing me into contact with the student generation, and with political activism on the various campuses. If I hadn't been teaching I might easily have found myself very isolated politically, and perhaps would not have developed. I feel I have learned a lot through teaching which I wouldn't have learned without it. And in some cases, like last year at MIT and the year before at Berkeley, especially, I experienced a marvelous sense of community with my students at times, and I'm glad not to have missed that. Of course I've always felt it with individual students, but I've twice felt it—not all the time, but some of the time—with a group of students. I think that was a very important human experience.

Q: *Are there areas in which you have generally found American students to be well-equipped when they come into a poetry writing class, or places where they are often deficient?*

A: Well, I can't compare them with, say, English students, because I was never a student in England myself, and I've never taught anywhere but in America. But I'd say that most American students are grossly deficient in their reading background and general knowledge. There are lots of people with lots of natural talent, and very, very few with any sort of useful background.

Q: *Do you partly blame television for that?*

A: I don't blame any single factor for it, but I certainly don't think that television has helped. It is definitely a generation of spectators, and I don't know that this affects student *poets* particularly, but it does affect students in the classroom. My students this year, for example, tend to want to be entertained, I think. They want me to put on a performance for them in which they can sit passively back and not participate. Of course, the more politically conscious students are, the more they really try to participate in discussion and in everything else that's going on in the class. They want to create their own education. The students I have this year are politically very backward, an economically elite group, I would say, and it's very difficult to get to each other. They don't have a sense of collective possibilities. Students, and people in general in this country, have less and less of a common culture. Even if you get a bunch of people about twenty years old together who have all read a fair amount and looked at some paintings and had other experiences in the arts, there is very little likelihood of their having read the same books or looked at the same paintings, and the only thing that they can count on for sure is usually certain TV programs, such as "Captain Kangaroo," which they watched when they were little. And that's the common currency, which is a very low grade of common cultural currency, the only dependably shared element. I think that's a pretty sad state of affairs, to put it mildly. However, as far as poets are concerned, it's very hard to say what is good or bad for a person of real talent. It's such an individual matter.

Q: *You've written about helping your students to experience a poem as a sonic entity, apart from its meaning. How do you go about that?*

A: By trying to get them to listen to the poem, to hear it a number of times over, before launching into discussion of it. A lot of students—I would say the majority of students—have somehow picked up the idea that a poem is a problem to be solved, and that one reads a poem efficiently by making a paraphrase of it while reading it, and by this process of paraphrasing you somehow *obtain* the poem. Then you can forget it, and go on to the next one. But they don't listen to music that way. Of course, if a person is a serious student of music he will learn about musical form, he will be interested in it, and he will recognize when a theme is transposed into another key, or when it recurs played by another instrument—all those little things that take place in the structure of a piece of music. But certainly the average person who cares to listen to a piece of music isn't constantly doing that, he doesn't regard that as the only way in which he can really get the music. It's a direct experience which is accepted as such by most people. Poetry presents complicated surfaces of denotative and connotative meaning as well as of sound-patterns and it's natural that people want to feel that they have understood what has been said, and sometimes a certain degree of interpretive paraphrase may be necessary if you want to talk about a poem. But you can receive a poem, you can comprehend a poem, without talking about it. Teachers at all levels encourage the idea that you have to talk about things in order to understand them, because they wouldn't have jobs, otherwise. But it's phony, you know.

Q: *Do you think the fact that memorization has gone out of fashion has anything to do with the modern reader's having trouble reacting to a poem as rhythmic sound? Poetic rhythms aren't established in his head, in his ear . . .*

A: I don't know. It's an interesting theory. I've never been able to memorize anything myself, but I think I have a strong sense of rhythmic structure. I remember a French teacher I went to when I was a kid being quite impressed with me because I read aloud a French poem in a metrically correct way, and she said she very rarely had a student who did that. I think that's because I picked up very quickly on the rhythmic structure of the poem, but it certainly wasn't through memorization, so I don't feel I'm in a position to pass judgment on that.

Q: *You have done direct translation, knowing the other language well yourself, you have also translated using a linguist, as you did with the* In Praise of Krishna *poems. Do you find the experiences very different in the degree to which you are able to reach the heart of the original poem?*

A: There's certainly a degree of difference. However, in those Indian poems, my collaborator was himself so deeply into the poems and was able to give such fine explanations of any questions I had, and his own versions which I worked on were so good, that in some cases I really changed very few words. In others I changed quite a lot. The degree of difference was not as great as it can be when you have a less sensitive collaborator. I once did that, and it just didn't work out. The big difference is that translating from a language you don't know at all, you have actually no idea what it sounds like. With the French, although I didn't try any sort of elaborate imitations of sound and structure, I did of course know what it sounded like and was influenced in my versions by the sound of the original.

Q: *Where, on a scale that ran from literal translation to adaptation, would you put your translations of the Guillevic poems?*

A: The Guillevic ones, with few exceptions, are very close to the original, I think. I noted the places where I knew that I had departed, and there are many places where I just goofed. With those exceptions, they're not adaptations. They are translations, but I tried to make them stand up as poems, and therefore it's not a line-by-line thing. You'll find some stanzas are longer, or possibly shorter, in mine than in the original because I broke the lines differently with the idea of English-American rhythms. With some translators, if a stanza has five lines in the original they have five lines, quite rigidly. I didn't stick that closely, but I never deliberately changed an image, added an adjective, except as noted in the text.

Q: *There are clear similarities between your poetic style and Guillevic's style. Do you feel one poet can successfully translate the work of another whose interests and methods are radically different from his own?*

57

A: I would think it would be very difficult. I myself would not be very interested in attempting it. I have to feel a certain affinity to be drawn to translate something.

Q: *Why do you do translations?*

A: It's to—to really get deeper into the poem. One of the things one is doing in writing poems at all is grasping one's own experience by transmuting it, one is translating experience into language, one is apperceiving, one is finding out what it is that one knows. So with poems in another language, I tend to feel that if I'm attracted to a poem I want to absorb it more deeply by the act of translation. It's already a verbal experience, but it isn't absolutely distinct from that basic impulse to grasp experience in language that a poet has anyway, I think. It's just an extension of it.

Q: *You've said you try to help each of your students find his own voice. When you came to this country to live, what impact did meeting the American idiom have on your poetic voice?*

A: Well, it certainly made a difference. Of course, it's impossible to predict what my development might have been if I'd stayed in England. I have always felt that I would not have developed very far because it was not a good time for English poetry. It was really in the doldrums, and I think I might have found it stultifying. I presume that I would have gone on being a writer because I can't imagine being anything else; and you know I had started writing very young and had had a book published before I came here. I think it was very beneficial for me to come to America at a time when American poetry was in a very live period. But, although it seemed so at the time, in recent years I've come to realize that it wasn't a dramatic break. My early poems are very kind of wish-y romantic poems, the ones in my first book, but they have in them the seeds of everything that I've done since, actually. Hayden Carruth pointed out to me that in the poems about my sister, and in the ones in which I am writing about my childhood, my diction becomes quite British. It was an unconscious thing, but in fact my language has always moved back and forth between English and American usage. It leads to problems for the reader, because there are ways I have of saying things, if I'm saying them in an English kind of way, that the American reader doesn't pick up on. As for the English reader, the English reader doesn't know how to read American poetry anyway, because the whole pace of American speech is very different. Of course, this has changed somewhat in the last ten or fifteen years because there is much more interest in American literature now in England, and people have seen so many American movies they're probably getting the feel of the American idiom. I feel that I am genuinely of both places, and that has simply extended my usage. I'm glad to have a foot in more than one culture.

Q: *To what extent do you feel a poet can use words in his writing that are not part of his normal vocabulary?*

A: He can, if he's not doing it for pretentious reasons, but because really, in looking for the accurate word, he comes upon a word which, in its meaning and sound, makes him say, "Aha! This is the word I need for this thing that I'm saying." At that moment that word becomes a natural part of his vocabulary. After all, the whole thing was once unknown territory to each of us. Our vocabulary grows as we grow. So I wouldn't exclude words that a person finds because he's looking for them. But the sort of deliberate showing off —occasionally you find somebody actually looking through the dictionary for abstruse words and sort of saving them to be used in some poem—I think that's just childish.

Q: *When a new poem begins in your head, do you start writing immediately?*

A: It depends on what is coming into my head. If it is a sort of vague feeling that somewhere in the vicinity there is a poem, then no, I don't do anything about it, I wait. If a whole line, or phrase, comes into my head, I write it down, but without pushing it unless it immediately leads to another one. If it's an idea, then I don't do anything about it until that idea begins to crystallize into some phrases, some words, a rhythm, because if I try to push that into being by will before the intuition is really at work, then it's going to be a very bad beginning, and perhaps I'm going to lose the poem altogether. So there is some feeling of when to begin writing, but it's really rather hard to describe, especially since it's somewhat different with each poem. There is often a kind of preliminary feeling, a sort of aura—what is it? An early warning?—which alerts one to the possibility of a poem. You can smell the poem before you can see it. Like some animal . . . Hmmm, seems like a bear's around here . . .

Q: *Do you usually hear a poem's rhythm from the beginning?*

A: Well, if it was the smell of a bear, you know, you might begin to hear it kind of going . . . pad . . . pad . . . pad around the house; but if, let's say, it was a kind of a rustle in the bushes, which might be a bird or a snake or a squirrel, it might start to go blipblipblipblip . . .

Q: *Do you revise a good deal?*

A: That again depends on the individual poem. Of course, the longer the poem, the more revision. The kind of poem that comes out right the first time is almost always a very short poem. When poems emerge full-blown, I feel that there's been lots of preliminary work done on them at a preconscious level.

Q: *Since you write in nontraditional, free forms, what determines the physical shape a poem of yours will take? For example, what most often decides stanza divisions for you?*

A: I've written about this in an article called "Some Notes on Organic Form," which has been published in a number of places. It was first in POETRY Magazine, and then it was reprinted in a NEW DIRECTIONS ANNUAL, and it's been reprinted again in an anthology called NAKED POETRY which Bob Mezey and Stephen Berg brought out about a year ago. I think of there being clusters of perceptions which determine the stanza. Of course, sometimes the stanza breaks in the middle of a sentence, syntactically, but the perception cluster, nevertheless, did pause there for a moment.

Q: *What do you consider in deciding the length of a line?*

A: I regard the end of a line, the line break, as roughly equivalent to half a comma, but what that pause is doing is recording non-syntactic hesitations, or waitings, that occur in the thinking-feeling process. This is where the dance comes into it. You can't get this onto your tape, but I can sort of demonstrate it for you (*stands, and moves to the center of the room*). You see, in the composition of a poem, thinking and feeling are really working together, as a kind of single thing, although they often get separate in other areas of one's life. We don't want to call the movement of that process thinking-feeling, it's too clumsy; and we don't want to call it thinking, it's more than thinking, and we don't want to call it feeling, it's more than feeling, so let's call it perception, as perhaps a not totally accurate, but usable, term. That process does not go on at a steady walking pace (*walking*). It doesn't

constantly dance around, either, but it may kind of hurry forward
(*little fast steps*), and then it will stop (*stops*), and then it will walk more
slowly, and it has definitely an almost dance-like movement to it, not
constantly skipping and jumping and running, but a varied motion.
For instance, when one is simply conversing, with feeling, with a
friend, even if one tends to think and speak in rather complete
sentences, nevertheless there are pauses in one's speech which are
expressive pauses—sometimes for emphasis, sometimes because one
has rushed forward to a certain point (*demonstrating*), and one doesn't
really know what the next word that one is going to say will be. These
are not syntactic pauses. The sentence is there, in back of them.
Sometimes the sentence becomes broken, sometimes the sentence is
never finished, often the sentences are complete. But articulations
—in the sense that our bones, our fingers, are articulated, right? they
have joints, they can bend—occur. These occur within the rationale
of the syntax, and the line break is a peculiarly sensitive means of
recording those things. So that one can pick up all the rhythm of
feeling, all the rhythm of experience, in ways which prose is perhaps
not as well equipped to do. Of course, good prose is rhythmic, too,
but it doesn't depend quite so heavily as poetry does on the finest
adjustments of rhythm and even of typographically indicated intona-
tion.

Q: *There is a remarkable variation in the speed with which your lines can
be read—sometimes there are several speed shifts within one short poem, such
as* The Singer; *and sometimes the change comes between sections of longer
poems, as happens in the one called* Six Variations.

A: It's never directly stated in that poem, but the six variations are
about language and what it can do. You know, it mentions Gertrude
Stein's dog Basket, and how she learned what a sentence was. The
section with the long rhymes, with the ashcans and the children on
the street, demonstrates the speed of polysyllabic lines—the lines are
longer, but there are lots of polysyllables in them, and the movement
is a sort of fast, rippling movement. And then there's a section with
many monosyllables that moves very slow and is about ". . . heavy
heart and/cold eye." So they are variations almost on how the syllable
works, variations on the theme of the function of the syllable? That's
not quite accurate, but . . .

Q: *You control line speed, then, by the length of the lines, and the number
of syllables, and—*

A: Not the number of syllables so much as the kind of syllables, and whether the consonants are sufficiently harder to enunciate so that they help to slow things down, too. However, when one talks about these matters, it tends to sound as if the poet were extremely deliberate and conscious, but, in fact, it is something that becomes second nature so that you're doing it instinctively. When you're revising you may find places where you've botched it, your instincts were not working well, and then you may deliberately try to achieve an effect by those means which you know will help to achieve it. But in the first instance one is working pretty unconsciously, I think.

Q: *Can you say generally, in deciding between several words for a particular spot in a poem, if you put more importance on sound or on sense?*

A: Well, the sonic effect would be the more important, but it's never a factor entirely separable from other things about the word. If you wanted a word that had something sort of thick about it, let us say, you might find a word which had that sonic quality and yet the associations of that word, or the fact that it was a homonym and the associations with the word that it sounded like were all wrong, would prevent your using it. Let's say you have a choice of adjectives, and one has an onomatopoeic quality which you want, but it also has a couple of "s's" in it, and the rest of the line, or the line just before it, is already pretty sibilant, but you feel that that line is right. You might have to forego the word that you've just found and keep on looking, because you can't have all those "s's" jammed up together. There's almost never just one factor to be considered. You always have to weigh the one against the other.

Q: *In your more recent poems you seem to be indenting less than you did in the earlier ones. Is there a reason for this change?*

A: Lately I've been doing it quite a lot again, I think. When I indent, I'm trying to do two things. One is very obvious. If I have something that approximates a list, a number of things mentioned in succession, in different lines, which form a kind of category, I sometimes like to indent them and line them up. They're like a subsidiary clause. And that's for reasons of clarity. But the other reason for indentation is that if the eye is going from the end of one line all the way back to the margin, it takes infinitesimally longer than if it goes only to the beginning of an indented line. Sometimes one feels that the next line *is* another line, it's not just part of the line before it, yet it is in some way intimately connected with that line in a manner which makes one desire to have that little extra speed for the eye, which transmits itself to the ear and the voice.

Q: *It's a psychological adjustment.*

A: It's a psychological adjustment which, however, is also, I think, a neurological one. I don't know if they have instruments which measure that—I daresay they do—but it's something one feels; one doesn't need an instrument to measure it. I'm pretty sure that it works because I have had the satisfaction of hearing people read poems of mine aloud who are not simply imitating me, because they haven't heard me read them, and they've read them right. The way I've deployed them on the page has been an accurate indication of how they're supposed to be read. Now just Wednesday, I had a sort of argument with some students who were objecting to that much direction by the poet. I defend it, absolutely, because I feel that it's exactly like the writing down of music. When music is written, it allows a considerable amount of interpretation to the performer, and yet it is always definitely that piece of music and no other. You get twenty competent pianists playing a Beethoven piano sonata, and each performance will be different. But it is recognizably the same piece of music. One may take the whole thing faster than another, one may make the loud parts louder and the quiet parts quieter, but the composer has indicated that here it's allegro and here it's adagio, or here it's fortissimo and here it's pianissimo. That is his privilege, and although we don't have such a generally accepted system of notation for the nuance, I see no reason why the poet shouldn't have the same privilege, and by that means obtain as fine results as composers have done. I don't feel that it is an imposition on the reader. It still allows him lots of freedom, and without that much care about the structure of a poem, I think what you have is a lot of slop.

Q: *How concerned are you about the way the entire poem looks on the page?*

A: What happens visually produces a certain psychological effect, there's no doubt about it. When you look at a piece of music and the score is very very black with notes, you get a kind of crowded, agitated, perhaps even busy feeling. And a poem that fills up a page has psychologically for some people, or perhaps for all people at some moments, a somewhat intimidating effect. You're not sure if you can get into it. A poem that has two-line stanzas and lots of space tends to attract the eye. But I think these are very secondary effects.

63

They're not essential where one is considering the nature of the poetry. The written poem is the written notation of a sonic effect. Which doesn't mean that the best way to receive poetry is to hear it and not see it at all. I think it's a question of eye-ear coordination. I'm not fully satisfied with poems that I only hear at a reading or on a record and never get to look at. I have to look at them, too. But by the same token, I want to *hear* a written poem, and I will either read it aloud to myself if I can't hear the poet read it, or even if I'm not actually reading it aloud I'm sounding it out in my head. I think the two things are equally important. Sometimes a poem will look absolutely, delightfully decorative on the page, but I think when that *takes over*, it's a mistake. They were doing it, of course, in the seventeenth century—wings, and crosses, and things—and sometimes it works out, but I don't think it's really a main direction for poetry. To hell with what it looks like, you know. Some poems that do sort of get all over the page, like some of Olson, or some of Duncan, I've actually heard objected to because they looked so messy. That's not the point. Never mind if they do look messy! They're indicating rhythm and pace, and all sorts of sonic values.

Q: *You often repeat words or themes in your poems. Do you have any theories about the value and effect of repetition?*

A: Do you mean, throughout all my poetry the same things come up, or within one poem?

Q: *Within one poem.*

A: Oh, well, there is the impulse to tie things together. If one feels them to be at all tied together, one wants to get that into the structure, instead of things flowing along to the point where they slip out of your fingers. Maybe it sounds a little compulsive, but in other works of art which I value I often see echoes and correspondences. I see the curve of the bushes in the corner of that painting by Howard Fussiner, echoed by the curve going the opposite way of the armchair down in the lower left-hand corner. I see the uprights of the delphiniums out the window, there, and the trunk of a tree in the distance, and the vase—they're all related to each other as uprights in that picture. It's the compositional sense; it's the impulse to create pattern, or to reveal pattern. I say "reveal," because I have a thing about finding form rather than imposing it. I want to find correspondences and relationships which are there but hidden, and I think one of the things the artist does is to reveal. That's the principle on which I've worked.

Denise Levertov

Q: *It's interesting that you mentioned Gertrude Stein earlier. Repetition was so important in her writing.*

A: Well, think of any work of art that you really value. Can you think of one in which there are not such things?

Q: *But sometimes there is more repetition in one work than in another, sometimes the repetition is especially obvious, and its effect is easy to feel . . .*

A: Where there's more of it, in any particular artist's work, I think it indicates that that artist has a feeling for denseness of texture; and where you find it very little, he is perhaps after a kind of transparence, an almost waterlike, flowing thinness of texture. For example, look at the very unstructured work of Gary Snyder, whose poetry I like very much. Read his statement in that anthology, NAKED POETRY, and compare it with mine. You'll see two very different sensibilities, in regard to form, operating there, and I think the differences in our work run naturally out of that difference in the way we want things to be. What pleases him is something more loosely formed, spread out. I certainly seem to have inherent in my nervous system more of a liking for pattern, not exactly symmetry, but I want to gather things together and see them in their juxtapositions.

Q: *Since your poems are such physical wholes, is the need to divide the longer ones up into pages a problem for you, when you put them into books?*

A: No, but I have had one typographical problem. Sometimes, if I have a long line, and it's wider than the page permits, then of course the last few words have to be sort of tucked under. And since I do so much indentation for structural reasons, it bugs me very much when I have to have a line broken up that way, because the reader might well think that that is an indentation. It's sometimes a little hard to make sure it looks like what it is. I have wished that poetry books could be different dimensions, as some published by small presses are, but my publisher tells me that it's very hard to change the dimensions of books. Bookshelves are designed to hold books of certain dimensions, booksellers don't like to handle books that are odd shapes, and distributors don't like to distribute them, so one is stuck . . .

Q: *Many of your poems reflect an experience of reality and of the present moment that is extraordinarily clear and deep. In THE COMING FALL, for instance, you speak of "A sense of the present," and ". . . a shiver, a delight/that what is passing/is here . . ." Are you able to maintain this awareness for long periods?*

A: Oh, that's a hard question to answer. Not very often, I would say, and perhaps rarely when not engaged in the writing of poems. But sometimes, as something distinct from writing, I've experienced it, too.

Q: *You often use the word "joy" in describing those moments. Once you say "terrible joy," and in the poem called* Joy, *you say, ". . . glad to the brink of fear." What is that fear?*

A: "Glad to the brink of fear," is actually a quote from Emerson, where he speaks of crossing either the Boston or the Cambridge Common on a cloudy, raw sort of evening (I'm paraphrasing now, because I can't remember the exact words) with nothing very special about it, and being seized with "joy to the brink of fear." Well, I suppose joy is a passion, and all passionate things are perhaps very close in nature to their opposites. Joy, pain, fear—there comes a point, perhaps, where one no longer knows which is which. I think that is what he was talking about, and I guess that is what I am talking about, too. What people call ecstasy is more like terror than it is like contentment, isn't it?

Q: *Some poets today are using drugs to reach a state of heightened consciousness in which they then write poems. Have you any feeling about this practise?*

A: Well, I smoke grass—I smoke it as a social pleasure and in order to relax, but I don't use it in order to work up poems. In fact, I don't smoke very much. It's kind of hard to get! I like to drink, but it's not something that I use in relation to writing, and I haven't taken any other kinds of drugs such as acid, mescaline, any kind of psychedelic drug. I've had experiences without the benefit of any such thing that I feel have been so close to what people describe having with drugs that I feel I don't want to disturb the peculiar balance of my imagination and my associative language. I feel that if others need to loosen up this way or that, well, that's their way of doing it. And I have felt a certain amount of fear of spoiling what I have got. It would seem kind of greedy. But if I came to a point in my life where I felt dried up and out of touch with my unconscious, with my imagination, then I guess I would try whatever seemed to be a good way to shake myself up again.

Q: *Your poems contain many religious words, such as "hymn," "psalm," "communion wine," "pilgrimage." You speak of ceremonies and*

Denise Levertov

rites. You often use the word "light" in a Quaker sense. There is a sense of joy like that of the Hassidim. In your love poems there is frequently a kind of devotional feeling along with a sensuous one. And, throughout your books, one recognizes themes that recall the Quaker, Jewish and Zen emphasis on the importance of the present moment. What does the word "religious" mean to you?

A: The impulse to kneel in wonder. . . . The impulse to kiss the ground. . . . The sense of awe. The felt presence of some mysterious force, whether it be what one calls beauty, or perhaps just the sense of the unknown—I don't mean "unknown" in the sense of we don't know what the future will bring. I mean the sense of the numinous, whether it's in a small stone, or a large mountain. I think at this particular point, that sense of joy which you've mentioned in my poems, and which I think is very real to me, and has been, is at a very low ebb. I think of my poem called LIVING, which says:

> The fire in leaf and grass
> so green it seems
> each summer the last summer.
>
> The wind blowing, the leaves
> shivering in the sun,
> each day the last day.
>
> A red salamander
> so cold and so
> easy to catch, dreamily
>
> moves his delicate feet
> and long tail. I hold
> my hand open for him to go.
>
> Each minute the last minute.

There's a certain apocalyptic sense in that, but there's also a kind of joy in the marvelousness of that green fire in the grass and leaves, and in the beauty of the little salamander. My feeling this winter, like many peoples,' is so doom-filled, the sense of time running out is pretty much squashing my sense of the beauty of the ephemeral being ephemeral. I've always hated artificial flowers unless they were just flagrantly and beautifully, sort of brassily, artificial. But the good imitations, the ones that you think are real until you get up to them,

67

and then there's that awful dead plastic, are really vile. And the reason why I think they're so vile is because so much of the beauty of a flower is in its very perishableness. One doesn't want it to last forever, and accumulate dust. And so there is joy in the very sense of mortality, in a way. But facing not just the mortality that we have always had with us, but the annihilation of all life, which is every day more and more a real possibility, one's feeling of anguish and despair certainly takes over.

Q: *Speaking of social protest, W. H. Auden has said, "I do not think that writing poems will change anything." Many people disagree with him, and you are one of the poets who, over the last five years, have written many poems of protest against injustice, particularly against the Vietnam War. That situation is worse now than it has ever been. What do you feel, at this point, a poet can do?*

A: To confine it to America of the last five years, let us say, I think the poetry of protest, indignation, anger and so forth, that has been written by many, many poets has helped to awaken many people to the situation. There were the Vietnam Poetry Readings that Robert Bly and other people organized, where slides of Vietnam, of napalmed children, and also of beautiful, still untouched villages—sort of alternations of terrible destruction and of what the country looked like before it was blasted—were combined with the reading of poems. Those things, back in 1966, stirred up quite a lot of people to become active in the anti-war movement. And the anti-war movement itself has grown very much and is becoming a more revolutionary movement in which people no longer see stopping the war as a single issue which can be divorced from racism, imperialism, capitalism, male supremacy. There are increasing numbers of people who understand, or are beginning to understand, the connections between all these things. And the poets have played some part in this consciousness-raising. There's a lot more going on in the way of organizing and educative work in local communities than there was two years ago. A lot of people who were activists in college, who have now graduated or dropped out, instead of also dropping out of the movement (which is the way it used to be) have gone further into it, but you don't hear so much about them because they're working in very sort of unspectacular, local ways. This is something about which in itself I'm not despondent. I don't think that the movement is a failure, and hasn't achieved anything, and so forth; but the fact is that we're working against time. And the factors, including ecological ones, against which people on the revolutionary side are working are so tremendous; they're such tremendous, heavy forces, that one just doesn't know whether there's going to be *time* for this new kind of patient, consciousness-raising work to produce its effect before a disaster is brought about by the other forces.

Q: *As for your own activities—do you feel differently now from the way you did in 1966 and 1967 about what you should be doing? Certainly you are now more concerned than you were then about time running out.*

A: Yes, well, all we could think of to do in 1966 was to have big, peaceful demonstrations, which got bigger and bigger. People as astute as, let us say, Chomsky, feel that those demonstrations did have a deterrent effect, that the United States might have gone further, might have used nuclear weapons by this time, if there had not been a strong, growing, anti-war movement in this country. So you don't measure the results of those demonstrations by positive results, you have to measure them by sort of negative ones, which is very hard to do. Now, most people feel mere demonstrations, mere massing of people, is no longer enough. There has to be definite civil disobedience action, and the spearhead of the movement is those people who have done sabotage, who have destroyed files—not only draft files, but the Dow Chemical files, and so forth—all those sorts of actions. If there are going to be more moratoriums, they're going to have to take a different form. I think there are a lot of people who are still back in 1966 in their political development, and they need to experience big demonstrations, which do have a radicalizing effect. When they get tear-gassed, and they see police beating up people with clubs at a demonstration, either they cop out and never go to another one (in which case they wouldn't have been very useful people anyway), or, step-by-step, it radicalizes them. What I personally am trying to do at this point is very, very mild, because I find myself teaching at a school which is back in 1954, I would say, and I'm trying to organize a teach-in. I think that the right speakers at a teach-in could stir those people up, and it would be a beginning for a lot of them, at least.

7
Galway Kinnell

Q: *In our craft interviews we have tried to be as objective as possible, and not get too involved with feelings and emotions about things, but stay with craft and style.*

A: All matters I don't know anything about.

Q: *Could you tell us something about your method of writing—revision and that sort of thing?*

A: Only that I usually do revise a very great deal.

Q: *And what about beginning to write at a certain time of the day, music, etc.*

A: No, I have no habits, no habits.

Q: *What about revising something that has already been published?*

A: Yes, sometimes after a poem has been published in a magazine I might change it a bit here and there before putting it into a book.

Q: *And your translations—your translations of François Villon—what function do you feel that translation has for a poet?*

A: There are people for whom translating is a way of making clearer to themselves the kind of poetry that they would like to be writing themselves. But for myself translating has just been a way of getting under the skins of poems I liked. I don't think it has played any important role in my own writing.

Q: *What about your recommendations regarding translations?*

A: For a person with time and energy to spare, translation is a marvelous thing to do. For one of a more plodding disposition, it can rob you of the strength you might put into your own work. Also, translation can be an escapist activity, for in translating there is much of the "fun" of writing and little of the responsibility and risk, the real excitement of writing. It's therefore a tempting activity. While you are engaged in translating it's easy to think you are doing something splendid and important, but at the end the true joy turns out to be missing. I have myself given up translating, because it takes me such a long time and my life seems so filled now I can't afford that time and energy.

Q: *How do you feel about teaching in terms of what it does for your own work?*

A: I don't think that it does anything for my own work. Teaching is exciting and interesting, and it is an honorable profession. But I don't think it nourishes a writer. Many of the people you are talking to are too much like yourself: it's too much like a conversation going on inside your own head. It would be much better if one could find a work by which you could enter a new world, a world different not only in its kinds of people, but also in its materials and terminology. As yet I haven't found for myself such a work.

Q: *Do you think this would bring you more reality experiences?*

A: Yes, I think it would keep you in relation with a wider world and help prevent academic atrophy.

Q: *What about workshops? Have you participated as a student?*

A: No, I never studied in a workshop.

Q: *How do you feel about them from the point of view of the new writer?*

A: All I can say is that I never met a writer who thought he had learned much from a workshop. On the other hand, many seem to have enjoyed the association with other writers and feel that the excitement generated in workshops brought forth more from themselves than a life in isolation might have.

71

Q: *What about poetry readings?*

A: I do quite a lot of them. They can be awful. There are few things more depressing than reading poems you have read many, many times, to people who aren't terribly interested in hearing them, who attend the reading because they regard you as a curiosity. The only way to survive such an evening is to read to yourself. But then it happens you meet an audience that seems at one with you; reading to them gives you a rather beautiful sense not so much of sharing your own feelings as of being the voice of everyone there. This can be thrilling for one who has lived much of his life alone. Furthermore, if you've just recently written a poem there is a matchless excitement in reading it to others. The great moment is when you become one with the poem and create it anew as you read it.

Q: *You were active, I understand, in setting up the University of Chicago Adult Education program, and the program at NYU. Could you comment on that in relation to your poetry? Was it all part of the same thing?*

A: It was a separate compartment. I would not be able to do the same thing now. I had a lot of energy at that time, enough to maintain compartments.

Q: *What was it you did in terms of the program?*

A: We tried to figure out what would be the education we would like to have had and to organize that kind of education into a program of courses. I don't think it's quite the kind of education I'd like to have now. Now I don't think I would do it in quite the same way.

Q: *What about adult education in this country and the relationship between poetry and education? Is there enough poetry in it?*

A: I don't think the way poetry is treated in colleges—whether for adults or undergraduates—is really the right way to treat it. Of course, I wouldn't like it *not* treated in colleges either. And yet the thing about poetry is that if you're moved by a poem you might not wish to say anything at all. You might wish to live with that poem in silence for a while. If you're not fully able to understand it, maybe if you just read it to yourself again and again, get it by heart, you will come around to understand it—and understand it in a way we don't have terms for expressing. In a class, however, they want you to analyze the poem, say exactly what it means, clear up the difficulties.

72

You have to commit two sins: eradicate the mystery of the poem and talk about it on demand, which is to say in someone else's critical language. But the university lives on talk, and so apparently that's the way it's got to be.

Q: *Would there be another way to present poetry to a class?*

A: Ideally, only ancient poetry should be studied in universities. The function of the study would simply be to compensate for all the time that has gone by. Contemporary poetry would be so available, so much part of one's life, that to "study" it would be superfluous. Of course this isn't the case. I don't think the solution is to submit contemporary poetry to the same objective scrutiny as ancient poetry, as universities now mostly do. Rather we perhaps should try to discover a whole new function for the teaching of contemporary poems. Perhaps we shouldn't teach them directly at all, but use contemporary poetry as pretexts for getting students to look into their own inner lives—their own deepest experiences—and to meet each other rather openly at this level.

Q: *Do you think we have failed to create an audience for poetry—in the basic education system—not just the colleges? Do you think it should be a spontaneous thing—and if not created do you think it should just die?*

A: I don't think the responsibility ultimately rests on the teachers. They themselves have been betrayed in regard to poetry—and all that mysterious life that poetry seeks to express—not by their own teachers but by the whole technological culture in which we live. The reason poetry is returning into the lives of young people is their revulsion against technology and technological alienation. We have all become a little clearer about what human life is.

Q: *There was an evolution from interest in the arts to becoming more pragmatic, an interest in the dollar, etc. Do you think this is a further evolution to the way back—the way it used to be?*

A: I think it will take a new unpredictable turn. We'll just have to see what happens.

Q: *Could you comment on your use of invented words—neologisms—in* Crucible *and* Body Rags, *the word regarding the porcupine "spartles across the grass."*

A: I have invented a few words but not many. What I have done more is to try to rescue certain ancient words.

73

Q: *Is it despair at finding a traditional word that makes you want to rescue?*

A: I think there is a danger our language will get too mental. We are discarding some of the great, sensual words in favor of more electric words, whether astronaut language, hip slang, or advertising talk. I would simply like to see as rich a vocabulary as possible available to us. English is a fantastic poetic language, and to lose any of its gorgeous words seems a waste. I guess we use the words which correspond to our feelings about reality. As we become more mental and technological, we discard the words which evoke mysteries, that don't interest us any longer.

Q: *You say you have no habits, but how do you write?*

A: Well, I never write on a typewriter. Sometimes I keep note-books, but since I tend to lose them I manage with scraps of paper.

Q: *Do you carry around a fragment or a line for ages until you use it in a poem?*

A: Sometimes I do.

Q: *Is that your usual way of starting a poem?*

A: You see, I don't really have a usual way. I have started poems that way, but other times I have written the whole poem out from the beginning to the end.

Q: *About six years ago there was a photograph in* LIFE *magazine with regard to your involvement in civil rights. How do you feel about involvement in any political activity for a poet?*

A: As poets are freer than most people to engage in such activities it's rather wasteful of them to decline. In the case of the protests against the Vietnam war, very few poets didn't take part in some way. No other profession or group was so overwhelmingly opposed to the war and so active in opposing it. As to whether they should or shouldn't: I only think that if they hate the war they should, if they don't hate the war they shouldn't.

Q: *In terms of enriching your poetry, do you feel involvement has any bearing on that?*

A: I think involvement in the effort to alleviate pain in the world, whether a militant cause, or just caring for a sick person, any involvement at all which seeks justice and brings you into a feeling of love and community is purifying and is bound to be nourishing—and this is true whether you are a writer or not.

Q: *We note in a brief biographical sketch about you in* A CONTROVERSY OF POETS *(Paris Leary and Robert Kelly, editors; Anchor Books, Doubleday, 1965) that you have spent some time in France and in Teheran. What about living away from this country—what effect do you feel it has had on your work?*

A: I was a rather backward person, I think, and living in France especially opened up worlds for me that probably would have remained closed if I had stayed in Chicago, where I had been living. I guess that's good for one's poetry. Traveling itself isn't particularly useful; it's what happens to you. I guess it can happen anywhere.

Q: *What about your poems* THE BEAR *and* THE PORCUPINE? *Bill Packard sees them as rather unique nature poems. Do you agree with his interpretation of them?*

A: As for the term "nature," I think we have to revise our understanding of it in regard to poetry. The "nature poem" as opposed to, say, the poem of society or the urban poem, doesn't have much future—and not much past, for that matter—we have to get over that notion we carry from the Old Testament on down that we are super beings created in God's image to have dominion over everything else—over "nature." We have to feel our own evolutionary roots, and know that we belong to life in the same way as do the other animals and the plants and stones. Then a nature poem wouldn't be a matter of English gardens, of hedgerows and flowers. It would include the city too: if the beaver dam is a work of nature, so is the city a work of nature. The real nature poem will not exclude man and deal only with animals and plants and stones; it will be a poem in which we men re-feel in ourselves our own animal and plant and stone life, our own deep connection with all other beings, a connection deeper than personality, a connection which resembles the attachment an animal has for an animal. We're going toward that sense of ourselves and we're going away from it simultaneously. Now, for the first time in a long time, there is a kind of countermotion toward the natural, toward connection with the life of the planet.

Q: *So it isn't a totally new development?*

A: No. Thoreau was doing precisely this 125 years ago. He had a kind of allergy to technology, an instinctive reaction to it—it made him break out in spiritual hives. Yet even he, because of the terminology available, kept making the fast distinction between man and nature.

Q: *He was the first?*

A: No, I wouldn't say so. I suppose that in all human societies from the beginning there have been both a drive to control and dominate nature and a hunger to be one with nature. These contended in some kind of balance. Only since the Renaissance did the drive to dominate overwhelm the other. Only in the twentieth century have we seen the catastrophic result.

Q: *What do you do about dry periods? Do you have them?*

A: Yes, dry periods, of course, but I don't think of them that way—more as complications of life—practical and emotional complications—which produce in me depressions, and when, therefore, I can't write.

Q: *So you wait as you simplify and it just levels off? Then you write again.*

A: So it's been true in the past. I can't say for the future.

Q: *What of your early influences?*

A: I had a teacher in college, Charles Bell, who was a powerful influence on me. Aside from him, really no one I knew. As for poets I read, when I was young Eliot influenced me much, later Yeats, Whitman and Rilke.

Q: *What about poets now? Do you read for influence or just because you like them?*

A: I read because I like them. If any contemporary poet influenced me at all I think it was Allen Ginsberg, in HOWL.

Q: *Do you think it is necessary for a poet to go through form and then break out of it?*

A: No. That was what happened to my generation—almost all of us began writing in strict forms and almost all of us gave it up. I don't think this will happen in the future. Those who say you have to "learn the rules in order to break them" are probably extrapolating from their own experience, and that experience was probably an historical quirk. I doubt it's necessary. I don't see any young people interested in form and I see them writing a lot better than we were writing at their age. I doubt that there will be a return to form even as an exercise.

Q: *Do you ever set up a form and try to write within it as a challenge?*

A: No, never.

Q: *Your long poem* THE AVENUE BEARING THE INITIAL OF CHRIST INTO THE NEW WORLD—*was it your intention at that time to write a long poem?*

A: Yes. When I began writing it I understood it would be a long poem. I can't even say I experienced much difficulty, it rather wrote itself and it surprised me that it came out as whole as it did.

Q: *Everything works so beautifully in the poem, the words, the specificity—did it just happen that way or was it predetermined?*

A: There was something terribly exciting about that neighborhood—those people, those things. Whatever poem came out of it flowed from that excitement. I don't think I set out to be specific; it happened.

Q: *You lived there or you just observed it?*

A: I lived there a couple of years.

Q: *What about young writers—is there any person or set of persons writing that you would feel the young writer should be aware of?*

A: I think the atmosphere is such today that young writers don't have any problem in discovering their kinsmen among writers of the world. I only think young poets should read the poets they love. Twenty-five years ago certain poets were kept secret, so to speak. There weren't too many people who knew of Neruda, for instance. Things have changed so much, there are so many translations available, word-of-mouth conveys so much, I don't think people have trouble finding friends among writers.

Q: *Do you think this was a purposeful thing in the past?*

A: No, it was due to the provincial quality of American letters. We were very Anglophile and a little Francophile—and that was it. Not too many people were doing translations and not too many publishers were interested in turning them out.

Q: *Whom do you read now?*

A: With some shame I have to say that in the last three years, while I've been working on my new long poem, I've hardly read any poetry at all, except poems by students and friends. Now that my own poem is finished I hope to read again.

8
John Ashbery

Q: *When did you first start writing poetry?*

A: When I was in high school. As a kid I was more interested in painting and wanted to be a painter; in fact I did up until I was about eighteen. It overlapped with poetry and I found that I was able to say better what I wanted to say in poetry than in painting, which I subsequently lost interest in.

Q: *We understand you always begin with a title. Does that mean you have the title before any conception of the subject matter or the form?*

A: I don't always do that but what happens is that a possible title occurs to me and it defines an area that I feel I'll be able to move around in and uncover. It's not that I feel necessarily that titles are important in themselves. I remember hearing Aram Saroyan telling students in Indiana what was happening in New York and one of the things he said was, "Titles are out, man." This may or may not be true, but in any case it seems to me that the title is something that tips the whole poem in one direction or another, doesn't it? I mean a satirical title can give a different color to a poem that might be very different if it were titled something else. As I say, I feel the title is a very small aperture into a larger area, a keyhole perhaps, or some way of getting into the poem which I suppose is my thoughts at any particular moment, which I find I can then organize by this means.

79

Q: *Do you find the beginnings of your poems in your immediate surroundings? notes or recent conversations? dreams? reading? painting?*

A: I'd say in all those, yes. I often begin writing a poem with a collection of odd notations that have come out of conversations, dreams, overheard remarks on the street and these, again, are a further definition of an area that I'm hoping to explore. Very often I throw out these beginning notes once I've finished the poem; but again they are devices which enable me to get at something I don't already know. I can't tell you why a certain overheard remark seems significant and another one doesn't except that when I'm in a state of attentiveness, waiting to write a poem, I can tell intuitively what's going to help me to write it and what isn't.

Q: *You always want a poem to explore unknown territory?*

A: Yes, that's what a poem is to me; I think every poem before it's written is something unknown and the poem that isn't wouldn't be worth writing. My poetry is often criticized for a failure to communicate, but I take issue with this; my intention is to communicate and my feeling is that a poem that communicates something that's already known by the reader is not really communicating anything to him and in fact shows a lack of respect for him.

Q: *You talked about an especially attentive state. Could you tell us about that? Is that something akin to inspiration?*

A: People often ask do you sit around and wait for an inspiration or do you just sit down and write. I think when I first began writing poetry I had the idea that one sat around and waited for the muse to descend; but now I have to program myself in order to find time to write since I have a job, and I've also gotten so much in the habit of writing critical articles and reviews for my work that I don't seem to have to wait any more. All I need is the time and a not too depressed state of mind to be able to start concentrating attentively in order to pick up whatever is in the air.

Q: *You have a constant accumulation of things waiting to be written?*

A: I hope so. I go at them one at a time; I can't look too far into the future. One never knows of course. Very often there isn't anything there but you have to proceed on the assumption that something is, otherwise you don't write.

John Ashbery

Q: *We understand that for your writing you keep a tape recorder by your bed. What is it useful for?*

A: I did that for a while but I haven't used it lately. I had one of those pocket kinds and I thought if I kept it by my bed I might wake up in the middle of the night with some great line that I'd be too lazy to write down, and I did this a few times. I've since found that those lines are usually not too memorable once daylight comes. I used to carry it around with me—I waste a lot of time before writing by going for long walks—and occasionally I would take this pocket tape recorder along, fish it out of my pocket and mutter something into it, getting strange looks from people; but I found a pencil and paper are really just as good. I jot down little phrases and ideas on pieces of paper, dig them out of my pockets and keep them around as I'm starting to write. And then, as I say, I get away from these once the writing takes over.

Q: *Do you actually compose at a typewriter?*

A: Yes. I used to be able to write only by hand and about ten years ago I'd become so used to typing that I began writing poetry that way. I think it was while I was writing THE SKATERS, which has very long lines in it; I found that I would often forget the last part of the line before I got a chance to write it down and the typewriter was more efficient for this. Now I use it all the time.

Q: *To go back a little, to what you were saying about eliminating the initial phrases, what is it about them that makes this necessary?*

A: They often stick out like sore thumbs even though they were what prompted me to write what came after them. As I say, they are devices and sometimes that's all they seem to be; they often don't fit into the texture of the poem; it's almost like some sort of lost wax or other process where the initial armature or whatever gets scrapped in the end.

Q: *In '69 when you appeared in Bill Packard's class at NYU you said you usually write listening to the radio or record player. Is the music a direct stimulus or a partial distraction? How does it work?*

A: The thing about music is that it's always going on and reaching a conclusion and it helps me to be surrounded by this moving climate that it produces—moving I mean in the sense of going on. I find too that I suddenly get into, as they say, a certain composer's work which seems to me to be a very good background for what I'm thinking about while I'm writing a particular poem.

Q: *So you actually choose people to work by sometimes?*

A: Very often. While writing one of the three prose poems which is in my book that's coming out I got to listening to Brahms' first sextet and it seemed to be the only piece of music that would work for this particular poem but it's hard to say anything very meaningful as to why. Poetry is mostly hunches.

Q: *What other composers have you used?*

A: I have very eclectic tastes in music as in most other things: Couperin is often very good. I played Elliott Carter's CONCERTO FOR ORCHESTRA a lot while I was writing THE NEW SPIRIT. Mostly, however, I would say my tastes run to nineteenth century music for purposes of poetry.

Q: *Traditionally a poet's craft or the way he wrote a poem was contained within a fairly fixed set of conventions: meter, rhyme, the most obvious. As a modern poet, do you have anything analogous to that kind of craft?*

A: Not any more. When I was younger I investigated the various forms and meters; I reached a point I think where I felt, if called upon, I could write a sonnet that had a beginning, middle and end and would say what a sonnet is supposed to say. And my early attempts to do without these traditional structures were not very successful. I feel that I've had to get a great deal of practice in the kind of free poetry that I write in order to be able to do it, I hope, successfully, and now it's something that I simply don't think about any more. I sit down to write without any questions of form or anything like that although it's not that I ignore them; I feel I've digested them for my purposes and can concentrate on the more important aspects of poetry.

Q: *With regard to revision, you've said that you "absorbed from Cage and Zen that whatever way it comes out is the way it is." Was it difficult for you to accept that idea?*

A: I don't know that I would make that statement now because I do a certain amount of revising, although I do less of it now; I used to go over every poem and change things constantly until often there wasn't very much left of the original, but this is something that comes with practice. Young people in universities always ask the question, "Do you revise very much?" because, I suppose, they're going through the same period that I did. I don't any more and yet I wouldn't say that whatever comes out is all right; it's just that I've, I think, trained myself not to write what I'm going to discard later on. I do a lot of small revisions but I think I've moved away really from the total freedom I thought I had when I was beginning to experiment with very free almost unconscious poetry.

Q: *In what book?*

A: A lot of these poems I've never published and there are a lot in THE TENNIS COURT OATH which are really like automatic poetry, which no longer interests me very much. For instance, the poem EUROPE, the long poem in that book, is one that's no longer very close to me. At the time I wrote it I was baffled as to what to do in poetry; I wasn't satisfied with the way my work was going and I felt it was time to just clear my head by writing whatever came into it and that's very much the case with that poem; and I think it helped me along but I don't value it as much as ones I've written since.

Q: *Your poem* THE NEW SPIRIT *appeared in the* PARIS REVIEW, *Fall 1970, and will be included in* THREE POEMS (THE NEW SPIRIT, THE SYSTEM *and* THE RECITAL) *published by Viking in February 1972. In* THE NEW SPIRIT, *there still seems to be operative some extension of this notion of acceptance that you described as coming from John Cage and Zen, the way you refer to there being many ways and how you choose or get pushed into one way but they're all valid.*

A: That's something that's part of the content of the poem which is a little different. Yes, that's an idea that probably keeps cropping up in my work but as far as the actual writing of the poem it doesn't have much to do with it.

Q: *Would you say you usually write a poem at one sitting?*

A: Shorter ones, yes, but long ones like the ones I've done lately I only work perhaps an hour at a time—it's very hard to write poetry for much longer than that—and so these are things that take a period of perhaps several months and it's something, of course, quite different from a poem written all at once because one's mind changes during the course of the writing; these changes are reflected in the poem, give it a diversity that the other wouldn't have.

Q: *Do you ever discard something you've written because it seems insufficiently poetic?*

A: I don't know exactly what poetic means.

Q: *We were just thinking that you might have some notion in your own mind, if not necessarily one to define at the moment, but some sense that something didn't fit within your notion of what is poetic.*

A: That I would certainly do but as I say the word poetic is one that we, of course, all use but I'm not really sure of what it means and it often has a pejorative sense. So, in this case, I would probably say unconsciously to myself that that doesn't work or that's no good or that doesn't fit; the concept of its being poetic doesn't occur to me in the process of writing.

Q: *Would you agree that you sometimes deliberately work to maximize content over subject matter?*

A: Yes, that's a very accurate phrase as far as my poetry goes, I think. My poetry doesn't have subjects. Not in many years have I sat down to write a poem dealing with a particular subject and treating it formally in a kind of essay. My poetry, as I indicated in what I said already, has an exploratory quality and I don't have it all mapped out before I sit down to write. I do have a very general idea which it would be very difficult to tell anybody about before I had written the poem; it would simply make no sense to another person and yet I know myself enough to know that it's probably going to lead to a poem.

Q: *What techniques do you use for staying away from subject matter?*

A: I'm not sure that I use any techniques to stay away from subject matter. I guess I feel that subject matter is, might well be, some tributary part of a poem; because I think when there is a poem—take a poem of the past, for instance, a poem by Hardy or DOVER BEACH or something like that where the meaning is perfectly clear. The subject matter is common knowledge and it's the other things that get included into the poem that raise it to the level of poetry and which are therefore the vital elements in the poem. I suppose one might say really that subject matter is a kind of structure which gets transformed in the process of the poem's being written so that it becomes something quite different. I guess what interests me in poetry is the difference, the ways in which the prose sense of a poem gets transformed in poetry and this I think is the area that I write in to the exclusion of a formal theme or topic. I find one can say very much more by advancing immediately to the poetry in the poem.

Q: *The poetry consisting mainly in the fluidity of thought rather than objects of thought?*

A: Yes, I think I'd agree with that.

Q: *Memory, forgetfulness and being are simultaneously present in much of your work, which prompts us to ask what tense do you like to work in?*

A: You mean a verbal tense? Well I guess in all of them simultaneously since these three things that you mention imply different tenses and they're certainly things that are happening in our minds all the time which I'm attempting to reproduce in poetry, the actions of a mind at work or at rest.

Q: *What is your fascination with dreams and daydreams? Do you try to reproduce dream qualities or techniques? Do you find they are truer than ordinary consciousness to man's relation to space and time?*

A: I don't know; maybe the dream aspect of my poetry has been overemphasized. I think in fact that the conscious element in my poetry is more important than the unconscious element, if only because our conscious thoughts are what occupy us most of the day. Unconscious memories, dreams that suddenly recur and seem to have an explicable signification or meaning all of a sudden also come into my work just as they come into our thoughts. But I would say that my poetry is really consciously trying to explore consciousness more than unconsciousness, although with elements of the unconscious to give it perspective.

Q: *It seems that your relationship to confusion has changed as described in* THE NEW SPIRIT. *Do you think that's so? You remarked in Packard's class about some of your poems being barrages of words and, in that earlier work, not wanting people to follow things item by item but to get a swarm effect; that's one way, and another way is related to your use of surrealist techniques.*

A: I don't know, I never thought of myself as having a relationship to confusion. Every moment is surrounded by a lot of things in life that don't add up to anything that makes much sense and these are part of a situation that I feel I'm trying to deal with when I'm writing; and yet I don't want to feel that in my poetry I've set up a standard of confusion that I'm either reacting to or trying to abolish. I guess what I'm doing is merely starting with the disparate circumstances that, as I say, are with us at every moment; maybe that's why I begin with unrelated phrases and notations that later on I hope get resolved in the course of the poem as it begins to define itself more clearly for me.

Q: *We have tried to get a sense of your geography by going through* THE SKATERS *to see where it takes place. It seems that you are indoors near a piano but your mind will travel as far as a label on a wine bottle, a painting or a postage stamp will take you back and forth across a placeless abstract area, and the voyages are as imaginary as that narrated in* THE INSTRUCTION MANUAL. *What is your relation to these imaginary voyages now? And did you at one time recognize your propensity towards them and make a deliberate decision to utilize the mileage they might give your poetry?*

A: First of all, to begin with THE SKATERS, that poem is a meditation on my childhood which was rather solitary. I grew up on a farm in a region of very hard winters and I think the boredom of my own childhood was what I was remembering when I wrote that poem—the stamp albums, going outside to try and be amused in the snow. I don't know whether that's what you mean by geography. Also an imaginary voyage prompted by the sight of a label or a postage stamp was again a memory of childhood—and also I guess of certain of Raymond Roussel's poems such as LA VUE, an epic-length poem describing a scene viewed inside the hollow handle of a paper knife.

Q: *What is your fascination with the repetition of words for time and its divisions?*

A: Will you give me an example?

Q: *Day seems to be your favorite, and afternoon, we'd say, would be your second favorite, and then months, and night.*

A: I hadn't realized that before. Day of course does appear very commonly in my poetry and I think all these things could be explained by the fact that the poems are setting out to characterize the bunch of circumstances that they're growing out of and a day might be said to be the basis for a poem, that one sits down to write a poem on a particular day and that's the beginning of the poem—the fabric of it—and afternoon and night are further aspects of day that moves on, and then it gets collected into months and weeks.

Q: *Is your work primarily about the sense of time, motion, change: is it, as Lawrence Alloway says, "continuum poetry?"*

A: Yes, I would accept that, I think, and that might again be another reason for the importance of music to me which is something that takes time and which actually creates time as it goes along, or at any rate organizes it in a way that we can see or hear and it's something that's growing which is another aspect of my poetry, I think. It's moving, growing, developing, I hope; that's what I want it to do anyway and these things take place in the framework of time.

Q: *Have you been specifically influenced in terms of a certain sense of indirectness, randomness, sense of time, by relativity, quantum mechanics or thermodynamics?*

A: No, not at all, I know absolutely nothing about physics; I never took it in high school, I took chemistry instead. My maternal grandfather who had a great influence on my growing up was in fact a physicist and the head of the physics department at the University of Rochester so perhaps through osmosis some physics has come down to me.

Q: *What about philosophical ideas?*

A: Philosophy hasn't directly influenced my poetry but the process of philosophic inquiry certainly has; again, sitting down to somehow elucidate a lot of almost invisible currents and knocking them into some sort of shape is very much my way of doing, but as for specific philosophical concepts, I don't think they play any role in my work.

Q: *In reference to communication it's often said that as randomness increases, meaningfulness decreases.*

A: In the last few years I have been attempting to keep meaningfulness up to the pace of randomness. I don't feel I've succeeded in doing this in poems such as EUROPE and the others I was speaking of before; but I really think that meaningfulness can't get along without randomness and that they somehow have to be brought together.

Q: *Is randomness more a methodology or is it more a subject for you?*

A: More of a content perhaps; but a methodology too. As has been pointed out by Richard Howard, among others, my poems are frequently commenting on themselves as they're getting written and therefore the methodology occasionally coincides with the subject. They are a record of a thought process—the process and the thought reflect back and forth on each other.

Q: *With regard to time, you seem to be aware of the end of something even before it has begun and that one is apt to experience something not necessarily when it does happen but later; as if nothing—no incident, thought or feeling—can ever be located in time, until perhaps* THE NEW SPIRIT. *What seems to go along with this is a nearly perpetual sense of something missing or a frequent overcast of regret or nostalgia. Would you comment on this?*

A: Awareness of time and regret and nostalgia are certainly important raw materials for poetry because they are things that I, and I think everybody, experience constantly. In a way the passage of time is becoming more and more *the* subject of my poetry as I get older.

Q: *You said in '69 that you wanted "to stretch people's brains a little." What was the rationale behind that? And would you still put it that way?*

A: That actually I borrowed from John Cage whom I once interviewed for THE HERALD TRIBUNE in Paris when he was having a new work done and said that he wanted to stretch people's ears a little so that they could hear a little bit more and this little is actually a lot, really, provided that the process keeps on going the only way it can keep on going. I suppose what I mean was to make people receptive to a more all-embracing or a little bit more all-embracing kind of poetry than they were before. That's my hope at any rate.

Q: *Are you interested in the occult?*

A: Not particularly.

Q: *You do use astrological signs and, for instance in* THE NEW SPIRIT, *those Tarot card figures.*

A: Yes, but those were really almost decorative elements in that poem and I think probably were there because they're something that young people today are involved in and were a way of situating the poem in the present—it is called THE NEW SPIRIT—but I don't have any very deep interest in them for myself. The occult is not mysterious enough.

Q: *You once expressed an interest in having no external references within a poem. Why? And what does the elimination of such references do to what happens within a poem?*

A: Because I want the reader to be able to experience the poem without having to refer to outside sources to get the complete experience as one has to in Eliot sometimes or Pound. This again is a reflection of my concern for communicating which as I say many people don't believe I have—but for me a poem has to be all there and available to the reader and it is, of course, very difficult to decide at certain moments what the ideal reader is going to know about and what he isn't going to know about; one has to do this by intuition as the cases come up.

Q: *Do you think of your poems as being autobiographical?*

A: Only in a general way. When I was talking about THE SKATERS a little while ago as being a kind of autobiographical poem in the sense that I was writing about childhood memories, I didn't want them to be specific ones that applied to me but only ones that anybody would use if they were thinking autobiographically; they were just to be forms of autobiography rather than special elements that applied to my own life and in fact many of them are made up things, not things I experienced as a child.

Q: *The islands, the ships and cruises and so on are the made up part?*

A: Oh, it would be hard for me to tell you which ones are and which ones aren't; those certainly would be made up since I never took a boat until I was much older. But those passages in THE SKATERS are no longer much related to childhood; it's mostly the first section which deals with that kind of imagery.

Q: *Would you describe the ways in which you use the personal pronoun, especially the word "you"?*

A: The personal pronouns in my work very often seem to be like variables in an equation. "You" can be myself or it can be another person, someone whom I'm addressing, and so can "he" and "she" for that matter and "we;" sometimes one has to deduce from the rest of the sentence what is being meant and my point is also that it doesn't really matter very much, that we are somehow all aspects of a consciousness giving rise to the poem and the fact of addressing someone, myself or someone else, is what's the important thing at that particular moment rather than the particular person involved. I guess I don't have a very strong sense of my own identity and I find it very easy to move from one person in the sense of a pronoun to another and this again helps to produce a kind of polyphony in my poetry which I again feel is a means toward greater naturalism.

Q: *What was your early interest in elaborate forms? You say you really don't think about form in that sense any more.*

A: I wasn't really thinking of elaborate forms which I used in my early poems when I spoke of forms before because they are highly artificial and arbitrary ones which are not the conventional forms we think of in connection with "form." Even the sonnet is not that artificial or elaborate. And I think when I spoke of forms before I was thinking of building a poem with elements that one had very clearly in mind, and using them to construct a poem in the traditional sense. These forms such as the sestina were really devices at getting into remoter areas of consciousness. The really bizarre requirements of a sestina I use as a probing tool rather than as a form in the traditional sense. I once told somebody that writing a sestina was rather like riding down hill on a bicycle and having the peddles push your feet. I wanted my feet to be pushed into places they wouldn't normally have taken; that's why I used these particular forms which I don't do much any more, perhaps because I don't like to repeat myself and also perhaps because I feel I don't need these props anymore.

Q: *What determines the lengths of lines and stanzas in your poems?*

A: That's difficult to say. I use a very long line very frequently in my poetry which I feel gives an expanded means of utterance, and saying a very long thing in place of what might originally have been a much shorter and more concise one is an overflowing of the meaning. It often seems to me to have almost a sexual quality to it in the sense that the sexual act is a kind of prolongation of and improvisation on time in a very deep personal way which is like music, and there's something of the expansiveness of eroticism in these lines very frequently for me although that's by no means a conscious thing that I undertake in writing them. And for stanzas the ultimate look of a poem on a page is something that I visualize in advance. Again it's the box, the framework, which is going to contain the poem and which is arranging it for the viewer. I think very much of the way that the poem will look, not just the lines, the stanzas, but even the form of the letters. All these are things that come into one's experience as one is reading poems which I, insofar as it's possible, try to take into account.

Q: *You're not influenced particularly by the notion of open field or projective verse techniques?*

A: It's nothing that I've ever codified or set up as a standard in writing poetry but I guess I certainly do it. I don't see very much relation between my own poetry and what is called projective verse although it seems to me that in fact that's what I'm doing.

Q: *But it came naturally rather than being an idea you picked up some place?*

A: Yes, I hadn't read Olson or his essay at the time I began doing it myself.

Q: *Why did you choose a ten line stanza for* FRAGMENT?

A: That again was the way I decided the poem was going to look before I wrote it; it wasn't that I felt it had any particular significance but that was going to be the form in this particular case. Also I had been reading Maurice Scève, the sixteenth century poet who wrote in *dizains* and I was impressed by the fruitful monotony of his form, as over and over again he says very much the same thing in the hundreds and hundreds of ten-line stanzas, constantly repeating the form and yet adding something a little new each time, and the ultimate cumulative effect of these additions is something I was aiming at although I didn't use the ten-line stanza with any very definite aim in mind or desire to imitate Scève particularly. It also seemed like a good in-between length; lacking the in-the-round effect of a sonnet and longer than a quatrain; a purposely stunted form which is ideal for these repetitions with minimal variations.

Q: *What criteria do you use in deciding between writing a free verse or a prose poem?*

A: I don't think I have any criteria. It's what seems suitable at the moment and I can't say any more than that. The prose is something quite new; I had written one or two prose poems many years ago and not found it a particularly interesting form and then it began to creep into a couple of poems in THE DOUBLE DREAM OF SPRING and then suddenly the idea of it occurred to me as something new in which the arbitrary divisions of poetry into lines would get abolished. One wouldn't have to have these interfering and scanning the processes of one's thought as one was writing; the poetic form would be dissolved, in solution, and therefore create a much more—I hate to say environmental because it's a bad word—but more of a surrounding thing like the way one's consciousness is surrounded by one's thoughts. And I was also very attracted by the possibility of using very prosy elements, conversation or journalese, what libraries classify as "non-fiction;" to extract what's frequently poetic and moving in these forms of communication which are very often apparent to us and which haven't been investigated very much in poetry.

Q: *It's still something that's quite unique in English, the prose poem, whereas it's become fairly standard in French.*

A: That's true, but there's something very self-consciously poetic about French prose poetry which I wanted to avoid and which I guess is what I found disappointing in my earlier prose poems; it's very difficult to avoid a posture, a certain rhetorical tone.

Q: *In THE NEW SPIRIT you say, "In you I fall apart, and outwardly am a single fragment, a puzzle to itself. But we must learn to live in others, no matter how abortive or unfriendly their cold, piecemeal renderings of us: they create us." I wonder if this has any bearing on your long poem,* FRAGMENT, *and its title?*

A: The title FRAGMENT for that poem was a kind of a joke because it's very long and yet like any poem it's a fragment of something bigger than itself. And it is a single fragment and a puzzle to itself as it is to others.

Q: *You don't have any Shelleyesque notion, do you, of individual poems being part of one great, grand poem?*

A: Oh, I suppose so, sure I do. I don't know as I'd use the word grand, but maybe great. As I say, each one is certainly part of something larger than itself which is the consciousness that produced it at that moment and which left out all kinds of things in the interests of writing the poem, which one is nevertheless aware of in the corners of the poem.

John Ashbery

Q: *Would you have anything to say about the content of* FRAGMENT?

A: I don't remember it very well. I think what I said before about its taking up again and again a single situation and repeatedly developing and then in a way casting aside what has been developed to start over again is the content in this particular case. I think it's like maybe all of my poems, it's a love poem; Scève's DÉLIE was a long cerebral love poem; and the actual situation isn't apparent in the poem, but it's what is behind it and is generating these repeated reexaminations and rejections and then further examinations.

Q: *You seem to have an increasing interest in longer poems. What do you aim for in them that you feel you can't achieve in short one- to two-page poems?*

A: I'm frequently asked this question. It seems quite obvious to me that one is given much broader scope to work with and, as I said before, the time that it takes to write and the changes in one's mood and one's ideas enrich the texture of the poem considerably in a way that couldn't possibly happen in a poem written all at once. And they are in a way diaries or log books of a continuing experience or, at any rate, of an experience that continues to provide new reflections and therefore it gets to be much closer to a whole reality than the shorter ones do.

Q: *In your* ART NEWS ANNUAL *article on* THE INVISIBLE AVANT-GARDE *you said, "Most reckless things are beautiful in some way, and recklessness is what makes experimental art beautiful, just as religions are beautiful because of the strong possibility that they are founded on nothing." Do you feel you have been reckless with poetry? Where?*

A: I think there's something quite reckless about my poetry in general; I think for many people it's quite debatable whether it is poetry or not, and it is for me too. And I can never be certain that I'm doing the right thing by writing this way which nevertheless seems the only right way of writing to me. I think the poignancy of this position gets into the poetry too and intensifies it. I could read you a passage from one of my recent poems which might clarify this: "You know now the sorrow of continually doing something that you cannot name, of producing automatically as an apple tree produces apples this thing there is no name for," which I guess is one of the places where my work is commenting on the work itself, and yet I should caution against reading my poetry too much in this light. When it is

93

commenting on itself it's only doing so in such a way as to point out that living, creating is a process which tends to take itself very much into account and it's not doing so with any attempt to explain the poetry or explain what poetry ought to do.

Q: *What types of diction are you aware of incorporating into your poetry?*

A: As many kinds as I can think of. In THE SYSTEM, for example, there's an almost pedantic, philosophical language and a lecturing quality and the poetry keeps running afoul of clichés and pedestrian turns of phrase. Again these are the result of my wish to reflect the maximum of my experience when I'm writing; these are ways in which one finds oneself talking to oneself or to someone else.

Q: *You do seem to use parody and certain types of diction or jargon, really, in a wry way. There is a humorous or satirical aspect to things that you write.*

A: Yes, but it's not so much satirical as really trying to revitalize some way of expression that might have fallen into disrepute. Again, just because it's a way that we frequently have of speaking, it deserves our attention and we should find out what it is that makes us talk that way and why it is that we do that. There's a good reason, I think, each time.

Q: *And the same thing would apply to parody?*

A: Yes, I don't think that parody as such is my aim when writing this way; it's not to ridicule.

Q: *What about lyricism? Do you think of yourself as being lyrical or trying to be lyrical sometimes?*

A: That's a word like poetic which I don't really understand; I guess romantic in the sense of romantic poetry I would understand and agree to; all my stuff is romantic poetry, rather than metaphysical or surrealist.

Q: *We've mentioned this before, but how has writing journalistic prose on a regular basis affected your poetry?*

A: I did that mostly during five years of my living in Paris when I wrote weekly articles in THE HERALD TRIBUNE. I don't think the way I was writing had very much effect on my poetry but the fact of having to sit down and do it for a deadline without really having much time to think about what I was going to say certainly made me less intimidated by the idea of sitting down and writing a poem and in that way I'm certain it was very helpful. On the other hand my reading of newspapers, which is something I'm addicted to, has certainly surfaced in a recent interest in discovering new poetry in what would ordinarily be considered prose.

Q: *Having written several plays and a novel as well as five books of poems could you give us some idea of what it is that makes you turn to one form rather than another?*

A: I think you're somewhat exaggerating the extent of my writing; the novel was written in collaboration with another poet, James Schuyler, and we began it really as an amusement for ourselves and never expected to finish it or that it would be published. And that is a work quite apart from my other writing. And the plays I've never really been very satisfied with; I've always meant to go on and do something more with writing for the theater because I feel that writing for a number of different voices is something that I am equipped to do and I would like very much to do it for the theater. I have some ideas about that but most of the things of mine that I think are the most important to date are poems.

Q: *You have said that for you and your friends contemporary painting was at one time more important to you than contemporary poetry. Is this still so? Do you read much poetry?*

A: I don't remember saying that; it never has been for me. But certainly at one point the most interesting experiments were being done in painting and therefore one wanted to keep up with them if only to have an example of what one might try to do in one's own art; but as far as painting itself goes, although I know I'm an editor of ART NEWS, I don't feel that the visual part of art is important to me, although I certainly love painting, but I'm much more audio-directed. And I don't read very much modern poetry. I'm quite ignorant of what's being written now; the poetry I read is mostly poetry of the past, from the 19th century back.

Q: *You say you wrote the French poems in* THE DOUBLE DREAM OF SPRING *in French first with the idea of avoiding customary word patterns and associations; and we've mentioned Scève and Roussel; could you tell us about some of the ways in which involvement with the French language and perhaps particular French writers has influenced the way you use English?*

95

A: I think French poetry on the whole hasn't influenced me in any very deep way although I have mentioned Scève and Roussel; I think those particular instances of influence were not really profound ones for the poems. I don't know that the French language has influenced me very much; of course, it does have a mathematical clarity to it which I might occasionally use in a poem for a change in tone that I might feel was expedient at a particular point. Sometimes in my poetry I feel a sense of things that we don't have in the English language like genders of nouns or the past historical tense; I think in fleeting moments I get an idea of a structure that doesn't exist in English, nothing very central to my poetry.

Q: *There is a general effect in a lot of your poems of talking things out, of trying to say things in a lot of different ways. Perhaps in* THE NEW SPIRIT *the effect of it is new.*

A: Yes, "the madness to explain" that I mentioned in one poem. And not only the talking things out but also the hopelessness of actually doing this.

Q: *Is one impulse of* THE NEW SPIRIT *an effort to live through and out of the Wasteland consciousness?*

A: What do you mean exactly by the Wasteland consciousness, you mean that everything is desert and with the decorative elements Eliot used?

Q: *Yes.*

A: Maybe, although that wasn't a conscious thought when I wrote it. Most people would agree that the Wasteland is a pessimistic poem; I think that my most pessimistic moments in my big poems are optimistic. In fact, there's a line in THE NEW SPIRIT which might be used to illustrate this: ". . . just as the days get whittled down to more and more darkness at the end of the year without one's wishing to be back at midsummer, for this is somehow a higher ledge though a narrower and bleaker one, so time running out does not make this position less worthy or any of the individual instants of light darker." I think also what you might feel about that poem I covered a little before when I talked about the fact that somebody is being born; in other words at the end a person is somehow given an embodiment out of those proliferating reflections that are occurring in a generalized mind which eventually run together into the image of a specific person, "he" or "me," who was not there when the poem began. In

John Ashbery

THE SYSTEM I guess you might say that the person who has been born as "he" has taken over in the first person again and is continuing the debate.

Q: *Are you working on anything now beyond* THE RECITAL *that you'd care to talk about?*

A: I am but I don't like to talk about my work in progress; I never do.

9

James Dickey

Q: DELIVERANCE *got us to thinking about the poet's writing novels—*

A: Almost every poet feels like it's incumbent on him to try to write at least one. That was my situation.

Q: *When did it start?*

A: DELIVERANCE? Or do you mean poets generally?

Q: *Poets generally.*

A: If you take enough time to try to write poetry, and you're serious about it, you build up an enormous linguistic skill. The poor human creature, the poet, cannot help thinking that, in a culture that rewards written things as it does the works of certain novelists, it might be possible for him to subsidize his poetry-writing out of the proceeds of a successful novel. For example, Karl Shapiro just has a new book called EDSEL, and I think this is one evidence of the tendency I'm describing. Hart Crane, in a letter somewhere, when somebody asks him why he doesn't write fiction, says, I've just never been able to think of anything with a plot. Neither have I, except DELIVERANCE. It just seemed to work out.

Q: *Do you feel it as an extension or another dimension of something you might have begun—*

A: Well, I would say this about my own relationship to the English language: poetry is kind of the center of the creative wheel; everything else is actually just a spinoff from that: literary criticism, screenplays, novels, even advertising copy. If you keep that part of your work steady, and you recognize it yourself as being central to what you're trying to do—then the other things can be done as well. For me, poetry has got to be the center of everything, but also the kind of options and word choices and things that poetry makes you attend to are additionally useful in other kinds of linguistic forms.

Q: *Was there any shift in adapting to a different form?*

A: No, it was fascinating. What I missed at first was what I had depended on as a resource for a long time; it was the poetic line. You don't have that in prose; you have the sentence and the paragraph. But you don't have the rhythmical continuity of the line. And I missed that for a while. But then you get interested in the other resources, the prose resources, and what the paragraph can do, for example. You carry your poetic, your word-choice ability into that, instead of into the line; it is interesting to do.

Q: *Is there anything on the adaptation from novel form to screenplay form to cinema that gave you trouble?*

A: One thing only. The difficulty was a lot of the novel is interior monologue; for instance, what the narrator thought or said to himself as he was climbing the cliff, and so on. You have to find a way to objectify these things in cinematic terms and show what in the novel you did in an interior monologue. When Ed is climbing the cliff in the novel, he's thinking about how to ambush this guy. He thinks it out, in other words. But you wouldn't know, in the film, exactly how he is figuring on going about what he's getting ready to do if you didn't have some way for the form to let you know that. So we do two things: we have him not thinking it out to himself but talking to Bobby about it before he starts. And we also have him talking to himself all the time. Which seems to work out pretty good.

Q: *Now if we can go over to some other roles a poet has, aside from pure poetry—his working as critic, or as teacher. As critic, you said: "I am for the individual's reaction, whatever extraneous material it includes, and against all critical officialdom." (Preface, BABEL TO BYZANTIUM) This was '65, '66—do you still feel the same way?*

99

A: Exactly. There are some things in BABEL TO BYZANTIUM that I was absolutely and dead a hundred percent, 180 degrees wrong about, but that wouldn't be one of them—yes, I do feel exactly like that. I was wrong about some of the poets I talked about. I've changed around about a good many of them.

Q: *Is it something new that a critic is able to be so much more open about something like that now?*

A: I think it is. And I think that BABEL TO BYZANTIUM had something to do with this. At least I hope it did.

Q: *Yes. We couldn't imagine certain critics in the post-war period making such a statement.*

A: No. You have, of course, a literary critic like Yvor Winters, for example, and you know that this fellow feels that he cannot afford to be caught contradicting himself. I think that's a lot of shit. I think you should have different opinions at different times. The whole thing should be open and fluid, and not locked into some straitjacket of a self-imposed critical system.

Q: *The function of criticism has changed, because—*

A: I hope it has.

Q: *—because that was a pretty dogmatic and tight attitude.*

A: It used to be more so than it is now.

Q: *Now criticism seems to be more trying to—what? See into the poetry?*

A: Why is it a critic can't say about a book or a poet, "I loved it last week; this week I dislike it"? Or, "I disliked it last week, but I'm crazy about it now." You know? Of course you can't have any system, but there's something about the human mind that insists on being dogmatic and systematic. I think it's a terrible mistake.

Q: *We don't seem to have any people now who are trying for any kind of definition of poetry.*

A: No.

Q: *What poetry is.*

A: No. Nobody will ever know what it is.

Q: *You also mentioned, in that Preface, Auden's idea of a "censor."*

A: Yeah.

Q: *Which you describe as—*

A: But he changes, too.

Q: *Yeah?*

A: I don't mean Auden, but the censor.

Q: *Along with the censor, you develop this idea: "the faculty or in-dwelling being which determines what shall and what shall not come into a poem, and which has the final say as to how the admitted material shall be used." You said that was derived from—Coleridge?*

A: Or something.

Q: *Is this—*

A: Yeah, that's what he calls, what Coleridge calls the "architectonic" faculty.

Q: *Is this something that can be taught? Or trained, or conditioned?*

A: It can be trained to some extent, and conditioned to a large extent. But taught? I'm not sure about that. I'm a college professor, as so many of my generation are, and I work with students every day of my life, and I've never been able to decide that.

Q: *No?*

A: I think there are some sensibilities that a teacher of creative writing of a certain kind can be extremely good for. There are also certain ones that you can be death and destruction for, even though you're doing the best you can. You can turn out to be the worst possible influence they could ever have come onto. You know? And I've been both ways, lots of times. The teacher really isn't God, all he has is his own opinions—and as I say, they change.

Q: *The younger generation now are teachers—*

A: But I've been an awful lot of other things besides a teacher. I was an Air Force career man, I was a professional guitar player, I've

101

been an awful lot of different kinds of things. But as somebody said somewhere, "The main problem for an American writer, or indeed for any writer, is to find a way to survive and get his work done and take care of his people." The University, for me, worked out badly at first. It works out badly at the lower levels for the writer. But at the upper levels, where they let you have your way, it's good. But as a teacher of freshman English, controlled by the syllabus, supervised all the time—that's humiliating, and that's why I got out.

Q: *This business of poetry workshops is, historically, a fairly modern thing. What do you feel is the value for a young person in going into a workshop to study under a known poet? Did you, looking back now on workshop experiences you may have had, feel they were very formative for you?*

A: I never was in one. I've taught them, but I've never been in one. I have a feeling it would have been bad for me.

Q: *Bad for you? Did you ever have the experience of a formal structure of criticism by your peers?*

A: No, none at all. I developed completely in the dark, and very haphazardly.

Q: *Do you feel there's too much emphasis now on group criticism?*

A: Yes, yes, I do. I do it, but I do it because so many people are doing it badly and destructively, and I figure that if it's going to be done at all—I mean, it's the same reason that I would take a position, say, as the chairman of the Pulitzer Prize Committee. Because if I didn't, they would get somebody in there like Robert Bly, and he would get somebody up there to make a political speech. That's doing poetry no good.

Q: *Your saying that raises the question about rivalries and the wonderful feuds that can go on in the world of poetry. Sometimes it seems to be a very healthy thing.*

A: Well, it is, but there's so many sick people doing it, we live in what I would call a kind of Age of Moral Blackmail.

Q: *Yes?*

A: So that if you were a poet, and if you didn't agree with me on Vietnam, I would say then that your poetry was no good.

Q: *Yes.*

A: It's that kind of thing is what's going on now, all the time: political opinions substituting for talent.

Q: *Yes.*

A: And that's wrong. That's wrong for us all.

Q: *In some ways, though, even back in the more tight academic periods when aesthetic theory was the vogue, there were feuds then, but they were more submerged.*

A: Yeah. Right. But there was not nearly so much name-calling. I mean, they had decorous articles attacking each other's opinions about Aristotle—in the back pages of the KENYON REVIEW! It was that sort of thing. Now it's all political.

Q: *We'd like to shift now to an article you wrote in 1965, called "Barnstorming for Poetry." That article described the poet as public reader, and we're curious to know how much you feel that experience may have had a subtle effect on the work you're doing now.*

A: None.

Q: *None at all.*

A: None. I write an awful lot of poetry that's not suitable for public readings, and I don't write anything just to be able to get up there and read it.

Q: *Do you feel the word placement in the poetic line has been at all altered by oral reading?*

A: No. No. I'm a very good reader, I'm told. But I don't do it for the money at all, and never would. If I ever did that, I'd get out of it. I've given my life to poetry—I wrote it on troop ships, and in airplanes. I wrote it going on business trips. I wrote it in American business offices. I wrote it on weekends and vacations—simply for one reason: I love it. It's been the central concern of my being and my character all my life.

Q: *You imply there are a lot of traps in the economics of poetry readings.*

A: Plenty.

Q: *And in the frenetic pace which some poets might not be up to sustaining.*

A: Well, it's killed a lot of them.

Q: *Yes. And altered their style.*

A: Yes.

Q: *To what extent do poetry readings actually complement the center of a poet's concern?*

A: Well, I've never really taken the time to think about that.

Q: *You never feel nervous.*

A: I tell you, yes I do feel—did you say menaced?

Q: *Nervous. But menaced also.*

A: Menaced, yes!

Q: *At times you feel you might be getting—*

A: Yes, yes!

Q: *—a little further away—*

A: Yes, yes.

Q: *—from writing poetry.*

A: Yes, I do, I do, because it's fatally easy to fall into this business of doing nothing but going around giving readings, and I've been quite guilty of that—

Q: *And then—*

A: Because after you've gotten up to a certain level, like Lowell and Berryman maybe and a few others, where you can get these enormous fees, you not only figure that you really don't have to write any poetry any more, you figure that it's better if you don't.

Q: *Yes?*

A: Because the reputation that brings in this dough is already there, and if you write more stuff, you're just giving somebody a chance to bust you.

Q: *Hemingway had that problem . . .*

A: Sure he did.

Q: *You have to keep the images straight, and see yourself basically as poet.*

A: The only thing that's going to save you is the basic love of *das ding an sich,* the thing itself: poetry. That's the only thing that's going to save you. All this publicity, the dough, the women—especially them—are fatally easy to come by.

Q: *Yes.*

A: And a certain type of person is going to settle for that. Me, I won't. I won't do that.

Q: *If we can shift a bit. You use a phrase, a concept you call "presentational immediacy"—*

A: That's a phrase of Whitehead's.

Q: *Well, you describe it as "a compulsiveness in the presentation of the matter of the poem that would cause the reader to forget literary judgments entirely and simply experience." Does this have to do with the oral presentation of the poem?*

A: No, no, I don't mean it in that sense. In fact, I'm using it in a different sense from Whitehead. No, I don't mean the presentation, say, from a reading platform. I mean, for words to come together into some kind of magical conjunction that will make the reader enter into a real experience of his own—*not* the poet's. I don't really believe what literary critics have believed from the beginning of time: that poetry is an attempt of the poet to create or recreate his own experience and to pass it on. I don't believe in that. I believe it's an awakening of the sensibilities of someone else, the stranger. Now if I said the word "tree," you and I would not see the same tree, would we?

Q: *We're not sure.*

A: What would you see—just as an experiment, what tree would you see?

Q: *A very gnarled old oak tree that's been blasted by lightning.*

A: Yeah. That's right. I'd see a pine tree!

Q: *Yeah.*

A: So if I use the word *tree* in a poem, this would be something that would bring out your gnarled oak tree to you, you know, when that wouldn't have been what *I* had in mind at all. It's an awakening of the sensibility of someone else. It's giving *his* experience to *him*. It's revitalizing his experience, rather than trying to pass yours on to him. You see what I mean?

Q: *Yes. "Presentational immediacy," then, would be in the composition. It would also carry over into the performance, into the reading of it. You mentioned, about 1965, you said "Of late my interest has been mainly in the conclusionless poem, the open or ungeneralizing poem, the un-well-made poem."*

A: Now you know I didn't know what the hell I was talking about! It sounded good at the time! Well I think what I did mean in that— the open, conclusionless poem—was that I was brought up on poetry that came essentially out of criticism. I was educated in the era of the New Criticism, and the neat poem with the smashing ending.

Q: *Yes.*

A: I think maybe we can do something else now. You know, you have to keep moving around. There's a certain type of poet who was young in the '40s, James Merrill was one, Wilbur was one, Anthony Hecht was one—fine writers, fine poets—but they got sold on that neat kind of poetic construction, and it turns out that the only work they've ever done that's good, that's remarkable, is what they've done to transcend what they were initially so good at.

Q: *Yes.*

A: You getting some stuff into that machine?

Q: *Well, we hope so.*

A: Well, we *hope* you are, but are you?

Q: *You did say before we began taping that* THE NEW YORK QUARTERLY *was the best poetry magazine in the country, didn't you?*

A: Yes. Yes, I'd say. Yeah, it is. Sure it is. It's very well edited.

Q: *NYQ began as a reaction against a lot of what you were talking about—the University periodicals, quarterlies which were too entrenched. But we were talking about "presentational immediacy."*

A: I've got to make a Whitehead reader out of you! If *you* can understand him, please tell *me*! He's the most difficult philosopher I've ever read.

Q: *What about Heidegger?*

A: Oh, but Whitehead's got so much more to him than Heidegger. When you read Whitehead, you know there's something going on up there, if you could just rise up to it. You just feel about Heidegger and his *dasein* and all of that business, that it's just philosophical jargon. Whitehead and Russell take a whole thirty pages of the beginning of PRINCIPIA MATHEMATICA to define what unity is—in other words, what is involved when you say "one." I would have thought that would be fairly simple, but it isn't, apparently. Oddly, I was a philosophy major in college.

Q: *Really?*

A: My major professor was a disciple of Wittgenstein, named Christopher Salmon, who was an Englishman, and a very, very good teacher. But my minor was astrophysics.

Q: *Great.*

A: I didn't really get into English until I went into graduate school.

Q: *Was that on the conviction that you did not want to be exclusively English literature department?*

A: Probably. I didn't want the kind of officialdom that that entails. Yeah, at Vanderbilt I had the best teacher that I ever—the two best teachers—the three best teachers I ever had. Old Salmon was one, who died this hideous, agonizing, humiliating death of cancer, rectal cancer. He was one of the three best, and the other one was Monroe Spears—I don't know whether you know his work—he's an American literary critic, eighteenth century scholar—he just had a book last year called DIONYSIUS AND THE CITY. It is very good, extremely good. And the other one was my astronomy professor. His name was Carl Seifert. He was killed in an automobile accident, a couple of years after I left there. But he opened me up to the magic of the universe. He's the only person that I have ever encountered who had feelings about the universe. Most of us, you know, we just take it for granted. Carl Seifert was fond of quoting Edwin Arlington Robinson's line from one of his letters: "The world is a hell of a place, but the universe is a *fine* thing!"

Q: *Did you continue an interest in astrophysics?*

A: Not as much as I wish I could. I always feel like I could get it back. I don't know if I could get the math back, but I could get some of it back. I used to do a lot of spectroscopy work, and analyzing calcium lines.

Q: *Could we look at an example now of "presentational immediacy." There's an image in* THE LIFEGUARD, *two lines:*

> *Beneath me is nothing but brightness*
> *Like the ghost of a snowfield in summer.*

Is this the beginning of what you would call "magical conjunction"?

A: Well, I would like to think so, but I couldn't say that myself. It would have to be said for me. Yeah, a moonlit lake would be like a disappeared snowfield. You know how pure a field of snow is, not even a track on it, no, nothing to disturb its purity—that's what I tried to get, anyway. The ghost—it's disappeared, it's gone, it's not a lake, the snow's all gone, in summer, it's all melted—but if it were there, if it existed, it would look like this.

Q: *Is there anything in its absence?*

A: Yeah, also. I hope.

Q: *Can we look at another image, in* THE MOVEMENT OF FISH, *in these eight lines:*

> Yet suddenly his frame shakes,
>
> Convulses the whole ocean
> Under the trivial, quivering
> Surface, and he is
> Hundreds of feet away,
> Still picking up speed, still shooting
>
> Through half-gold,
> Going nowhere. Nothing sees him . . .

This reads like onomatopoeia, as if you had actually recreated the sudden disappearance of the fish.

A: Yeah, you've seen fish do things like that, you don't know what's scared 'em, they just jump and they run like hell. There's nothing bothering 'em . . .

Q: *So much of that seems to work through what you've done with the placement of the lines, that suddenly the fish is gone.*

A: Yeah, well I don't really know. You see Buckley and me the other night talking on FIRING LINE?

Q: *No.*

A: We were talking about poets. As poets we're committed to the life of the imagination and the sensibility, and almost everybody wants to be that kind of a person. But what's really doing us in psychologically is exactly the effort to be like that. It's being over-sensibilized, and overimaginative, and above all, overanalytical.

Q: *You mean that all you have to do is observe the fish accurately and try to see the way the fish actually moves.*

A: Yeah, right. What we are doing to ourselves is that we've made it so that we can't peel an apple without self-consciousness. We can't do the simple things that used to give such pleasure to people who were able to do them without excessive self-consciousness about it. But the paradox is that poets are dedicated to excessive self-consciousness. You know what I mean?

Q: *Yes.*

A: And everybody wants to live fully and be creative and imaginative and intelligent and so on. But some of the happiest people I've ever known in my life were dumb, stupid people. They didn't have any of the hang-ups that the intelligentsia has got. An excessively cultivated sensibility killed Randall Jarrell, it killed James Agee, it killed many another—

Q: *Hart Crane?*

A: Hart Crane, especially him. And now it's killed John Berryman.

Q: *Could we look at another image, this one from* THE MAY DAY SERMON, *just a part of a line, the one describing the young man starting the motorcycle, and it's divided into units:*

> *. . . he stands up   stomps   catches   roars*

Here the space units work in recreating the physical act of starting the motorcycle. Is this an example of what you couldn't do when you went over into prose, you couldn't try to recreate the river using unit phrases?

A: No, no, it wouldn't work. You know, I see that split line stuff that I've done, I'm not doing it any more, but I see it in almost every book of poetry that I pick up in bookstores. It's sometimes very effective, it's just like any other device, it's good when it's used rightly, and it's bad when it's used wrongly.

Q: *Do you feel that about any theory of placement, like breath line or variable foot?*

A: Well, it also has to be used with tact and intelligence. To get back to Coleridge, to get back to what we call the architectonic quality, you've got to know when to do it, and how to do it, and when not to do it.

Q: *How long did the composition of* THE MAY DAY SERMON *take?*

A: I could go on record as saying that's the best thing that I've ever written. A lot of people like FALLING, but it's too much of a *tour de force*. If I can do more poetry like THE MAY DAY SERMON, I'll be very happy with my life.

Q: *How long did it take you?*

A: Oh, years and years. Years and years. I'm doing another long thing I've been working on for ten years, called THE STEPSON, which is about work, the relationship between sex and work. It's about working in a candy factory, as a dropout. I used to work for Tom Huston Peanut Company, making candy bars. And there's a very real relationship about workers and what they do and their sexual life that I don't believe I've ever seen anything written about.

Q: THE MAY DAY SERMON *doesn't seem cinematic, because it's so telescoped—there are so many images working at the same time. There's the sermon to the women, and the whipping of the girl, and the previous action of the sex with the motorcyclist—there are these several realities going on at the same time, it doesn't seem like it could be cut down to one plane for cinema.*

A: Yeah, if anything could be said good about that poem the best thing that I would like to have said about it is that in it, especially toward the end, there is an authentic frenzy.

Q: *You seem to be a part of all of it.*

A: Yeah, and the fog and the motorcycle, I'd love to *do* something like that, I'd like to be the guy on the motorcycle, I'd like to be the girl and the father, I'd like to be the chickens and the snake—

Q: *The poem seems to be like Jeffers'* APOLOGY FOR BAD DREAMS, *in that it begins with such a strong image, in the* APOLOGY *it's the whipping of the horse—*

A: Which is tied up by the nose or something like that—

Q: *—but the Jeffers poem is more on a lineal plane, like he gives you the image, and then he gives you the meditation on the image, and then he gives you the statement.*

A: You know, he's very underrated, isn't he? Jeffers. I'll tell you why I think so; I think he's one of the few American poets we've ever had who had an authentic sense of grandeur. Beside Jeffers, the poets that are paid so much attention to now—Anne Sexton, for example, or Sylvia Plath—they're just so many scab-pickers, you know? They concentrate on their little hang-ups, and bitch about them. If I have to read one more poem of Anne Sexton's about middle-aged menstruation, I'll blow my head off! Those things exist, of course—but those gigantic schools of fish and those flights of birds, they also exist, in Jeffers' imagery! Marvelous *big* imagery, galaxies, oceans.

Q: *Jeffers was writing out of a locale, a region, and you're also writing out of a specific locale and region. Is this some new kind of regionalism, different from Sandburg's and Frost's?*

111

A: Well, in a way, I don't know—people say so, but I don't really know. The fact of being a Southerner, as far as that conditions you as a writer, or conditions me as a writer, is simply an accident. I don't have anything doctrinaire to feel about it. I would not, for example, as the people who taught me did, like Donald Davidson and Allen Tate and Red Warren—people who were agrarians and had a political stance based on being Southerners, and a poetic stance, and a sociological stance—I would not have anything like their orientation. I'm not like that. My Southernness or my regionalism or whatever you choose to call it is simply an accident. Now Wendell Berry is a fine poet, but he's much more of a Southerner than I am and attached to a locale, and so on. Isn't he *good*, though, Wendell Berry's awfully good! We need somebody like him, who really is rooted in the land and believes in it and lives on it and loves it and writes about it. Wendell Berry's the kind of writer that Jesse Stuart should have been, you know. But we need him, because the land is disappearing, and we're not going to do anything from now on except live in places like New York, those huge metropolises of chromium and glass.

Q: *You once wrote: "To be a white Southerner in the mid-Twentieth Century is to realize the full bafflement and complexity of the human condition."*

A: Damn right! It is.

Q: *So that it becomes less a hard regionalism than an existential predicament.*

A: Yes, that's essentially what it is. You cannot transcend your origins, no matter how much lip service you give to political ideas. You cannot, no matter what. If I see a Negro with a white girl at a party, it's offensive to me. It's not my fault, it's not his fault, it's not the girl's fault. That's simply the reaction that's aroused. There's nothing to be done about it. I could go over and talk to them, he's probably a terrific guy, you know, and yet that first gut reaction—you have it, no matter what.

Q: *And the poet is—*

A: He's a creature of gut reaction, he has to be, he certainly does. Now, see, your background is not my background. You might not feel what I feel. But with all the business now about race, and so on, that Black Pride and Black Power and all of those things: the Blacks should have those things. No man wants to feel helpless. Every man should have his pride.

Q: *What about Black poetry?*

A: I wish there would come along some really good Black poet, but I haven't found him.

Q: *Do you feel that political statements, or social statements, are concerns which are not the immediate business of the poet?*

A: I think you must be eternally wary of poetry that has newspaper value, topical value, don't you think? Great poetry has been written, as we all know, out of the heat of public occasions, like Yeats' poetry, EASTER 1916, and those things. But the tendency now, with Robert Bly and some of these people like him, and Ginsberg, who's really not a poet at all, is simply to use poetry as an occasion for making Bohemian speeches, which is a terrible, terrible mistake. People who go to those readings, and who seek out these authors on that basis, really don't care anything about poetry. If you go to a reading by Ginsberg, one of these awful group readings, and so on, you hear all this applause, say, where he works in material about Bobby Seale and the Chicago trial and the political conventions and that sort of business—and the audience applauds wildly—they're not applauding the guy's poetry, they're applauding themselves for holding the current fashionable social and political opinions that this guy gets up and tells 'em about. That has nothing to do with poetry.

Q: *We'd like to get into some very practical aspects of being a poet. We gather your work takes gestation time before you actually start writing it down.*

A: Yeah, if I have one principle, rule of thumb, I guess you could say, as a writer, it's to work on something a long, long time. And try it all different ways. I work as a writer—let me see if I can come up with a metaphor or analogy—on the principle of refining low-grade ore. I assume that the first fifty ways I try it are going to be wrong. I do it by a process of elimination. No matter how back-breaking the shoveling is and running it through the sluices and whatever you have to do to refine low-grade ore, you have the dubious consolation that what you get out of it is just as much real gold as it would be if you were just going around picking up nuggets off the ground. It's just that it takes so damn much labor to get it.

113

Q: *Is this labor in actual drafts or worksheets?*

A: One after the other, yeah. I tell you what you can do, and it might be interesting for you to do. Washington University Press has my papers, and they've got these huge stacks of three, four, five hundred pages of work on a single poem, and you could see what I did from that.

Q: *A poem like* THE MAY DAY SERMON, *we imagine, would have gone through a tremendous amount—*

A: Two or three hundred. And that's typing it out laboriously time after time.

Q: *Most of your work is done at the typewriter?*

A: Yes, yes.

Q: *How much work is done in longhand or pencil?*

A: I do it any way. I attack the problem any way, with hands, typewriter, feet, teeth, everything else, everything I can get!

Q: *On your travels, you spend so much time on the road, do you carry a notebook?*

A: I do, I don't use it very much, though. I also carry one of those tape things.

Q: *Do you compose into the tape?*

A: No, I do other kinds of writing on the tape. I have a new book out, I did that way. It's called SORTIES, which is a lot of journal entries and things taken off of tapes and also some new essays. It's called SORTIES.

Q: *What about dry periods, when you just are not able to get going?*

A: No, there's never one of those, no! I've got so many ideas, I've got stacks of ideas and new projects and so on, enough for twenty lifetimes! Most of them will never be written. There's a sense in which you assign priorities: one is the poem that I just can't keep my hands off, that's the one I do.

Q: *You never experience any blockage—*

A: No, no, it's the opposite, I just don't have the time, enough time. You think you about got what you want?

James Dickey

Q: *On the interview? Just about, yes.*

A: Well let's end up with one thing that I would like to make in a statement, a very simple and a childish and a naive kind of a statement: What you have to realize when you write poetry, or if you love poetry, is that poetry is just naturally the greatest god damn thing that ever was in the whole universe. If you love it, there's just no substitute for it. I mean, you read a great line, or somebody's great poem, well, it's just there! I also believe that after all the ages and all the centuries and all the languages, that we've just arrived at the beginning of what poetry is capable of. All of the great poets: the Greek poets, the Latins, the Chinese, the French, German, Spanish, English—they have only hinted at what could exist as far as poems and poetry are concerned. I don't know how to get this new kind of sound, or this new kind of use in language, but I am convinced that it can be done by somebody, maybe not by me, but by somebody. I feel about myself as a writer like John the Baptist did, when he said, "I prepare the way for one who is greater than I." Yeah, but look who it was!

10
Muriel Rukeyser

Q: *When did you begin writing poetry?*

A: Since I was a little child that's what I did—that's all I did as a matter of fact.

Q: *Just rhymes?*

A: Yes. "Tis winter" on the first winter day.

Q: *Then what particular early influences led you to become a poet? Did you have any home background which was conducive or did certain poets you admired influence you? Or a teacher perhaps?*

A: It was otherwise. It was the silence at home. It was the river to which I have just come back and didn't realize how much I needed. Books were the BIBLE and the BOOK OF KNOWLEDGE. It wasn't a reading family. They were busy building up New York. It was very much that. No. I ask people now how old they were before they knew there were living poets. How old were you when you realized there were living poets?

Q: *(You're asking me?)*

A: Yes.

Q: *I was pretty old, although I did begin when I was a child to write little*

verses and I had a little family newspaper, which included poems. I wrote a
play when I was in high school—all rhymed verse—

A: High School. I was reading then. But writing for the first
time—the poems get into one before one has language. I was
reviewing some Mother Goose books the other day, and these are the
things that happen before one is in language. They say it comes
with the beginnings of language, but it's before that. You point to
a toe and say, *"This* little piggy went to market . . ."* Colling-
wood said that's how we learn "toe." And I think after you have
"this little piggy went to market" then contemporary poetry just
follows.

Q: *And then you came to the winning of the Yale series of younger poets*
at the age of twenty-one with the collection THEORY OF FLIGHT.

A: I had been writing before this. The poems in that first book
start in the second year of college.

Q: *Did that affect your poetic career—winning that prize?*

A: Well, of course it did. The way it was published affected me. It
was turned down the first time, and Stephen Vincent Benet, who was
then editor, wrote to me when he turned it down. He said there were
two manuscripts that had come in that year. One was James Agee's
and one was mine. And he was going to publish Jim's and he thought
mine could go to a trade house. He wrote three letters, to publishers
and an agent, one of which I used, and after that the book was turned
down by eleven publishers. Then Mr. Benet did something extremely
generous and out of line. He asked for the manuscript back. And he
said of course it would have to go in with the rest, and that's how it
was published. And a lot of that is in the general form of things
for me. The no first, and then the yes. If I've been able to go on
writing during times when everything does not go well. At my parents', it meant that there were cigarettes on the dining room table.

Q: *Do you think there are any poets who influence the body of your*
poetry?

A: All sorts of influences come in, I think. People always expect
the answer to be in terms of poets, and last night I was giving a
reading of Blake, and thought how Blake came in for me, and the
Bible. When you asked for first things, they were silence, the river
and the Bible. Yes, Blake, and Keats, and Donne, although Donne

117

was not read. I went back to look at the high school anthology that was used, and Donne was not in it. It was a different day. The great poets are the bad influences. Anybody coming too close to the method of Whitman falls into a pit.

Q: *An imitator?*

A: Yes.

Q: *Do you find that certain physical conditions are conducive to your writing?*

A: Yes, but I don't know what they are. They can be anything. A lot of this is unknown to me. I've written under all sorts of conditions. This place feels very good to me. Airports feel good. I've written —you know, the question of a large space directs thoughts to oneself—in relation to space—or a small space like a telephone booth.

Q: *Have you actually written poems in a telephone booth?*

A: Yes—and in an airport. The telephone booth poem was a very short poem.

Q: *How about an elevator?*

A: No, although elevators are good because there's nothing about money in them.

Q: *Well, then you don't necessarily discipline yourself by regular hours?*

A: Not about poems—prose is a different fish. But there is a feeling of a poem arriving—a pressure of a poem that one has not been able to come to that has almost presented itself. There is quite different work after the poem is down on paper and the critical work is there. But I don't know—I couldn't say what conditions—a lot of this is unknown to me. I know I do work all through the night, the further into the night the better. But I think this is about a long stretch. If I can get a twelve- or fourteen-hour stretch I'm better off in anything I do.

Q: *Without any interruptions?*

A: Well, without any interruptions that I don't fall into.

Muriel Rukeyser

Q: *Do you keep a notebook?*

A: Yes. I carry a little notebook around with me. Some poems come out of it. The big poems in which there are many meeting places come out of those.

Q: *Do you have a method of filing them then? I find that notebooks can be quite baffling.*

A: Very baffling. I can deal with that kind of baffle, though. I thrive on that. This is one of my notebooks and I carry one just like it in my pocketbook at all times. I certainly do.

Q: *Is it even by your bedside?*

A: No, scraps of paper, envelopes, things that I sometimes can't read in the morning.

Q: *Do you wake up sometimes and perhaps put down a line that has occurred to you?*

A: Well, I began that way. That's how I knew in the beginning, because in high school I had a friend, a best friend, in high school who wrote very well and played the piano very well. She seemed to me marvelously making in all things. There was some kind of quarrel—I don't remember what it was about—and she said to me, "Stop writing poems or I'll never speak to you again." Now the "never speak to me again" was a terrible threat to me. That was a punishment at home. The silence. That was only part of the silence that I mentioned. That was a real threat, and I promised that I would never write another poem. A promise is an absolute for me. For four weeks I didn't think of anything, and then a poem began; but I had promised, and for two weeks and two days that went on, then in the middle of the night I got up and wrote the poem. The next morning first thing I went to her and said, "I'm sorry, but I haven't been able to keep that promise." And she said, "What promise?" I knew at that moment. It was nothing as far as she was concerned, but I knew what it meant to me. I knew at that point.

Q: *We're glad you did. Galway Kinnell said in an interview with NYQ that the complications of life both practical and emotional brought on for him periods of depression during which he could not write. Do you have such dry periods, or what produces your dry periods?*

A: I have terrible periods. Depression is a mild name for it. Sometimes it means not being able to write. Sometimes something will pierce through a period like that, and then it will go on strangely. That is, I can't tell you the rules. I know that the pit is frightful, and what I find myself doing is translating because I like to have something I care about out in front of me, and not have to send everything out of myself. To have a wonderful poem and do that folly, folly on a madness on a stupidity—translation, I like.

Q: *That is just what Paul Blackburn said about translation, that it fills in his dry periods.*

A: Well, it's the reservoir and one goes to it. And one finds the poets one loves in that way.

Q: *Do you find that your teaching or your readings or your lecturing have helped you in your poetry?*

A: I don't know. I don't teach now. I found that I didn't write when I taught. I wasn't able to. I don't think it's about energy either. I think it's something about the quickness with which one gets a response in the teaching. And one goes away and does not write a poem that day. It's a response that never comes or that comes years later, in writing—that comes out of the silence in which the poem is made—and the teaching seems to crowd that very much. I admire the people who can do it. Well, for instance this year in January, I was asked to come back to the college where I have worked right along, and I said I wouldn't come back for teaching in the scheduled year, but I would come back in the week between semesters, and I would read poems with people, not just with undergraduates, but with students and faculty, and with people who worked in the plant. The man who ran the bookstore was there, and the head of the nursery school. We read poems every afternoon and every evening, all week, having conferences in between. And a great deal came out of that, out of not letting go.

Q: *That wasn't exactly teaching.*

A: No, I don't know what to call these things. I can't answer some of your questions because I don't know these answers. I've heard people jeer at the word Workshop, but I know what I do is and is not teaching. I think of it as reading poems with people.

Q: *You give readings before audiences too, do you not?*

A: I read Blake last night and Wednesday I'm reading at Cooper Union. I like to read.

Q: *Do you read your own poems at any of these times?*

A: Yes, that's what I've been doing.

Q: *Does this have an effect on your work in progress?*

A: It postpones it, I think, and I think that is the sin against the whole thing. And talking about Blake last night I reminded them and myself that Blake's patron had said "Postpone your epic and support your wife." And this is one of the curses—or three of the curses right there.

Q: *Rilke said in his* LETTERS TO A YOUNG POET *"Nobody can counsel you, nobody. There is only one single way. Go into yourself." Do you agree with that statement or do you seek the advice of other poets in regard to your work? The classic example, of course, being Eliot and Pound.*

A: I think it's the ultimate way. I think, though, there are moments in relationships. I don't think of advice, but I think with another person something can be struck like the thing that is struck between two elements in a haiku. It is a bringing together that is in all of poetry. This is in one's relation with another person, and out of that clash comes either half a line in a poem or sometimes the instigation of the poem—I think it comes almost as much in relationships as it does in going into oneself. Although the going into oneself is a curious relation with something else. Going diving. It seems to me that the awful poems are written from someplace into which the poet has not dived deep enough. If you dive deep enough and have favorable winds or whatever is under the water, you come to a place where experience can be shared, and somehow there is somewhere in oneself that shares. And I know with the poems that I thought were most private, most unsharable, the ones I would not show, would certainly not print, later when I have shown them, they were the ones that people have gone to.

Q: *You said that at the Barbizon Plaza. You read a poem you were working on, and you wondered if it would ever be printed. Do you happen to remember what poem that was? Was it the one that was published in NYQ?*

A: Yes. Yes, it is. That was one that I simply put in with the pile of worksheets.

Q: *We were speaking about translations and how you do translations. Your poems have been translated into many languages.*

A: Yes, I've been lucky.

Q: *Have you been satisfied with the way they have been translated?*

A: The word doesn't come into this life, not with the poems one writes or the poems one translates. I don't know—I stumble very much in other languages and sometimes the translation of poems is a way into another language. But I don't know about being satisfied any way in life. I get very happy somehow almost every day for a moment. As far as satisfaction in what one does, one is—it's always the poem one is in at the moment.

Q: *You collaborated with Octavio Paz.*

A: There was some back and forth with Octavio Paz in translating two books of his. We are reworking one of those books now.

Q: *Another area—the games that many beginning poets play, such as anagrams and found objects and acrostics. In your collection, THE SPEED OF DARKNESS, you have three poems from a section called games: THE BACKSIDE OF THE ACADEMY, MOUNTAIN: ONE FROM BRYANT, THE FLYING RED HORSE. Would you like to tell us something about your conception of these poems as games and the techniques you used in developing them? Each seems different.*

A: Yes, I selected those out of many that I wouldn't print. I've been doing this, all along. I did serious poems based on a principle that started as a game. One thought of the sounds of a poem as climbing up all the way to the last breath of a poem—doing the modulations of one sound, and I call that "held rhyme" and have printed some of those. But no one ever noticed that anything was in them. When one writes sonnets one doesn't think of them as sonnets. We all do that. I've published sestinas and a sonnet of mine has found its way into the Jewish prayer book, which astonishes me. It is absorbed into the prayer book all in Hebrew and English and without signature. One feels that one has been absorbed into the line and it's very good. In the games in SPEED OF DARKNESS, BRYANT is simply run backwards, and it's almost as if one ran a film backwards. A very curious poem. The Academy one: I was living on the street in back of the academy and my son played there. And it is the back side, which I am very interested in—the back side of houses. I have a poem called DESPISALS—a new one—which is about the backs of things, of all things—people too, especially, and what they think of.

Q: *Have you ever done a poem on the motion of people?*

A: Some of that, I think, is in the OUTER BANKS. There was a question about verbs. You said there are very few verbs. I've made a list for you. The quality that I was trying for in that group of poems was the shifting of things, and the shifting of the sand bars. And, I tried to hold it and to get to the main verb in each poem, and that's what happened. I was very glad you picked that up.

Q: *Do you think that a poet should begin early to submit work and to enter contests, and do you advise him to slant his submissions for certain markets?*

A: I don't know how to slant my own submissions. The advice that I have asked for is not like that at all. I think of something that I go back to—the question of a black woman student who met me after class and said, "I thought poets were all universal people. Who is the universal poet?" That's an unborn poet, of course. Of course, hatred, and dealing with hatred may be possible in a solving man or a solving woman. It isn't a question of no hatred shown. It's the use of all the motions, it seems to me. But as far as sending things, I get things back from magazines now. I advise people to make waste baskets out of their rejection slips. There is something very comforting about throwing something away in a waste basket which is covered with rejection slips. I have made such waste baskets for friends of mine. But I tell people, if it breaks them to be refused or refused for no reason or for reasons one knows are nonsense, to get a friend to send out the poems for them. I don't know how much can be learned from the refusals, but surely something can be derived. But, as far as method, I have no idea what makes magazines or publishers move or not move. I don't want to stop it with an answer like that because one does send—I think there is something wrong with the word "submit." I'm perfectly willing to give or offer or sell them, but I don't like to submit. There is something very curious about that. Although I am willing to submit to many things.

Q: *You use a great number of rhetorical devices but you rarely use the simile. Is that correct?*

123

A: I tacked up before me for a long time the saying *Poèsie farcie dé comme* ("Poetry stuffed with like"), and I have tried to discipline myself to avoid my faults that became very evident to me. And Horace Gregory helped me with this very much. He helped me with the elimination of a kind of running start which I used in the beginning, in which, say, the first two lines were simply getting going and could be thrown away. And anything that can be thrown away in a poem must be thrown away. There is no possibility of marking time or even the use of the rest as in music, although you can space it certainly on the line, on the page. But anything that does not absolutely belong must be got rid of. And very often the "like" and the "as" that are made in identifications. One wants the correspondence and resemblance but if I can get to the unmediated relation, I like to be able to do away with the "like" and "as" and similes.

Q: *You also use repetitions?*

A: I also use repetitions.

Q: *In your poem* ORGY *you used the lines ". . . and he then slow took off his tie, and she then slow took off her scarf" and you repeat these phrases throughout the whole poem. And then in the "self-portrait" section of the poem* KATHE KOLLWITZ *you used the words "flows into" repeatedly and both of them come out as musical refrains.*

A: Thank you. They are my rhymings. People ask me why I don't rhyme, and I find it impossible to answer. Because I rhyme, and go beyond rhyme. The return once is not enough for me. I will carry a phrase through. Or a sound, that may not be at the end of the lines, but I try to carry any sound that is important in the poem so that it comes back many times. I find returns very romantic in all things. I love the coming back at different times of all things, including sound, including words.

Q: *Are you a musician as well as a poet?*

A: No. I wish I were. I was sent to a music teacher as a young girl, a very skilled piano teacher, who worked with concert pianists before they performed. I was awful. What I really wanted was to study harmony. I brought an exercise book to him; he said I would go home playing eight more bars of Chopin.

Q: *Do you see those returns as related to something seasonal and a closeness to life?*

A: I mean recurrence in all things. What they call repetition. The phrase in a different position is new, as has been pointed out by many poets. But I think I use this as other poets use rhyme. It's a time-binding thing, a physical binding, a musical binding, like the recurrence of the heartbeat and the breathing and all the involuntary motions as well. But in a poem I care very much about the physical reinforcement, the structure in recurrence. And I love it myself.

Q: *That establishes the pulse of the poem in a way.*

A: Well, the pulse of the poem is established in the first breath. The poem is established in the title. The ODE TO A NIGHTINGALE is established there. The two words are very difficult for us, are almost out of the language for us, but for Keats—Keats did not need to say nightingale once he had it in the title. He could say "bird" from then on.

Q: *You use slow rhythm in some cases.* POURING MILK AWAY—*you have to read slowly. Again* A SMELL OF DYING IN THE MILK-PALE CARTON. *In your poem* SPEED *we say you have established your rhythm in the title—then reinforced it with such lines as "the jet now, the whole sky screaming his name; speed."*

A: I hope so.

Q: *Also in your poem* CANNIBAL BRATUSCHA *you not only combine rhythm but you combine opposing styles in the last line of each verse.*

A: There is a recent poem that might interest you. I was working with some young writers and high school people who were beginning to write, in East Harlem, and to put off going away each day the way we white people rush out of Harlem at the end of the day with our portfolios, I would go across the street to a hot dog stand that had a counter open to the corner. There were two tanks on that corner, there always are. One says "Orange" and one says "Grape." The man, whom I had begun to know, was pouring that day, dark purple into the tank that said "Orange," bright orange into the one that said "Grape". And I said "How are we going to believe what we read and write and do and say while you go on doing that?" And he looked at me and smiled and went on pouring, and I thought it was very much like everything else, and it worked on me, very much like anything else, and I thought a poem was beginning and I thought I don't know what form this could possibly move into. And I thought I'll be damned if I write a ballad and it's THE BALLAD OF ORANGE AND

GRAPE. It's that ballad with a long line at the end of each verse, like a long casting out and pulling in. You see and hear it in songs like Miriam Makeba's songs. Casting out and pulling in.

Q: *This is an example of one of your verses that is in the* CANNIBAL BRATUSCHA:

> *Spring evening on Wednesday,*
> *The sky is years ago;*
> *The girl has been missing since Monday*
> *Why don't the birches blow?*
> *And where's their daughter?"*

A: I would like to go back to one thing which I think I skipped, evaded and dodged, and that's about advice. I care very much about working with young poets. I'm lucky in that young poets come to me. I didn't mean that advice was not possible, but by advice I think more a kind of confirming of what they're doing. Somehow setting things out for them, something that works against what's always called depression. Something that allows them to keep going. I would very often say "NO." I would say "No" always when a poet says, "Should I go on writing poetry?" I would say "No" and then I would say "If they can't go on writing poems in the face of that No which they will get from everybody, they are not going to go on writing poems." If they would bring the poems back to me then, I would be glad to do whatever I could.

Q: *I know you have taught children—two years old up through teens.*

A: And college, and graduate students, and continuing education and labor school.
I like to read poems with people.

Q: *How do you feel about punctuation? You use spacing a great deal too.*

A: I like punctuation very much. It is breathing. I had a rubber stamp made—"Please believe the punctuation." I have needed that very much in dealing with printers. It has saved me a great deal of everything.

Q: *Maybe you should have also "Please believe the spacing."*

A: Yes, that I think has to be added onto another line. But I care very much about the air and the silence let into a poem, and I would like to work with other poets on ways of making this visual. Certainly the placement of a poem on the page can do most of it, but many readers do not take that meaning to be what it is, a metric rest. It's a question of a measured rest in the poem. I've tried to work out a visual form for rest but it clutters the line very badly.

Q: *Would you say that your poems come easily or are they somewhat of a struggle?*

A: Oh, all different ways. Sometimes they come right through as single units, some of the short ones in the group THE SPEED OF DARKNESS. I've been struggling to bring through a poem that I'm now working on which is searching/not searching, a poem out of the long digging for a lost man, a lost set of meeting places in man and history, and all the things I was not searching for during that time I want to get at, and I want the poem out of that. What about all the other things not done at that time?

Q: *In your poem* TO ENTER THAT RHYTHM WHERE THE SELF IS LOST *you seem to equate the feeling you get from* WRITING A POEM, LOVEMAKING AND BRINGING TO BIRTH.

A: Yes, and of course the extreme joy in coming into those rhythms. The three rhythms. The feeling that these are the rhythms most to be alive. There is extreme joy. As far as satisfaction with the poem, joy is a better word. It is the thing that is present as one travels through the making of a poem. That seems to me to be alive in a rhythm which I want, which makes me feel most alive.

Q: *Yet where the self is lost.*

A: Where the only way to move into self is to know that it is lost. I know that it is a way of moving, as a verb.

Q: *As for subjects, are there any particular things that interest you?*

A: I don't think I work that way. It's much more the meeting place, the coming together of a theme (if it is a theme) with something which is extremely immediate and present in my own mind. My work—poems at the center, and the other things—seems to me very much a coherent thing, not a set of discrepancies. But I think it is held together by something other than theme, other than specific forms, and it would be very hard for me to say what is it that holds it

127

together. It is what holds me together. And there is sometimes great difficulty in that.

Q: *You've said, "In poetry, form and content, relation and function, reach and merge." You yourself use a great variety of subjects and a great variety of forms. They seem to come together and to merge.*

A: They merge in what I suppose is the voice—a recognizable voice—a recognizable music if they work at all. Again I am unable to get outside of my poems. I had great difficulty in making a book of SELECTED POEMS; I can choose according to kinds of poems in a way but my poems don't fall into kinds from where I look. Maybe from where you see them.

Q: *You spoke of the* ORANGE AND GRAPE *that did take the form of a ballad.*

A: I want to do another ballad about the Jews and the Blacks. I see those as ballads.

Q: *And you called the one about Timothy Dexter . . .*

A: No, it's not a ballad. It's the form of a person's life. I worked at that again and again. That was satisfaction, it seems to me. It is a fan-shaped form, in which choices are made—the form which cannot be seen until the entire life is accomplished and sometimes not until long after that. Again, going back to Blake, one sees very much what the AUGURIES OF INNOCENCE were, what the refusals to accept anyone else's ideas of innocence were, and the establishment of his own ideas of innocence. He had to know what his own ideas of experience were, and the great trust in experience. He had to be able to make something of that experience, had to be able to make the great structure of poems. That stamp of a person, that music, that voice unifies.

Q: *It has been said that your poems come out of myth and dream. Certainly the word* dream, *with various connotations and images, occurs and reoccurs especially and naturally in your collection* BODY OF WAKING. *Would you describe your poem* CLUES *as defining your use of dreams?*

A: I would be willing to go according to that. That's a use taken from the Thompson River Indians who paint their dreams on their bodies, that is, they do not let them go. I saw MARY STUART the other night and I thought of that piercing thing of Queen Elizabeth and dreams and not acting on her dream in respect to Mary Stuart, and the necessity to act on it. And this acting through art, the painting of the dream itself on one's body. I suppose it's related to the machine in the Kafka story in which one cannot read what is engraved into one's back. The first step is to take what one is deeply, deeply saying and one does not sometimes hear—take it into the waking life. It's rather what is thought of as the uses of poetry, which is an expression and still remains very good sense and now people are talking again about what effect a poem has. One does not know at all. But it is like dream. It can be accepted, or not, as with a curse. It takes two; you have to accept it. You must to let it be a curse. With a poem, with a dream, you have to take it back into your life, to see what it becomes.

Q: *As for myth, when your poems come out of myth—in* THE POEM AS MASK *you say "No more masks! No more mythologies!"*

A: And then the myth begins again. At that moment "No more masks! No more mythologies!" the god lifts his hand.

Q: *Then it is an acceptance actually.*

A: As soon as the refusal is made. It's a movement that brings together things that are very far apart. That is what I care about very much.

Q: *Robert Payne says you have "Launched a new and serious mythology, a mythology in which people of the world assume heroic and even divine stature," that you have "Charted a landscape of hope." Do you remember those words?*

A: I remember them very gratefully, when I lose hope. But it is in that relation of the least human impulse—there is no scale in any of this. That landscape is without scale.

Q: *Each person can have his little personal hope as well as a large landscape of hope.*

A: And personal despair.

Q: *Besides poetry, you have written prose and you said researching for your biography* THE TRACES OF THOMAS HARIOT *led to the* OUTER BANKS. *Has this happened in other cases?*

A: It was the OUTER BANKS that led me to Hariot and then Hariot led me to the poem. But I had gone to the Outer Banks long before I knew there was a Hariot. I went to the Outer Banks years ago interested in flight and the Wright Brothers. And in beaches. As a child I played on sandbars here. Sand means very much to me, because my father's business in the building of the city was sand and gravel. This is a poured city. This is a concrete city by now, and when people speak of concrete poetry it should be of poured poetry and I wish to do my kind of concrete poems.

Q: *Do you think that the writing of poetry serves as a discipline for the writing of prose?*

A: The writing of poetry is a discipline for many things. Prose is really a footnote to the poems. The Hariot book is a footnote to the Outer Banks poem. The Gibbs book was a footnote to the Gibbs poem. And I don't know what in the future. They have also been ways of surviving, during the writing of poems. They were a sustained work. If I hadn't had to do that I might just have done the reading. And not done . . . I don't know. I have no way of knowing. They became obsessive hunts. Each of them was having to look for the material. I haven't been particularly interested in doing anything where the work had already been done.

Q: *You did say that in prose the search may be for the* mot juste. *But in poetry you have to go further and find the* sound juste, *too.*

A: The sound structure in prose is certainly part of it.

Q: *But don't you think it's more important in poetry?*

A: I think everything is more important in poetry.

Q: *Your interest in* Akiba *and your poem by that name—Did it spring from your possible descendency from him?*

A: Our mother told us that we were descended from him. Now that isn't anything that anybody can trace or prove. It was a total gift to a child. My mother was a very strange and non-reading woman, except for the BIBLE and Emerson. Many of the things that she did and said even when most damaging were marvelously suggestive and open.

Q: *Do any of the other poems in your* LIVES *have a personal connection? What was the common denominator of the people you have written about? There was a composer, an artist, a painter, a physicist, an anthropologist. Was there anything that drew you to these particular people?*

A: I think it had something to do with what we were talking about before. The structure of a life being an art form. About the ways of

Muriel Rukeyser

getting past impossibilities by changing phase. The reason I think that I came to do Gibbs was that I needed a language of transformation. I needed a language of a changing phase for the poem. And I needed a language that was not static, that did not see life as a series of points, but more as a language of water, and the things are in all these lives that I try to see in poems. Moving past one phase of one's own life—transformation, and moving past impossibilities. Things seen as impossibilities at the moment . . . Or the transformations that come in any great life. It seems to me that the language of poetry is the best way. Music certainly does hold transformation, but without the verbal meanings that I need. Poetry is a clearer metaphor, if you will. More like a transformation than anything that I know. That meaning is a religious meaning. And a very common plain one, too.

Q: *How do you account for such an early breakthrough of your own voice as in* EFFORT AT SPEECH BETWEEN TWO PEOPLE *written as an undergraduate?*

A: I think that was in answer to the silences, the things left out that I wanted to hear about, the—I suppose many of my poems are things that I wanted to hear—and certainly something that has gone through all the way from EFFORT AT SPEECH to a poem called FRAGILE in WATERLILY FIRE—about the nature of speech and what action takes place in speaking. And the relation of speaker and listener.

Q: *Doesn't your poem* WATERLILY FIRE *end on that note?*

A: No, it's contained within the singing at the demonstration outside of City Hall. It feels like that. The poem FRAGILE that I spoke of relates to something I saw on TV. There was an interview with Suzuki, by an American. . . .

Q: *Oh, yes, but those—are they not all different parts of the poem?*

A: Of the poem called WATERLILY FIRE—when Buddha says "I speak to you, you speak to me"—Can I tell a story? What is the most important moment in Buddha's life? And Suzuki says "the moment when he holds out the lotus." And the young American says, "Isn't that fragile?" And Suzuki says, "I speak to you, you speak to me. Is that fragile?"

Q: *This element of personalism continues to be strong in many of your poems. In your recent poem* YES, WE WERE LOOKING AT EACH OTHER *published in the sixth issue of* THE NEW YORK QUARTERLY, *this element seems to be fused with a commitment regarding the outside world ("We fought violence and knew violence," "We hated the inner and outer oppression.") plus also a feeling of sensuality and love. William Packard has suggested that this might be some sort of an* ars poetica.

A: Well, certainly all you say and all besides. That's the center of it, but it's that in relation with. Even in a solitary condition it's in relation with. There is no way not to. It's the interior space of one's life. The poem seems to be a meeting place just as a person's life is a meeting place. And a dance of all these things is held, by whatever art can be given to it. We allow it because it is perceived as having its art. And it seems to me that one's perception is clear or human or not obstructed, really, that these things exist and that they're life entire and that the great devastating activity in life as we know it is to shred all the unities one knows. It isn't that one brings life together—it's that one will not allow it to be torn apart. And not only the wars but the thing that wars are images of, the tearing apart of life entire in ourselves and in our relations with each other. It isn't a question of making them come together. They are together. It's a fighting that they not be torn apart and killed that way.

Q: *Speaking of wars, would you call some of your poems protest poems? There is an element of protest that runs through many of your poems. The poem* ENDLESS *for instance, or some of the Delta poems or* WHAT HAVE YOU BROUGHT HOME FROM THE WARS? *And some of the poems certainly from your book* U.S. I *are protest poems against the disease of dust.*

A: I can't stand a lot of things, a lot of things have killed and mutilated people I love. I will protest all my life. I am willing to. But I'm a person who makes, much more than a person who protests, and I think we are that, and I have decided that wherever I protest from now on, and a number of people are doing this too now, I will make something—I will make poems, plant, feed children, build, but not ever protest without making something. I think the whole thing must be made again. I think Beethoven said "Everything I see is against my religion" and I feel that way.

Q: *Then you want to make an active contribution along with your poetry?*

A: I will not protest without making something. I hope other people will do that.

132

Muriel Rukeyser

Q: *Some years ago you attended a gathering, quite a few years ago, of international poets in Spain.*

A: I landed in Spain by a fluke the first day of the war in Spain. There wasn't any gathering. Oh, I know what you mean. It wasn't poets. It was athletes.

Q: *But Aragon, Ralph Bates, Stephen Spender and Auden were there.*

A: Not at that time, later. This was the first day of the war. There were no anti-Fascist games. The people I was among were the Catalans. These were anarchists—a united front in which anarchists and socialists and communists were within the republic which won its war. It was that extraordinary sight of something that then did not take place. I saw the war won in Spain by the republic. By the time we left it was at peace, and people had gone out to help the Madrid armies. But there was this curious vision of a republic that had expected help from their brothers from the United States which had already won for what was the government. Even the gypsies on the docks in Barcelona were with this. It was a curious vision of a Twentieth Century world which would not take place. It may still, but it has been beaten down in place after place, from Spain to Vietnam and many, many places in between.

Q: *How did you arrive at the title for the poem* WATERLILY FIRE?

A: That was a fire in New York, a fire that burned one of the Monet Waterlily paintings. In that building which cannot burn, the Museum of Modern Art. And I was going there that day and the glass was falling and the firemen were rushing in and the painting was burning.

Q: *In that poem you have fused various seemingly unrelated elements —autobiographical, political, philosophical, religious.*

A: I would have to defend that. I think they are related. I use my . . . I see it as a childhood in New York, the Indians of New York, the building of New York, the demonstration in New York, and underneath that bound by much more than place. The idea of the waterlilies burning in a fireproof building. And the pilot image was making and discovery of burning things is seen as being fireproof. The gathering of poets, by the way, was really there, because people were singing in City Hall Park, several of the poets. That island was

133

Manhattan and was New York and was us at that time. People do think of these things as seemingly unrelated. I hate to explain poems. This kind of showing I'd be glad to do as with the verbs. Because they are there. I don't work without verbs. I don't work with unrelated elements.

Q: *Will you explain your comparison of the techniques used in the writing of modern poetry to the techniques used in the movies or on TV?*

A: Well, I was trained professionally as a film editor, a film cutter. The work with film is a terribly good exercise for poetry although many people have been seduced away to writing for film. But the concept of sequences, the cutting of sequences of varying length, the frame by frame composition, the use of a traveling image, traveling by the way the film is cut, shot, projected at a set speed, a sound track or a silent track, in conjunction with the visual track but can be brought into bad descriptive verbal things and brought into marvelous juxtapositions.

Q: *Which you have used in your poetry?*

A: Yes. But I was speaking of exercises. These are games actually.

Q: *You have said that poetry has no acknowledged place in American life today?*

A: I have in THE SPEED OF DARKNESS four lines which I think say it for me. It's called IN OUR TIME.

> In our period they say there is free speech.
> They say there is no penalty for poets.
> There is no penalty for writing poems.
> They say this. This is the penalty.

Q: *You spoke of fear of poetry.*

A: That was when I was beginning. It still exists but it's in a quite different form now. I have an eleven-year-old nephew who said to me the other day, "Most of the kids in my class are poets." You have a thing now of a great many people writing poems. And a great many of the elements of everything, but a kind of note-taking. But this was always true. People told lies about poems, about poets, and about the rareness, the weirdness, of any man or woman involved in writing poetry. I have always asked the question in any hall I speak in no matter how small or how large: How many of you—all critical questions aside—how many of you have ever written a poem? And I get nervous when I ask this. There is a moment of hesitation, and then very slowly almost all the hands go up. In a big university they will look around to see whether the basketball team is putting their hands up. But almost everybody—and if I stay around afterwards with any luck the five or six people who did not put their hands up will come up to me and each will say something like "Well, I was fifteen, it was a love poem, it stank." This is a human activity, and they tell us lies about it.

Q: *But that's writing poetry. What about reading poetry?*

A: Well, one doesn't know when a person reads a poem, how much is read. Suppose every person in the country is writing and is writing bad poems, where are we? We then have to come to the critical questions.

Q: *How to make a bad poem good.*

A: Well, if you can make a bad poem good . . . I had a very funny job when I was in high school. My English teacher asked me to write the tests that were later used at Teachers' College here, in which you took a lyric and you messed it up four different ways. You made it into a kind of rocking Kipling, you made bad free verse. It was made up as a test. Five examples were given to students and they were asked to say which was the real poem and defend their choice. Of course a lot of students will choose a messed up variant and defend it. So you have only opened the question. The fact that the poem is needed by people—when people will come out in stormy, rainy weather to hear poems—or a marvelous summer night. It's partly curiosity and it's partly a need—that you feel the culture works against. But there is a real and very often a buried need in everyone. And the people who cut it out of themselves are deprived and do not know they are deprived. They can be reached; they will say things like "I haven't had any time for poetry since I was fourteen" or "Poetry bores me" and when I hear those things I know there is something right underneath. But that need in everybody is what comes through the devastating inert force that is around us now.

Q: *Do you feel that the present time provides a fitting setting for the poet. You have spoken about the Elizabethan age, considered the much-vaunted age for poetry. But what about the present age?*

135

A: Well, one of the attacks on me for writing that Hariot book spoke of me as a she-poet—that I had no business to be doing this and I was broken for a while and looked out the window for a while. And then I thought, yes, I am a she-poet. Anything I bring to this is because I am a woman. And this is the thing that was left out of the Elizabethan world, the element that did not exist. Maybe, maybe, maybe that is what one can bring to life.

11
Richard Wilbur

Q: *How long are you likely to work on a poem?*

A: Long enough. Generally pretty long. The last poem I finished concerned a mind reader whom I met in Rome in 1954. Very shortly after I met him, I commenced to think of writing about him. In the intervening years I've now and then jotted down on an envelope, or in a little book, some phrase that might belong to a poem about this man, but it wasn't until three years ago—that is, fourteen years after I met him—that I actually got going on the poem, and now it's taken me three years to finish it. It is, to be sure, a long poem for me, a hundred and some lines. Occasionally I've had the luck to write a poem in a day, but that's not commonly my experience.

Q: *When you say, "in a day," do you mean first version or completed?*

A: Over and done with. I don't actually revise, or it's very seldom that I revise. What I do is write so leisurely that all the revisions occur in thought or in the margins of the page. It can make for a page which is as dense, graphically, as some men's-room walls. Which is not to say that a poem is like going to the men's room.

Q: *Is this a recent development, this slow process of writing?*

A: No, I've always been that way. Always extremely slow. And I think perhaps it has something to do with my respect for the written

137

word—even my own. I don't dare set things down, for fear I'll leave them there.

Q: *But you do take notes.*

A: I take very, very fragmentary, suggestive, or wispy notes. I never write out the matter of a whole poem in prose or in jottings, and then proceed. I'm aware that some august people have done that, but I couldn't do it; I think it would take all of the surprise out of the experience, so that there wouldn't be any carrot to lure me on. Sometimes, to be sure, I've got lost in detail toward the end of a long effort, and have made a little outline so as to discover its argumentative dimension.

Q: *What you do write down before, it would be a snatch of an image, a word?*

A: A word, yes, or, in a sketchy way, the central idea. Not always do these little notes which I put down (and I don't keep anything in the way of a continuing notebook; I'm not like Ted Roethke), not always do these little jottings actually appear in the final poem. They're just a way of reminding me that there's a poem I might be thinking about.

Q: *Do you keep these little notes in any organized fashion?*

A: Pretty disorganized. I have a little blank book in which I've been making jottings for perhaps ten years, and I may have used fifteen pages of it. And then there are scrawled-on scraps and sullied envelopes here and there—tucked into that blank book, or stuck in the drawers of desks.

Q: *What form does the "carrot" take which lures you on? Is it a vision of a completed, crafted work of art? Or some kind of emotion?*

A: Both, I should think. I do aim at making a good thing, working out a poem which shall be well constructed; at the same time I wouldn't be interested in writing a poem if it weren't getting a great deal of me and of humanity off my chest. I believe I'm not expected to feel this way, but I agree with Emerson that it's not meter but meter-making argument that's important. To go back to what we were saying earlier, I probably denied too flatly that I do any revisions; but the revisions are likely to be small and local. I showed this poem just finished to Bill Meredith, who's a fine poet and is also the sterling

138

kind of friend who can look at a poem of yours and discuss it neither in a flattering nor in a malicious way. I pretty well trust him. He's pointed out some four words or phrases which he thinks I might profitably tinker with. And I think perhaps I will, in at least two of the cases. But that's the kind of revision I do: finding a better word for the end of some line in a long poem. If there's too much to be done, I tend to throw the poem out altogether.

Q: *Do you experience in this process of revision a separate distinct critical faculty?*

A: I don't know that I can be so analytic about my feelings on such occasions. But I'll try. I do know that, like everybody else, I feel that I have to achieve a certain distance from what I've written before I can mess with it. That must imply, then, that one is allowing the critical faculty a little more prominence and isolation than it had during the process of writing. You become, then, two people, the advocate of your poem as you wrote it and the critic of it. That's dangerous, and should be avoided save when necessary. The poet should be wary of the usurping critic in himself, who is capable of concerning himself with ambition, fashion, publication, and book reviewers. The unitary poet, in action, never thinks of such rot.

Q: *You wouldn't revise, then, after publication.*

A: Very seldom. Once or twice I've found that a poem of mine was needlessly confusing, and that a change which was in no way a disreputable concession could increase the precision of the poem, the intelligibility of the poem. I haven't minded making changes of that kind.

Q: *You have used notes to explain references and allusions. Do you append those after you have written the poem?*

A: Yes, it would always occur afterwards. When you offer notes, it's just a matter of being civil. I don't think of it as a patronizing or show-off gesture. There are a great many things which—although I keep my mind fairly busy and self-respecting in intellectual matters —I just don't know, and need to be told about. I expect my reader to be tolerant of being told this or that which I happen to have stumbled on. I had a note in my last book in which I unburdened myself of much that I had lately learned about the constellations. I'm sure that many of my readers had not just read the little Simon and Schuster astronomy book which I'd picked up in a drug store.

139

Q: *Also by using a note you can keep the explanation out of the poem itself?*

A: Yes, it would be wretched economy to build all one's information into a poem.

Q: *Do you have a poet who has served you as a model?*

A: No, I don't think I've had any *one*. When I was in high school I read all sorts of poets in an extra-curricular way—it's so often extra-curricularly, I think, that we read the poets who matter to us—and they were as widely separated as Joyce, whose poems are very Elizabethan and conventional, and Eliot, and Hart Crane, and Robert Frost. And I read Wordsworth in class with good will though I found much of him damnably earnest, and still do. All of those would add up to a quite varied set of influences and models. And I think that most of my life I've been in luck in this respect. I've seldom been overwhelmed by the influence of any one writer so that what I wrote myself was too imitative. There's a piece of mine that's probably got too much Yeats in it, and which probably resulted from my having taught a seminar on Yeats at Harvard with John Kelleher. There are one or two poems which show how much I've liked Robert Frost, or Baudelaire. I expect there are some rhythms out of Gerard Manley Hopkins in my first book, and maybe I stole a word or two from Emily Dickinson somewhere. But I've never enlisted under anyone else.

Q: *You don't mention Auden?*

A: Well, Auden has been a constant delight to me ever since I began to read him. I feel that, at the moment, he's the best presence around—our most civilized, accomplished and heartening poet. I don't know whether at any time I've sounded like him, though Roethke thought my poem THE UNDEAD showed traces. I can't tell about that. Very often I think we fear that we've been perceptibly influenced by another writer, and yet we're too much ourselves, and too safeguarded by our ineptitudes, for it to be perceptible to others.

Q: *Or perhaps that influence becomes subconscious.*

A: Yes, that can happen. Once I was composing a poem called THE DEATH OF A TOAD, and at the end of the first stanza of it I had an odd feeling of self-approval, the sort of feeling I don't usually have when I start in to write something. That made me self-mistrustful, and after a few minutes' pondering I became aware that I had reproduced a sequence of adjectives out of Edgar Allan Poe's DREAM

LAND, and that's why it felt so proper to me. Needless to say, I revised. I suppose every poet ought to be wary of self-approval, it most likely indicates that there's some kind of hidden thievery operating.

Q: *Do you have periods when you're not writing?*

A: Indeed I do. I suspect that everybody has dry periods. One advantage of getting older is that you have been through it before and before and before: though it doesn't do very *much* good, you can tell yourself that you will come out of it, that you will write again, and therefore you can stay somewhat this side of despair. It's odd, isn't it, that when you have written, and it's mattered to you and to other people, you feel guilty as well as impotent when you're not writing. I don't think this necessarily has anything to do with the parable of the Talents, but you do feel a kind of guilt—or is it shame—as if you were not being quite a man.

Q: *How long are such dry periods likely to last?*

A: They've lasted for many months with me. Happily, I've never had to go through a whole year without getting my hand in again, however briefly. One thing I do when I find that nothing is coming out of me, is to turn to translation—a risky thing to do, of course, because translation is easier to do than your own work, and it can be a way of distracting yourself from poems of your own which you might do if you left yourself exposed to the pain of your impotence.

Q: *Do you have a work schedule:*

A: No, I've never had a schedule. I go simply by impulse, whim. What I do try to do is to keep my life uncluttered when I'm not teaching, and therefore be able to harden to the first whisper of any idea. I very much mistrust, for myself at any rate, the idea of sitting down clerkishly every day at a certain hour and making verses. The Trollope regimen won't do for poets. What would happen in my case, I think, is that I would write more poems, but I would write my poem about the mind reader ten years before it was ripe and spoil it. Oh, I may have spoiled it now, but it would have been worse if I had done it back then in the fifties.

Q: *Could this method of working have to do with the fact that you write short poems?*

A: That's quite true, I think. When you're engaged in a long poem you do have to keep plugging at it, or thinking of plugging at it, because you're waiting not for one inspiration but for a sequence of inspirations. Also because, I think, in any long poem there are going to be non-Crocean stretches, connective tissue. There are going to be architectural problems which you can face and cope with in a state of imperfect frenzy. I remember Robert Frost, one time, talking about the dullness of Wordsworth. He used "dullness" as a term of approval, speaking of Wordsworth's willingness to write prosaically so as to fulfill the structure of his longer poems and make bridges between his more intense passages.

Q: *Do you find, just averaging things out, that you're more of a day or night writer, more of a summer than a winter writer?*

A: I've never figured it out in a seasonal way. I've got to pay some attention to that and see if Cyril Connolly is right. He said something about the month of October, I think. He said if you're going to write a work of genius you will do it in October. I expect that was a little personal.

Q: *Probably, Keats wrote his great* Odes *in the Spring.*

A: I used to be a night person, used to be able to work until three or four in the morning, and now I find that I get sleepy after midnight, and do a little better at other hours of the day. Unfortunately, I'm not old enough yet to be an early morning person. I sleep extremely well in the morning, and can't get up at five as some of my slightly older friends do. I'm stuck with the middle of the day, alas—the period in which the phone rings and people drop in on you.

Q: *On to less practical subjects. What is the importance, in your mind, of traditional forms in poetry. Are they essential?*

A: If by traditional forms we mean meters, stanzas, rhymes, that kind of thing, I don't think any of those has any meaning in itself or is absolutely essential to poetry. There are some poets who are no good at these things. William Carlos Williams fully proved in his early work that he was no good at writing with the help of such means. He found himself, and began to delight us, when he moved into the use of a kind of controlled free verse. And I have no case whatever against controlled free verse. Yet I think it is absurd to feel that free verse—which has only been with us in America for a little over a hundred years—has definitely "replaced" measure and rhyme and other traditional instruments. Precisely because trimeter, for example, doesn't mean anything, there's no reason why it shouldn't be put to good use now and tomorrow. It's not inherently dated, and, in ways one really needn't go into, meter, rhyme and the like are, or can be, serviceable for people who know how to handle them well.

Q: *Perhaps their demands put your imagination into places it wouldn't go otherwise?*

A: Yes, that's something which is not always recognized, the freeing effect of a lot of traditional techniques. They are not simply a straitjacket, they can also liberate you from whatever narrow track your own mind is running on, and prompt it to be loose and inventive, to entertain possibilities it hadn't foreseen.

Q: *Do you ever write a poem just for whimsy, a toy poem of just pure craft and little else?*

A: I have a desire to go for broke, I think, whenever I start writing. I find it hard to do anything which is foredoomed to triviality or to the character of an exercise, although I don't mind at all writing children's poems—I've been doing some of that. That's a conscious step, however, into another genre of poetry in which your expectations change.

Q: *How about traditional forms, like the elegy?*

A: Well, you're working in such a case with certain expectations of the convention; and, of course, you're working against them. If you can't make it new you won't allow it out of the shop. It is a help to have a form that you're working with and against. I teach Milton here very often, and I suppose the greatest example of working with and against a convention is LYCIDAS.

Q: *Is bad art bad, then, in a contemporary way? That is, it seems that in order to be a trumpet player you at least have to know how to move your fingers to call yourself one, or know how to draw in order to call yourself a painter. What do you have to know in order to call yourself a poet?*

A: There are no widely acknowledged qualifications at present. I'm on the Board of the Wesleyan University Press. Actually, I've been on a year's leave from the Board, because I got sick of reading poetry, and I've just gone back. Rather grudgingly, too, because I don't feel very much attuned to a fair part of the work now being done. I don't feel able to distinguish between the better and the worse of it, because the fashionable aesthetics seem to me so distressing. I don't like, I can't adjust to, simplistic political poetry, the crowd-pleasing sort of anti-Vietnam poem. I can't adjust to the kind of Black poetry that simply cusses and hollers artlessly. And most of all I can't adjust to the sort of poem, which is mechanically, prosaically "irrational," which is often self-pitying, which starts all its sentences with 'I,' and which writes constantly out of a limply weird subjective world. There is an awful lot of that being produced. If you are given a box containing twenty manuscripts of verse, and eighteen of them are in that style, it's in the first place depressing, and in the second place you are unable for weariness to say that this is better than that. It's bad to be bored out of exerting one's critical faculty. I imagine that a lot of poetry which is deranged in a mild way, and more silly than funny, is trying to suggest drug experience, trying to borrow something from the excitement that was recently felt about the drug experience. There are even some good poets, writing in other styles, whom I suspect of having been subtly influenced by the drug cult's notion that vision and self-transcendence are easily come by. It's not so, of course; it's hard and rare as hell to get beyond yourself. *Beside* yourself is another matter. I like Robert Frost's saying that before you can be interpersonal you have to be personal. It seems to me that's what Timothy Leary forgot.

Q: *Would you, then, agree with the statement by Valery that "a man is a poet if his imagination is stimulated by disciplines?" Some kind of discipline.*

A: Yes, I would agree. The idea of letting go is very attractive to people nowadays; for some, fingerpainting and happenings are the norms of the art experience. But I don't think the kind of art you and I like to consume was ever produced in a spirit of simply letting go. One only arrives at a useful precision in spontaneous art if there's been a lot of discipline in one's life earlier. Dr. Johnson said, "what is written without effort is in general read without pleasure." I have trouble with some of my students and some of my friends at the moment about this matter of precision. I always say that art ought to be a trap for the reader to fall into, and that he ought to know when he is caught, and what has caught him. There are some people like Jim Dickey who express a blithe willingness to have the reader's subjectivity collaborate with the poet's in producing a hybrid which will be the reader's experience of the poet's words. I think I'm less generous than he in this matter, and that, given a good reader, a good poet should make him think and feel precisely what he wants to and nothing else. But perhaps I've overstated my case. It is obvious that we all take possession of art as we can, in the light of our own feelings and experience—every statue is going to be different for every beholder, depending on where he stands, but having admitted that, I'm all for demanding of the artist a maximum control of his audience. One of the few ways of judging a poem or a painting is to say that it does or does not make you experience it within a certain range of meanings.

Q: *In a recent interview Jorge Luis Borges suggested he thought the way poetry worked on people's imagination to "trap" them, as you say, was through metaphor. That the poem as a whole was a metaphor which brought the reader from the concrete to the abstract. How do you respond to that?*

A: I think it would be true of some poems I've written, like THE BEACON, which is all one metaphor. The poem is thinking about how much we can know of the world, what the kingdom or province of human thought is, and the poem does its thinking in terms of a lighthouse, and the sea, and night. There are a lot of lesser but connected figures in the poem, mostly having to do with ideas of empire, province, kingdom, domain. I'm sure that I could think of a good many other poems which could be reduced in this manner to a field of thought and a scene or situation in which the thought is embodied. I know that's true, for example, of my more recent poem, ON THE MARGINAL WAY. There are certain—I shan't say what all the thoughts of that poem are about—but there are certain thoughts on tap, and they're all connected with the stones of a particular cove off the shore of Maine, and the geological history of those stones, and their changing aspect as the light changes, as the sea rises and falls back. I don't think all poems can be described in this way. It seems to me that there are some quite fine and legitimate poems in which the one really pervasive element is the argument, and the metaphors and other figures appear as illustrations of it, are treated in a subordinated fashion. I think a dramatic poem might well do that.

Q: *Then the argument would be what would, in a sense, hold the poem together?*

A: Yes. Metaphor, in the small sense and the large, is the main property of poetry. But there are other elements in poetry, and I see no reason why any of these shouldn't be lead dog once in a while. You wouldn't want to blackball certain epigrams for being nonfigurative. Much modern French poetry, and some English poetry written under French inspiration, suffer from being wholly metaphorical, wholly lacking in statement, and thus too difficult to get ahold of. It's interesting to turn back to the Metaphysicals and discover how, in spite of what we were once told about them, the figures are often not sustained and a dramatic argument is the thing most prominent.

Q: *On the question of personal style, do you feel your poetry has been evolving or is evolving into new modes and styles?*

A: I've never tried to initiate blue periods or green periods in my work, and I've always distrusted self-manipulation. All I can say about that matter is that, yes, I do feel changes of direction beginning, but that I can't offer any prognosis. It would seem wrong for me to know or to guess. I'm getting older, and, as Bill Williams said, age gives as it takes away, and I'm just going to wait and see what age gives. Undoubtedly it will give new perspectives.

Q: *Do you feel that your later work, as in* WALKING TO SLEEP *might tend to be less ornate than the earlier poetry? The language more simplified and direct.*

A: I think that's probably so. Another way of saying it might be to say that there is less gaiety in the later poems. I do think that, very often, what may have seemed ornate or decorative in earlier poems was, for me at any rate, an expression of exuberance. I expect that progression may continue, but I do hope not to end in a dull sincerity. I hope to preserve some feeling of exuberance. To lack it is to lack one access to the truth of the world.

Q: *You teach classes in literature and in writing? How do you go about teaching your literature class?*

A: I don't think there's anything peculiar about the way I do it. The course I was teaching this year started with Anne Bradstreet and ended in the middle of Williams. It was inevitably somewhat cursory, but perhaps a little less silly than most survey courses in that almost our whole business consisted of the study of individual poems —putting them on the slide, as Ezra Pound said—and understanding, for example, as well as we could, four poems of Anne Bradstreet before going on to Taylor, and doing four of Taylor before we went on to Philip Freneau—in some cases, of course, slowing down and being very careful that we understood what Whitman was up to in the whole of SONG OF MYSELF. I suppose that I do about ten or fifteen minutes worth of generalizing in a class meeting of about an hour and a half, and for the rest I simply talk over with my students—who this year were simply marvelous in their preparation, intelligence and enthusiasm—what's going on in a poem line by line, and, where we can, how this poem might be illuminated by comparison to its neighbor, or why William Carlos Williams' poem THE CATHOLIC BELLS reminds us of Walt Whitman. That kind of thing.

Q: *When you go line by line are you trying to determine what the poem "means" or how it was made?*

A: I think we do both. We talk about how it got its effects, how it made its points, but also what the general position of the poet seems to be—not so much position as concern; that's what we aim at finding out, what's eating the poet. Of course, every now and then there's a dissenter from the method who would prefer to have a somewhat more swooning and less argumentative relation to the poem. My answer to that is that what we do is what can be done in the classroom, and that while extra-curricular swooning is admirable, we simply cannot swoon profitably in class. I'm probably making it sound too dry. It isn't dry at all, and we always read the poems aloud. And we allow ourselves parenthetical vows.

Q: *Many teachers try to impose symbols and meanings on a poem, how do you feel about that?*

A: I try to be uncertain even where I feel pretty strongly, not to impose any one way of reading, and to entertain seriously every decent suggestion which comes from the floor. The only time I've stamped my foot this year was when somebody took too seriously the girl-drying-her-hair simile in BIRCHES and suggested that the whole poem had to do with climbing girls. I wouldn't have that.

Q: *How would you scotch that kind of thing?*

A: In this case I simply said no, no, and I wouldn't talk about it because it seemed to me so intolerably untrue. But that was, I think, the only time that I ever played authoritarian this year. It won't do to do that; and I'm not in the least disposed to impose archetypal, Freudian or other patterns on the poems we read. In general my attitude about criticism and about teaching is that you look at the thing and see what it wants you to say about it.

Q: *You've lived in Europe; could you compare the state of poetry teaching here to that in Europe?*

A: I think we probably do it much better than they do it in Europe. That's my guess. I'm judging mainly from the attitude of foreign students who come here and are astonished by the openness of our discussions. The French student is likely to be extremely docile, and to have been taught to treat the great poetry and drama of his tradition in a very prescribed manner. There are certain things he *is* to find, so that he can answer questions about them on important examinations. I don't think that we feel there are obligatory findings to be made; and indeed I'm glad when people go off on tangents, if they're not perfectly mad. I'm glad to see people take poetry personally—I guess that's what it amounts to.

Q: *From your experience with your poetry writing class, are there any poets who you detect to be large influences on the present generation of young people?*

A: Oh, I suppose I couldn't produce any names which would surprise you. Any poets in Untermeyer's Anthology are likely to be having a continuing effect. It seems to me that most of my students are interested in Stevens, in Pound, in Williams, in others of that great generation. But the ones who are very strong about poetry, and very concerned with writing their own, also attach themselves to writers of the moment, like Creeley, Snodgrass, Ginsberg—it's a very long list. Most current styles seem to have their adherents, in one year or another. If you'd asked me the question last year, I think I would have said that people who write a kind of tricky confessional poetry were the strongest influences on our students. But this year I noticed in our verse-writing seminar (in which I don't try to coerce people at all into writing this way or that) an astonishing number of voluntary villanelles, sonnets, quatrains and so on.

Q: *Any foreign poets influencing your students? Baudelaire for instance.*

A: The individual student poet, who is also a French major may well catch fire from Baudelaire, as a student of German may learn from Rilke. But there seems to be no foreign poet in fashion, not even Neruda.

Q: *What do you do in your verse-writing seminar?*

A: I ask them to write an original poem every other week. These poems are printed up, anonymously, and distributed to the class. We criticise them collectively. I also criticise them myself in writing. For the odd weeks, I suggest various well-tried exercises—I'll have them write a riddle, for example. Once in every semester I'll ask that they look through a dictionary of poetic forms, find some form which interests them and write in it. But that's as far as I go in that way. Then I'll suggest things of this sort: I'll say, "It's generally thought enhancing to compare aeroplanes to birds; make a comparison of the reverse nature, comparing something that is presumably exalted to something that is presumably on a lower imaginative plane." Some students will find that such an exercise jars their imaginations in a good way; for others it'll make no difference at all.

Q: *"The worlds revolve like ancient women gathering fuel in vacant lots"?*

A: That's right, that's exactly the kind of thing I hope to get by that exercise. I have a number of others, all of which are meant simply to shake up the mind a little, to disturb its habits.

Q: *Wesleyan just recently admitted women. How is it having coeds in the class?*

A: It's very civilizing. There are qualities of feeling missing from any poetry class if you don't have girls there. And the effect of it is to mature the male students very rapidly. I think they don't linger in their prep-school or high-school attitudes very long if there are girls with them, raising the tone and legitimizing delicacy.

Q: *Do you think there are different difficulties with which male and female poets have to contend?*

A: There used to be special difficulties for men, way back when I was first thinking of writing poetry. When I was an undergraduate at Amherst, poetry was associated by some with effeminacy, and I knew one man at Amherst, a poet and teacher, who rather overstressed his abilities as a boxer in order to reassure the world about his masculinity. There's none of that any more. I'm very sure that it's possible to distinguish between male and female sensibilities—but I should think that there's now no subject matter that you would expect to find in a man's book but not in a woman's. Everyone seems to have access to everything, and the girls seem to have found out how to write about the whole range of masculine topics.

Q: *You don't think a man might not have the problem of saying things just for their own sake whereas a woman might have more of a problem detaching herself?*

A: I think women have less capacity for nonsense than men do. And so, if I understand you, I agree with what you've said. A man

149

can be a complete abstract-minded ass in a way in which most women can't be.

Q: *Now, we'd like to talk a little about translation. Hayden Carruth in his recent anthology* THE VOICE THAT IS GREAT WITHIN US *describes you in terms of the neoclassic French dramatists you have spent so much time translating, and refers to your "courtly tone of respect for order to mask fundamental metaphysical uncertainty." To what extent do you think a poet is attracted to poets in the languages he has translated?*

A: Well, it seems to me that Carruth offers a very good description of something which happens in Racine. In Racine you have the finished and sonorous surface, and underneath that an awareness of violence, irrationality, disorder. However, if I try to apply Carruth's words to myself, as you quote them, it looks as if he's implying some kind of faking or bad faith. Is he? That word "mask" troubles me. Actually, what he seems to be saying was said once before by Theodore Holmes in a review in POETRY. He said that I had a cheerful, elegant surface and a fundamental despair. Where Mr. Holmes got his information about my fundamental despair, I don't know.

Q: *You said you felt you were fortunate in not being overwhelmed by any poet enough to imitate him, but what about translation as a kind of imitation?*

A: You write a translation because someone else has written a poem which you love and you want to take possession of it. I think it also is a matter of imposture, too. You want to speak in the voice of that poem, which perhaps you could not do in your own poetic person. I think I've felt myself drawn to certain jobs of translation in that way, feeling that they would be somehow an expansion of me, and might perhaps lead to my coping with a certain area of subject matter, striking a certain kind of attitude, using a certain tone. I detest exercises. I've never done any exercises myself, and I've always sympathized with my students when they've said, "I refuse to do exercises, I'll just write my own stuff, if you don't mind." But doing a job of translation can have some of the benefits, I suppose, of an exercise. It can be an exercise in the use of someone else's palette.

Q: *Robert Lowell has said, in reference to translating, that poetry is a matter of tone. How do you feel about that?*

A: I think Lowell was right in saying that. It's not the only matter, of course, but it's crucial. The translator must catch and convey not only what the poet says but how he means it.

Richard Wilbur

Q: *Would it be more difficult to translate an ironic tone, do you think?*

A: Perhaps it's a little harder to translate the special ironic dissonances of a language than to translate the pure vowels of some unqualified emotion. Think how hard it would be to render John Crowe Ransom in Afrikaans. Still, I think anything can be done, with luck.

Q: *You have done both translation from poets in languages you are thoroughly familiar with and translating, with help, from languages you don't know. Could you compare the two?*

A: Translation from languages you don't know works only if poems are well chosen, well assigned, in the first place. And then the linguist must do an extremely good and patient and sustained job of mediation. Working either with Max Hayward or Olga Carlisle, I've asked that the poem be read over and over again in Russian and then, out of my tiny knowledge of Russian, have asked all sorts of detailed questions about the words of the original. I've asked, too, about the meter of the original and its relation to the tone and matter of the poem. I've asked, indeed, almost all of the questions you ask, in a somewhat other way, of yourself while you're composing a poem of your own. Given three days with Max Hayward and a couple of bottles of Scotch, I think you can become quite intimate with two or three Russian poems, and be in a position to take your notes and write something which will be at once faithful and a work of your own.

Q: *Has Voznesensky seen your translations of his work?*

A: Oh, yes. He seems to think well of them, I'm glad to say.

Q: *Do you ever have a wish to be doing something else to support yourself aside form translating and teaching?*

A: Yes, there are other things I've felt an itch to do. I should like to be a farmer. But that, I suppose, would get altogether in the way of writing poetry, it's so hard a life. I've been drawn to a number of other professions, and, of course, one reason I've felt restless at times is that teaching literature and writing poems are far too much the same thing. I find, especially as one grows older and as one outgrows one's initial infatuation with poetry, it's easier to feel after a hard day's preparation and teaching that one has had enough of poetry for the day and doesn't want to go home and write any. At the moment, I think things are working out pretty well. I enjoy teaching and I very much like my students here. I teach only in the fall, and sometime in December I become a free man and write until September. That's good enough. Indeed, I feel pampered.

Q: *One final question. Would you recommend poetry as a profession?*

A: Oh, yes. For someone who doesn't mind a bit of discipline.

Q: *What are its advantages and drawbacks?*

A: There's nothing so wonderful as having constructed something perfectly arbitrary, without any help from anybody else, out of pure delight and self-delight, and then to find that it turns out to be useful to a few others. You have it both ways, if you're lucky: you do exactly as you want to do, you're as lonely and as happy as a child playing with his toy trains, and then it turns out that people are grateful to you for providing them with some sort of emotional machine.

12

Robert Creeley

Q: *When did you begin writing poetry?*

A: I didn't write really as a younger man, when I was still in high school, going to school, and I think the time I felt it would be a distinct possibility—something I wanted to commit myself to, had been when I had just finished school and was now contemplating college. And at that time in my life I still wanted to be a veterinarian. That was my ambition and I applied for scholarships to the University of Pennsylvania and to Amherst, and also I applied to Harvard, growing up in Massachusetts, that was Jude the Obscure, huh? That seemed to be the place. Amherst and the University of Pennsylvania both had good pre-veterinarian preparations and Harvard, of course, didn't. And I was accepted at all three and given scholarships to Pennsylvania and Amherst. But I chose Harvard, I really did because at that point in my life I decided I wanted to be a writer, not a poet particularly but a writer, and so it was really at Harvard that I began to write in a distinct manner.

Q: *What poets have influenced your work?*

A: Oh, most decisively Charles Olson. Also most decisively, William Carlos Williams. I learned a great deal from Ezra Pound, in the sense that his critical work, his writing about poetry, was to me very decisive. He emphasized the whole condition of writing as a

153

craft, and as a craft separated usefully from academic uses of it or from even, say, senses of literary tradition in an academic context. He really put a very distinct emphasis on the fact that writing is the possibility of doing something, and it has, therefore, conditions particular to itself and if you intend to be involved with it, you better pay attention to what it is. And really pay attention to what is happening. So, both Pound and Williams at the time I was in college, let's say, were really my imagination of what writing could be. I learned a lot from, say, Wallace Stevens, but I loved his thinking, I loved the way his mind worked, and I loved the play of his intelligence in his work. It was to me extraordinary and very, very pleasing. But I found that the mode in which he said things wasn't really appropriate to what I had to do.

Q: *What about Louis Zukovsky?*

A: I really didn't come upon Zukovsky's work until I was certainly older. I was introduced to his work by Edward Dahlberg and I was then living in Majorca, and he said that I should get hold of Louis for work to be published in the BLACK MOUNTAIN REVIEW. And I was frankly ignorant of it and I dare say a lot of my contemporaries were. Not long after that I met Robert Duncan. He came to live in Majorca for a year. And he had with him Williams' review of Louis' book ANEW. And he in turn had some texts of Louis' I think. And when I actually held the work in my hands it was instantly something I could use. Its economy, its modality was absolutely attractive to me.

Q: *Your work has been described as a bridge from Williams.*

A: Well, I know what's meant by that. That has to do with literary history which isn't my interest. Not my ability either.

Q: *Under what physical conditions do you work best? At the University of British Columbia, you said if you wanted to change the mood of your poem, you changed the color of the paper?*

A: Not quite. This was the so-called Conference or Gathering of Poets, 1963, Vancouver, and the company was extraordinary. Allen Ginsberg and Denise Levertov, Robert Duncan and Charles Olson, Phil Whalen, Mgt. Everson, and various other, younger, writers, and I realized at that point how boxed in my own possibilities had become. Because of the physical habits of my writing. Up to that time I think I wrote primarily—always a typewriter, I never wrote anything in longhand or with pencil. Now I have gone almost entirely the other way. I write prose still using a typewriter, but poetry I seem to write entirely in notebooks. Because I realized that I had boxed myself in to a circumstance which only let me write when I was literally in a room with my own typewriter because I never learned to type properly so I depended on the familiarity with my own typewriter. And also I had to have a particular condition of paper. All kind of a fetichistic circumstance that gave me permission to write. And I really envied both Charles and Robert and Allen, all of whom wrote—you know, Charles composed on bits of paper, envelopes, anything that was physically to hand, and then he'd work from that collection to the actual draft that he would consider the finished poem. And Allen equally could write anywhere. And that to me was the pleasure that I really coveted and wanted, so beginning with really WORDS and entirely the poems in PIECES were a shift from that earlier habit.

Q: *That gave you a little more freedom then.*

A: Far more. It lets you write when you can write instead of when you find yourself in the physical circumstance—only in a bleakly incidental manner. I tend to write now in a very conventional notebook sort of style. I tend now to write in a continuity rather than in a single instance. I have another book coming out later this year, and it follows the conditions found in PIECES. It's a kind of continuity. In fact, I'm hopefully persuading Scribner's not to put in page numbers and get rid of all that. I want it to be one continuity instead of a single poem, a single poem, a single poem.

Q: *That would make it a little difficult for the person who wants to specify a certain page.*

A: Not any more than a novel. I don't see why one would have that problem. I'm trying to say that the poem is not a single instance. In the kind of text I'm interested to get hold of. On the other hand, I can't say that it is like the CANTOS or . . . there is no index in the CANTOS, is there? No. People seem to find their way around. Well, PATERSON doesn't have an index either.

Q: *In a discussion of yours on free verse, you quote Louis Zukovsky as saying he wrote out of a deep need.*

A: That made absolute and lovely sense to me. A great diversity of writers, poets, particularly in conversation with younger people . . . I remember Tony Scott saying to someone younger who was interested in writing poems, he said: "If you don't have to do it, don't

155

do it." And I think that's reasonable advice to give the young. Because they do understandably get involved with their sense of the social reality of the poet. It's certainly not the thing to do if you don't feel the demand upon yourself to do it.

Q: *In relation to notebooks, do you keep one nearby at night to note material from dreams?*

A: No I don't, simply because I don't usually recall material from dreams. Robert Duncan does a great deal of his work which has been initiated from dreams. Denise does. I don't know if Allen does or doesn't. I think it tends to go in and out for him. But myself I don't tend to get material in that way. And frankly, let's say I wake up in the morning and children are ready to go to school, and that's where I am in waking up. We live in a happily dense kind of family state. The day begins with a sort of pleasant abruptness. There really isn't that occasion. I have a shed I work in which is just back of the house. I simply go into that shed when I want particularly to do something. My wife has another happy little shed on the hill. She's a painter and she goes here when she wants to do something.

Q: *Do your kids have a shed, too?*

A: They have the whole world.

Q: *Is there any particular time?*

A: I think if I were to recall the times I wrote, I think I wrote most accurately say, starting at eleven in the morning and writing until about four in the afternoon. I tend to wake up as the day goes on. I can't really do anything in the early morning. And by the time the night has come I'm almost too excited. That way I can't sit still long enough. I sort of work most easily from midday until late afternoon.

Q: *Does the area you live influence your work?*

A: We live now in a deeply pleasant town. It is the most extraordinary meld of diverse living styles. There is an incredible context of people. Variously the sounds will be like some rock group practising, or some person playing a flute walking down the street or kids playing, and it is a small town, not too many cars. One thing I deeply respect in this town is that if one is working, all you have to do is put a note on the door and literally no one will bother you. No one will feel offended that you haven't got up to greet them. I have friends say that they heard the typewriter and knew I was working so didn't come by. We all have that kind of respect for each other.

Robert Creeley

Q: *Is it a town of many artistic people?*

A: Well, we have everything from members of the World Bank to members of the Jefferson Airplane to an extraordinary cabinet maker who has a show presently in the Smithsonian, to painters to dairy farmers to small local businessmen people who commute to the city, a lot of hippies, for example, crazily diverse people, two lawyers are our neighbors across the way, the lady who wrote the I HATE TO COOK BOOK, Peg Bracken, lives there. One thing it does seem to have is a community of circumstances that people who come to live there have really got to the other side of this continent. And you can't keep thinking of possibilities over there. Either it is going to be made here or it isn't ever going to be found. Growing up in New England I understandably had the feeling that there were greener fields elsewhere. By the time you get to the Pacific Ocean you realize that that's as far as the land's going to go.

Q: *Is there anything about the climate that affects your writing?*

A: Well, being born in New England I really love the various climates of the Pacific. There is a kind of lovely shifting weather. The mean temperature is around sixty-five, never very hot, never very cold. A lot of weather comes in from the sea. We have mountains to the back of us so you get a various weather pattern. You have a remarkable diversity of what you call microclimates. You find yourself in a situation where you can move a mile and find yourself in a different environment. It's extraordinary in that way.

Q: *What part of California was Robinson Jeffers in?*

A: Not too far. He was down the coast in Carmel. That area down toward and around Big Sur. That's a beautifully dramatic coastline there. We live in a rather light coastline. It's coincident with the earth condition. When you have mountains literally bordering on the sea you have very unstable land form. It's a very dramatic situation in which to live. We live right on the St. Andreas fault, it literally goes down the road in front of our house. But that's only one of several, actually. I know that various neighbors are concerned about their houses falling into the sea. We are right on the edge of the national seashore. I even forgot the point we were talking about.

Q: *Whether the change in climate affected your writing.*

A: I find in a kind of way . . . I tend to a . . . not a cold climate, but coming from New England I like the weather to be decisive, and

157

to be various, and . . . I lived for a time in Guatemala. The heat was . . . I found myself sluggish. I just didn't have the energy I tend to have in a more temperate climate.

Q: *Argentina has the same weather as we have, which is reflected in the work of the Argentine poets.*

A: Sure. I think it's true. I mean the whole so-called sensibilities are based on one's sensual environment, and would seem to be absolutely a modification and/or a condition of what one experiences. I think Jasper Johns, really because of being a Southerner, does do well in a warm climate, and he is thinking about buying land down in St. Martin's in the West Indies, and plans to work down there. It must be hard to get anything done down there, but one can understand that the climate probably is attractive to him.

Q: *Do you think there is any connection between the life style of a poet and the so-called life style of his work?*

A: Well, sometimes it's rather willfully present. For example, the one person I think of instantly would be Charles Bukowski whose life style is very much present in his writing. And not in a strictly parallel sense but obviously Allen Ginsberg's life style is deeply present in what he has to say. And there are circumstances . . . I remember years ago when I was at college and Wallace Stevens had come to read at Harvard, I was then a student with Ethel Mathewson, so he had a long conversation with her, and he reported to us that at one point in this conversation which was very intently involved a propos poetry, Wallace Stevens just suddenly broke out and said, "Wow, what if the boys back at the office could hear me now . . ." So in that case, the life style had literally no actual connection, and there must have been a very schizophrenic circumstance. I don't think that life style is of necessity reflected in the writing. Or vice versa. I think that's a very interesting circumstance a propos "creative people" in that they just don't conform to a pattern of person. Some of the poets that I have as friends are extraordinarily discreet in their behavior, very formal, very "middle class." Others are quite the contrary.

Q: *Well, talking about Allen Ginsberg, as a person is he not quite a gentle . . .*

A: Extremely gentle and extraordinarily humane. And again I think it's a misapprehension. Allen's poetry is, let's say, responsive to kinds of violence he has met in the world but it has nothing to do with his initiation of that violence. In other words you can be a very gentle man, but if one goes to jail he becomes a jailbird.

Q: *What would be your reaction to the statement that unless a poem communicates instantly, the poet rather than the reader has failed?*

A: I think that's a rather absurd contention. I did once hear an apocryphal but nevertheless lovely story that some people in company with Eliot asked him if he would help them by explaining a particular section of the WASTELAND, and he simply said I don't understand it. The assumption that the poet understands all he writes is to me absurd. I don't understand my own children. And I certainly don't understand all of my own poems.

Q: *In your opinion, are most contemporary poems ironic? To a greater or lesser degree?*

A: No. I felt that that was the prevailing mode in the forties. Primarily through Eliot's attitude and impact on the practice of actual writing then. And also Allen Tate and John Crowe Ransom. Irony gives one a rather quick location of attitudes toward content. It is easily recognized as an attitude and it is a kind of use of what's being said that's pretty simply available. I think irony is one of the simplest attitudes to gain. And make manifest. But I don't think at the moment that irony is one of the . . . it's one of the modes of statement obviously, but I don't think it's the prevailing mode.

Q: *But you use some irony?*

A: As a younger man I used it a great deal. It was simply that that was a way of holding one's own with the dismays and confusions of daily existence. But at the moment in my own writing now, it doesn't seem to me to be the most insistent attitude.

Q: *You have given your interpretation of the term free verse as being related to the literal root of the word verse. Will you explain that?*

A: I'm a little confused.

Q: *Well there was a quotation "If one thinks of the literal root of the word verse, a line, furrow turning—Vertere—he will come to the sense of free verse . . ."*

A: I understand . . . well, it's simply to qualify what's meant by free. I don't at all agree with the contention that free verse is like playing tennis without the net. What I was trying to emphasize was that verse is an activity that doesn't really require attention but insofar as it is happening specifically, there are limits and responsibilities that can be recognized. I love that quote of Olson's: "There are limits to what a car will do." If you consider verse as the possibility of a farmer's plowing, then that locates what's happening in some specific sense. And the way it turns, as verse does, in contrast to say prose, would be an actual place, an actual circumstance, of that turning. If it becomes simply a farmer's meandering all over the field, one who has not as yet mastered either the horses or the plow, it will look simply as such, a man wandering over a surface, which is rather incoherent. Although there will be lines. And if they do somehow gain a coherence in that wandering, then that will be interesting. I know that Williams in his later life particularly began to be very both dismayed and depressed and in some ways even confused about what were the actual possibilities of coherence within this context. The very term to me indicates a reaction to a previous sense of order, a particular kind of order, that which we call a poem. One could use set modes of coherence—Sonnet or whatever the mode might be, and could gain a very lovely articulate patterning within that structure.

But again, you see, our times, so to speak, have really confronted head-on a very altered conception of how the world seems to be. Not only in poetry but in a great variety of contexts we have had to yield this. Music, probably, at least in the arts, led the way into that problem and began to make the most articulate solutions. So that free verse is really close to a situation, let's say, that is like the music of Stockhausen or Cage or so many other younger composers who we would be very familiar with. Senses of duration . . . senses of the modality being a diversity instead of one containment. I have felt that to continue forms arbitrarily, no matter how pleasant, that they had been used. I didn't want something really new, not necessarily in my own writing, but I did want to know what did the possibilities of coherence have other than what was previously the case. I remember Cage saying he felt it was a little presumptive to tell twenty men to sit quietly and play what you told them to. First of all, it is extremely expensive to get one who sits thus still to work, to hire a full symphony orchestra. So therefore he was thinking of this. He also questioned the kind of music that only used as he put it one quarter of the spectrum of sound that was possible. That from great noise to silence. He pointed out that great music was . . . up to the Nineteenth Century . . . only used about a quarter of that spectrum. He said being American, he wanted it all.

Robert Creeley

Q: *Well, do you think it's necessary for a poet to write first in traditional forms?*

A: I think it would be rather regrettable and a little dumb not to make use of the full context of what's been done, in light of the available material the poet has to draw upon. I know in teaching, when I am asked to teach the classes in writing, I become rather nervous and it almost seems to me a little specious for poets or writers generally. One has all this incredible range of example. Just go to your local library and see what's been done. I think that if you're going to write, reading obviously is part of the process in the lovely sense that Duncan once made clear. He said there were times when he couldn't remember if he had written something or read it. And therefore any of us have to pay attention to the range of the possibilities as we have them.

On the other hand, I've been reading a book on Francis Bacon by John Russell. He is speaking in the text of Bacon's respect for and use of previous painters. And there would be particular things that Bacon had in mind to do. He wanted, for example, almost an air of implication or ambiguity, which wasn't quite resolved, and he was therefore very interested in any painter who could manage that. For example, he respects Corbet on the grounds that Corbet really paints people naked as actual presences of that nakedness, and he said in contrast, Reubens for example, and Renoir, I think that's the painter he speaks of, gave the whole body a kind of lushness that was to him distracting. He wanted to see if it was possible to locate that meat in a way that would be descriptive but wouldn't be presenting, in the sense that Pound says an image presents. So when painters or writers go for certain suggestions or solutions, they find other writers. I think it's very important to emphasize that poets and/or writers are not reading simply to be entertained, or simply to say that they read the right books. They find suggestions and possibilities for their own activity. I read for pleasure, obviously, too, but I read also to find out what's possible and who's got some useful answers.

Q: *Wallace Stevens said that he never read poetry for fear that he might imitate it.*

A: Someone might find it out.

Q: *Related to your teaching, how do you feel about this in connection with your poetry?*

A: Well, you see, I began teaching when I was about thirty and I was both grateful and relieved to find that there was something I could do in the world that had use for others and also gave me an income, which I then obviously needed as a younger man with a family. Last year, teaching in San Francisco State, and I think coincident with the sad upheaval of education in its daily condition, and also in its attitude toward its own function, I suddenly found myself almost irrevocably bored, really entirely dulled with this insistent confusion. I didn't suddenly get tidy and neat, but I was just bored. Bored out of my head and then I unhappily began to be resentful. I was driving let's say thirty miles in to teach and then home again, and I wasn't really being asked to go in that frequently, only about twice a week, and we would sit around in this extraordinarily desultory fashion and I couldn't help but feel that I was accepting money under false pretenses, and all the people I was teaching would be far better . . . and I found myself thinking why in heaven's name can't you find something specific for your lives, or else get out, go.

And I realized that all my students who were stuck in that circumstance did so because they were really rather intimidated by the fact that at least for the time being, they had an income provided by being in school. Then I questioned their ability to do the kinds of things that majoring in English used to train one to do. Straight-on research, that kind of ability. Reading was extraordinarily desultory if they were majoring in "creative writing." I thought it was really sad, I thought it was a fraud to give people a degree in creative writing. And I felt that gives them no condition either with respect to writing or the ability to find a place in the world of some use and self-respect and to get on with it. It just left them in limbo. To go to the usual publisher and say, I got all A's in creative writing, and they'd say, well, that's nice, you know, but that isn't going to assure you that your novel or whatever it is going to be published.

Well, it's reflected in my decision. I had previously been teaching full time and I was now in my forties and I had had an almost . . . I was confused, I think, about was I actually committed to writing, or was I in a sad sense copping out by leaving teaching? I was living in a town where I found myself in company with at least a dozen other younger writers, primarily I saw them improvising means to keep themselves together and I thought well, I really respect their choices more and more. So I began to think, do I need to be a full professor at the

Robert Creeley

University in Buffalo? I mean how much of that do I need? It was pleasant to take one's family to London for two weeks, but was that entirely necessary? I mean if that's the only way one could find relief from the nine months of otherwise doing it. So I figured to get out of it as much as I could. When I was teaching I found myself fresh and responsive to the people I was involved with. I think the saddest thing in the world is a burnt out teacher. You know, plodding on. He or she really resents the students all the time and has nothing that way to give them. That rancor. So I wanted to cut back to teaching a semester a year. And I continue happily in an association with Buffalo because I respect the faculty and students there. At San Francisco State I sadly didn't. And it got to be problematic because I certainly liked the people. But couldn't respect the institution at all. I think it's a sad, sad place. The sad fact is that I remember a student once at Buffalo who was a very active young woman. I was very impressed that she was the character of student there, and that we were getting this thing together. But then she pointed out to me, very truly and quickly. You know frankly to constitute a group in the proportions of this university, I represent five percent at best. That leaves ninety-five percent who sadly but truly are the status quo. And who completely refuse to be otherwise. And so it's very hard to avoid the bleak and contemptuous metaphor of the sheep. In a kind of almost goofy or grotesque parallel I went to Julliard Theatre to hear Virgil Thomson's first opera. Apparently there was the possibility that Kenneth might do the libretto, Kenneth Koch, and that would have been beautiful. Those two men would have gone together in a beautiful manner. Instead, you have this incredibly tedious and pompous and dull, ridiculous take on Lord Byron. We sat there for three acts. I couldn't believe our own stupidity. I watched the cast come out and take curtain call after curtain call, and this incredible audience—bravo, bravo, and you think doesn't anybody in the place have ears? Wasn't anybody there? We really came out looking like we had just seen Dachau for the first time. Just white with shock and outrage. Just incredible—thousands upon thousands of dollars, a Ford Foundation grant, cast of millions, all for this incredible muck. Not that it was just so bad, but it was a travesty.

Q: *Why are some of your poems titled and some of them untitled?*

A: It seems to me simply that they have no particular relation to a title. A title to me, at least in earlier writing, was most often present to locate a context which was my imagination of the location of the emotional situation being set. So a poem which would be titled: THE KID, has a task of a signal to the reader that this poem would involve some imagination of, or feeling of, feeling young, feeling inadequate, then the poem clarified the particular sense of kindness that I had in mind. It was a way of signaling to the reader or to whomever was listening to the poem that the poem was going to be involved with this particular context. Then I realized that a title might overemphasize something that was going to take place and I really didn't want that to happen. It didn't seem to be appropriate.

Q: *Gives it away?*

A: Yes. Gives it away, simply has no use.

Q: *You still do title some of your poems?*

A: Yes, some poems seem to me to need titles. Say, for instance, Shakespeare's sonnets where there doesn't seem to be any need to title them. And others of his poems obviously he felt needed the location of a title. It really speaks better of the poem not to have a title. I think of Cummings primarily. He used a title if I remember very rarely.

Q: *Your poems are characterized by a certain spareness. Do they originate in that form? Do you revise?*

A: No. I certainly deeply respect other poets who work through the process of revision. I think the word revision or revise—to see again—that has taken place, and a poet say like Louis Zukovsky has endless revisions upon his initial writing, he then gets the thing in the most incredible . . . it's like tuning up a motor. He really isn't satisfied until all the elements of the statement are for him utterly working in congruence. I would love to be able to do that at times. I find that I can't go back. I lose the initial energy or impulse. And the poems tend to dilute or refute what's been said. And that's true both in prose and in poetry. I tend not to revise. If something's not working, that is if the motor won't start, I usually give it up and try later.

Q: *In the original manuscript of* THE FINGER *which was in the Paris Review, the first three stanzas only had one word change. Then after that it changed considerably.*

Robert Creeley

A: Yes. What happened there, if you look you'll see there's a false start, and in the full manuscript you would see what happens. Those lines are crossed out and then you start again at that point and that impedence or that difficulty hopefully gets past. When something isn't working for me I stop, say, something that's going to go on for a while, then I usually start back up and try it again. You would say like in a car that wasn't getting through a ditch. Or else possibly find a way around it, but more usually back up and have another try. And if it just can't get through the ditch, then I just get out and walk home.

Q: *Dudley Fitts has called your poems "lyric epigrams."*

A: Yes. He generally is reviewing FOR LOVE. I don't think that the basic character in my writing has altered that significantly. But I think that the kind of tightness that was so insistent in those earlier poems has modified. Well, the kind of emotional crisis one seems to live in daily in one's twenties in a difficult situation or marriage—there is a need to get it as tightly together as it can possibly be done just to survive in an emotional nexus, except that emotions seem to be curiously diffused and vague. Now I feel much more relaxed and therefore don't have that necessity to make everything so uptight. I think those early poems, although I really liked them when I wrote them, seemed to me really uptight.

Q: *There's a widely influential quotation attributed to you—the one about "Form is never more than an extension of content." Would you comment on that?*

A: I still feel that to be true. The thing to be said tends to dictate the mode in which it can be said. I really believe Charles' contention that there's an appropriate way of saying something inherent in the thing to be said. Which is really not formally more difficult to apprehend than, say, what's the case when you take a glass of water and spill it on the ground. It takes place on the ground in the nature of itself as water, being fluid, etc., and in the context of the ground that nature and circumstance that it's now met with. I found that statement actually in a variety of other writers from other times, for example, Flaubert, says something very akin to that. And I remember finding it some time after Charles had quoted me, and feeling almost dismayed, I was a younger man, that this had been said most succinctly—and certainly Emerson had it much in mind, in his sense of spontaneous form. I was thinking of Waggoner's insistence that all American verse is from Emerson's, not tutelage, but from Emerson's perception of its nature. In other words, his senses of how poetry takes place were crucial for American writers.

Q: *What do you think of Peter Jay's descriptive term that your works are verbal miniature sculptures?*

A: I don't really like the word sculpture. I remember there was a lovely thing in Wallace Stevens. He said something like, there are those who speak of form in poetry as though it were some derivative of plastic. And I think the word sculpture is a little assumptive. I can see what he means. But I don't think poems are sculptured any more. It's like saying someone is very poetic in school. I can sympathize with the intention and the assertion but if someone took it seriously, then what would they do? They would have to assume a three-dimensional condition in the book they were reading. And the pages didn't fold out or nothing to touch. Except old paper.

Some of my best friends are sculptors. But I'm an absolute failure as a "visual artist." I can't even take a decent photograph, which is something where one has every aid. Although I realize being a photographer is obviously more sophisticated than just having a camera in your hand. For a long time as a younger man people would clarify my writing as having almost no experience of visual condition. The room was never described. In fact all the writing seemed to take place in a room. Which must have been very bare indeed, because nothing was ever reported as being in it. Only two people talking. I have tried in the last two years writing that simply says: the road is going this way down the hill and there are trees here. I mean sit down and deliberately say I want to make a statement of what seems to be physically actual in this place, and I really don't want to involve more than that in the statement. I don't feel I have any particular prowess in the visual aspects of my work. It really isn't something I can do with much confidence.

Q: *You seem to have many aphorisms in your writing.*

A: Well, Pound again, in that kind of circumstance he found so useful when he spoke of writers, or poetry, as having several modal possibilities: phanopoeia, logopoeia and melopoeia, that is. The writer might be primarily decisive in one or more of these modes, and probably the phanopoeia situation in my writing is the weakest. The image-making quality in my writing is really not what's happening seems to be the case. I think it's logopoeia—head trips—are what I'd be into.

Q: *They say the great poems combine all three.*

A: All three. Well, one day. Not in my time perhaps.

Q: *One poem of yours starts: How the fact of seeing someone away . . .*

A: That's from PIECES.

Q: *That seems to consist of one aphorism after the other.*

A: I'm fascinated by the way you state something and this very curious activity, not merely compressing, but this very curious activity follows. For example, I really love people like Lichenstein who can so state the case that it creates an entire, not merely possibility but creates an entire activity in the statement. As a younger man, for example, when it came time for me to go to college I took college boards and I must report sadly that I was somewhere in the upper two percentile in mathematics whereas in literature and English I was down sluggishly in the middle or lower fifties. At least in that kind of testing I didn't seem to have any particular aptitude, or the average aptitude for what reading and writing seems to involve. In the kind of intellectuality that's involved with mathematics, I seem to have a very high ability.

Q: *That shows up in your poetry?*

A: I think that's true. I know people, friends and otherwise, who feel that there are qualifications to understandably make about what I'm doing, really think that I think too much. A generous friend like Allen would say: We have too much mental garbage in the world and I don't think there should be any more of it. I would not argue that kind of emphasis, but I would not want to get away from the pleasure that thinking can be. I don't think that one can go mindless in order to accomplish experience. It's as much the body as the fingers.

Q: *The mind's eye.*

A: Yes. Well, that is like Melville's "The eyes are the gateway to the soul." Archie Moore charmingly quoted when asked after a particular fight how he managed to keep on top of his opponent, well, he said, keep digging at his eyes. The eyes are the gateway to the soul. He could tell what his contestant was into by just watching his eyes. Also the brain surfaces in the eyes directly. The physical eye is like the brain surfacing. It's where the brain comes literally. Outward from its own physical place. If you put your finger in your eye, you put your finger in your brain.

Q: *You quite often use an unexpected end rhyme. Is this a device or does it come to slam the poem shut?*

A: It comes from impulse and to lock it up so to speak when it can be locked up.

Q: *And you also sometimes end your poems with an ingenious turn of thought—with an epigram.*

A: Yes.

Q: *That* POEM FOR WCW *you end: "In time of trouble a wild exultation." Which is almost an oxymoron.*

A: I know.

Q: *Does that derive by any chance as a connotation from the words of the Apostle Paul, "Rejoice even in our troubles"?*

A: I wasn't familiar with that. A few weeks ago I found myself possessed by the statement, not from this particular source, but make a joyful sound unto the Lord. And it was always paradoxically true. I found a great energy field and paradoxically a great interest in voices that had extraordinary and sometimes painful difficulty. Other friends regretted that it did prove so insistently the case that the ideas came so insistently and so directly from situations of human crisis and pain and agony and even some statements like: "After every major war a major literature." It did seem that they were energized by situations of extraordinary crisis. And that is what I think I meant by the great exultation. Williams did really seem not merely to thrive on difficulty but at least in some very actual way to depend upon them.

Q: *In his medical career?*

A: No, in his personal life, I think. The kinds of difficulty he felt as a man were very fruitful. If one goes through his poems, especially his later poems, you find that there are periods of happiness which are not so much meager but they are not the periods in which his most intensive writing took place. Also Charles Olson's emphasis on the difficulties once more. Again, paradoxically and obviously unhappily, human beings tend to find location in difficulty. And find and build happiness.

Robert Creeley

Q: *To speak of images, your images are more of real things.*

A: Yes. This is what you could call particularism or literalism. I'm by nature and circumstance a very literal man. There was a sign over a diner as one drove from Albuquerque to Santa Fe, and it said: Ly'n Bragg. For years I drove past that cafe and it never occurred to me that it was a pun. Lie and Brag. I thought that the one owner's name was Ly and the other's name was Bragg. As far as being literal, I can be extraordinarily dumb in that way. I begin by believing that you put your name on the cafe and accept it as the name.

Q: *Don't you have trouble interpreting cartoons then?*

A: You mean such as political cartoons or comic strips? Yes, sometimes I find that I don't get the joke. I find that most truly when I try to tell a joke that I find has tickled me, and I find that I get so involved with the literal thing that happened that I tend to lose the joke.

Q: *Then you would say you do not use the surrealistic images?*

A: With no intention they occur at times but again they come out of literal states of feeling. They are found in a literal circumstance rather than a fantastic. This book that I've written for Marisol has many surreal situations in it that are literal. They are surreal but they are literal. I was again thinking of Bacon, Francis Bacon, the presences of the images that one finds in his painting are surreal, to put it mildly, but the impact on consciousness are that they are a literal reality. They're not about something. It has to be actual, otherwise it's simply an echo of something or a description of something that's not present.

Q: *In some of your poems you seem to leave it entirely to the reader to create his own images. The poem you have: "Before I Die./Before I Die./Before I Die./Before I Die."*

A: It's called Four. There the insistence was not intruding merely but was insisting. That insistence was unavoidable. I don't know why but that's what I was speaking of earlier that there began to be noticed about the time I was getting into my forties, this sense provoked by biological fact and also other sense provided by experience, that one's life was finite and the condition of what one hoped to do and realize was absolutely contingent on that existence. And so Before I Die is a small ritual of that conviction.

169

Q: *You have a period after each line. Is that the finality?*

A: That's to let it be insistent instead of some accumulating statement. Each time it says it, it is insisting that that be recognized. I wanted it as flat as possible.

Q: *To what use do you put punctuation generally?*

A: Well, things like commas I tend to use to help phrasing, pauses, the thing being said, and then commas are certainly presence. Commas are used to make manifest the physical thing being said. How it should break or how one's feeling of breaking or hesitating or moving. Things like periods or question marks for example. I tend to use question marks when there is otherwise no indication that the thing being said is a question. I really respect Gertrude Stein's notes on punctuation. I can't quickly recall the title of the piece, but it's in a book of her writings that's published by Beacon. She indicates, why use question marks when the thing being said is obviously a question. Then it's only an addenda. Also like situations: Why did you come. Is a very different statement than: Why did you come? Why did you come. Seems to me to indicate already a resolution in the speaker's mind who doesn't really want to hear an answer, just wants to experience this person's presence. The period there simply emphasizes that there's already a resolution in the speaker's mind. If you put a question mark, then you do want an answer.

Q: *You use punctuation to direct the reading of the poem?*

A: Sure. I can think of no other use for it. The reading of the poem and the physical way I want it to be said and also at times in simple syntactic circumstances. Like colons or dashes. Semicolons I use very rarely.

Q: *Do you think it's characteristic of contemporary poetry to make the reader as well as the poet work? More in contemporary than in previous ones.*

A: I wonder. I was thinking in a conversation with Tom Clark a few days ago. We were talking about radio and then we were thinking that various wonders of television reflected in the discussions of the various political candidates for the presidency. One thing that happens to things being said in television is that the sensory demand of all else that's being seen means that the focus upon the thing being said is much diffused and is diminished. I was thinking of old time radio plays in which the door closing and the squeaking door had incredible effect whereas if you saw a contemporary TV drama with a squeaking door you'd be watching the door and saying it looks like it needs oil or something. It wouldn't have nearly the impact. The focus, you see, is diffused because simply there is more happening. I therefore wonder what was the experience in a culture where when you heard something and/or read it you didn't have the diversity of other things happening to divert or distract you from that kind of occupation or focus. I think equally that as the world changes in its own experience of itself, I think that humanly we are at a time of great crisis. Not simply political and social but biological. And I think that the apprehension of that either as attitude or just intuition are going to mean to the reader he is not going to work harder simply to be a good student but that the demands upon his consciousness are now very large indeed, poetry obviously being one of them. I think that the complexities of experience which are now in our consciousness, we tend to insist that they be there. They are going to make great demands on the reader and the writer alike.

Q: *Your work is well-known for its use of the colloquial.*

A: It's a language I feel very at home in. One thing that dismayed me when I was younger, still in college, was the predominant interest in a poetry which I felt myself excluded from by virtue of diction and social situation—in the same way that, let's say, contemporary Black writers feel that the norm of white American writing isn't part of their vocabulary. I felt that to a much lesser degree. Nevertheless, as actually, I felt that the writing of Tate or Auden or Eliot was all the habit of the diction and therefore of an experience which was not mine. I mean, I literally grew up in the depression years when my mother was a public health nurse in a small New England town. And I sure couldn't come on like T.S. Eliot. It would be absurd. You know. So the colloquial was part of my daily material. John Chamberlain said in a lovely fashion—someone asked him why he used old cars as materials for his sculptures, and he said: Well, Michelangelo seemed to have a lot of marble in his backyard and what he had was a lot of rusty cars.

Q: *Do you ever visualize the work of a poem on the page?*

A: No, I don't. I was thinking of a recent poem of Michael McClure's. It's always very intriguing, Michael's sense of the formal sense of that appearance which in one sense you superficially think:

Wow, that looks like George Herbert or something. I think it's really involved with the phrasing or the way he wants it read as a sequence of emphases or rhythmic states. He has a way of giving the lines that telescoping and then expanding. This is the way he accomplishes it. I'm only interested in the typography and/or the visual appearance as to how it will inform the reader as something he can hear. I use notation in the same way a composer uses a written score.

Q: *Would you say that the subconscious played any part in your poem* THE FINGER?

A: Yeah. Sure. From the situation that gave it its primary material, the whole experience with LSD, then how it came to be written was the dictation of that subconscious.

Q: *A little different from your—most of your poems?*

A: Well, but that woman, whether it be the woman of that particular poem, the poem called THE WOMAN IN WORDS, or the woman in the door for example, that woman was very insistent, and she comes apparently from my subconscious. In fact, somewhat sadly about two years ago now, I really was feeling in some crisis and couldn't locate it, and was in Boston and went to see a psychiatrist at the Mass. Medical Center and we got talking very briefly but nevertheless—much the same as I had been to a psychiatrist in San Francisco. For only a period of three or four visits and both of them told me that the nexus or the circumstance of this woman for me was not located in a literal person. It wasn't my wife. It wasn't specifically my mother, it wasn't specifically my sister. It wasn't specifically a person who had created this experience, it was a rather dense and complex thing. And so the woman of THE FINGER, the guise of that presence is to me most relieving really. The woman can also be the woman in a poem called THE CRACKS, and that woman is really pretty scary to me. It's a poem that is toward the end of FOR LOVE. That woman is really kind of threatening.

Q: *You have made the statement: I write what I don't know.*

A: I lean heavily on Franz Kline. Mitchel Goodman and Denise were at that time living in the city on Seventeenth Street, and I was having a sort of messed-up time in my own life and was teaching at Black Mountain, and when I was in the city I'd usually stay with them. And I'd go every night to the Cedars and spend time there until four in the morning. Then I'd come home halfway discreet. I didn't make a lot of noise or anything, but I'd babble what an incredible man Franz Kline was. And Mitch after hearing this morning after morning simply said: Aren't you really masking the fact that you're spending an awful lot of time in the local bar? I really question Kline, not so much his painting, but I question his whole condition as a painter. Simply that I don't think he pays any attention to other painters. Anyhow I persuaded Mitch to come with me one night to see this and happily Kline was there, and not hostily but very politely questioned Kline's interest in painting that might have little to do with his own activities as painter, and he spoke of a particular show of a friend of Mitch's that was then on. And he said: No, I haven't been to see it but let me tell you what it looks like. And he described every fact of those paintings. And Mitch kept saying: Yes, that's true, but, and then Kline would continue to tell him even the kind of framing. He told him all the dimensions. He told him every color, he told him techniques. He told him, you know he told him all the physical qualifications of these paintings. And after he had finished this recital he then said: Now, if I paint what I know, that bores me, if I paint what you know, that bores you, so I paint what I don't know and I paint very little of what I do know because that's a repetition of what's already in hand. That made great sense to me. Hopefully I write what I don't know.

I know in teaching simply telling people again and again what you know or what they know, the whole thing sags entirely. So it's a delight to teach in a circumstance where something's to be learned. The teacher has equal possibility with the students. In fact also one time when I was teaching in Black Mountain, they asked me if I would teach biology. And I said: that literally is the one thing I know nothing about. Somehow I never had it in high school and didn't have any involvement with it in college. How can you propose that I teach these college students and he said: Ideal circumstance, man. You'll be learning along with them. Which was the best possible state.

Q: *And in this connection, what about poetry readings? What are your feelings about poetry readings?*

A: They're lovely feedback. Sadly, having seen Virgil Thomson's opera last night and seeing the audience's response to it which was ostensibly one of approval . . . they should have thrown stones at it or some awful thing but to me public readings are most interesting feedback and doesn't have to be something like "Gee, that was a great poem you wrote" and discuss it analytically. One can tell pretty quickly what the intuitive response of the audience is, not to the performance reading but to the actual place that they are given to be as they are hearing something. I lived a great deal of my life in isolation humanly speaking, that is, in a very close intimate nexus of persons . . . I was so extremely shy that the sense of reading poems in public when I was say twenty-five, that would be impossible . . . I just literally couldn't see how it could be accomplished. Then as I got older and got confidence and literally took the risk as I think everyone has to, in the world rather than in some sheltered small place, public readings began to be a lovely information as to what was getting through and what wasn't. And I realize too that there are various kinds of poems that can't be heard in public and have no reason to be heard in public, in the sense not that they're private in their information but they just can't be heard. And going down in the middle of Times Square and starting to read one of Shakespeare's sonnets, I don't think many people would get much out of it. On the other hand, you could read kinds of poems.

I have been teaching the plays of Sophocles in New Mexico to a class of about twelve people, and they asked, does he have to keep saying: "I think I see them coming now." We saw that a page ago, and here's the lookout saying "Here they come even now" and they said that at least five times. There must be some reason for this. So I went to look up what was the condition of Greek theatre and found out that this was about forty thousand people. So you had to say it five times to allow for the possibility that someone was eating popcorn or something else. Readings really give you a lot of information about what the . . . what's getting through. In a kind of intuitive way. For example, Saturday night I'm going to read up at a friend's loft. In a literal sense it's a public reading. Probably the audience will be primarily a nexus of friends here in the city. That's a good group to read to because I'm going to get some very useful information as to what the condition of what I've been involved with seems to be. It will be really useful to me. The only times when I don't like public readings is when it becomes just like show biz or when one is writing out the single scene. I mean you don't have to do it fifty thousand times. I mean, Yeats being asked to read THE LAKE ISLE OF INNISFREE once more. He apparently loathed being asked to read that poem. Because that was the poem that everyone wanted him to read. And he had read it *ad nauseum*. I think as Olson put it, one is always interested to read what one has just finished writing.

I've always been suspicious of drama for myself. I think of a friend or a poet as Kenneth Koch who has made drama a lovely playful and aesthetic kind of writing, some of my friends can work very ably in that mode. Duncan is another. For me it turns phony. It's false and I can't locate the emotional field and I can't get ahold of it. It tends to blow up the condition, the thing being said, in a way I can't keep track of. So dramatic poetry for me is really bad news. I would then go again to prose and write a prose narrative, a story. That's the only drama that I really have any ability with.

Q: *You read your poems in a contained manner.*

A: Well, I've had a lovely meeting with a lovely old timer in Los Angeles who wrote a book THE HOLY BARBARIANS, Lawrence Lipton. Allen Ginsberg took me over to his house to meet him and he had no sooner said hello to me when he said, "You have literally the worst reading style of anyone I have ever heard. I'm going to read you a poem and you take note, young man, and see if you can't improve." A lot of people have come up after I've had a reading and said, "We really felt for you. You seemed so nervous—so distraught—you kept stumbling over the lines." I don't like to argue about it but I say, actually I wasn't as nervous as you perhaps thought I was, this is really the way I want those poems to be heard. They are written in an intensity of that order and it is hesitant in what it feels it can say and to read it as though it weren't the case would be to mistake its actual condition.

Q: *Different poems require different readings.*

A: Well, I would hope so. Much as I admire him in roles involved with Sherlock Holmes, I sure don't want Basil Rathbone to be the great reader of our time.

Q: *Have you read in connection with the American writers against—*

A: Yeah, I've read with resistance groups.

Q: *What poems of yours would you designate as being protest?*

A: Very few. A poem called AMERICA is one such instance. A poem called THE SIGNBOARD. But basically I haven't been able to write a poem of direct political protest. I excused myself but I did not want to let the war, let's say, eat that up too. It's as though you're sitting in the house with your wife and family and it doesn't mean that you're safe but you're aware that you have that as a possibility and you don't want to yield to that demand. I know that Denise, that dilemma has eaten her very harshly. It entirely occupies her attention as a writer.

And I deeply respect that. But it would be false for me to say it has done that to me. Politically and humanly and socially I protest the war, but I haven't been able to speak of it in the way that she has or that Allen has or that Duncan has or that Robert Bly has. When it comes to reading the poem that paradoxically I remember getting an extraordinary response from audience in terms of protest, was THE FINGER. I keep thinking if we could simply state or gain a situation of experience that would make the war seem as bleakly and painfully and brutally unnecessary as it obviously is, then possibly people's minds might change concerning it. People walk away and just refuse it as a commitment. Just not accept its quasi- or phony-serious demand. If the distortion and ridiculousness of that conduct was simply revealed as such and admitted as such, then possibly we could stop. In painfully small instances like refusing to pay taxes insofar as they are used to support the war, but really ridiculing all those people. I felt that Ed Sanders had possibly come closest than any of us to protesting the war when he got that lovely permission to exorcise the Pentagon—which wasn't really as "funny" as it might seem. I think that kind of address to the war might be very useful. I think that in like sense Abbie Hoffman was an extraordinarily alert political intelligence in his way of demonstrating at the Democratic Convention. I heard a lovely tape of him talking about the whole situation. There were literally four or five yippies present and all the news media were reporting like a takeover of the Democratic Convention. One is coming tonight. We'll have five thousand federal troops facing him. I think what I mentioned would be far more useful, not useful, but would probably work far better. Either walk away or laugh or ridicule them out of existence. Out of their procreation of existence. Once you engage it in terms of argument, it's like tar baby. You're stuck with it.

Q: *Your little poem* CHANGE:
   Turning/One wants it all—
   /No
   /Defenses.
Does that poem have any special significance?

A: It was written for a friend's birthday—Ted Berrigan—and when it was printed it had a dedication to him, and it simply is that when there's a demand in one's life that one change, it's like Williams's now that men heretofore had been unable to realize their wishes. Now that they can realize them, they must either change them or perish. And I believe that entirely and when there are demands upon one's life that one change, there can be no defenses.

Robert Creeley

You know, you can't take anything with you. Someone says: Get out of the house quickly. It is on fire and momentarily going to collapse, you can't start worrying about whether you can save the radio or even the baby bleakly. You have to move. You have no defenses against that demand.

Q: *Did it have any significance as far as your work is concerned?*

A: Only in the sense that when there was a demand that I change some habit or some circumstance, that had become a habit and had become reassuring, there was no defense that could provide for the possible risk of the change involved.

Q: *Would you like to comment on what you have termed your present writing and situation generally?*

A: At the moment involved with prose, as it happens. I have in mind a short novel using much the same approach that I've used with this book for MARISOL, and poetry is interesting to me but I simply haven't been writing it . . . I've been writing occasionally . . . we have something that delights me—birthdays are celebrated endlessly, so people write odes to somebody and all kinds of pleasant manners. That's really the poems I've written mostly in the last six months. They're lovely. You can't throw them away in contempt but then you don't have to worry about them. Now I'm much more able to explore what's on my mind with prose than I am with poetry. I don't worry about losing it but I'm more involved with that. This book, A DAYBOOK will be—again coming to that change in my life—which moving to the West Coast really meant—not just the change of a physical place but the change I had to get into my own physical consciousness about life. Take it in hand and really accept its reality. The poems of that book go through that consciousness.

13

Erica Jong

Q: *How do you start a poem?*

A: That's a very difficult question. My way of writing has changed considerably in the past few years. At this point, I usually get a first line. I don't know where that first line comes from and I don't know who says it to me. It may be the Muse. (I really believe in the Muse, by the way.) But the process seems to be that I get a line and write it down as quickly as I can and generally from that I allow things to build. I follow the images one after the other seemingly automatically. That doesn't mean that my poems are not revised or edited, but they come in a very mysterious way. Almost by dictation.

I didn't always write this way, however. When I was in college I wrote in a much more premeditated manner. I would struggle from one line to the next, poring over a rhyming dictionary, counting out the meter on my fingers. Although I now write very freely, I'm conscious of the oral qualities of the poetry and of the rhythm. Also, I don't let everything stand. The second draft is written extremely critically. Most of the process consists of striking out the crap—the bad lines.

But I can't tell you where my first line comes from. I do know that I recognize Osip Mandelstam's description of the kind of foretrembling which precedes writing a poem. It's a weird kind of excitement which feels somewhat like sexual tension and somewhat like anxiety. It's as if an aura exists around you—and you know you're going to write a poem that day. The real question of beginning is when you get the hook into the poem, and that hook is the first line. It may not always *remain* the first line. It may become the last line, or it may drop out of the poem altogether, but it's the line that starts your imagination going.

Q: *Do you usually finish the poem in one day or work on it for a while?*

A: It depends. Some poems are finished in one day. Others take years. Sometimes the process is merely a question of refining, and sometimes you have to grow into a poem. I have a poem which is just beginning now, and I haven't the faintest idea when I'll finish it. There are two lines that really live. Two images. But they haven't grown into a poem yet.

Q: *It's working?*

A: It's there working, yes. I'm reminded of the motto Kafka had over his writing desk—"Wait." And it's true. You're not always conscious of working on a poem. And then it happens. It erupts like a volcano. Your imagination is working all the time in a subterranean way. And when it comes time for you to write the poem, the whole thing explodes.

Q: *What about ideas for a novel—is it a whole section, a chapter . . .?*

A: FEAR OF FLYING was written in such a funny way that it's difficult to describe the process. I had been working for years on sections of it and I had attempted two earlier novels that I didn't finish. I had been collecting autobiographical fragments, fantasies, character sketches, ideas. When the framing device for this book —the trip across Europe—occurred to me, I suddenly found a way to make a coherent story out of materials which had been obsessing me for quite some time.

Q: *One of the questions we were going to ask you was about the Muse. Because you do mention her in a very specific personal way sometimes.*

A: How do you mean?

Q: *You talk about her in a very familiar way as if you met her and she's right there beside you. Could you talk about it?*

A: Well, I used to think that all this talk about the Muse was a lot of bullshit. But I was wrong. I'm convinced that there are powers we

179

cannot find names for. Maybe the Muse is really the same as the collective unconscious. I don't think it matters. Maybe the Muse is one's own unconscious which connects with the collective unconscious. Or maybe the Muse is a supernatural being. But I think there are forces we have no way of scientifically codifying, and inspiration is one of them. Why is it that at a given moment in your life certain elements come together and fuse in a way that makes a poem or that allows you to write a novel you've been dreaming of for years?

Q: *So you call it the Muse?*

A: Yes, but that's just one of many possible terms. That quality of inspiration, that sudden chill, the thing that makes your hair stand on end . . . I don't know what else to call it. You see, I think part of being a poet is learning how to tap your inner resources. Probably poets are born, not made. But the training of a poet consists in learning how to tap that secret part of yourself which connects with the communal unconscious. So you spend a lot of time imitating other people's poems. Writing on subjects that, let's say, aren't of interest to you but were of interest to the poets you admire. You're learning your craft. But what you're really learning during those years of apprenticeship is how to explore yourself. And when that happens—(I've said this in the poetry seminar about a million times)—when craft and the exploration of self come together, that's when you become a poet. All the stuff you produced before that was derivative apprenticeship work. And you usually know it when that point arrives.

Q: *One of the quotations you had in your article "The Artist as Housewife" was "Everyone has talent, what is rare is the courage to follow the talent to the dark place where it leads." What has helped you the most to go into those dark places?*

A: I had to learn to trust myself. I had to learn to trust that part of my mind which had the potential of being original. I think lots of things helped. Getting older and having more confidence in my own voice. The other thing (unfashionable as it's become) was psychoanalysis. Artists tend to be afraid of it. They think they'll lose their creativity. But what analysis teaches you is how to surrender yourself to your fantasies. How to dive down into those fantasies. If you can do it on the couch—and not all people can do it on the couch either—then, you may learn to trust the unconscious. To follow its meandering course. Not to look for a goal. As in an analytic session where you begin meandering. "Oh, this doesn't make any sense at all. I'm saying X. I'm saying Y." And then at the end of the session you discover that it does make sense. It makes more sense than most "rational" discourse. There are a lot of dreadful analysts around —just as there are a lot of incompetents in any other profession. But about two percent of them are artists, and understand artists. I was also lucky to have a couple of teachers who knew where I was going. And who encouraged me when my poetry began to take the inner direction. Mark Strand, for example, said at one point, when I showed him my early poems, "You haven't really been fucked by poetry yet." I don't know if he would remember having used that phrase, but I've never forgotten it. Then, when I showed him the first draft of FRUITS & VEGETABLES, he said, "Now you're into something! Keep with it." He recognized that I was dealing with sexuality in a way that was more daring for me and that I had begun to allow my imagination free rein. His encouragement was vital at that time.

Q: *You mention voice in that same article. You say that the poet's main problem is to "raise a voice." How did you find your voice and how do you suggest a poet find his voice? Going into himself?*

A: Well, I remember my gradual realization that the person I was in life and the person I was in my poems were not the same. When I wrote poetry I assumed a kind of poet-role. It probably came out of some old grade school notion of what a poet is. We all have that and it somehow stands in our way. I realized that in life I was a clown, alternately very solemn and serious—and at other times, kidding around wildly. But I never had allowed that range in my work. I had always been attracted to satire, and even in my high school and college poems, I had tried to write satire. But it was a kind of formal satire. It wasn't really open and spontaneous. I had to learn how to let spontaneity into my poems.

Q: *You speak frequently of the need for authenticity. Is the need for authenticity the need for trusting yourself?*

A: Yes, because all you have to write out of is your own kinkiness, the idiosyncrasies of your personality, the special spectacles through which you view the world. If you censor those things out in deference to some fear of exposure, fear of what your family, your husband, your lover, or your friends may think, then you're going to lose authenticity. When you write, you're not writing for an outer social world that approves or does not approve. Writing is for that inner place, that inner place in other people, too. That's what I mean by authenticity. And it's very hard to get past this obsession with trying to please. It's especially hard for women. Men are afraid, too, of course, but in women the fear of self-exposure is even more cultivated.

Q: *Many of your poems refer to specific people who seem to be in your life. There is a poem called* CHINESE FOOD, *for example, where there are specific people by name. And in some of your recent poems you mention your mother. Do you deal with these poems that are maybe biographical in one way, maybe nonliteral in other ways—how do you deal with this issue of speaking from your voice and also other people?*

A: I don't think that any of the people in my poems are real people in a strict biographical sense. Obviously, they are people frozen at certain moments in time. My real biographical mother is not merely like the mother in that poem. And she would be the first to say so.

I don't think that biographical question is a fair criterion by which to measure a poem. There's a wonderful quote from Jerzy Kosinski which I used in my novel. He says that you can't have such a thing as straight autobiography or confessional writing because even if you *try* to write down literally what you remember, memory *itself* fictionalizes and orders and structures. Even if you make a film or a tape, you have to edit it, and in so doing, you put a controlling intelligence around it. It ceases to be the same as biography.

What you're talking about in my poems is that they refer to—yes, I have a mother—everybody has a mother—I could have written twelve other poems about my mother in different incarnations and I probably *will* as time goes on. But I don't see the people in those poems as real people. The Chinese food poem mentions people who were present at a given dinner. But those people aren't really depicted. And I don't see my poems as confessional at all. I see them as "structures made to accommodate certain feelings." (The phrase Kosinski uses.) Obviously they come out of my life. But then all poets' poems come out of their lives.

If the people in the poems were just people in my own life, and hadn't any universal meaning, nobody else could connect with those poems. They would be so personal that they would mean nothing to anybody but *me*. That's why I think the term confessional poetry is an absolute misnomer. I don't think there *is* such a thing as confessional poetry.

182

Erica Jong

Q: *One term you do use is "author" in the sense of authority. What would you say is the author's particular responsibility as an author writing today?*

A: When I talk about authority, what I mean is: You are the person where the buck stops. You are responsible for what you write. You cannot write a book in committee, nor with a certain editor, publisher, or reviewer in mind. Writing is one of the few professions left where you take all the responsibility for what you do. It's really dangerous and ultimately destroys you as a writer if you start thinking about responses to your work or what your audience needs. That's what I mean by authority. And that's why I say again and again to my poetry seminar: "Don't even listen to *me*. We're offering criticisms of your poems and we're saying—'OK, that line works, that line doesn't work.' But if you want to ignore it, go ahead and ignore it because learning to be a writer means learning to ignore people's advice when it's bad." You have to reach that place in yourself where you know your own sound, your own rhythm, your own voice. That's what it's all about. You'll find that with many great authors of the past, their strengths and weaknesses are so intertwined that one can't unravel them. A contemporary author like Doris Lessing is a good example of this. She can be incredibly hard to read, even boring at times. And yet she's a great writer. It's the very heaviness of her writing, the way she works out a detailed portrait of a society that makes her so good. How could an editor sit down with THE GOLDEN NOTEBOOK and excise passages? God knows there are sections of it that are very heavy going. Yet the strengths of the book and the faults are so interwoven that editing it would be impossible. You can't make THE GOLDEN NOTEBOOK into an E.M. Forster or Elizabeth Bowen novel. It's a different animal. You try to refine your work as much as you can. But ultimately you have to say: "I am I. I am the author." That's what I want everyone in my seminar to learn eventually.

Q: *You mentioned earlier some of the problems of being a woman poet. In your article "The Artist as Housewife" you said "Being an artist of any sex is such a difficult business that it seems almost ungenerous and naive to speak of the special problems of the woman artist . . ." What are those special problems?*

A: There are many. Despite the fact that we've had Sappho, Emily Dickinson, Jane Austen, the Brontës, Colette, Virginia Woolf, etc., there is still the feeling that women's writing is a lesser class of

183

writing, that to write about what goes on in the nursery or the bedroom is not as important as what goes on in the battlefield, that to write about relationships between men and women is not as important as writing about a moonshot. Somehow there's a feeling that what women know about is a lesser category of knowledge. It's women's fiction, women's poetry, or something like that. Women are more than half the human race, and yet since the culture has always been male-dominated, the things men are interested in are thought to be of greater importance than the things women are interested in. Also, there is still a tremendous condescension toward women in reviewing. Whenever people tote up the lists of the greatest writers now writing, you get the same male names over and over. Roth, Malamud, Singer, Updike . . . the same old litany . . . You don't get Eudora Welty, Doris Lessing, Mary McCarthy, Adrienne Rich, Anne Sexton. Why? There is a kind of patriarchal prejudice which infuses our whole culture. I think it is not *always* malicious on the part of men—it's often purely unconscious. The psychological reasons behind this are many. Probably womb-envy—that most unrecognized phenomenon—plays a significant part. Since the majority of psychologists and anthropologists have been male, they've been reluctant to recognize it. Men have the feeling that women can create life in their bodies, therefore how *dare* they create art? A book I'm very interested in is THE FIRST SEX by Elizabeth Gould Davis. It deals with male envy of the female and its manifestations throughout different cultures.

Q: *Do you think women writers have more difficulty getting published because of this?*

A: It's hard to generalize because women are being published now for faddish reasons. Let's just say women don't have difficulty being published. But they do have difficulty being taken *seriously* as writers. Certain kinds of commercial writing are almost exclusively done by women—Gothic romances, children's books. Yet being published is quite a different thing from being accorded respect as an *artist*. Second-hand bookstores are strewn with books which were published and forgotten.

Q: *You mentioned women writers. Do you find it more often that women are reviewed as women than as writers?*

A: I've never seen a review of a woman writer in which her sex was not mentioned in some way. And frequently reviewers do things like comment on appearance. Carolyn Kizer was reviewed (I think in TIME or NEWSWEEK) as "the Mae West of the poetry world" or some crap like that. There are many good looking male poets and people don't go around saying "Isn't W.S. Merwin a cutie?" I mean, he's very handsome. Richard Wilbur is very handsome. Mark Strand is very handsome. I hope I haven't left anybody out. But people don't talk about that in reviews of men. With women they *always* talk about it. And if a woman's ugly, they harp on that too. Did you see that reference to Gertrude Stein's "fat ankles" in the TIMES a few weeks ago? It's as if you're a piece of meat. Besides condescension and not being taken seriously, there's that awful category of "woman poet." *Women's* conflicts—as if they weren't applicable to *all* of us.

Q: *Now when you go in to your workroom and begin to work, and you're a poet and also a woman, what special kind of traps do you have to look out for because of this scene in terms of your craft? In terms of your voice?*

A: As I said in the "ARTIST AS HOUSEWIFE" article, I went for a long time not dealing with my feelings about being a woman, because I had never really seen it done before. In college I read Auden, Yeats and Eliot, and imitated a male voice. I didn't think of it as a male voice, I thought of it as a *poet's* voice, but it didn't deal with the things that I wanted to deal with. Perhaps the reason Sylvia Plath was so important to my generation of young women was that she wrote about being a woman and she wrote about its negative side. She dealt with birth, menstruation—all the things that male poets don't deal with. So she liberated us. Now I think we can go on beyond that. We don't *always* have to write about female rage.

Q: *Do you have any work habits? Isadora writes in the nude. Do you have work habits like this?*

A: I *don't* always write in the nude. Anyway that's not a work habit.

Q: *Do you have any—certain papers—in longhand?*

A: I write in longhand and I write very fast. I like to have a pen that flows rapidly because when the words start coming they come so fast that my handwriting is virtually illegible. I can't compose on a typewriter, although my second draft is typed. It gets pasted into my notebook side by side with the scrawled first draft and I refine it from there.

Q: *Do you keep a journal?*

A: I don't really have time, though I would love to. I've kept journals at many times in my life, starting from when I was about thirteen or fourteen. But it's boring and contrived to keep a journal every day. Better to write as the mood strikes. But I don't even have time to do that except on rare occasions. Writing a novel, writing poems, writing letters to many correspondents, trying to keep notes on poems that come to mind—there just isn't time to keep a journal. Also you use up the energy that might go into poems.

Q: *Do you write every day—your poems, your novel—Do you write at a set time?*

A: Writing a novel is a very tough discipline. Poems can be written in spurts, irregularly. I sometimes write ten poems at once. But of those ten, perhaps one third will eventually be published. With a novel it's a whole different thing. You sit down every morning and push that pen across the page, and you have to get from one point to another. You know that you have to move your character to a certain city and out again and you must do it that day whether you feel like it or not. You don't always *start out* inspired, but as you work your way into the scene, things start happening. You begin pushing that pen along, and then maybe after two hours you're really going. Things you hadn't expected are happening on the page. There's such a hell of a lot of sheer plugging. Sometimes you write chapters and chapters and wind up discarding them. But you plod along day after day. You have to get up every morning at 8:00 (or whenever) and sit down for at least three or four hours.

By the way, I think that you can be a writer with four hours a day to write. Although you may need two hours of warmup time before, and two hours of winddown time afterward.

Q: *We were talking about serving your apprenticeship as a poet and becoming a poet.*

A: There was something I wanted to add about that. You have to find that place in yourself where you have great control, yet great freedom. Control over your craft so it's almost automatic. And at the same time great freedom to deal with unconscious material. That's the point at which you become a poet. Both things are not always operating at optimum pitch, however. You may sit down in the morning and feel that you're going to write a poem, but the poem you produce may be just a warmup for some other unwritten poem.

Q: *Do you use special exercises like free association exercises or games to get you going?*

A: No, I don't, but sometimes I read.

Q: *Which poets?*

A: Lately I've been reading a lot of Neruda. God help me for saying that. Every time you mention a name in an interview, you get haunted by that name from then on. Critics will clobber me with "influenced by Neruda"—but the reason I read him is that he shows me the possibilities of the imagination. I love the way he associates from one image to the next. It gets my mind going. But when I write, I write poems very different from the ones I've been reading. I may read a poem by Neruda that deals with death. But that doesn't mean I'm going to write a poem about death.

Q: *What do you do when you are plunging underwater and you hit a block, when you can't write anymore, when the poem doesn't mesh and when you sense it's a block rather than just being finished for that day?*

A: You leave the poem in your notebook and come back to it eventually. Months or years later you may see it very clearly. I save all my notebooks, and from time to time when I don't know what I'm going to write, I read them over and find the first line of a poem which I started but couldn't finish and sometimes I'm able to finish it. Nothing you write is ever lost to you. At some other level your mind is working on it.

Q: *Are there times when you can't write anything? How do you get around them?*

A: One of the happy things about writing both prose and poetry is that you always have something to do. We have a funny idea in this country about overspecialization. Lately I've been writing poems, articles, and prose fiction and it's been a good combination for me. Obviously you're not going to be at the peak of inspiration every day. And if you're not writing poems, why should it be dishonorable to write an article?

Q: *Then you don't have problems with blocks?*

A: Not at the moment. God knows I had lots of them in the past, and may have again in the future. Knock on wood.

Q: *In your article "THE ARTIST AS HOUSEWIFE" you wrote about the willingness to finish things being a good measure as to whether one was adult or not. Could you talk about this willingness to finish work as a special problem of the artist?*

A: I went for years not finishing anything. Because, of course, when you finish something, you can be judged. My poems used to go through 360 drafts. I had poems which were rewritten so many times that I suspect it was just a way of avoiding sending them out.

Q: *You can see it very clearly now.*

A: When I look at some of those drafts, I realize that beyond a certain point I wasn't improving anything. I was just obsessing. I was afraid to take risks.

Q: *Is this more of a problem with women, do you think?*

A: It's hard to generalize, but since women are encouraged not to have responsibility for their own lives, I suppose they *do* have more of a problem in this respect. Of course throughout history there have always been women who didn't give in to the demand that they remain children. Nevertheless, a woman's time tends to be more fragmented. (I can just hear all the male poets I know who have office jobs screaming and yelling). But perhaps it's not a problem of sheer time; perhaps it has more to do with not trusting yourself. Also women want to find men they admire and look up to. And that's very dangerous.

Q: *What started you writing?*

A: I don't remember a time when I didn't write. As a kid I used to keep journals and notebooks. I wrote stories and illustrated them. I never *said* I wanted to be a writer, but I always wrote. Still, it was hard to make the step of saying "I'm a writer" before I had published. I would shuffle my feet and look down at the floor. After my first book was accepted for publication, I began to think "Gee, I'm a poet." Talk about being other-directed.

Q: *You mentioned once that your early poems were in traditional verse form and that you came rather late to free writing. What would you say about that kind of classical training for a poet?*

A: I think it's tremendously important. You get letters from people saying: "I love to write poetry and I have twenty-six books of poetry in my desk drawer but I never read poetry." The country is full of "poets" who have never bought a book of poetry. If every person who sends poems to magazines would just buy one slim volume of verse, poets would not be starving. I've spent years reading poetry. I went to graduate school and read ancient and modern poetry, imitated Keats, imitated Pope, imitated Browning . . . Learning is good for a poet as long as she doesn't become a professional scholar.

Q: *Can you write prose and poetry simultaneously?*

A: For the first six months when I was writing my novel, I wrote poems simultaneously. But then when I got very deep into FEAR OF FLYING (when I got past the 200-page point) it really took over—and from that point on I couldn't write poetry. Many of the poems in HALF-LIVES were written the year before FRUITS & VEGETABLES was published, and many of them were written the following year. Some of them were written during the time I was beginning the novel. But fiction takes over your life. The final section in FEAR OF FLYING (the chapter where Isadora is alone in Paris, abandoned in the hotel room) nearly did me in. I felt that I *was* Isadora and was abandoned in that hotel room. It was ghastly. Then I spent months writing chapters which never found their way into the book at all. The ending was finally rewritten about seven times. The last chapter, which is now about six pages long, was rewritten so many times you wouldn't believe it. And I finally wound up with a minimal amount of words but just the *right* sort of indeterminate feeling I wanted. I had written it every other way imaginable.

Q: *Other endings?*

A: Yes. And I won't tell you what they are.

Q: *Was it a coincidence or were you working toward prose poem form that one of the last poems in* HALF-LIVES *has long prose poem sections in it?*

A: I think I'm going to do more of that. Prose and poetry intermingled. It didn't really have to do with my writing the novel, but I'm very interested in mixed forms. Even the novel has a few poems in it.

Q: *You mentioned once that you raised your own consciousness as an artist while your home was in Germany. Then you mentioned just now that*

Paris became a locale for you. Generally speaking, how do you feel your locale affects the way you work as a poet?

A: The German experience was complicated because it made me suddenly realize I was Jewish. I had been raised as an atheist by cosmopolitan parents who didn't care about religion, and living in Germany gave me a sense of being Jewish and being potentially a victim. That opened up my poetry. I wrote a whole sequence called THE HEIDELBERG POEMS, some of which were published in the BELOIT POETRY JOURNAL under my maiden name. They dealt with a kind of primal terror and with being a victim of Nazism. After writing those poems, I was able to explore my own feelings and emotions in a way I hadn't before. The experience wasn't pleasant, but it was a deepening one.

Q: *How do you find the New York locale as a place for a working poet?*

A: I must say that I don't give a lot of importance to locale despite what I just said about Germany. At that point in my life it was important to be in touch with those feelings of terror. But I don't think it matters where the hell you write. You write where you are. You write from your head. You don't write in Paris or London or Heidelberg. But perhaps I'm too harsh about this because I'm not a landscape poet. I write about my own inner geography.

But there are other things in New York that are very distracting. Too many parties. Too many telephone calls. Too many people. Yet when I found myself last summer at Cape Cod sitting alone for hours and listening to the ocean, trees and stuff, I would call long distance to New York because it was too quiet. I couldn't stand it. Still, I do think it's kind of phony when young people say: "I'm going off to Europe with my notebook in my hand. I will be inspired by the fountains of Rome or sitting in a cafe in Paris." What crap. (I did it, too, of course.) You write best in a place where you're familiar and can stack papers on the floor. But beyond that, locale doesn't matter.

Q: *When you talk about that room of your own, what do you mean particularly?*

A: I mean a place where you can close the door, make a mess if necessary, and nobody bothers you. My mother, who is a very talented painter, never had a room of her own, had to set up her easel in the living room and put away her paints if people were coming over. That's very destructive, especially for a woman. Staking out your territory is the big definition of identity that you win within your family or with the man you live with. That in itself is a very important struggle. When you can say to the person (or people) you live with: "This is the place where I work," then part of the battle of your identity as an artist has been fought. And in a very tangible way.

Q: *Could you comment on the question of the selfishness of the artist to demand time and space—the whole question of selfishness as a working condition.*

A: We all suffer about this. If you want to have human relationships, it's very hard to say: "Now I am closing the door to work." But the people you live with have to be aware that you are not shutting them out and it's not a rejection of them. It's very hard to be a writer because it means taking seriously your own nightmares and daydreams. If you're a young, unpublished writer and you're closing yourself in a room, neglecting other people, it seems very selfish. Almost like masturbation. But you have to believe in yourself. It helps a lot if the people you live with respect what you're doing. My husband respected my work at first more than I respected it. He'd say: "You have to work." And I'd say, "Help, let me out!"

Q: *Like Colette.*

A: Well, not quite. Willy locked her in a room to turn out these Claudine novels. He was exploiting her financially.

Q: *You once suggested writing a poem from a dream and dream images. How do you feel about using dream material?*

A: Again, that has to do with total self-surrender. But I've always found that if you try to use literal dreams in your work they're very boring. It's like waking up in the morning and trying to tell your dreams to somebody at the breakfast table. Fascinating to you but to the other person, incredibly boring. "There was this floating apple and a winged eyeball and blood." It doesn't interest anyone else. So when you use dream images in poems you have to universalize them. Like any other poetic images.

Q: *How do you feel about the use of drugs to get into a poem?*

A: I've never been able to do it. With pot, all I want to do is sit around and eat. I don't have any interest in writing whatsoever. Alcohol also makes me incapable of writing. Hashish is like pot

—only more so. And I've never tried LSD. I tend to think that drugs are useless to writers. But that may just be because I have not been able to use them. I think when you write you need a combination of great control and great abandonment. What the drug gives you is great abandonment, but the control goes all to hell.

Q: *What special things do you want to happen, do you think can happen in a workshop?*

A: The best things that happened to me when I was in a workshop at the School of the Arts was that I met a lot of other poets. They turned me on to lots of books. Also I got feedback on my work. I met people I could exchange poems with. And from time to time somebody would say something that made me think hard. I don't think a workshop teaches you how to be a writer, but it serves its purpose in indirect ways.

Q: *What assignments do you find helpful for beginning writers thinking over your own workshops?*

A: That's hard. Some students come to you with too much freedom. They cannot censor themselves at all. For those you have to stress craft. Other students come to you so hung up on craft that they have absolutely no freedom. For them you stress freedom. What works for one student doesn't work for another. So to say something in an interview like: "Craft is the most important thing" is misleading.

Q: *Did the workshops help you in your own writing?*

A: Yes. But that was because I went around a lot and worked with different poets. It's dangerous to have only one mentor. What you'll do is pick up all that poet's prejudices and imitate them. It's much better to study with a variety of people.

But the most important education you get is on your own. It's like what Rilke said in LETTERS TO A YOUNG POET: "There's only one way—go in to yourself." You learn in solitude from reading other writers. And from writing and writing and writing. A workshop can accelerate that process, but the basic learning you do is alone.

Q: *You've run workshops for high school students and for adults. What do you find happening in the two age groups when you get started?*

A: It's really not all that different except that (as you'd expect) a high school student is less sophisticated. I honestly think it's a rare high school student who has her or his own voice. You must have a certain amount of maturity to be a poet. Seldom do sixteen-year-olds know themselves well enough. You can work a lot with students at that level, but it's really preparatory work. I go into shock when I see a South American poet with a first book at the age of nineteen. In North America we tend to have a prolonged adolescence. We're more likely to publish around the age of thirty. I think it was Neruda's TWENTY POEMS OF LOVE AND A SONG OF DESPAIR which was published when he was nineteen or twenty. But in South America they tend to grow up faster than we do. It must be the heat.

Q: *It may have to do with the competitiveness of the publishing business.*

A: I don't know anything about publishing in South America. But I do know from my experience with other writers that most North Americans don't come into their maturity until they are at least twenty-five. I hate making generalizations like that because I can see people writing it down and saying—Ah, until I'm twenty-five. . . . There are always millions of exceptions.

I used to sit around reading books and comforting myself. Virginia Woolf didn't publish her first book till she was past thirty. Katherine Anne Porter was thirty-three when she published her first short story. I would pore over such facts. If I had known someone in high school or college and saw something published by him before I was published, it threw me into an envious rage. Being unpublished is so painful.

Q: *How do you feel about publishing? Do you feel it's important for a poet to be published?*

A: Obviously if you write, you want to communicate with other people. To say that you don't is phony. But I'm not sure that publication always reflects quality. Magazines buy poems for very strange reasons. And for a young poet to determine whether or not his work is successful, dependent on whether or not he gets published, is a very dangerous business. I think the best poems in my first book never got taken by magazines. My name was unknown, so nobody cared. Also, many of them were long, and lots of magazines use poems as filler.

Q: *What about sending out?*

A: Yes, I think it's helpful to send work out depending on what kind of reaction you have when it's rejected. If you take that as a final judgment, it's dangerous. But if you do it in a kind of lighthearted way (who does it in a lighthearted way? Nobody!) it's okay. You must realize that people who accept or reject your poems are not always right.

Q: *You can be affected by the recognition after publication.*

A: I was helped by the freedom it gave me. You see, I was one of these people who was very hung up. I had all kinds of blocks and problems and didn't believe I was a poet, so when people began saying to me: "Hey, you really can write," it gave me a lot more confidence and it made writing easier. But this is tremendously individual. I think for somebody else, it might be ruination. I am very self-critical and don't publish everything I write. I sometimes get requests from little magazines which say: Send us anything you have. And my theory is I'm *not* going to publish anything I have. If I publish a poem I want it to be something I care about.

Q: *What about poetry readings? How do they affect your own writing?*

A: They've made me very aware of the rhythms of my poetry.

Q: *Would you rather have your poetry read on a page or heard as a poem?*

A: Both. I like people to hear me read because I think that they understand the poetry better. When I read, I feel I'm giving life to the poem.

Q: *Does this desire to have your poetry read influence some of the forms you use like the list poems or the poems where a certain word or phrase is repeated?*

A: No, it isn't premeditated. I do think my poetry has a kind of sound quality. Very often it uses repetition. But I think that poetry by *nature* is a form brought alive by the human voice.

Q: *Could you comment on what you think poetry is?*

A: It's voice music. Ancient poetry was all produced for that purpose. And that's still a very strong tradition. I don't think it was produced by the "reading scene" of the late sixties and early seventies. This was the ancient function of poetry. We haven't created a tradition—we've just rediscovered it. There was a period in American poetry in the 40s and 50s when verse was very difficult, involuted, and meant to be studied and read on the page. That was partly the influence of The New Criticism. Since tight academic verse was being written by a certain segment of American poets, those of us who went to college at the time thought that to be the nature of poetry. On the contrary, that period was actually rather aberrant. Poetry has more often been a spoken thing than a difficult metaphysical puzzle. When I write, I always hear the voice in my head. I'm baffled that there is even a question about it.

Still, since we're into definitions of poetry, I think I ought to add that condensation is essential. Images are important to me because the image is a kind of emotional shorthand. Poetic language must be rhythmic, fresh, interesting language, but it must also be condensed and pack a lot of meaning into a little space.

Q: *Are there any contemporary poets that you feel particularly close to?*

A: I could name them, but then the people I hadn't named would wonder why I hadn't named them and it would only be because they hadn't popped into my head. There are so many.

Q: *Do you think there are many good poets around?*

A: I think we're living at a time of great renaissance for poets.

Q: *You mentioned once that when you were a beginning poet it helped to get together with small groups of poets and read work in progress. Do you continue to do that?*

A: I have a number of friends who are writers and who read my work. There were specific people who were very important to me when I was putting together my first book. I used to get together with Norma Klein and Rosellen Brown and Patricia Goedicke. I think it's very important to find friends whose prejudices you know. And who care about you and your work and will be honest with you. You must share enough values with them so that you can trust each other. Finding such friends might be the most important thing a young poet does. You need a critic, but it can't be just *anybody*. The idea of sending your work to a stranger is perhaps not such a good idea. You need somebody whose prejudices you know.

Q: *There must be a need for criticism. So many manuscripts come in to the* QUARTERLY *with requests for criticism.*

A: Yes, and it's so hard to honor such a request because you don't know the person. And often you don't know what kind of psychological problems are going on behind the request. It's not as simple as it looks. If you write a critical letter to somebody, you may absolutely destroy that person. Or make him furious.

195

Q: *Do you get manuscripts from strangers?*

A: Yes. Everybody does. It's just impossible to deal with. You don't know how this person is going to react to what you say or what you may be stirring up.

Q: *Do you have a favorite poem?*

A: How can you have a favorite poem? Your favorite poem is always the one you just wrote. The others are not quite real to you. I read HALF-LIVES now (those poems were finished about a year ago and other people tell me they're enjoying them), but I can't enjoy them. They seem very remote from me now.

Q: *What will your next book of poems be like?*

A: It's too early to tell. I think I will do some more combinations of prose and poetry like FROM THE COUNTRY OF REGRETS. Overlapping of forms. I'm also working on a long poem which looks like it might become a self-portrait in verse. I'm writing on very traditional subjects again and poems that rhyme occasionally. I'm writing a poem to Keats and a poem to the moon and a poem to Spring. After all the wild stuff in my first two books, here I am writing poems to Keats and to Spring.

Q: *You've spoken about the frustration of writing from the point of view of a woman. Did you get to the point where you felt trapped by your subject matter?*

A: It took me a long time to break through to the freedom of writing out of a woman's voice, and then it seemed to be *all* I was writing about. Now I want to go beyond that. Sexuality is an important part of life, and sometimes it seems to be *all* of life. But there *are* other subjects. One tends to become impatient with oneself and doesn't want to repeat the things one has learned.

Q: *That doesn't mean you won't come back to it.*

A: I don't know. I don't have any program. I just sit down and write. When I have enough poems, I'll see if they make a book. I didn't realize that HALF-LIVES was a book which dealt with fulfillment and emptiness until I began putting the poems together. Then it became apparent to me that I had subterranean rivers of imagery in those poems. Certain themes repeated themselves and I saw that a lot of the poems dealt with emptiness, wholeness, halfness, and so on.

Erica Jong

And a book began to come together. So I arranged the sections the way they naturally fell. I can't tell you what the third book will be "about" until I see what poems accumulate. But I am quite sure that at certain periods in your life you deal with certain themes; and if you grow, those themes have to change.

Q: *We wanted to ask you some questions about translation. Have any of your poems been translated into other languages? And then do you ever do translations? Do you read poetry in foreign languages?*

A: I don't read poetry in foreign languages. Although I know some foreign languages tolerably in a kind of school way, and used to be able to speak some of them when I lived in the countries where they were spoken, I don't really know any language well enough to translate. I suppose I don't try translation because I write prose when I'm not writing poetry.

Q: *When you speak of translations as the kind of thing poets can do, what recommendations would you make to a young poet about choosing something in a related field like translations or teaching or something entirely different to be a way of surviving economically while he struggles?*

A: I think the best thing for a young poet is to grow up in Latin America. And to be made a diplomat.

Q: *Like a Neruda.*

A: We don't have ways of rewarding our poets like that. I don't know what a poet can do to survive. Everything you think of has terrible disadvantages. If you're a college teacher, you're always up to your neck in bad student writing. If you're an editor you get so weary of books being thrust at you that the printed word almost loses its force. Advertising is not the most joyous profession. (I know poets who do all these things.) Maybe the best "profession" for a poet is to be born very wealthy. When I was in graduate school, I was told to get my Ph.D. in English and to use my summers to write. I found that getting a Ph.D. in English was not conductive to writing at all.

Q: *How do you feel about confessional poetry?*

A: Who the hell was it who invented that dumb term? There is no such a *thing* as confessional poetry. Anne Sexton gets loaded with the term and it's absurd. It has become a putdown term for women, a sexist label for women's poetry. People who use the term are falling into the subject matter fallacy. Subject matter doesn't make a poem.

And so a critic who uses that term is showing his total ignorance of what poetry is about.

There is this tendency to think that if you could only find the magic way, then you could become a poet. "Tell me how to become a poet. Tell me what to do." Is there a given subject that makes you a poet? Well, that's ridiculous. What makes you a poet is a gift for language, an ability to see into the heart of things, and an ability to deal with important unconscious material. When all those things come together, you're a poet. But there isn't one little gimmick that makes you a poet. There isn't any formula for it.

Q: *In general modern poetry requires: (underline one): more vegetables, less vegetables, all of the above, none of the above.*

A: The answer is: All of the above.

Q: *That gets into your whole minimal vs. maximal poetry. You want everything.*

A: I do want to get everything into my poetry. I want to get the whole world in. Colette had a term for it. She said that she wanted the "impure." Life was impure and that was what she wanted in her art—all the junk and jumble of things. Wallace Stevens also uses the image of a man on a dump: the poet—the man sitting on the dump. Life is full of all kinds of wonderful crap. Splendid confusion. Poetry should be able to take it all in.

Q: *What do you think of interviews?*

A: You always read them and say, "Oh, no. That's not me." No matter how candid you are, you *hate* the person you seem to be. But I understand the impulse to get a person down on paper. I'm reading my novel in galleys now, and thinking: "Who wrote this book? What kind of shit is this?" And I'm thinking that the only way that I'll ever get it all down is to write another book because I don't like this one anymore.

Q: *You made a statement a while ago about writing from your inner landscape. And yet you also talk about writing as a woman poet. At a point when women poets are having a renaissance, how do you see this relationship between writing from this inner landscape and writing as who you are quite apart from where you live and the time you live in? And also being alive in a moment where there are lots of forces—psychoanalysis, the women's movement, moving down to the end of the century, and that kind of thing.*

A: What should I answer first? One question at a time . . .

Actually, I don't think those things conflict. If you're writing about your inner landscape, you're writing about that inner landscape as female. It's female first and then beyond that, it's human. The two things don't cancel each other out. It's just a question of how you get there. Of course you're affected by the movements of your time, but not in a direct way. Look—I was not living in the United States between 1966 and 1969—which was the explosion of the hippie subculture, the flower children, the student revolutionaries—and yet there were many people who, on reading FRUITS & VEGETABLES, saw me as a sort of flower child of that generation. If you're a poet, you *do* have your navel plugged in to the zeitgeist, and you *are* tuned in to the currents of your time. And not in a literal, obvious way. But your antennae are working. You don't plan it.

Q: *A completely different question that we didn't ask you is if there are any reference works on the craft of poetry. For students to read or that you particularly love yourself.*

A: You know the books I've recommended for my seminar. And some of the other books I find really indispensable are: THE GLASS HOUSE, Allan Seager's biography of Theodore Roethke; Rilke's LETTERS TO A YOUNG POET; Keats' letters; Mandelstam's HOPE AGAINST HOPE (which shows you what it's like for a poet in a totalitarian country); books on mythology like THE GOLDEN BOUGH or WOMEN'S MYSTERIES or THE GREAT MOTHER. I would certainly recommend THE BOOK OF THE IT, a book that really loosens up the imagination. I would very much recommend Theodore Roethke's STRAW FOR THE FIRE, Virginia Woolf's WRITER'S NOTEBOOK, Colette's EARTHLY PARADISE. Those are not books, strictly speaking, on the craft of writing, but I don't think you're going to learn much about poetry from reading about iambic pentameter, spondees, trochees and things like that. If that's what you're thinking of—a handbook. (There are many good handbooks of poetry. There's Untermeyer's THE PURSUIT OF POETRY which is very complete and good.) But for the most part you learn to be a poet (as Rilke says) by going into yourself and by reading lots of other writers. I think I once told you that when I began writing free verse, I read and reread Denise Levertov's books. I figured that *she* knew where to break a line. Her white spaces on the page *meant* something. So I reread and reread her books trying to figure out where she broke her lines and why. I might have gone to William Carlos Williams too, because that was where she learned. You learn to write by reading the poets you love over and over and trying to figure out what they're doing and why they're doing it. You read Galway Kinnell's BOOK OF NIGHTMARES and you see the way he interweaves certain images throughout the book. Study the poets you love. Read them again and again. That's how you learn to be a poet. Unfortunately though, talent is something you're born with. And that's not very democratic. A gift for language is essential. So is a feeling for the rhythms of prose and poetry. The other gift is stamina—that willingness to *do* it and *do* it and *do* it. I don't know where you get that. I knew many people in college who had plenty of talent, but never became writers. They gave up. A good portion of the struggle is just that willingness to keep on doing it. Ultimately, I would say I write because it gives me a great deal of pleasure to write. I would rather write than do almost anything else. Somebody will say to me: "Oh, you've been very productive," and the implication is that I've been disciplined and plodding. But writing is such an incredible joy and pleasure that at times it scarcely feels like work. There are also bad times, though.

Q: *Have you ever thought of another career?*

A: I thought of being a painter and for years I did paint. There was a time when I wanted very much to be a doctor. At one time I thought I was going to be a college professor. And, of course, I still teach. But I think writing is the only profession which has enough surprises in store to hold me for the rest of my life. If you keep growing and changing, writing is an endless voyage of discovery. The surprises never stop. All that runs out is time.

14

Diane Wakoski

Q: *Could you tell us when you began writing?*

A: I really did start writing when I was a little kid. I wrote my first poem when I was seven years old, about a rosebush, and then I wrote a lot of poetry when I was in high school. I got seriously involved in college, which was when I decided I would spend my life as a poet—right about the time I was taking Thom Gunn's workshop. That workshop was a wonderful workshop because Thom was very gracious when he said I didn't need a teacher, but what he meant was that there was an unusual situation in that particular workshop. There really were five extremely talented people who would have learned from each other whether he had been there or not. He did what a gentleman and scholar would do. He quarreled with us enough to present his objective, but he also respected the fact that we all were just passionately involved in what we were doing. And would do it. In the true sense, we didn't need him. On the other hand, he really did help us because he understood that. He didn't try to mold us or do anything else. That was a formative period. I was just beginning to find my voice and write the poems that—my publishable poems date from that year.

Q: *That was* COINS AND COFFINS?

A: Yes. You know, there really are events that happen in your life that are significant at the time they are happening. No one else may

201

notice that they are significant, but they are obviously partly significant because you think they are. But you also felt they were because there was something significant about them. And the event that I will always remember from that period—and I date my poetry from that period, though I wrote poetry much longer than that—was the result of Thom's workshop being very prestigious in a strange sort of way. The Poetry Center, which was just beginning, invited him to pick five students from Berkeley or people who wrote poetry seriously, and obviously Berkeley had a reputation, and put us on a program in January of 1959 called "Berkeley Poets." For me it was a really significant event. The other poets—they were all men if that means anything—it didn't mean anything to me . . .

Q: *So you would say that that was your most important apprenticeship —that experience?*

A: It really was. The first thing Thom Gunn made me realize was that there are lots of rules about poetry that have nothing to do with poetry in the abstract. Poetry is a human art, and we're really talking about our lives, and poetry which is most readable is that which is most intimate and touching. At the same time, it requires a tremendous kind of craft to talk that tightrope of talking intimately about feelings or talking feelings and not producing a certain amount of gush. Thom made me immediately aware of the fact that—he didn't say this in so many words—I had a proclivity to like beautiful things, that I thought poetry was about beautiful things. I still think that, by the way, but I have a different idea of what beautiful things are now. He made me realize that if I was going to get any tension at all in there I would have to stop writing those pretty things. I would have to write something more powerful. And he did this partly, I think, by being British. You know, Americans are very susceptible to a British accent. It carries a certain authority, especially when you're young.

Q: *Do you have your student poets read their own poems?*

A: I do. I really very much subscribe to the idea that what contemporary poetry is about is partically an oral phenomenon which can only be understood and really appreciated if you hear it. I know for a fact that the experience of hearing the poetry reading is dynamic to many people who would not have had that experience reading the poems on the page. I'm not talking about the poet himself or the good reader of poetry or the scholar who obviously can find many kinds of pleasure in a poem. I really do think that if there is any such thing as a possible wider audience—and even for any of us who think of ourselves as experts having specialized in one poet—the experience of having been to a poetry reading is much more vivid to us than reading the book. Consequently, I think the people should learn to do it. I used to be very, very interested in the prospect of poetry as theatre and having some actors get involved in it. I am against it at the moment. I still believe it's an interesting prospect but I've come to realize, from talking about this to many people, that isn't really what poetry is about these days. Poetry is about poetry, which means the poet reading his poems. This gives the poems another dimension in the same way that when you try to talk about film as an art as opposed to theatre as an art, you can make all kinds of generaliza- tions. The point is that right now in the times we live most people find the film experience a more vivid one. It's only those of us who have certain kinds of knowledge and certain perceptions that like the theatre just as much. I think that's pretty generally true about poetry. I see no reason why if a person is really serious about poetry, it shouldn't be one dimension of his education. If he reads it, and reading it means presenting his personality as another dimension, then that's part of the poem. There are poets who have resisted this and their argument is a perfectly good one, a good poem comes alive on the page. But perhaps that isn't really that much to think about right now. We do and we don't. We have a much different idea about poems lasting. It makes me think that if a poem lasts eighty years, it has really lasted a long time. And I do expect poems to last eighty years. Although they don't always. I know I tried to reread Shelley this summer, and found it impossible.

Q: *Do you have an imaginary audience in the back of your mind during a reading, the way you really want an audience to be, the way you'd like them to respond?*

A: Yeah, I think so. I think I have several imaginary audiences. First of all, I always write my poems with the feeling that I am speaking to someone. Or some group of people. So I obviously have people in mind. And I wrote poetry because I had a very narrow and circumscribed deprived life, and it was a fantasy world. And the Diane who's in my poems is not a real person. She's a person I would like to be, that I can imagine myself being. Even though I put all my faults in my poems, it doesn't mean I'm not a fantasy or imagined person. I didn't create a fantasy that was unreal. I'm smart enough not to have done that. But the Diane in my poems really is fantasy. I don't care how happy my life ever gets, there's always a part of all of us that feels deprived in some way or another. We don't have everything and what the poem speaks to is that fantasy part of ourselves—and no matter what my life is and no matter how it's fulfilled, there are many things that I will not be, and those are the things that I will fantasize. Part of my imaginary audience are always those people who have not loved me or are not in my life because I am not the Diane I fantasize. In a way I'm always having a kind of duel with my audience. I don't ever believe they'll ever like me. And they are the very people who in real life probably wouldn't like me.

Q: *Your early poems have been called "confessional poetry." What is your definition of confessional poetry?*

A: I'll give you my parting line first, and then—the term confessional has been a real misnomer. A critical school, I don't know if it was M. L. Rosenthal who coined it or not. In general, people think that it is, when he was writing about Plath and Sexton and Lowell. The one thing that Plath and Sexton and Lowell all had in common —and most twentieth century poets have this—is they liked physical imagery. They all had been in mental institutions and all had either suicidal impulses or alcoholic behavior. They had, in some way, had antisocial patterns in their lives. And I use the term advisedly because the term confessional is related to poems and poets who are talking about experiences that were not acceptable to normal people—the fact that you've been in a mental institution, the fact that you're an alcoholic, the fact that you tried to commit suicide, the fact that you were a conscientious objector—whatever. They were things that you were supposed to be ashamed of and so to talk about your impulses was to confess them. I think that's a real misnomer becuase first of all even Plath's poetry, which comes closer to that term than any other, is not confessional in the sense that none of those poets are ashamed of what they did or felt that anything they felt should be condemned. They felt they had human experiences. In Sexton's case her poetry was only made possible by her experiences of madness because what her personal experience did was obviously shatter a kind of bourgeois insulation—I don't mean that all bourgeois people are insulated, but that life is one that insulates you very easily. And to break through to a kind of feeling perception of the world is something I'm sure she would never have arrived at without her nervous breakdowns. Plath has often been said to glorify suicide in her poems. She's certainly not confessing it as a bad thing. I think in order to read her poems with real sympathy you have to have a tragic vision of the world and it has to be a kind of grand thing accomplished by itself. Sexton's poems really do point to the fact that when you go to bedlam and back and get something good out of it, it isn't a bad thing at all. Lowell's poems, which are the source of that term, are simply autobiographical poems. What he does is speak about being an aristocrat with a certain amount of humility, showing that it wasn't all that it was cracked up to be either. But none of them are confessing. Lowell doesn't feel it was an original sin. He wants you to understand that whatever condition people have, it's a human condition and he glorified it.

Q: *Could you tell us about your George Washington poems? Why did you choose him?*

A: Because I'm basically interested in symbol and allegory. And Washington is the father of our country. And we live in this very paternalistic society, and he stands for the kind of masculine values that have strengths but for many of us have their frustrations. They do stand for the opposite of what poetry is about. For me he's really the symbol of the material world that doesn't appreciate enough how you feel, and for me the revelation that that frustration comes out of not any of the things like materialism or the kind of philistine attitude that penalizes but really comes out of our inability to communicate which I equate with our unwillingness to communicate. For instance, nobody ever understands anybody else. The people we think we understand or feel we communicate with are simply the ones who have tried to talk to us and we have therefore been aroused to try to talk back. Washington, as an historic figure, stands for that kind of aloofness that just doesn't give. For me it's the antithesis of what poetry is. It's also basically what I fought in myself all my life. I am extremely shy. It's really hard for me to talk to people. It took many years of writing poetry and then approaching people by talking to them about poetry to get away from this. I sat in Greece for three months this summer and literally did not have a conversation with anyone except one huge quarrel that I had with a man about poetry. And it's not because people bore me. It's because I'm really frightened of them and I am not able to give and they don't want to communicate, and then do seem boring to me. It's always been easier for me to go off and read a book. Poetry is the next thing to reading a book. By putting it down on paper and then by publishing it, you're doing the same thing to people as if you had a conversation with them. But for me it's easier because I can do it by myself. I still really fear to communicate with people, unless I have that symbol.

Q: *Do you think your surrealism goes closer to the tremendous emotional impact of all that is in conflict?*

A: Surrealism is a fascinating subject, and it's very easy to have a different idea about it every day. What I would say today about surrealism is that, as a technique for writing, it's a fascinating way of trying to combine your intellectual perceptions and your emotions about it. All those bizarre placements of things have to do with the fact that every day of our lives we have this bizarre mind living in a body that could be someone else's. Seeing too much and knowing so much more. I've never been an athlete or had any kind of physical prowess of any sort. And I often wonder if athletes, people like those Russian gymnasts, or acrobats you see in circuses, have a different kind of control over the world because I keep feeling how helpless we are. We know—I wonder for instance if they have more control over their emotions.

Q: *Because they seem to have so much practice.*

A: To me emotions seem to come so much out of the body. A lot of my imagery is physiological imagery. I really do perceive my emotions as if they come out of different parts of my body. Different parts except my head. And I wonder if people who are wonderful athletes have in some way more of a sense of continuity with their emotions. My emotions are very strong and athletic, but my body just doesn't follow. I really think that's part of what surrealism is about and why it's such a twentieth century technique is that we have all developed our minds so much. They still live in these bodies which are so separate. It's a very good way of presenting that separate but together bizarreness.

Q: *What about recurring images in your work—oranges, blood, jewels, flowers—have they evolved?*

A: Yes. I didn't start out knowing what I was doing but after a few years of writing poetry I began to realize that there were certain things that were part of my fantasy life. Usually images are what to me seem very beautiful or very terrible things. And I realized that

206

even before I became a poet I was going to be repeating myself. Those were the things I wanted to write about. I think at the point I became aware of that, was the time I was taking Thom Gunn's class and, even more important, I was for the first time reading Wallace Stevens and beginning to understand that beautiful early poetry of his, and I was reading Lorca for the first time, and those are both poets who used very, very sensuous physical imagery, and it was particularly notice-able in the case of Lorca but equally true of Stevens. He used over and over again the same images. And I realized that they used them as symbols—that their landscape became part of their trademark or their voice, and it suddenly was one of those awarenesses that you have known for a long time without realizing it. That was so obvious. There was no reason why I had to keep trying not to write about those things. The thing to do was to be superconscious of writing about them and to make them into a network. So all of those things did stand for my own sense of what is beautiful and durable.

Q: *Also, the very short words, the very strong short words. Is that part of this network of symbols?*

A: I think that has a lot to do with the fact that I always wanted to read my poems aloud and that I come from California and that we have a—I don't know what a good adjective is for the way we speak—but it's very matter of fact, and poetry in general cannot have a matter-of-fact tone. One of my greatest battles is how to get my matter-of-factness, which I consider part of my vision of the world, into lines and still make it sound like poetry. It's very natural for me. It's my matter-of-fact way of trying to describe things. It's something that I have deliberately allowed myself to use and tried every possible way of using it to see if I could get away with it.

Q: *Another one of the things in addition to the short words is the assonance. Is this sought or does this just happen?*

A: That's a very hard thing to talk about because it's talking about your perception of the use of language. I don't know if anyone, including a linguistic specialist, has really figured a successful way of assessing what that is in a person. I know that my own view of it is that I studied music for many years, that I started writing Shakespear-ean sonnets, that in the back of my mind I'm always going de-da, de-da, de-da, and that's the test for me, by the way. If my language gets too prose-y, too short, it means that at the back of my mind I've said: boy, you haven't been iambic for a while. I don't mean just iambic, but that's the easiest one to use. When I feel that there haven't been any regularly recurring rhythms, even though I don't feel required in any way to make even-length lines or subscribe to theories of meter (that strange thing which poetry is all about), I still keep pulling back to that kind of thing. Poetic language is everything that's beautiful. In some way it always comes out singing. And I'm sure that that has to do with my literal sense of what music is, and the way poetry is related to that.

Q: *What about the parallel line and the parallel structure that you use? That relates back to music, doesn't it?*

A: That relates back to music, yes, and it also relates to the way I like to put things into neat little piles.

Q: *Do you find yourself practicing exercises to keep yourself in shape, writing sonnets and so forth?*

A: I write short poems as exercises. It's hard for me to write short lines in short poems. Although in retrospect I've written an awful lot of them. Whenever I begin to get very long and discursive, which is when I'm writing a poem that I really wanted to write, I begin to feel myself just kind of dissolving out. I have a strong urge to just kind of pat things back in shape, and I write short poems. I haven't for a long, long, long time, done any kind of experimentation with what is referred to as metrical forms. Because I started writing poetry that way. In high school poetry was a game for me. I don't mean I didn't take it seriously because I think when you're young, games are a serious part of your life—they were challenges—using language in certain rhythms, you'd get a rhyming dictionary, a Thesaurus, it was really fun to do. The only thing was you couldn't say too much that way. And that's ideal for young people because you don't have much to say then except this is fun, who am I. You can boil it down to two or three statements, and you don't have to think about experiences to write about unless you want to write for SEVENTEEN magazine. So I think game-playing is a very good way of starting poetry. If you start writing poetry when you are older, I don't think that's a natural concern—unless you have the particular sense of language which goes with that, which by the way is not a twentieth century sense of language. But I periodically go into doing it again. I found a wonderful book of forms this summer. Its name has escaped me. It has, I think, every peculiar form ever invented. What is that crazy little book of forms and who is he?

Q: *But you do write in form. You have a sestina, for example, in* INSIDE THE BLOOD FACTORY, *which was five years ago, wasn't it?*

A: Sestinas are fun. If you break the rule for iambic pentameter, which I insist is an English rule and not a French rule, it's a fun-organizing form, because you keep coming back and back and back like a refrain. If you make yourself very conscious of making very long lines and very short lines then there are really interesting musical sounds to the language. I'm not sure that I could write an iambic pentameter sestina.

Q: *That was a free form sestina.*

A: Yes. The idea of making thirty-six lines all the same length is like being in jail.

Q: *Do you keep a journal?*

A: Oh, I'm a hopeless failure at keeping a journal. The most I can ever do is several weeks at a time.

Q: *What excuses do you make up for not keeping a journal? What excuses do you make when you don't write?*

A: Well, I have a lot of excuses. I'm still enough of an old Puritan to have to have an excuse for myself when I'm not writing. I truly believe in my own self-discipline and that I write when I'm ready to write and if I'm not, nothing valuable will come out. I wrote very little this summer except a few critical articles, and my excuse is that I really am going through a big change in my personal life and in my poetry. This year is a very retrospective year. I'm looking back on what I've done. I don't feel very compulsive about writing anything. As far as I'm concerned I've written enough so that I don't have to worry about not writing any more. So I don't feel obliged to write. On the other hand, I write because I like to write. I am going to write again when I'm ready. I wrote three or four poems this summer which will be included in my new book, some that I like very much. They're moving in other directions, much more—if you can make these distinctions—Apollonian than Dionysian—and much more interested in prose as a component of the poem, and for the first time in my life I'm really interested in writing some amount of criticism.

I'm very interested in theories of poetry, and ideas of poetry and how poetry has changed in the last years and what it means, the kind of poetry that works, and why it works and so forth, and these never interested me. I mean, they interested me in terms of how you made a poem but not in how you made articles out of it. I sat down and wrote articles this summer because I really wanted to.

Q: *What writing method do you find most conducive to producing your work, writing in longhand or writing at the typewriter?*

A: I'm very unhappy these days working in longhand which is another reason these journals are not kept up. I don't write letters in longhand. I really like my typewriter. I started—I can remember being appalled once when someone told me he composed his poems on a typewriter. To me it was appalling, and he said: Have you ever written a short story, and I said yes, and he said: Did you write it in longhand and I said yes, and he said well, what's the difference? But I do notice that the more I compose on the typewriter, the prosier my poems are. I never compose those kind of exquisite little things—lyric poems—on the typewriter. I don't see any way of possibly composing a lyric poem on the typewriter, because that's the kind of thing where every word means something and the way you write it down and the shape of it. I have notebooks from when I was in college that have an almost shocking little strange, elegant hand—my hand was very sloppy—that the poems were composed in. It was like a different state of organization.

Q: *The handwriting had to match it.*

A: Yes, it had to match. There was a kind of elegant slowness, and just the act of writing down a line and then another line, I can just feel it. Every once in a while I get in that mood again. It's not the usual mood.

Q: *Do you have to be in a special mood to write a poem? Or if you feel one coming on, do you know . . .?*

A: I do. I think that's probably fairly typical. I can sit down at any time and write something. But the good things, the better things that I write—every once in a while I just sit down and write. My favorite poem last year—I was writing a letter to someone and I wanted to include a poem and I didn't have a thing I had written, so I just sat down and wrote it out and it's my favorite poem from that time. Actually I had done a lot of things that got me in the mood to write that poem, and I became aware of it in the process of sitting down and writing the letter.

Q: *How about revision? Do you revise a great deal?*

A: I don't revise a great deal, but I revise after I read a poem aloud, and if there are what I call dead spots in it, I bring all my rhetorical skills to bear on it.

Q: *When you say read aloud, do you read to yourself or before an audience?*

A: Preferably before an audience. But to myself if there is none. It's very hard for me to type something up which is one of the reasons I appreciate hiring a typist. It's very hard for me to type things up and not want to change. My kind of revision is not what Dylan Thomas would call revision. Fifteen drafts or anything like that.

Q: *Then most of it comes through your original impulse.*

A: The one part of every poem that I subject to rigorous rewrite is the last three or four lines. I love the last three or four lines of poems, and I think they are the easiest part to rewrite. You can rewrite a poem five days after you've written it and completely change that poem's meaning by changing the last four lines. Or you can turn what was a mediocre poem into an exciting poem. It's impossible for me to put a book manuscript together without meddling a little bit.

Q: *You were talking about craft before in relation to that workshop in California. Do you think craft is a conscious thing or something that just happens when enough bad stuff gets discarded in the process?*

A: Well, obviously I think craftsmanship is something that can be acquired in a lot of different ways. Because I've always resisted authority even though I'm a very authoritarian person, it's hard for me to learn neat, methodical ways and yet I always want to see other people learn that way. So the hit or miss method is my method of learning. In terms of the craft of writing, I think that you learn it by reading. I just don't see any other way for learning it. I think you learn more from reading than from hearing people talk. I don't see how anybody who writes poetry conscientiously for ten years and reads can help but get better. I just don't see any way. In a way that's almost a dilemma with so many people writing today and so many, many creative writing programs because it means that any person with a certain amount of time and effort, with a lot of reading, and

211

who has a certain kind of intelligence can write a respectable poem. That presents a whole other funny vehicle for poetry these days. No one really trusts reading one poem by a person. On the other hand, if you read one poem that you really like, you will remember it and you will go on and look for something else. Most people don't even see one poem that they really like in a magazine. On the other hand, they like the magazine. They say this is interesting, this is interesting and that could be and so forth. But it's a very controversial subject of what the value of publishing poems in magazines is. I know one value it has and that's purely professional, and that is you can't get a book published until you get published in a lot of magazines. They are your credentials for publishing a book. And they are the way a lot of people can get to know your name. But I don't know of a single positive value that I would say derives for people from reading poems in magazines. My feelings about this in the past few years have forced me to forget to submit poems to magazines. Lots of magazines ask you for poems and I'm always perfectly glad to submit them, but I never quite get around to typing them up, and by the time I sit and think about it, I know that those poems can be put in a book. The book will definitely have some readers. It's a very complicated subject, because if you ask me now if my conclusion is: should there be no poetry magazines, I wouldn't say that. I'd say it's even great to have poetry magazines for young writers to publish in. I can't reconcile that with the fact that I really don't think people read magazines. Obviously somewhere I'm working with a prejudice. Maybe my prejudice is that the magazines aren't good, or maybe my prejudice is even if they're good, you shouldn't submit to them.

Q: *What books do you recommend that your students read for craft principles? You said before that they have to read a lot. What do you recommend?*

A: Well, there's just so many good books. I would like to suggest something very different from specific poets for people to read to learn craft. I think the way you learn craft is the same way you learn criticism. And that is by reading everything that you can find. I don't think you learn any kind of discrimination if you only read masterpieces. When you read a masterpiece, you may not like it. It may seem awful, and it's not until you read about a hundred more pieces that are nothing like masterpieces that you suddenly realize how good that was. When you start reading things that are badly written, and you suddenly recognize how badly written they are, you have already learned some craft. You can see students doing this, but you can't see them doing it if you say: Now, read Sylvia Plath, and notice how she uses imagery here and so forth. There's nothing wrong with doing that in retrospect after they've read a lot, but if that's the way they learn, they will know that that's how Sylvia Plath knows how to use imagery and they know that Auden's lines are all scanned, and they know that and that, but they don't have any idea of why that is good poetry. They don't have any of the sensation that that's really exciting. When you go through a magazine and there's nothing that you can even stand to read and then suddenly there's this beautiful poem there. That's the experience they don't have because they only read masterpieces. They don't seem as masterful when they don't have a lot of schlock around them, when we don't have a whole life of reading to compare them with. I think at any given time it helps to have models to write from. I learned to write from models. I think most people do. Anybody who learns on his own uses models.

I started imitating Shakespeare's sonnets when I was in high school. It's still the best way to learn many, many things. So I don't see anything wrong in putting whatever five or six books together at any given time, and I'm sure they change over the years, and reading them because it will give pleasure, and pointing out what you really like about poets, and they'll get some ideas. I've seen students that I would be willing to swear will not become poets, even if they have a certain amount of talent, write some nice pieces because they found a poem by someone that really excited them and they imitated it. And it was an exciting experience for them. But my real feeling is that if you read five books and that's all you're going to read, you're almost doing them a disservice. There should be some way that they could go out and have a lot available. This is done in the universities because the libraries are getting better and better and better. But you still have to go to the rare books room for most of the poetry books, and most students are shy about doing that. So they don't really get to sample anything.

Another article that I wrote this summer—and it's a letter, a response to a man who teaches English at Kent State—and the whole subject of the letter is how it is possible to teach poetry today without being exclusive because I think that's what the most exciting thing should be for the student—there's just this huge gamut of interesting stuff being written. Any time you make a reading list, it doesn't become a reading list, it becomes a list of what you leave out. And that's the biggest problem. And if you're in some place like Kent

213

State, Ohio, maybe you stick around because you had a good teacher for a few years but if you're in an ordinary college town, you don't have anything to browse in, to really see what's going on. So if they have one professor there who teaches Robert Lowell, they don't even know half the time that someone like Ginsberg exists. And Ginsberg is a different case because he's been in LIFE magazine. But they don't know the possibilities of poetry, they know that there's one, but they don't know that that one doesn't have to be in a quarrel with any other one. And they often don't find out that there are really ten or twelve things going on instead of two in a quarrel with each other. Because usually if somebody is teaching Robert Lowell and then he teaches anybody else, he'll teach someone and say: now this poet doesn't write anything like that. And they'll spend the time going over how much less good he is.

Q: *And you can't do that in writing. It destroys the whole idea of creativity.*

A: The whole idea of making literature competitive—the great story of your life if you are an artist and you love nature, is savoring the beautiful things that you've read and you've heard, the masterpieces, but the masterpieces aren't beautiful because they're famous. They're beautiful because they're things that really hit you and you really like them, and there's no way that some young person is going to have your masterpiece experience. I may have loved Beethoven when I first heard him. But I didn't feel he was a master the way I now feel. And the real problem is that you have—I sometimes think that instead of lectures given by experts, the best teachers would be people who didn't know anything. I think the problems of teaching poetry today has to do with the *way* poetry is going to be taught in the schools, and I can't—I'm usually very good at thinking of ideal systems, I can't think of any ideal system of teaching poetry. I just cannot think of it. Everything seems to be lacking. No matter what you do, you seem to be putting something else down, or leaving something out. Maybe that's the way the poetry world is. They're always at each other's throats. You don't seem to be able to praise one poet without putting down another one.

Q: *How do you feel about the need for isolation in the life of a writer and how does it affect personal relationships?*

A: Well, as I told you, I grew up extremely timid and shy and it was very, very hard for me to even be interested in making friends with strangers. And consequently I always had a lot of enforced isolation in my life. And I grew up hating being alone, being terrified of being alone. And yet I spent a lot of time alone and it took me many years to learn to be alone and not freak out, to begin to appreciate that I really liked being alone and I didn't have enough privacy for being alone, and I got equally disturbed. And I approached it from the opposite side. I feel like you have to have a certain amount of privacy to sit down and work. But I don't feel that people interrupt that. I don't have that closed door sanctuary attitude. I really am very seldom annoyed if someone disturbs me when working. And that's a result of compensation from when I was a kid and I would have been delighted if someone had disturbed me. My attitude is that it's natural for me to be alone, and if my life just flows its own way I'll find myself alone anyway, that I'm grateful when there are people there that I can talk to. I'm very much less flexible about it if somebody I don't like interrupts.

Q: *Have you ever done any experimenting with concrete poetry?*

A: Not in the most literal sense. I've done a little series of what I call spells and chants. I did these a few years ago, many of which are just repetitions of words. I think of them as sound poetry. There is very little informational or emotional content. I think of that aspect of poetry as precisely that, an aspect of poetry. I'm not very satisfied with poems that only appeal to your eye on the page or can be listened to by your ear. It seems to me that an exciting poem can be seen on the page, and can sound good, and can also have all those other things.

Q: *Do you feel that you have a public image because of your readings?*

A: I think that it's inevitable that anybody who gives as many readings as I do and I tend to give fairly consistent readings—I read many of the same poems—I present myself in one of two or three ways.

Q: *Is it a public image or images?*

A: Well, that's a good question. I think the people think that I'm just as willing to talk to them in private as I am in my poems. Which may be true. I may be willing but my old shyness and inhibitions arise and I don't find it very easy. And there's a real intimacy when I read my poems because many of them are very intimate gestures. And there's no way I could have a first conversation with a stranger that's anything like what I say in a poem. Now I think that's a hardship because I think they are disappointed. I keep telling people that if you love me, you should love me in my poems, and I could be a mass murderer or something. In fact, I have always felt that there is too much personality and silliness in the poetry world, so that if you like someone, you try to like their poems. I'm a victim of this, too. You dislike someone, you find something wrong with their poems. I'm a very perverse person, and recently I've developed a dogma that you should be able to insult a person, somebody that you don't want to have anything to do with, you don't like him, you think he's stupid, and still like his poetry. And if you do, then he's written good poetry. Because you can transcend that. Now there are some people who just aren't honest enough to do that. I always admire people who can write wonderful poems and be rotten. It seems to me that they have achieved something. Poetry is a heroic form. People are idealizing themselves in a poem. I don't care what you say about confessional poetry and all of us presenting our weak sides, or our crazy sides, or whatever, we are presenting them to be loved, and we are presenting them in our most lovable form.

Q: *Do you write best early in the morning?*

A: Yes, and I find it almost impossible to work at night. I don't find the dark conducive at all. I like real light, the sun, coming in.

Q: *Do you have a certain number of hours a day that you set aside for writing poetry?*

A: Like my journals, I'm always trying to do that but I'm afraid it never did work out.

Q: *Do your dreams provide images for you?*

A: They haven't for many years. I haven't written many poems in the last three years using dream imagery but I don't really know why that is.

Q: *What do you do about fragments and unfinished lines?*

A: I've always thought that's what journals ought to do. I have one in that journal.

Q: *Do you usually use them right away?*

A: No, sometimes I use them five or six years later. I tend not to look through stuff like that. Because it's not exciting to me to keep a journal. I don't know and yet every once in a while I go through my papers. Sometimes when I'm going to edit a book and I want to put some poems together, I'll find fragments and write a poem from them. It always seems such a waste to have a fragment when you could sit for an hour longer and have a whole poem.

Q: *We talked about early workshop experiences, but was there any writer that you felt or you feel now did influence you when you began writing poetry?*

A: Well, when I was younger I really didn't think anyone influenced me. It was all absolutely out of my head. But in retrospect, you see things slightly different. I really think Jerome Rothenberg had a profound influence on it. He was one of the people I met when I first came to New York and published my first little book of poems, which he liked because they used those surrealist kind of dream images and had a haunting sense of being terrified. It was a way of presenting the world that interested him. He translated a lot of German and Spanish poetry and he himself had this kind of Hassidic tradition. Even though I'm not Jewish I've often felt like I've had a lot of the same emotional experiences in my life that the Jews associate with their history.

Q: *Do you have a sense of where you want your poetry to be, say, in five years?*

A: No. I don't really know. I guess the best thing I could say is that I want to create the possibility of being as discursive as possible. And discursiveness is not really an attractive quality in poetry. It's like looking for ways to do something that I think basically unattractive.

15

W. D. Snodgrass

Q: *You've been called a confessional poet. How do you respond to that label?*

A: As far as I can see my poems aren't what you would usually consider confessional—either having something to do with religious belief or with a kind of lurid sensationalism—revealing forbidden activities. Although sometimes my poems talk about "forbidden" activities, I try not to be lurid. And it doesn't even seem to me they often *are* about such things.

But at the time I came through school it was forbidden to write about any of your personal affairs—even though this is something poets always *had* done. The poems that brought me this title, "confessional," were the kind of poems that a hundred years before *anyone* would have written. I was moved in that direction by some of the German poets who wrote about lost children, dead children. Our children don't die as often, they get divorced.

In school, we'd been taught we had to write poems about The Loss of Myth in Our Time, and I was sick and tired of the loss of myth. I'd written all the standard poems about that; but then I wanted to write about what I really cared about—problems in my love life, problems with my daughter, feeling lonely. But the standard dogma said you couldn't write about those subjects; we lived in too complicated and too impersonal times. That seemed to me silly; it seemed at least worth trying to do something different.

218

W. D. Snodgrass

Q: *In other words, it was thought the proper response to this "depersonalization" was to write depersonalized poems.*

A: Yes. Exactly. We misunderstood Eliot's poems and we believed his criticism, which was very foolish indeed, since like most poets, he only wrote criticism to keep people from understanding his poems. By now, of course, people have begun to notice that all his poems were about troubles in his personal life, his love life—his own sterility and impotence and his first wife's nymphomania. Now we read THE WASTELAND and begin to see that it certainly isn't about all those things we thought, all the things you could get a Ph.D. for saying. Eliot had read out of the canon all the poets who had written about many of the standard subjects. Those things had been ruled out for long enough so that it looked like an area where you could make a discovery, do something others weren't doing. But weirdly enough, those subjects that poets always *had* written about, seemed very daring for a little while; many people felt that poetry had to be serving some kind of metaphysical aim, some particular religious belief or political program, some system of ideas. So they belittled our poems with a title like confessional.

Q: *Isn't it, then, a subject-matter question, that is, the difference between using psychology or ideas as subject matter?*

A: Yes, and very often ideas are the least important part of the poem anyway.

Q: *Is the fact that we know about the poem's having roots in Eliot's impotence really the question any more than knowing it's about some idea or other?*

A: It seems to me you're getting much closer to the poem when you get away from ideas and into emotions, which always seem to me more valuable, more important in people's lives, in their poetry, in anything.

Q: *Isn't it a danger to treat poems as an extension of biography?*

A: There are many poets that, without knowing something about their biography, I could never have begun to get a grip on them. Say Rimbaud.

Q: *But isn't there a danger in reading the poem only as a document of somebody's psychic troubles or whatever?*

219

A: Depends on what you mean by danger. If that's what interests people, I'm not about to say they shouldn't be interested. I suppose they're allowed to come to the poem and take what they want.

Q: *But wouldn't you say that limited the piece?*

A: I would think so, but then some people take a benefit from limitations. Somebody may come to the poem and find it useful for statistical analysis. That isn't what *I* want to do, but who am I to say they shouldn't?

In any case, when you're dealing with the poem's ideas you're almost never close to the poem; when you're dealing with its emotions you're getting much closer. It may be, though, that you'll get closer to that not by dealing with whatever it *says* about its emotions, but by what its texture, say, will reveal about the nature of its emotion.

Q: *So, in that sense, you might do that even with Dante.*

A: Absolutely. I've been writing, myself, a paper on Dante, analyzing all kinds of unconscious things in his poetry which have to do with his emotions and not very much with his ideas at all. (Though, as a matter of fact, his ideas and his emotions gear together rather tightly.) Anyway, I've been reading the INFERNO as a kind of psychoanalysis, a journey through the soul.

Yet until you get to the poem's music, and the richness of connotations of words—whatever is meant by things like *terza rima* and by the way a particular poet handles that—only then are you getting really close to the poem. In a certain sense, I can't ever hope to get that close to Dante because I can't really get the texture of it in the way a native Italian can, although I suppose a modern Italian is blocked off from it a little bit, too.

Q: *Are you saying that the colorings of the words indicate the emotional quality?*

A: I would think so. Since that is less conscious, it's more liable to get you close to what really counts in the psyche. Nobody knows, consciously, what things like texture mean, but in the long run they're likely to be much more meaningful, more likely to get you in touch with a deep area of the psyche, past the shallow areas where there are all kinds of false clues and false impressions.

Q: *When you say deep areas of psyche could you be more explicit? Intuition? Insight?*

220

A: No, merely that in writing a poem you're wanting to get people deeply involved with what it's like to be human, and that has to be done at a level way below the conscious.

Q: *Because the conscious is largely concerned with ideas?*

A: Yes, and with the impression we want to give to people, the lies we would like them to believe about us. You have to get down into how things *really* are, below the conscious level. It's there, it seems to me, that all real actions are driven and all the important decisions of our lives are made.

Q: *The popular conception of confessional poetry amounts to, I'm going to tell all my ideas about myself.*

A: Which is the least interesting part about you.

Q: *Not confessing at all.*

A: Not a bit, not one bit. Yeah, the analyst always asks, What kind of man are you, then he turns off his hearing aid, 'cause he knows you're not going to say anything.
On the other hand, there *may be* men in the world who can tell you in abstract terms something interesting and different about themselves. I never met any, but there could be. When I read a philosopher—if I *ever* read philosophy—I read for personality. Spinoza. Really, who cares about his ideas? But about Spinoza you can care enormously; the same with Plato. The ideas seem to me historically interesting because of the great effect they've had on other people, but in themselves they don't seem very interesting, at least not after you've known them a little while.

Q: *The ideas go out of vogue.*

A: But the personality doesn't. Socrates as a character is a really interesting, dreadful, snobbish, marvelous, wretched person. God, he was an awful man; he's very fascinating. At least the dramatic character created by Plato is very interesting. The way he *made* those people execute him—or that's the way it seems to me. They wanted to let him off, but he was enough of a peddler of moral and intellectual superiority that he was just going to force them into the wrong no matter *what* they did.

Q: *Which is consistent with the dialogues, where he got you to say the wrong thing.*

221

A: Exactly! But of course young people are very fond of ideas. Starting college, I was all hot for ideas.

Q: *You seem to be much influenced by psychoanalytic thought.*

A: I doubt if I've been much influenced by psychoanalytic theory. I haven't done much reading, but I have been in psychoanalysis: once in shallow therapy for a while and later in very deep analysis. It had a very great influence, I should think.

Q: *You found it useful.*

A: Oh, enormously. Well, I went into both when I'd been frozen up for periods of about two years each. And in both cases, it helped me get out of a bad marriage and into a better one and also to get me writing again, to get me loosened up.

Q: *From all this, can we say you see poetry as a way of opening things up, getting past the form and ideas?*

A: I hope so, although one needn't think of it in that way, and I'm sure that most readers don't. But they don't think consciously of what happens to them when they read a piece, anyway. Of course, nowadays it's harder to read something innocently; you're bound to have a certain amount of second-hand and degraded psychoanalytic ideas lying around and to be misusing them in your application to a text.

I've just finished a book of criticism, which is why I'm full of this right now. I've been writing, among other things, about DON QUIXOTE; it seems to me that if Cervantes were alive today he wouldn't have written DON QUIXOTE. He wouldn't have dared—in the book, he's made a mockery out of everything he believed, everything he loved: Christianity, the Spanish empire, his own life as a government official, his own life at the battle of Lepanto, all the things his conscious life revered and admired. In the book he makes a laughingstock out of the whole business without knowing it, and his readers loved it, without knowing it. Nowadays we'd all have to know, and he'd have been the first one to burn either the book or the person who said the things that book implies.

Q: *Do you have any observations about how one transforms personal experience into a poem—as opposed to ideas?*

A: Not particularly. It doesn't seem particularly different from other kinds of poems: narrative poems, highly symbolic poems.

222

Above all, you're aiming to give somebody a new perception of what a human being is like.

Q: *Do you have any preconception of where you're going when you write?*

A: You may not *know* that you do. Sometimes a student will come up to me and show me something new about my own poems. I think, "Holy God, I've got a chance—you know, something I didn't put there to make people feel sorry for me or to think what a nice guy I am; something I just couldn't *help* putting there." That delights me enormously.

Q: *When you're writing a poem or when you're through with it, is there any point at which you realize that, in the process of writing, you discovered something?*

A: Sometimes. Sometimes not. Sometimes the poem just feels rich—like somebody could investigate it at great length to good advantage. But you may not know what they'll find.

Q: *Can we make a distinction between your feeling the poem's richness and intellectual delineation of that richness?*

A: Absolutely; you can produce that richness and you can tell it's there without consciously understanding it. I've been doing another paper about the Impressionist painters. We're a hundred years past them and only now do we begin to figure out what those painters were about, and what the Symbolists' poems were about. We certainly know more about their subjects than the artists ever did.

Q: *Do you find you alter the physical facts or the physical terrain in order to render the "emotional" elements?*

A: When I do alter the facts, it's almost never for that reason. In a poem dealing with my personal experience I do much better simply saying exactly what happened. That will usually carry more emotional depth. When I'm trying to get to what I really feel about something, I usually do better just sticking to the facts. For me, those are the facts that call up that body of emotion; they're more likely to summon up meaningful qualities of voice and movement.

If I change the facts, it's usually for other reasons: to protect the guilty. Very often there are people who can be damaged and you don't want them hurt by your poem more than necessary. Or there may be practical reasons: you want to link two events, have them

223

happen on the same day or something, because it makes the telling easier.

Q: *One has the impression reading your poems that you're very careful about making the details of the terrain figurative. For example,* THE MARSH, *where the end of the poem sends us back to the terrain to find symbolic resonance in the things the narrator sees. You couldn't do that if you just selected details at random.*

A: Oh, I don't select details at random. But generally speaking, I don't make them up. After all, I didn't *see* them at random, either, the day I was out there walking in that marsh.

Q: *Do you ever make up a scene, a pastiche out of previous scenes?*

A: Sometimes, yes. For instance in HEART'S NEEDLE there's a poem that does that: two museums get merged. It's one of the last poems in the cycle where you're taking the child through a museum full of stuffed animals. One of those museums is in Iowa City where I actually took that child; the other is in Ithaca, where I went alone—a veterinary museum at Cornell, full of all kinds of dead things and diseases. In the poem, though, there'd be no insight or gain in setting a whole new scene for the second museum; it would be complicating and silly. I suppose you have to be careful to see you're not manipulating the facts to make them more palatable, to hide what they really mean. In this case, it just seemed more practical.

Q: *Quite a few of your poems, perhaps even most of your poems, use the physical detail to give a kind of resonance, so the whole poem stands as a kind of metaphor or symbol.*

A: That may have to do with the kind of teaching I got at Iowa. You know, we were under the aegis of Eliot and Pound and Baudelaire and Rimbaud; so, above all, we were making "objective correlatives." Of course, anybody does that all the time anyway, and finally you discover it isn't even an interesting term. It would be impossible to look at anything which wasn't an objective correlative, since the subject-object dichotomy has completely broken down. No serious thinker talks about it; it would be impossible for me to see *except* in terms of objects correlative to me as a subject.

Q: *What strikes off a poem for you?*

A: Anything. Maybe somebody says will you write a poem for next week; maybe I get a line; maybe I get an image; all sorts of ways. I don't see any pattern.

224

Q: *You get a poetic feeling.*

A: Oh yeah, and when I do I can be sure it's going to be a rotten poem. Very often you write the things that are any good when you're not even noticing. You find it on the desk and think, "When did I write this? Well, it's my handwriting." And you find, "Gee, that isn't bad!"

Q: *In other words, if your ego is invested in writing a poem, it blocks you up.*

A: It sure does. One of the dangers with writing is that you are working so much more consciously; you can get yourself all tied up in knots in a way painters and musicians don't. We didn't get all these writers' cramps and blocks until fairly recently, until the whole thing became much more conscious than before. I don't know—at least it seems that way.

Q: *Perhaps the entrance, with the Romantics, of writing as psychological caused these problems.*

A: Yes, and so much involvement of the ego with it, whereas before you simply didn't tend to think of writing in such egotistical terms. But then you didn't think of marriage or business or anything else in such egotistical terms in those times, either, at least so far as we can judge another period from our own.

Q: *In other words the idea of a personality, individuality comes into it?*

A: That tricky, sticky, very self-deceptive business. Like any other kind of freedom it has its great dangers and is liable to bind you up tighter than most forms of tyranny.

Q: *Do you have a usual process for a poem developing? How do poems come to you?*

A: I can tell you more about how it was ten years ago; then I sat down and thought about how it had been for the ten years before *that*. Since then it's changed and I really don't know what the process is like lately. I have written a little bit about this in several places, but I'll go over it again.

We were taught in a very highly intellectualized school which was very valuable in certain ways. Empson was my first love as a poet; Lowell was my second love. We all read Dylan Thomas and Hart Crane and all kinds of incredibly difficult poets and were raised on the symbolists and metaphysicals. We were taught to write an

225

intellectually packed, symbolically loaded poem. This was a very useful kind of learning but something I had to rebel against also, and move toward something much more emotional and much less intellectual. Still, it's not too far a jump from intellectual loading to emotional loading. The first drafts of my poems were nearly always like the kinds of poems I was taught to write. They look very labored over, but, if I'm lucky, the final draft will look kind of tossed off. It'll be about three times as long and probably won't have any very obvious symbols. And it won't have much showy language, rhetorical grandeur and all that kind of stuff—which is what my poems in school all were like—full of hyper-gorgeous language. Rewriting was a process of going into that material and opening it out less consciously, more intuitively rather than intellectually and rhetorically. That was true for about fifteen years. But in the last five or ten years my poetry has changed a lot and I'm not quite sure what the process is like now.

Q: *Does it involve skipping the symbolic step?*

A: I truly don't know.

Q: *Did you find that having the symbolic base was particularly useful, that it made you feel secure?*

A: Yes, but often it was too binding, also. You know what Frost said: if the best part was thought out first and saved for last, that's a fake. Very often that would keep me from advancing the poem. Also, in revising I would often find a certain amount of material that didn't fit; my first urge was to throw all that out. Then I had to get rid of that urge and put it all back in, develop it and figure out why I wanted that stuff in and what did it mean that I'd put it there. So instead of making the poem tighter and narrower, a more hermetically constructed box, you get a more open kind of thing, with a greater range, reaching out in more directions—though it may be less perfect (or less simple) as a construction. The way we were taught—and I am not attacking my teachers; I really revered them—we tended to write a sort of one-subject poem. It tended toward the conceit. What I came to is more like the sonata form, where you're building it out of opposed themes, at least two main themes and probably more. Those themes have to be in radical opposition to each other or the poem won't have space and range.

Q: *Then you're going for tension between the two themes?*

A: Absolutely. So that things are not in harmony. Dissonance above all.

Q: *Do you write on a schedule?*

A: I don't. The one time in my life I had something that could be called mental health—or some such awful term—I lived a very regulated and scheduled life; now I'm awful. If there's one thing I can be counted on to do, it's to break down schedules, especially ones *I* have set up. If someone else sets up a schedule there's some hope of my keeping it.

Q: *Is that part of the loosening-up process?*

A: As a matter of fact, I suspect it's part of the *tightening*-up process. Before I write a poem I usually get very blocked and tight, sort of building up my own steam, getting a lot of energy charged up. When I finally do get started it comes with a good deal of force, maybe because I feel so guilty; I haven't been doing anything for a long time. I'm tortured and, in the meantime, I've been biting my wife and kicking the dog and behaving badly generally. It seems to be part of the regular process; it can be counted on.

Q: *A kind of, "Who am I if I'm not producing poems?"*

A: Yes, and a "What am I here for? How much time have I got left?" I've had other ways of finding guilt, also, which also seems to build up into a kind of pressure that may come into the poem. A lot of people have: Dostoevsky, Van Gogh. I must say if I had my way I would like to write a little less overheated kind of work than that and to live a little less overheated kind of life.

Q: *How long are you likely to work on a poem?*

A: I work very slowly and doggedly. Eight or nine years doesn't surprise me at all; I think I've got one that took me about fifteen. I mean I carried the experience around that long, trying it in this poem, that poem, finally getting one that I thought worked. I just finished an essay I started well over twenty years ago.

Q: *What about revision?*

A: A terrible amount of revision. When I get through with a poem I may have several inches of paper. So far as I can tell it doesn't seem to affect whether the poem's good or not. Some of them are bad that

227

came both ways, some of them are good—or at least seem to me good—that came both ways.

I think I talk against ideas so much because I tend to get idea-bound; they're a great threat to me. You know, I've got a lot of crud in my mind. I've got to tell all the lies first. I guess it's like psychoanalysis that way; you have to go through all the disguises before you can get to the thing under it, but the disguises are part of the truth, too, so you don't want to get all the lies out of the poem. That'd be a lie, itself, because your mind is made up of all kinds of half-truths and lies and disguises and evasions. It would be a kind of spurious moral superiority to set up the poem as some sort of pure revelation of a naked truth. A lot of people talk about naked poetry. I must say that doesn't interest me much, any more than naked people do, except under very specific circumstances. I confess I'm more interested in people at costume parties than at nudist colonies: people really show something about themselves by the kind of disguises they put on.

Q: *Do you ever do any revision after publication?*

A: Oh, yes. The poem of mine that I like most to read out loud is one about an old man dying in a hospital. That first appeared in NEW WORLD WRITING in a version only about half the present length and full of high-flown fancy metaphors and rhetorical language; it seemed sort of like early Lowell.

Q: *Who do you feel has influenced your style the most?*

A: At first Empson; then Lowell. Jarrell helped more than anyone else to get me out of that. He said, "Snodgrass, do you know you're writing the very best second-rate Lowell in the whole country?" After that, my major influences came much more to be musical.

Q: *In what sense?*

A: Well, I was a musician before I was a poet, and you can almost say I'm a musician *since* I'm a poet. I still do write poems, but more of my time goes into music.

Q: *What kind of music?*

A: Early music in particular: early monody. For about fifteen years, I've been translating early songs to sing in English: Troubadour, Renaissance, more lately the classical folk ballads. But I've also been learning to play the instruments and to unravel old notation.

W. D. Snodgrass

The poems I first got known for are the ones about my daughter: HEART's NEEDLE. In those poems, I was very much influenced by Mahler's KINDERTOTENLIEDER, based on poems by Ruckert. I first began by trying to translate those. About the same time I also tried to translate THE MAGIC FLUTE. That never went anywhere except that I did one little poem based on the characters. As for the Ruckert-Mahler KINDERTOTENLIEDER, I ended up writing my own poems rather like Ruckert's pieces. Although as I think of it now, those poems seem more like certain of Hardy's poems which I perhaps didn't even know then. Anyway, I wanted to do something that was direct, dealing directly with the emotions, and the KINDERTOTENLIEDER very much influenced me that way.

I was also influenced by one of the first early music recordings: a record by Hugues Cuenod, the great Swiss tenor, called FRENCH AND ITALIAN SONGS OF THE SIXTEENTH AND SEVENTEENTH CENTURIES. I can still remember where I was and what I was doing the first time I heard it twenty-five years ago. My scalp just stood that high—that incredible, direct, passionate utterance. He's one of those marvelous Swiss tenors who sings right through the nose; none of that soft, gorgeous, gloopy Italian *bel canto*. And he sings with *incredible* passion. These were pieces by Scarlatti and Renaissance song composers.

Q: *Those are actually quite formal pieces, aren't they?*

A: Yes, but absolutely saturated with passion. It seems to me that a poem doesn't need to be clear, but if not, it's got to have some kind of passion, surface magic, something of that sort to carry you through to the other levels. And my poems didn't have that; they were obscure and very muddy in texture, emotionally muddied. They were intellectually clear. But that doesn't count. What counted was the clarity that would carry you into the poem.

Also, I must say one of the things that influenced me here was going into short-term therapy. It only lasted about six months and was done under special conditions, but this therapy consisted of simply restating the problem over and over until I finally got it in my own language. Then, it counted. When we started out, one of us in that room sounded like a psychiatry textbook, and it wasn't him. It was just a fake until you got it in your own language.

Q: *Isn't that the distinction between understanding something and having an insight into it?*

229

A: And how! Or understanding it as opposed to experiencing it.

Q: *Then is that a kind of distinction between the two kinds of poetry we've been talking about, the poem of ideas and the poetry that aims at making you experience something?*

A: It seems to me that there *might* be a valuable poem of ideas; it isn't likely, but there might be.

Q: *But if it's really a poem, wouldn't you have to* experience *the ideas in some way?*

A: It's possible, you know, for a person to get a new idea. One turns up every now and then, every couple hundred years, and it might be a poet who found it.

Q: *Wouldn't that sort of poetry end up like Lucretius?*

A: Exactly; that's one example I was thinking of. Lucretius is a very valuable and a wonderful poet. But compared to the ILIAD? You know, you'd tear up ten of Lucretius for one book of the ILIAD, which is above all experience. It simply slaughters you in ways Lucretius never could.

Q: *For example, in Marvell's* ON A DROP OF DEW—*one tends to teach it as a poem of ideas, but of course it's not a poem of ideas.*

A: Right; the real subject is something far different, having to do with the joy of making all those images, this texture, that clarity and so forth.

Q: *So, in terms of influence, you moved toward the song, the lyric.*

A: I think that's true. My recent poems, though, have moved in quite different directions. They seem less obviously lyrical, less obviously formal. Earlier, I kept most of my formal work and threw out my free verse; it didn't seem as good. Nowadays, I throw out most of my formal work and keep what at least appears to be free verse. Strangely enough, though, even if my work now *seems* less lyrical, it seems to me more deeply influenced by my work in music. I don't think I can explain that.

Q: *You said somewhere that you were influenced by the Texas poet S.S. Gardons.*

A: That would seem a reasonable statement. And now that he's dead I think I can say that. Yes.

W. D. Snodgrass

Q: *Can you make any other comment about how you feel your style has changed over the years?*

A: I almost never write about directly personal subjects now. I write much more indirectly, at least partly because, in a way, I already did that. You wouldn't be trying to write if you didn't want to do something you couldn't do.

Q: *Could it also be you no longer need that personal aspect to get to the poem?*

A: When I try to write personal poems now, they don't convince me very much. It's too easy to fall into an imitation of what one did before; it seems better to start a different kind of poem. Then you don't have that temptation to just look for the line that sounds like the way you're used to ending a poem, or whatever. When you made up that style you wrote something down because you had to; you thought, "Jesus, maybe that's rotten—and it probably is—but that's the only way I can do it." Then later you got used to it, even fond of it, and you end up imitating yourself. Even if I did finish a poem of that sort now I wouldn't feel particularly pleased because I already knew I could do that—although, come to think of it, I'm not really sure I *can*.

Q: *Knowing you can do it may mean you can't do it.*

A: Right. Catch-22½. Of course I still do write poems on a somewhat personal level; for instance, I write poems on my relation to my wife, or something like that, but they are not so direct. Right now I'm working on a whole cycle of poems on the last days in the Führer Bunker, and I was never there. As a matter of fact, the only time I even tried to go there was last year, and I was surrounded by jeeps full of East Berlin soldiers *that* fast. There's nothing but a bump in the field there. Everybody told me, "Don't bother; it's just a bump in the middle of a field," but I said, "I've been reading about it for twenty-five years. I'll look at it and think a big thought." I looked at it and thought, "Yechhh."

Anyway, this is a very different kind of poem; I'm enjoying working on it very much. It's material I started trying to make a play out of right after World War II. But none of my plays have ever worked. Then about two and a half or three years ago this material started going into something like monologues. It might end up being a sort of voice cantata.

Q: *You have a piece in* AFTER EXPERIENCE *about Eichmann.*

A: That's about Eichmann in a different way, about seeing Eichmann in yourself as you stand looking at a sort of mirror-window.
These recent Hitler poems are about the actual, historical persons, in
their own time and place. Of course, it's also about my experience, as
I suppose any poem is. But it's not about places I've been; none of my
former wives appears in the poem; on the surface, it's much less
personal.

Q: *You feel that's a development?*

A: It's different. It's a bigger subject. I mean, to have lived
through such a period—it's an enormous gift of terror (or something)
simply to have lived during the time Hitler came into power, to listen
to those rallies over the radio at Nuremburg, the speeches, the
shouting. That was the greatest collection of freaks ever got together
under one tent. It's a magnificent subject; I'm delighted to be into it.
Maybe I have a form for it now that will work for me.

Q: *Do you notice a tendency in your later poems, for instance in* AFTER
EXPERIENCE, *to use more technological imagery?*

A: Probably; I have no idea what that proves. I was born in a city,
or rather a town—I come from Joe Namath's home town—and so all
sorts of country images have a great appeal to me, living in the
country appeals to me. Most of the people who live near me in the
woods were born in New York and have fled to the country; the
people who were born in the country all moved to the city. I suppose
I tend to associate those country images with a kind of lyrical
impulse, whereas I tend to associate the technological things with a
more dramatic poem, a poem that perhaps is more sociologically
inclined or interested, politically interested.

Q: *If you were initially moving from the symbolist to the lyrical it would
be natural to use the natural images. It makes an interesting mix to carry that
lyric tone over now into technological objects.*

A: I think that for a poem you've got to have one of three things:
either a new idea, which is awfully unlikely, or a new set of details or
a new style. It always delighted me if I could get some detail into a
poem that nobody ever used before—all right, so you preserve one
thing that was in the world. I used to call myself the catheter poet; I
think I was the first ever to insert one in a poem—that same piece
about the old man in the hospital. It's just there as a literal fact.

W. D. Snodgrass

Q: *Of course in the context it becomes figurative.*

A: I guess it does, in a way, though I didn't think of it like that. The first published version of that poem had a lot more open symbolism; for instance, the suggestion of some sort of crucifixion was very overt. But I began to think, a ward aide working in a hospital doesn't think that way. You just don't throw around crucifixion imagery, not even in your private thinking; it may get in there, but not consciously. You'd get embarrassed by it and choke it back down or throw it out altogether.

Well, if there *is* more technological imagery, I think it has to do with a desire to write a different kind of poem, a less lyrical, less romantic, much more realistic poem—not "committed" in the usual sense—but more in touch with political problems, economic problems, rather than just love problems, as in my first book. I think. Maybe.

Q: *What's your feeling about the formal aspects of poetry, rhyme, meter, etc? You've used them.*

A: Not nearly so much now as I did before. And many of them irregularly.

Q: *You think they're essential.*

A: I think that's an individual matter. Not only is it different from poet to poet, it's different from moment to moment in your own career. I probably use such formal aspect, less now because having been through a great deal of analysis, I think maybe I can live with more freedom both in and out of the poem, can put a certain amount of creative freedom to good use. It seems to me that most people are almost totally crippled by great freedom. The average man said, give me freedom to show how creative and phallic I am and, boy, he sure showed. We ended up with the most anal culture that ever existed. Nobody's got off their ass for the last hundred years. They just sit there in front of the television set hollering for more beer. My wife and I've just come from Eastern Europe and it seems to us that most people there are much happier and more creative simply because they haven't so much freedom—which *is* also an enormous loss. You have people like Whitman who can put great freedom to a very great use. People like that have had a very rough time in Eastern Europe. I'm not picking one system over another, but most people certainly appear to be a good deal happier with a good many restrictions. At the same time, I confess I'm hoping to do something outside the range of most people.

I should add that I didn't go into analysis until I had a good deal of freedom and power and money; while I was poor and confined and couldn't get girls, I got along fine. Then suddenly people give you awards, girls line up outside your door—it really unhinges you; you become floppy and loose and uncreative. Anyway, I hope I'm now better able to live with some of these freedoms.

Also, since I spend a lot of time translating early songs, any need I have for restrictions is certainly satisfied there. Not only do you have to translate in exactly the same meter, the same number of syllables, the same amount of stress, probably the same rhyme positions, but it's got to be singable, too. And that involves all kinds of problems I don't understand at all consciously—and I don't think anybody else does, either. Anyway, boy!—if you need restrictions, that's where you'll find them. So, even if these recent poems about the Führer Bunker are in completely free verse, it may be that I feel free enough for that because of all the restrictions in translating folk ballads.

Q: *Do you still employ formal elements?*

A: In a way. Many of my poems are based on a theme-and-variations form—like the poem on Van Gogh in AFTER EXPERIENCE where much of the poem is based on the sounds of the last line in different variations running through the poem. There I'm very much influenced by Whitman. Many of his best poems are based on variations of a rhythmic theme—above all, OUT OF THE CRADLE, ENDLESSLY ROCKING. He does things like that with incredible inventive power.

I have a poem called OWLS which looks like free verse, and maybe is, but every line is a variation on the call of the Great Horned Owls. We have lots of them near our house and I go around and tape them at night. Or there's a poem that has a scene in a belly dance bar in Detroit where all the intellectuals hang out. Once I was talking to some students about it; I was saying that the basic theme, which comes twice in each line, goes, "da DA da; da DA da da DA da; it's the rhythm of the old song 'HEAT WAVE.'" A couple hours later I realized that it must have got into the poem because in Saratoga we used to hang out in a bar for black transvestites where there was a stripper called "Heat Wave" who always danced to that song; I must have associated that with those belly dance places in Detroit. Until somebody asked me I wasn't conscious of it, but I'm sure that's what brought it into the poem. I just picked what I thought was a random rhythm that might be useful—different from any of the rhythms Whitman had used.

W. D. Snodgrass

Q: *So you're doing an informal metrics?*

A: I think so, yes. But it looks like free verse. Nobody looking at the poem about Van Gogh would think of "Zoo heen kan gaan," (the last line of the poem), and as a mirror of "Row on row, the gray frame cottages." I did that very consciously, though I don't think a reader would ever be conscious of it.

Q: *You mentioned translation; do you work with a collaborator on your translations?*

A: Always. I don't read anything except English. By now I've picked up a little German, but not enough to even read a newspaper.

Q: *Do you find it a profitable way to work?*

A: Yes, I love that. You meet some marvelously interesting people . . . musicologists. You see, for about fifteen years I haven't done any translations except songs. That's a kind of translation I can do that other people can't since I have a big background in music. And I simply love the early music so much I want to put my time there. And it gives me a chance to work with musicologists and specialists in languages who have been far out into areas most people think are dry-as-dust. When you get there, you find their life is really a riot. These people are just dying to give you all this they've stored up. They're often the most marvelous people in the world.

Q: *When you translate, do you find that you have to rewrite the poems, in effect?*

A: Somebody else could probably judge that better than I can. My impression is that I translate very literally. I never go off, say, the way Lowell does, making my own poem. But, frankly, if you have any mental richness—and this doesn't criticize Lowell in any sense—you have millions of choices inside the terms of literal translation. Some people think that if you're rhyming you have to say something different from your original. That's only true if you have a very narrow brain or if you're in a hurry to publish.

Q: *Do you try to capture the tone?*

A: The tone is something I'll never understand; it could only be understood by somebody who had the original language very, very completely. For instance, I'm doing a lot of Provençal songs. It's up for grabs whether *anybody* can tell what the tone of *any* of those songs is.

235

Q: *Whether they're being ironic.*

A: Exactly. Or how literary they are or how slangy, how much they may be joking about this, that, or the other thing. In the last ten years we've completely changed our ideas about what those poems mean, what the music is like. Still, in many ways I'm not trying to catch the poet's tone; I'm trying to make a convincing tone in English. When I translate a poem I'm usually trying to make a satisfactory English poem; when I translate a song I'm trying to make a song that will be a delight to sing in English. My Hungarian friend, Lajos Vargyas, says, "You're making a new ballad." At the same time, I almost always stay close to the literal meaning of the original language. Of course if my original's way to say "get out of the room" is "get out of here," I may translate that "vacate the premises" or "skidoo" or "vamoose." Perhaps that's not a literal translation of his words, but it may convey the tone of his words better. Or again, I may not get *his* tone at all, since I'm trying to build a structure of tones in English.

The same way, the French saw things in Poe that we can't see. And we're right—he isn't as good as they think he is. But he means something to them and I imagine there might well be French translations of Poe that are better than Poe.

Oh-oh I lied—I'm *not* only translating songs. I may be the only man alive who is translating a cemetery—a marvelous one in Romania called "THE JOLLY GRAVEYARD"—I'm translating the verses on the grave markers.

Q: *Switching from translating to teaching, you have said you feel a teacher should represent an authority figure.*

A: I think he *does*, whether he should or not.

Q: *How does this express itself in your classroom?*

A: Again you could find that out better from the students than from me.

Q: *Do you push them to write "your kind of verse?"*

A: No, of course not. They almost never seem much inclined to write my kind of verse anyway. Here and there I will hear a line that sounds like me, but that's very seldom. I've only had to mention it once or twice.

It seems to me if you establish an authority, you make it plain that you ask for a very high level of performance and try to perform at a very high level yourself. Above all, you show that you are able to read a poem better and grasp it more thoroughly, to help them see what they can do with their poem that might move it in a better direction, help them see some of the places they're faking, that sort of thing.

Even more, you set a standard of performance: "We will have insights at this level." You show them that you believe they are capable of very great performance and you demand that. If you take it for granted that they can, the chances are they can. People, you know, tend to become what you tell them they are. If you assume they're brilliant and say, "Okay, say something brilliant," they do.

There are other kinds of authority, of course. If somebody starts to break up the furniture, you kick him in the head or you throw him out—a couple of years ago you had to do that, too.

I probably don't take as authoritative a position on many things as I wish I did. I'm sure many of the students would benefit if I insisted that they write a certain amount of metrical verse or experiment in certain kinds of metrical forms or things like that. They wouldn't like that and I would simply have to order them to do it. I guess I'm lazy; also I'm lax. I like to be liked, which is very bad. One would do better to forget about that. Also I tend to feel they should have *had* that a long time ago.

Q: *Do you feel there is some distinct advantage to be gained from teaching poetry?*

A: Keeps you from starving. In most creative writing programs it's going to do more for the way people read than anything else. Very few people at any one time ever write poetry that is any good. But surely all of them will read it and teach it with greater sympathy and understanding for having tried to write some.

Q: *What about the people who will become poets?*

A: That's another matter. I must say I couldn't have written anything if it hadn't been for the creative writing school at Iowa. They were just wonderful teachers and I couldn't have done anything without them, even though that also meant opposing them. But I wouldn't have been equipped to oppose them if I hadn't had them first.

Can you teach *somebody* to write? Yes, you can; you certainly can't teach *anybody* to write. Again, there are people who will get it without being taught, or will teach themselves, or will find different methods of instruction. But after all, even Beethoven had to go to school to Haydn. One way or another, you learn your art from your predecessors, from other people, usually slightly older people working in your art form.

Q: *You also teach poetry reading.*

A: That's one of the things I most enjoy about teaching at Syracuse. My students bring in all sorts of poems that I would never see otherwise. And even with the poems I know well, they give beautiful readings in ways I could never have imagined. Surely one of the best ways to get close to a poem is a good reading, to embody it and bring the emotion across. It's an exciting class.

Q: *You have different people in class reading the same poem?*

A: They do this themselves sometimes, although I don't ever assign it; I'm afraid of the wrong kind of competition. I usually have some speech majors or actors and also some English majors. They're very valuable because they've usually read more and often understood it better, but they've never taken any speech classes or faced an audience so they can very easily be hurt.

I often have them pick partners at the beginning of the class and then prepare dual readings to give that same hour. This does a great deal to jar them loose. They have to respond to the other person's tone of voice and begin to hear how they've cut down on their own range. It forces them out of their habits of performance.

Q: *As far as teaching poetry goes, do you have any feelings about what the poem does for people that other things don't?*

A: I suppose that's up to the people. It isn't my business to say what the poem should be to anyone else.

Q: *What marks it off from other things?*

A: From other kinds of literature? It's more compacted, compressed, more, if you like, forceful in its focus, in its technical resources.

Q: *How does teaching affect your own work?*

A: I don't know if it helps my work. It keeps me out of jail.

Q: *You don't feel it is detrimental, as some poets do?*

A: No. It's always easy to fantasize another life would be better. Well, maybe it would, and maybe it wouldn't. How can you tell? If I

238

didn't have to work I suppose I would quit teaching or doing anything but poetry and music. But it's entirely possible I'd quit writing poetry altogether; that was the result when I had a lot of free time earlier. Again, that fantasy that you could live better without any limits! It's great to talk about it until you try it. As I said, I hope I've gotten so I can stand a little more free time, now. All the same, after my year off, I was sort of glad to go back—I'd been stalled for a couple of months, other problems were getting in the way and I was getting pretty frozen up again. It wasn't bad to have a regular schedule to keep and pay off a few guilts by just getting to class on time and doing something I didn't specially want to. But then, it was fun too. Where else in the society would you find somebody to talk to? The university isn't a place where thought is rewarded, but it is a place where thought is possible. And every now and then somebody will really jar your thinking processes loose and something will happen. That might happen in Joe's Diner down the street but it sure is less likely.

Also, if most of the Chinese poets at a certain time were tax gatherers, it must mean that that was the best way to keep alive and be in contact with the intelligent people, the composers and painters —to make a living and have enough time to do some work on your own. If most writers these days are professors, I suppose it's for much the same reasons. At the same time, just because the other poets are doing that, it might be specially valuable to do something different —it might give you a different background, a different set of details. Now I'm really glad that I got drafted, had to work in a hospital, had to work as a night clerk in a hotel.

Q: *As a final question, would you recommend poetry as a profession?*

A: Oh, by no means. Never. We all feel that way at Syracuse. People are always bringing their poems and asking; "Should I write poetry?" To quote my friend George Elliott, without even looking at the poems you say, "No, not if you can possibly help it. The chances of having a reasonable reward or a reasonable life are ever so much better doing almost anything else. This will force you to see things that will be unspeakably painful and probably mess up your life continually. The lives of most artists just fill you with horror. It may be true that truck drivers are equally neurotic, but the neuroses aren't so valuable to them, they don't depend on them. If you can be happy doing something else that will be less trouble, why not do that?" But if they *can't* be discouraged then they're ours, and we'll have to look after them because they're going to be in trouble.

16

May Swenson

Q: *So many musicians start earlier than poets, in knowing what they want to do. When did you begin writing poetry?*

A: I think I was about thirteen. My father had a typewriter, an old-fashioned Underwood. I had been keeping a diary. I had been writing down my thoughts. And then I'd been doing school papers. That was what you were supposed to do in school. I remember my dad left the Underwood on the dining room table. I didn't know how to type, but with two fingers I copied something that I had written on this typewriter and it came out in a form on the page that looked like a poem. The lines were short. And I think I said: "This is a poem." I think it happened that way.

Q: *Do you do most of your writing on the typewriter?*

A: No, I do it in longhand first.

Q: *Did anybody in particular influence you to write poetry?*

A: No, not in the early days. One thing that made me write was that I was never a social person, and I didn't have a terribly jolly childhood. I had a lot of brothers and sisters. I was the oldest one. It would seem that there would be a social atmosphere; but I was always escaping from the family, from taking care of the kids, and going off

240

to be alone. Then I guess I got a little too lonely, and I began to create things to amuse myself.

Q: *Being an innovator and an independent stylist, have you ever tried the traditional forms, the sonnet and the villanelle?*

A: No, I never have. I develop my own forms, but I don't begin by saying: "I'm going to invent a form in this poem, and it's going to have so many lines and perhaps such and such a rhythm." It doesn't happen that way. I mean I don't predetermine.

Q: *You've written two books called* Poems to Solve *and* More Poems to Solve, *containing what many call "Riddle Poems." Could you tell us something about the Riddle Poem?*

A: Well, those two books are really selections from my other books. They were issued by Scribner's as books for young readers. I chose these poems from my other collections, thinking that young people would be interested in this particular device.

They happen in this way: If I am observing something, I don't think about its name or its label to begin with. I think of how it is affecting me. Take this ashtray, for instance. I think I look at it the way a painter would. Unless I were going to diagram an ashtray or make a picture for a Sears Roebuck catalog.

But for a painter, the thing that interests is its form and its particularity, its characteristics, what it does to him—his eye, the way he sees it. And the very last thing he would write at the bottom of his painting is: "Painting of an Ashtray." The label is the least important thing. In my way of perceiving things I think I approach it that way, that I don't give it a name. So, the Riddle Poem is called that because the name of the thing that's being talked about is not in the text and not in the title. But it is hinted at so particularly in the poem that, for whoever is reading it, it will become defined for him without his having been told its name. That's what makes it a Riddle Poem.

Q: *And these are compilations of these poems which have happened from time to time? It's not that you worked into that particular direction—they happened and they still happen, is that it?*

A: Yes, although they haven't happened for quite some time. I think the last one that happened was a few years ago, a poem called Speed that *THE NEW YORKER* published. What it is, is about insects and butterflies being smashed on the windshield of a car that's moving very fast through meadowland. This kind of painting, as I call it, gets splattered on the windshield. When the car stops you can see all these butterflies and things which have died in this way. As you read the poem, I think you gradually find out what it's talking about.

The first Riddle Poem I published is called, By MORNING. It's about snow falling. That happened to be the first poem that *THE NEW YORKER* ever bought. But *THE NEW YORKER* insisted on calling it SNOW BY MORNING, which made me mad. That gave it away.

Did you know that Emily Dickinson wrote Riddle Poems? She has one about snow:

> *It sifts from leaden sieves—*
> *It powders all the wood—*

The curious thing is that I hadn't read hers at the time I wrote mine. And I saw it later and was so amused and interested that she had one like that.

In SEVEN NATURAL SONGS (which was the earliest one I made), I put the answers at the bottom, in tiny print. After that I didn't put any answers. There are seven different things of nature in it.

Q: *Would you like to read one of your Riddle Poems? Here's one:* LIVING TENDERLY.

A:
　　　　My body a rounded stone
　　　　with a pattern of smooth seams;
　　　　my head a short snake,
　　　　retractive, projective;
　　　　my legs come out of their sleeves
　　　　or shrink within
　　　　and so does my chin.
　　　　My eyelids are quick clamps.
　　　　My back is my roof;
　　　　I am always
　　　　at home.
　　　　I travel where my house walks;
　　　　it is a smooth stone.
　　　　It floats within the lake
　　　　or rests in the dust.
　　　　My flesh lives tenderly
　　　　inside its bone.

242

Q: *That's a turtle.*

A: Yes, a turtle. And also I guess it's me. I realized afterwards that I had described myself.

Q: *In your poems do you make a conscious effort to use poetic devices?*

A: When I notice something of that kind happening, if I like it, I let it happen, and then I make it more emphatic when I do my revisions.

Q: *In that poem* OF ROUNDS *there is a use of repetition, isn't there?*

A: I got that one just from going to the Hayden Planetarium and watching the model of the solar system which they have there. The little sun and the planets around the sun relate to each other the way they actually do in the sky. That's what started that poem.

Q: *You say that all your stimuli come from the environment. Do you ever use anything from dreams?*

A: Yes, I do. I think dreams are a part of your environment. Things can be very vivid in your dreams. Dreams have this aspect of mystery, and not quite understanding what is happening. But it's very significant. And you don't know quite why it's significant. And dreams come from your subconscious. Art comes a lot from your subconscious.

Q: *What about notebooks? Do you keep a notebook by your bed?*

A: Most of the time when I'm working on a poem I'll have a copy of it wherever I am, if I'm walking or riding. And of course it will come to bed with me—on my night table—so that if I'm able to solve something before I go to sleep I'll do it.

Q: *How do you feel about rhyme?*

A: I use rhyme occasionally. I usually don't use it with absolute regularity.

Q: *In* THE WAVE, THE FLAME, THE CLOUD, AND THE LEOPARD *it is used. This is one of your most regular poems. There is an a-a-a-a—*

A: That is probably the most regular poem I have ever published. It's very incantatory.

243

Q: *And then in* THE ENGAGEMENT *you use an a-b-c-b rhyme. But you are not conscious when you read your poems of the rhyme, which makes it all the more clever—to incorporate the rhyme and not be conscious of it.*

A: Yes. It's very boring to have a rhythm at the end of each line, especially if you have regular rhythm within the rhyme. Unless you have a good reason for it.

Q: *Some of your rhymes are most unusual. For instance, you have* burlap *and* dapple—*rhymes like that.*

A: I do internal rhymes a lot.

Q: *Yes, and random rhyme and assonance. You use them all very effectively, but they're concealed. In one of your notes somewhere you mention using sound symbolism, verbal texture, allegory and organic metaphor. Just what is organic metaphor?*

A: Where the metaphor moves all the way through the work, and it builds with just one metaphor.

Q: *Do you use punctuation very much?*

A: Well, strangely, I started out with none. My early work doesn't have conventional punctuation, but rather a substitute for it. There might be spaces, or the lines so arranged that you have to read it with pauses. I would begin with a capital but would not use the period. Then later on I began to use punctuation, and more and more I used it, until I use it entirely now. Isn't that odd, because it's sort of upside down? I am discovering there is a reason why punctuation was invented. And it can be clarifying, and there's no real reason for leaving it out.

Q: *Some of your uses of spacing are very interesting. In your poem* A WISH *you have between each word a space, which makes you read the poem in a very deliberate manner:*

> Out   of   an   hour   I   built   a   hut
> and   like   a   Hindu   sat
> immune   in   the   wind   of   time

A: That's exactly what I wanted. To slow down your eye, which will slow down your thought which causes a rhythm and causes you to think in a sort of—it's that sort of a philosophical-mystical poem that you would want to do this with.

244

May Swenson

Q: *Your poems do have a great deal of detail and precision, sometimes as if you were writing right on the spot. Do you actually do that—write on the spot?*

A: In a lot of my work, the impulse has come right out of what I would be doing, or where I would be, what I would be looking at, or what I'd be feeling. And I would stay with it, right on that spot, until I had a first draft.

Q: *You use a great many cloud images; you have* Swollen-Breasted Clouds, Skins of Clouds On Torn Blue, The Cloud-Shell.

A: Now that you point them out to me, I realize I do have many cloud images. I didn't know that. It's true that one is not conscious of one's own consciousness. You don't know what your mind is tending to do. You are at least two people. There's your mind, and then there's your mind following your mind. It gets very schizophrenic. The things that the mind does are unconscious. And yet it has a kind of logic, somehow.

Q: *How far does the original impulse carry you before you begin to rewrite work?*

A: If you can get a first draft done while you're still in that fresh immediacy or being struck by something, it's right. There have been times when I've been trying to finish a poem and have been distracted, and not only does the intensity of it fade in your mind and in your emotions, but also your mood about it all fades away. You let an hour go by, and go back, and you say, "Well, this isn't so hot. Why did I bother with that?" You might give up. So I've learned to try very hard to stick to the first draft until the poem is brought round to an end.

Q: *Do you keep notes, in order to get your original impulse back?*

A: Yes, I get it from the first draft and from reading it and from notes. And from research. I have a long poem called First Walk on the Moon. I wrote that secondhand. I got it from the TV, I got it from reading—and from imagination.

Q: *But not many of your poems are that type that you have to do a lot of research. What about revision? Do you revise extensively? Do you have an average number of times?*

A: Yes. One always has to revise—with rare exceptions. There's a poem that's been anthologized a lot; a line from it is in Bartlett's

QUOTATIONS—it's called QUESTION,—and that came as it stands, almost, in its entirety.

Q: *Do you like being called a nature poet?*

A: I certainly don't mind being called a nature poet. I think that's one of my things. But I have other things.

Q: *Do you write on the subway?*

A: Yes. RIDING THE A was one of those. I think I finished it up at the Cloisters on the lawn.

Q: *Do you have a special time that you set for yourself every day when you work on your poetry, or does it just happen sometimes?*

A: It's an up and down thing. It's either something that comes very, very easily and with great enthusiasm so that ideas for poems are proliferating in my mind and I can't wait to get them down. Or else nothing's happening.

That reminds me of this poem called How EVERYTHING HAPPENS, which is about how creativity happens. "When nothing is happening/ something is stacking up to happen." That's the way it is with the tide. When there's space between the breakers it's because it's pushing up to make a bigger breaker. So I tell myself that. You're going to get on the pinnacle of a breaker.

Q: *Do you have a strategy to get yourself going again?*

A: Sometimes I'll just sit down and empty my mind. Everything comes out. Even if it's just: "Nothing's coming out, nothing's coming out, nothing's coming out," I just type that. I just keep typing and whatever enters my mind I will type that down. Two sheets single-spaced of that. And then I'll read that over and there will be something there that will attach itself to something else. It will lead to something that happened yesterday. A kind of concretion will take place. I'll be reminded of something that I wanted to write about and that I never quite got to. It will sometimes start something.

Q: *When you say the environment influences your poetry, the city environment and the country environment and the sea and all, then you're exposed to other environments?*

A: Well, I find that traveling is good. I always write a poem if I take an airplane trip. Very often a poem will start in the airplane. I'm having a new experience. I'm seeing something new or I'm just generally excited. Or—it's long ago, now. It's over ten years ago that I went to Europe. On the ship going over I was writing like crazy. Travel seems to do it.

Q: *You give poetry readings. Do they stimulate or slow down your writing? Does it help you as a poet to give the readings?*

A: It helps my ego. To that extent I suppose it's useful. But anything of that sort that interrupts my writing—like teaching, too—I find that I can't teach and write successfully. I become so absorbed in my students' work that it tends to take the place of my own, which makes me jealous.

Q: *What do you think about poetry workshops?*

A: I've conducted them on occasion.

Q: *Did you ever attend one?*

A: No, I never attended a poetry class or workshop. But I think that's the way poets are being developed these days. I think there are several different ways of being creative. I wouldn't say that one way is better than the other. My need is to find my own way, and quite alone. To be in a workshop trying to do my thing while exposed to other people's things, would not suit me.

Q: *How do you conduct a workshop? You said that you seek originality and that you don't model. Do you suggest that your students model?*

A: I suggest that they do what works for them. I attempt to discourage them from imitating, because I think that imitation and creation do not get along together. You can do imitation, I suppose, as an exercise.

Q: *Do you assign exercise poems?*

A: No, I never do that when I am teaching. What I do is give them assignments that exercise their senses and their ability to be attentive, to become more observant and particular and precise.

Q: *Do you think there's enough discipline in craft today for young poets?*

A: I think there's an awful lot of bad poetry being published, in fact an awful lot of non-poetry. I think that discipline is a part of art. I think the artist learns how to discipline himself and how to discipline his work. And yet it seems that the tendency is to be free. Anything goes. Let's spill it all out. But I hesitate to criticize because it might

247

mean that I just don't understand what's happening these days. And that I want it to happen like it happened with me.

Q: *But aren't there some kind of craft principles?*

A: I think that there is an order. I think that the work of art finds an order. I don't think it needs to have an order imposed from the beginning. I don't think it has to fit into an order, but I do think the order has to be found in the process. It's almost synonymous with the word "Art." I just can't see it any other way.

Q: *What about your students? How do you transmit this idea to them, that there has to be an order?*

A: Well, I do it by considering their individual work. When the poem is before us I will say something like, "I don't understand what connection this line has with the rest of the work," or "I don't understand why you can't leave this line out, why it has to be this way." In other words, everything in the poem has to be inevitable, so that if anything is changed it's going to ruin it.

Q: *Of modern poets, are there several whom you would suggest?*

A: Poets that I find healthy to read: one of them is Theodore Roethke. Some of the older poets like Whitman, Hopkins, James Stephens, Emily Dickinson. Among living poets, some that come to mind that I have strong respect for are James Merrill, Elizabeth Bishop, Bill Meredith, W.D. Snodgrass, Anne Sexton, Dick Wilbur, Tony Hecht. There are others. When I was starting to write, Cummings interested me a lot. His playfulness. Marianne Moore interested me. I have to say that I don't read other poetry in order to be stimulated to write my own. When I'm stimulated by literature it's generally not by poetry. Science, or the news of the day—new discoveries. Reading other poetry doesn't generally bring out mine.

Q: *What is the significance of that centaur image that has been talked about so much? There was something that led up to the poem that you call* THE CENTAUR, *which appeared first in* A CAGE OF SPINES.

A: THE CENTAUR, you know, is a childhood memory. The girl in this poem (who is myself) feels herself to be the horse. So that's how the centaur image comes into that. Then there is a poem called ANOTHER ANIMAL, and it starts out with the centaur. The centaur is part human and part beast. I think the significance of it relates to my feeling for animals, my love for horses which I always had. Monsters are mythical beasts. You know, I do have a lot of animal poems. I've

248

always felt myself to be an animal, so to speak. I can really accept the idea of having evolved from the animals.

Q: *Then it's an image for you that's in your life experience?*

A: Well, the poem THE CENTAUR, which is a remembrance of a childhood experience with a hobby horse, was really experienced. I think this is what makes a person an artist: to live yourself into something so thoroughly that you become this thing. When I was ten and I was riding this switch that I cut from a willow tree, it was really true that I felt I was riding a horse, to the extent that I became this, that I was experiencing it so vividly that it was as though I became it. I think this happens with the artist. What you are making, you really live at the time. That is expressing the experience.

Q: *You may speak about yourself in certain images, but you don't speak about yourself directly. There are other themes which have interested you besides nature in your poetry.*

A: Science comes into my poetry quite a bit. The space program, the astronauts' experiences fascinate me. Many of my poems are from the sciences. There's a recent poem called TELEOLOGY—it's many things at the same time. It says:

> The eyes look front in humans.
> Horse or dog could not shoot,
> seeing two sides to everything.
> Fish, who never shut their eyes,
> can swim on their sides, and see
> two worlds: blunt dark below;
> above, the daggering light.
> Round as a burr, its eye.
> its whole head, the housefly
> sees in a whizzing circle.
> Human double-barreled eyes,
> in their narrow blind trained
> forward, hope to shoot and hit—
> if they can find it—
> the backward-speeding eye
> in the cyclops head of the future.

I think that's a poem that when you get to the end, you'd read it over again to find out what it really says. What is the Cyclops head of the future? Why is it called teleology? Teleology refers to the end result of

249

something, the target of the future, the prediction for it. So that's an "-ology." The various -ologies, they interest me.

I'm not religious. I was brought up very religious; I was brought up as a Mormon. They are very religious; they call themselves the Latter Day Saints. They think they are the Chosen People. My parents came to this country as the result of their conversion to the Mormon Church from the Lutheran. I was brought up very strictly in a religious way, which made me turn away.

If there is any hope for understanding the world or understanding the universe, I think that the closest thing we have to it is the discoveries of science. I don't know how close that is, but I also think the artist is on a little search. I think that is one of the impulses of the artist—that you have to unravel the mysteries. Something is going to be revealed to you, and if you keep your senses very sharp, you're going to have a vision. The whole pattern is going to be somehow magically seen.

Q: *Do you think that in addition to science, the artist holds the interpretation to all this?*

A: That's it. The artist and the scientist are our two hopes.

Q: *What would you say are the most important attributes of a poem?*

A: A number of attributes have to work together, and it's the combination—a poem is a complex. What makes it poetry instead of prose is simply the way the language is handled, as far as its sound, its image, its texture, its motion or muscularity (not even to mention *what* is being said) is woven together naturally—all these are important. The way every word is joined with every other word. The complex of it. And then concision, having it tight. The other nice thing about a poem is its small size along with great weight.

In the old days you could hear its rhyme and its rhythm. Of course what's happened today, instead of poetry we have the modern troubadors, the singers with their guitars. What's committed to memory is the tune and the lyric of it. But originally poetry was like that. The language used to be in your head, in your ear, and you'd quote it.

Q: *What poetic devices do you use, for instance, in your poem* THE LIGHTNING?

A: That's one of my iconographic poems, and the first thing you notice about it is the way it looks on the page, with the lightning streak of space running through it. So that it has a visual metaphor before you begin reading it, and it says:

> The lightning waked me/it slid under/my eyelid a black book
> flipped open/to an illuminated page then instantly/shut/
> words of destiny were being ut-/tered in the distance./
> Next day as I lay/in the sun a symbol for conceiving the/
> universe was scratched on my eyeball/but quickly its point
> eclipsed and/softened in the scabbard of my brain/my cat
> speaks one word . . . /he receives with the hairs of his body
> the whispers of the stars/he is held by a thread to the eye
> of the/sun and cannot fall into error./Any flower is a
> perfect ear . . . /When will I grope my way clear of the
> entrails of intellect.

It's about trying to find a pattern, or have a vision, the power of the unconscious. It's sort of what the artist expects and wishes for—to be given some kind of extra knowledge because he's ready for it, always looking for it. Because really what do we know about the reasons for things and about the origins of things and about the ends of things? It's all very mysterious. Unless you can believe in a God with a long white beard in heaven sitting on a cloud. We really don't know. We really don't know anything. But it always seems that we are about to know something. We are going to get ready to know something.

Q: *How do you feel about poets interpreting their poems?*

A: I think the poem should be autonomous and should explain itself. But the poem needs from the person who is reading it whatever he thinks it needs. Sometimes the poet can't explain everything that's in there.

Q: *There's always something in the poem that the reader gets, that is revealed to him, an interpretation of his own.*

A: I think so. The reader has a right to interpret the poem in his own way. What it means to him is important. He shouldn't feel he has to be confined by what is told to him by the poet or anybody else. That's the whole thing.

Q: *Do you consider the revision as much a creative act as writing the poem itself?*

A: If you were to transfer it to another art, let's say sculpture, the beginning thing in sculpture would be the figure modeled out of clay. As a whole, it would have the general shape that the artist intended. But in refining it, you would have to do an awful lot more to it to bring in the details. Little attentions must be given to it, and that's what revision is. If you have a good general beginning, a draft, you want to make it more so. You want to make it more itself.

Q: *Some poets insist that they revise very little. Robert Lowell says that he revises over and over and over and over and over again.*

A: Sure he does. And you know Auden would sometimes revise after his poems were published, so there are various published versions, and the latest version would be the only authentic one.

Q: *Have you ever revised after publication?*

A: I've been tempted to, but I haven't done it. I don't think I would, even if something could be improved. I don't think I would want to impose my new self on my old self.

Q: *You wrote an essay in* POETS ON POETRY *about similarities between the poet and the scientist. And yet there are dissimilarities.*

A: They have dissimilar methods. But I feel that the artist and the scientist are after the same thing. They are after truth. The way things really are. And to make that actual to people.

Q: *Well, the scientist seems to get definite results, but the poet . . . Do you think that poetry has really an influence?*

A: On the scientists?

Q: *No, on the general public.*

A: The only thing that has influence on the general public is advertising. Don't get me into that, or I'll rant and rave!

Q: *And now we must come to the shaped poem.*

A: Except that I'm through making shaped poems. ICONOGRAPHS was published in 1970, and that's already seven years old. Since then I've done two or three others, and that's the end. I took it as far as I could go. I had satisfied my eye enough. "Iconograph" is a made-up word of mine, which means image writing. After the poems were done—and I wouldn't even know they were going to be shape poems or anything—I would give them a typographical arrangement on the page. The shape that you would then see would have something to say about what was being said in the poem.

Q: *The poem came first? And the shape afterwards?*

A: Yes. Always. This is not really concrete poetry.

John Hollander has done a book of poems he calls TYPE SHAPES. They're very interesting and clever. But he did it the opposite of the way I did it. He did the shape and then fit the text into the shape.

OUT OF THE SEA EARLY is a shape poem that appears in HALF SUN. It's also a riddle poem, so it's several things in one.

The trouble with iconographs is that you can't usually get the printer to do what you want him to do. OUT OF THE SEA is supposed to be round, because it's about a sunrise. It shouldn't be perfect on the edges, but it should be entirely round. The poem ZERO IN THE COVE is supposed to remind you of a mirror. These poems are actually my manuscripts which have been photo offset and reduced. This is the way I made it on the typewriter. If they were not typeset, there would be less room for error. That was the idea.

Q: *It's very interesting to pick up a book and have each page have a different shape.*

A: I just thought it would be interesting to the eye. It is part of my playfulness with poetry. I designed this cover myself. It's supposed to suggest a giant typewriter ribbon. But it doesn't really matter if people don't understand that.

Q: *Shape poetry really combines the medium of sound and the use of the eye. Whereas poetry originally was just to be heard and sung.*

A: The shape poems are a combination of the two elements. I guess it's the centaur! But I think I go toward being simple rather than sophisticated.

Q: *You say you are going in other directions now. What are these directions?*

A: I was afraid you'd ask me that. I won't know until I get there. I'm just halfway down that road and until I get there I won't be able to define it for you. One thing that I am doing is something like prose poetry, but it's not really. I don't think it is. I'm working with some prose things which just have the label "visions" on them. It's not patterned poetry. It's away from that. And yet it's not prose either. It's an in-between experiment, and it's just part of the search. It's part of the search and part of my insistence on invention. And not repeating myself and doing something different.

Q: *You spent time this fall watching the migration of the birds. Will that figure in your work?*

A: Well, I've been trying to keep them out because I'm very bird-y. And if I let myself, every poem would have a bird in it. I'm doing a poem right now; the first line is "A flicker with a broken neck. We laid him on the lawn." Those are the first two lines.

Q: *Have you been influenced by your religious upbringing?*

A: Yes, I think I would say so. I have a poem called GODS: CHILDREN. I wrote this soon after my father died. It's really a poem about evolution, I guess. I have a poem that hasn't been published yet about my mother's death. My mother died last summer. The name of that poem is NATURE.

Q: *As a woman poet, has it affected the way you were received? Do you find any solidarity with other women poets?*

A: I have a poem that anthologists keep asking for now. It's called WOMEN. But I haven't sat down to write any Women's Lib poetry, although I see myself a Women's Lib person. I always have. About being a woman and being an artist, I think that in a way it has been sort of lucky. Just as in a certain way, to be Negro is a little luckier these days.

Q: *Do you feel you have been discriminated against as a writer and as a woman?*

A: Well, there's general discrimination. Obviously it happens. If you turn to any general anthology, you will find that the number of women poets is about one-fifth that of men. But not in a personal way. I think there are lots of women poets who are defending that area today and who are doing it more effectively than I. It doesn't always lead to art to be a polemicist. To be on the battlefield. It can take away. I do what comes to me. What asks to be done.

17

Richard Eberhart

Q: *Would you describe the physical conditions of writing your poetry? Are you always at a desk? Do you do first drafts on typewriter or with pencil or with pen? On what kind of paper? As poems progress, what do you do with worksheets that you no longer need?*

A: I almost always write with a pen on typewriter-sized paper, or in a large notebook of that size, am often at a desk, or sitting in an armchair. I save first drafts—as a matter of fact, I am a saver and keep all changes in any poem, whether few or many, and have always been fascinated by the look of the text as it develops. I believe in the mystery of creation and have gone on record that some of my poems which are considered my best ones have been given to me, as it were, as if the poem used the man, not the other way around, or as if the personality were a vane on which the wind of the spirit moved to make the poem. Not automatic writing, but I use an old and now little-used word to convey the meaning, the word *inspiration*. These moods are strange and not to be accounted for by strict rationality, yet the idea of inspiration where poems come whole from the spirit, the hand and being the agent of communication, has governed, I should say, a small percentage of my poems. Therefore there is a kind of sacredness to the markings on the page when inspiration has been the compulsive force, and I look at these pages sometimes with amazement. I would not change a word or stroke of the original

255

manuscript due to my belief in the value of the mysterious origins and strange making of a poem.

THE GROUNDHOG, for instance, now over forty years old, was given to me in the way suggested and composed in perhaps less than half an hour, without the need to change a word, or perhaps one word was changed, I cannot remember. I used to study the manuscript closely, but alas somewhere in time it disappeared and is lost. In most poems there are few or many changes and all changes are kept to study with a cool mind. Many poems have undergone revision, light or heavy, but because of the ideas I have just expressed, I have often been doubtful about the value of revising one's initial force or thrust in writing the poem. It has occurred to me that there is no guarantee, in matters so subtle and delicate, that one can necessarily improve his work by taking thought, by using a cold rational intellectual gaze at the display of words, for any single change ramifies through words, sense, and lines and may decrease rather than increase the effect desired. Yet it is obvious that in many instances one can improve poems by careful analysis of every option available to thought. I am not dogmatic about anything, but being a subjective rather than an objective poet, I value what comes from deep compulsions, from the subconscious essence of being or soul, I respect what is compelled, and I have been, as I said, in some instances afraid to change a word in some poems where the poem was the gift and I its vehicle.

Q: *When you are away from your desk or writing area, do you carry a notebook with you? What do you do with thoughts or impulses that come to you when you are unable to record them easily?*

A: When away from my writing area I do not carry a notebook with me. Once Eliot told me that he wrote slowly, word to word, as if (but he did not use this comparison) a bricklayer were cementing one brick to another with great care. Once Frost told me that he would be walking in the woods and a whole poem of, say, thirty lines would form in his head and that he had so much control of the lines that each was etched definitively on his mind and that he felt no compulsion to write them down. He said that sometimes he could draw this poem off maybe ten years later precisely as it came to him in this way. In both these instances I was amazed and realized that my mind was of a different kind. I felt that my mind was wild and tempestuous in the comparison, volatile and Shelleyan. When words were flowing and churning, sometimes, I would lose a poem or part of one if pen and paper were not to hand. I would have to catch the poem out of the air immediately or it would be lost. HARDENING INTO PRINT deals with this problem.

About catching words out of the air, I recall waking at dawn once with a line, "The river of sweetness that runs through the meadow of lies," unaccountably repeating itself. I was half awake and in a kind of panic because I knew I would lose this line unless I found pen and paper at once, which I did. It caused the poem entitled HILL DREAM OF YOUTH,/ THIRTY YEARS LATER, which would not have been written except for the strange eruption of this line out of the subconscious when I was half awake. To answer your question directly, if I could not easily record my sometime thoughts or impulses I would lose them forever. It would be impossible to get them back. The creative word-cauldron is something seething, sometimes, I do not say all the time, which has always been a mystery to me.

Q: *What would you say about revision? Is it a creative act with you? Have you written anything that did not need extensive revision? Do you have any special procedure for revising a poem?*

A: I have talked about revision; I do not have any special procedure for it. I can see that revision can be creative too, its aim is to create something better. I conceive of revision as coming from your best, cool and rational mind, but I do not believe entirely in rationality. Indeed I think irrationality works in the seething cauldron theory, although I wish I could invent another term for what I mean.

Q: *What do you feel is the value of poetry workshops for a young poet? Did you take any when you were beginning to write poetry? What do you feel about student criticism of each other's work?*

A: When I began writing there were no poetry workshops; it would have been an unthinkable idea. We were fewer in number as poets and seem to have been radically individualistic. I feel now that workshops can be valuable for a young poet. Immediate student criticism of each other's work is now taken for granted and must be of great help to the beginner. Criticism is essential to poetry. Poetry is inconceivable without criticism. It cannot live in a vacuum of itself. Culture intends that the poet and the critic should go together. Just as men and women in the real world create the future of mankind by producing children, criticism brings to birth the future of poetry by preserving the best works written at a given time, insuring the pleasure of readers in a long extension of time.

I think of criticism in two main categories. First is professional criticism, which explains and evaluates the poetry of a time or age, and may be written by competent learned persons or by great perceivers such as Aristotle, Sidney, Dr. Johnson, Shelley, Arnold, and others. The second category is the criticism of the poet himself. He cannot create a poem without the critical awareness of what to leave out, as well as what to put in, or without using his rational mind, however irrational his creative impulse may have been, in perfecting every line and phrase and word of a poem. The Lockwood Library at Buffalo has Thomas manuscripts showing over a hundred changes in a poem to perfect and produce the final poem Dylan Thomas wanted to express. Likewise, most of us have examined elaborate changes made by Yeats in some of his poems, changes dictated by the critical intelligence.

Poetry is complex, very ancient, going back to primitive responses; it is deep in us and essential to us, and it is married to criticism as I suggested in the analogy of men essentially connected to women.

One of the many great things said about poetry by great critics was the statement Coleridge made in the BIOGRAPHIA LITERARIA that poetry gives most pleasure when only generally and not perfectly understood, thus giving on to endless delights of speculation and contemplation, making criticism a continuous, living thing.

Q: *Do you ever experience a dry period in writing, and if so what do you do about it?*

A: I have written more or less continuously since I was fifteen or sixteen and have never had what I would call a significant dry period. In late years I have recognized what I would call long swells of ups and shorter periods of downs. This is somewhat perceived after the event, as it were. There might be a year of intense upsurge of creativity, then a corresponding down-thrust of creativity, maybe of a few months; but I would not characterize the latter as dry, rather a difference of intensity due to unanalyzable reasons, just as I never could understand the long uprush periods, either. These fluctuations have to do with one's entire life, over which often we have little control, although we live as if we seem to have control of our lives and know what we are doing and why we behave as we do.

Q: *Do you ever play games with the craft of poetry, prosody, for the fun of it, or for what it might lead to? Anagrams, palindromes, etc.?*

A: I used to invent arbitrary forms for poems, an abstract *a priori* structure, then invent lines to fit this architecture. This would come

258

under the rubric of poetry as play, about which much has been said. In my entire life, however, this means would be rather slight.

Q: *What do you feel about the need for isolation in the life of a writer? How does it affect personal relationships? Professional activities such as teaching?*

A: I cannot speak for other writers. In a sense Hopkins was isolated all his life, except for communications with Bridges, Dixon and Patmore. If he had become Poet Laureate, as did his friend Bridges, would he have written better poetry for being a public figure? Probably isolation made and saved him. Take the other side of the coin, if Auden coming to New York in 1939 had written little and been known to a few poet friends, would his work have been deeper? It is impossible to say. Isolation is relative, in any case. Whitman partook of his times and the War but was isolated from the fame he now enjoys until long after his death. And it is difficult to think of Emily Dickinson as anything but an isolated poet. We do not think of her in the context of the worldly success of a Millay.

Some poets thrive in isolation, some do not. In a sense Jeffers isolated himself from mankind in favor of the vast impersonal realities of the California mountains and ocean. He had none of the social charm and social beliefs of William Carlos Williams. Frost, early thought to be isolated on New England farms, came to woo large audiences, college presidents, and a President of the United States.

For me there has always been the tug of the spirit and the world. To live only for the spirit would be to be isolated in some sense. My nature turned me to the world, but realism without spiritual meaning is devoid of something sensed as deep and primitive in all of us. I have never got out of dualism, the dualism of spirit-flesh, time-timelessness, tragedy-comedy, hope and despair, sorrow and joy, hatred and love. In A WAY OUT I went to nature as a unifying principle.

Some say one cannot teach poetry. You cannot teach genius, maybe you cannot teach talent. These will emerge and reveal themselves beyond the teacher, no matter what the means and the enthusiasms. Teachers can instruct in techniques, in systems of thought, in evaluations of meaning, in subtleties of being and feeling. I was delighted to be taught poetry when I was young and to teach it in the last twenty-five years of my life.

Q: *Have you ever received lines of poetry which you were unable to incorporate into a poem? What would you do with them, as a rule?*

A: I said something earlier about catching lines out of the air. There are many lines you write which you reject, for one reason or another. These are discarded and do not get into poems, but the pages are kept for study. Recently I sent a poem written in Florida to Spender suggesting that I should excise the third line from the bottom. He objected, said I needed this for the rhythm. The poem is entitled NIGHT THOUGHTS, recently published in TLS.

Q: *If a poet is about to fall asleep and suddenly thinks of an interesting poem or some interesting lines for a poem, what should he do?*

A: This is rather whimsical. If he is sleepy enough he will fall asleep and lose the lines. If not, he may wake up and use the lines to whatever problematical effect.

Q: *What reference books do you feel are useful for a young poet to have on his desk for consultation?*

A: What a question! The *OED* and perhaps Hutchins' hundred books, but he couldn't afford them. He could look out of the window and read the book of nature. He could look in his heart, as has been said, and write. Returning to the isolation problem, if he were to live on an uninhabited island for a year, should he not take the Bible, Shakespeare, Dante, Milton, the Greek dramatists, Wordsworth, and I would take along Blake? But think how many great exemplars this list leaves out! What about Buddha and if here a practical young man, Confucius?

Q: *Do you feel we live in a particularly permissive age so far as education and discipline in craft are concerned, and if so, what effect is this having on the present stage of poetry being written today?*

A: I believe that poets cannot escape their time, indeed are enmeshed in it. Poets of the thirties wrote differently than poets now writing in the seventies. In the forties and fifties they would have been influenced by the New Criticism and the so-called well-made poem. Poetry reacts to the acts of every man and woman in the society. These acts vary and one decade is not like another. Since World War II poets have written without rhyme, in long lines, about anything in the world, in what I have termed spewed lines. The poems in this fashion may be as excellent as those of the well-made poems of the middle of the century. There is no reason to limit the styles and force of poetry. Everything changes, including poetry. I am reminded of Dame Fortune, the Lady of Permutations:

Richard Eberhart

> All earth's gear
> she changes from nation to nation, from
> house to house
> in changeless change through every turning year.
>
> No mortal power may stay her spinning wheel.
> The nations rise and fall by her decree.
> None may foresee where she will set her wheel:
>
> she passes, and things pass. Man's mortal reason
> cannot encompass her. She rules her sphere
> as the other gods rule theirs. Season by season
>
> her changes change her changes endlessly,
> and those whose turn has come press on her so,
> she must be swift by hard necessity.
>
> (Ciardi's translation)

Q: *What poet do you feel would be a good model for a young writer to begin learning about poetry?*

A: Each young poet will choose his or her model or models by preference or by chance. Since there are so many poets it would be futile to name any one model.

18
Helen Adam

Q: *Having been born in Scotland, and spending a good many years in San Francisco, do you have any feelings about origins for a contemporary American poet?*

A: Well, I think one's origins are always fairly important, because although I've been an American citizen for many years now, I always feel myself as still Scottish, and all my strongest memories are of Scottish countrysides, and the extraordinary unearthly quality in the lonely places, in the moors and glens. I've never found it anywhere else I've traveled—however beautiful the countryside has been, it hasn't that weird quality that Scotland has, when you're really alone. I always loved the gloaming in Scotland, the long-drawn-out evenings, so you could walk or climb.

When I was a girl I loved to walk all night in the hills. I once spent a holiday in Skye, and idiotically told my family that I was going to climb one mountain in the Black Coolins, then I started out alone, and changed my mind and climbed another instead. It was brilliant moonlight, fortunately, because I had underestimated the time it would take, so I was out all night, and it was most weird because the stones move under your feet all the time, and I was only wearing canvas gym shoes, and the great stones rolled under and over my feet. If I had sprained an ankle, nobody would have known what mountain I was on, but nothing like that happened, and I have always remembered those black stone hills in the blazing moonlight, and the dark sea far below.

Q: *Just as Burns sort of inherited a musical tradition, do you feel that in your work there is a natural metric working?*

A: Yes, I think I do, because I was practically brought up on the old ballads, and also on the Scottish hymns. D. H. Lawrence says somewhere every poet should know the hymnbook in general. It does have good tunes, set to preposterous travesties of the gorgeous Biblical language—you know, it's twisted around—there are only two hymns I remember as poetry. But as a child I was not too critical of them, it was just more or less sung every Sunday. They're all very simple rhythms.

Q: *In the Donald Allen anthology* THE NEW AMERICAN POETRY *your work is the only work that is regularly metrical. You manage to combine the traditional love of metrics with a very contemporary voice.*

A: I don't really feel it's contemporary very much; it usually more or less belongs to the fairy tale or the archaic world—in fact, one critic called me a pre-Christian poet, which I think is nice, because I think I probably am—most of my poems are about an eye for an eye and a tooth for a tooth.

Q: *Is that the pagan world we feel in* MACBETH?

A: Yes, I think so—well, Shakespeare in MACBETH has always seemed to me to have a magnificent feeling for Scotland, greater than any English poet has ever had—because it's entirely and authentically Scottish in its feeling, the savage revenge and the courage and the wildness and the black magic all through it. We used to live close to Duncan's castle, near Inverness, and also near the blasted heath—it's just like any other long low-lying moor, if you didn't know it was the blasted heath.

Q: *Have you ever seen a leprechaun or heard the rustle of dry leaves when it ducked behind a tree? Do you think there's a link between second sight and the special vision of the poet?*

A: I think it's absolutely true that there must be a link between second sight and the vision of the poet. My mother had second sight, but I don't. And unfortunately I've never seen a leprechaun or any of the fairies, although I've felt their presence—I have seen a ghost or two. But I do think there is a definite link between the vision of poets and a belief in the supernatural, way down deep. And what's called the supernatural—to me the fairies are not supernatural but are absolutely natural—I've met many people who have seen them, who lived in the Scottish highlands, and who felt their unearthly presence. Second sight—my mother had knowledge when people were going to die. The whole thing of the magic feeling of ancient ballads—I've always loved that verse in Thomas the Rymer:

> O they rode on, and further on,
> And they waded rivers aboon the knee,
> And they saw neither sun nor moon,
> But they heard the roaring of the sea.

—surely in itself I think that's the queen of elfland, too.

Q: *Blake saw visions, too, but they were different visions—*

A: Oh, Blake of course simply lived in the real world. I think it's such arrogance, all the pithy little people who say that Blake was mad—he wasn't mad, he simply was living in the real world in which he saw into the astral world. I think it's very interesting today the terrific interest in witchcraft, the occult, and astral projection, although a lot of it is obviously promotion—all those things that have always been believed in the past. And Blake—of course actually almost all Blake's drawings and poems are straight out of the world of vision.

Q: *Do your poems come with the tunes to them?*

A: Yes. I can't write anything unless I'm writing it to a tune. I've very, very seldom written unrhymed poems. Even them I chant. The rhymes always have a tune.

Q: *Not many other American poets are doing that—*

A: Well, Duncan often sings his work, and he often gets extremely good tunes, too, some lovely haunting tunes.

Q: *Do you feel there's been any new interest in incantatory poetry through the Rock music?*

A: Well, the Rock music sometimes is real poetry—it certainly was in Bob Dylan's poems. I do think those were poems on any level, particularly with his marvelous gritty voice singing them, one of those voices that was absolutely right. Bob Dylan wrote his own, and

264

so did the Beatles. It interested me that Allen Ginsberg is writing a lot of rhymed ballads and blues songs now. There's one really marvelous one, To THE BONEYARD I AM BOUND.

Q: *What are the physical conditions of your work? Do you work in notebooks, do you work at a desk?*

A: I usually work outside—I go to the sea, to Coney Island in the off-season—I walk, and if I'm caught up with a poem I do it while I'm walking and I can chant it. I very, very seldom sit down and write in a room—I have to be outside. Here I can only do it in Central Park, the streets are so crowded. I never write it down, onto a typewriter. I know a lot of people do that these days. I have to write it out in longhand, the first rough version, then I can correct it—some of my poems take months and months and months to get right, and then I come back and look at the first version, and it's ludicrous! Just occasionally I write something and I don't change it at all.

Q: *What do you think of the idea of something's being "given" to you?*

A: Oh, yes, that I believe in absolutely, that I'm sure is true —anyone who's an artist at all does occasionally get in touch with something. When I was writing SAN FRANCISCO'S BURNING, I would say, "I need another sea chanty," and I would go to sleep, and when I woke up it would be written for me. That's a marvelous feeling. But then I go through long, long periods when I don't write anything at all. I remember when I was a child I was singing awful little bits of dreadful doggerel—like the wind being in love with the pretty rosebud, and I often did it all day long.

Q: *When there is a dry period, is there anything you can do to get out of it?*

A: I usually read a great deal, but then I'm always reading anyway, so that doesn't really count. Sometimes, though, I find that if I'm reading a lot of another poet, then I'll start writing something that's a bad copy of that poet, and that starts me on my own again.

Q: *What do you feel about poetry workshops?*

A: They were a real value for me, because I met Duncan through one. I think they're good, if they make you write. Jack Spicer's was one of the most interesting—it was a magic workshop; he did it with Tarot cards, and he gave everyone a Tarot card. He gave me that one that's very like me, the Two of Swords, in which the blindfolded girl is holding two swords, and behind her is the great moonlit sea, and she

265

won't turn to look at it. And I thought there was something magic about it just because Jack chose it for me.

Q: *You say poetry workshops are valuable because of the need for community, but that presupposes the tremendous isolation of the artist—and some people are not up to that isolation.*

A: Every artist really has to be isolated; the act of creation is lonely, anyway. Performing arts are not so lonely, but even an actor thinking out a part is lonely. And the creative arts are even more solitary.

Q: *When you are working on a strong metrical poem, do you ever have to go back and parse or do scansion to find out what you're doing?*

A: Oh, yes, of course I do. I have to go back—first, I more or less write it quickly, then I go back and work at it.

Q: *You mentioned Shelley and Blake and Burns and the great ballads —are there other poets who were terribly important to you?*

A: Well, Milton—I was brought up on Milton and the Bible. The great poems of Milton, particularly the shorter ones, COMUS and LYCIDAS, I learned by heart as a child.

Q: *You learned the whole of* COMUS *by heart?*

A: I learned the whole of COMUS; I don't know if I could remember all of it now, but I loved it so much—and then the Satanic parts of PARADISE LOST—

Q: *That was your choice, to memorize* COMUS?

A: Oh yes, no one ever told me to. I believe a way far back I had some great grandmother who wrote hymns. I loved a great many of the Irish poets: Yeats, always, from very young; and I'm very attached to some of the poems of James Stephens and James Joyce and to the Pre-Raphaelites, both as poets and artists.

Q: *Why is it that the greatest lyrics—the ballads and the songs, have come from the periphery of England—the Irish, the Scotch, the Welsh—*

A: It's very strange where poetry seems to flare out every now and then. Ireland's folklore was always on a gentler level than Scotland's, you know—it isn't nearly so savage, it has the charming mischievous fairies and not so much some of the creatures that Scotland had like the water horses and things, all of which were absolutely deadly, the fetch—of course Ireland has the Banshee, but the banshee is very nice. I have always liked an old saying that seems to me to express the real awe associated with the Scotch world of the supernatural: "If a man tells you he has seen the fairies, look if he be shaken. If he be not terrified, be sure he has not seen."

Q: *Most of the images we're talking about are either pagan, the Scotch and the Irish, or else the Egyptian—and they're mostly outside the Judeo-Christian tradition. Have you ever worked with Judeo-Christian images?*

A: I was brought up completely orthodox, Scotch Presbyterian, but as soon as I was old enough to think at all, I realized I didn't really believe in it. I think if I'd been brought up a Buddhist, I would probably have believed in Buddhism all right. I really can't think of a Christian ballad—

Q: *Is the ballad form itself alien to the Judeo-Christian tradition?*

A: Well, yes, I believe it is. There are one or two ballads about Christ's nativity, but they're really just songs.

Actually, I think the Egyptian gods are very real—the whole concept of them—the animal heads are simply symbols of the power of the god. I know Anubis seems to me—Anubis was worshipped for 6,000 years, and Christianity is only about 2,000 years old.

Q: *Of course the most striking difference is the polytheism—that there are many gods—as opposed to monotheism—*

A: Yes—well, I think—all the Hindu gods, there must be literally hundreds—and devout Hindus all say these are simply various aspects of the one reality, which I'm sure is the truth.

I love the Tibetan Book of the Dead, especially the part about the moment you die, the instant you die, you're faced by this incredibly blazing wonderful light. Very few people can stand it, and if you rush right into it you won't be reborn, because this is reality and your true self. But only the very saintly are able to do this.

Q: *Have you ever done translations?*

A: No.

Q: *Do we have a strong heritage of the weird in American poetry?*

A: Well, I think so. Certainly Melville, Hawthorne—the whole atmosphere of The Scarlet Letter is like a ballad, that brooding sense of evil—a lot of his short stories, too—and Poe, of course.

Q: *How long did it take you to write* SAN FRANCISCO'S BURNING?

A: Oh, I don't know; it took a year, I think. It's sort of a nonsense play. People always ask me if I did a great deal of research, and I think I read one book about the fire and all the dreadful things that happened to the poor seamen, even if they decided they wouldn't go ashore—

Q: *It's interesting what you do with time in your poem* HOUSE OF THE MIRROR—*you use the present tense throughout, but somehow there's a feeling that you're merging the past, present and future.*

A: Well, perhaps I was. That was based on a memory—when I was a child we lived in old Scottish manses—the rooms there were always very big, and they were full of huge Victorian furniture, and in my bedroom there was one of these old-fashioned wardrobes with three very high mirrors, almost to the ceiling, and I always felt it was rather strange, especially just before going to sleep in the half-light, these towering mirrors, and the images in them seemed to move, they seemed to float away—and I think that sort of stayed in my memory.

Q: *You use initial rhymes in your poem* TURN AGAIN TO ME *in NYQ # 18—a consonant followed by an* r, *as in Prince, Brandaris, drowned, tryst, break, grass, tree, crowned, cruises, drifting—at first reading it seemed a little strange, the sounds seemed to need getting used to—*

A: Well, it has to be sort of sung. When you're reading any poem of mine you almost have to make up a tune for it—it's really meant to be sung.

Q: *You've never done any teaching, have you? All of your work you support by doing odd jobs?*

A: I have never done any teaching. I don't think I know enough about anything to do any teaching. I've done all sorts of odd jobs. My weirdest was raking up gold dust off the floor when I was messenger in a gold place on 47th Street. We had to do it with a broom like in Grimm's fairy tales, and sort the gold dust out of the ordinary dirt. I only lasted there about three weeks. Then I did things like being a waitress, and odd jobs all the time.

The only one I ever enjoyed was during the war, when I worked with the land army, and I loved that. In the summers, up at Lake Erie, gathering apples and we were out very early in the morning, grapes growing, and it tasted so delicious—and also the little halo of light you'd sometimes see around peaches. They only barely paid your

268

keep, and that was working from morning to evening. You know, there were professional migrant workers who could do it far, far faster. That was terribly hard work, of course. But at least you were out in the open air. It's amazing, too, at first it seemed so tiring, constantly stooping and bending, and then you got good at it, and you enjoyed it, and you felt the power of the earth coming through.

Q: *But you never did anything remotely connected to literature?*

A: No, no, I never did a job like bookkeeping that you had to keep your mind on; I would have just gone wild if I'd gotten an idea! As for teaching, I've never been much good talking about poetry. I like to read poetry, my own and others'—but to talk about it in front of a class—it would sort of freeze me instantly.

Q: *You do a lot of reading—*

A: Well, readings depend so much on the individual audience —there's nothing more fun if you've got the audience, it gives you a lift. The only thing I don't like are readings I have to do in the afternoon. It must be like matinees in the theatre. Everybody's dead and you just feel dead yourself. I've never done a successful afternoon reading.

Q: *Do you go to readings?*

A: Not often. I do if it's a poet I really want to hear, but—I used to go to a lot more than I do now, I've just got lazy about everything, you know. And then I get mad at myself, I've missed this or that!

Q: *The books you're constantly reading—are they primarily history, or fiction?*

A: Well, I do read history if it interests me, but only things like the Egyptian. My history—it's only purple patches here and there I remember—even British history I don't know a thing about, I'm ashamed to say.

Q: *Do you ever work in prose, non-fiction, short stories?*

A: Well, yes, a short story, but I don't know if that's going to work out—this last witch thing I tried to do. I've struggled with that wretched thing for over a year, and it's still not right! This couldn't happen with a ballad, you know; if I worked a whole year on a ballad, at least it would work in the end!

269

19
Gary Snyder

Q: *How did you begin writing poetry?*

A: My mother writes poetry, and wrote poetry all her life, and before I could even read, she read poetry to me every night. In particular I recall the works of Edgar Allan Poe. And at a very early age it occurred to me that poetry was a respectable thing to do, and a pleasurable thing to do, and so I began to make up poems and transmit them to my mother, who wrote them down for me.

Q: *The way you describe it, poetry is an oral kind of thing—it didn't come to you through the written word, it came through the spoken word.*

A: That's how I first heard it.

Q: *As most of your poems look on the printed page—they're staggered left, right, or indented or something, spaces here and there—are you after visual effect, musical effect, or both?*

A: Well, I consider this very elemental. Most poets I know, most of my colleagues, who follow that open form structuring of the line on the page, do it with full intention as a scoring—as Charles Olson pointed out some years ago in his essay on projective verse (from Chapter VI STATEMENTS ON POETICS in THE NEW AMERICAN POETRY, edited by Donald M. Allen [Grove Press/Evergreen Books, 1960, p. 386]).

270

The placement of the line on the page, the horizontal white spaces and the vertical white spaces are all scoring for how it is to be read and how it is to be timed. Space means time. The marginal indentations are more an indication of voice emphasis, breath emphasis —and, as Pound might have called it, *logopoeia*, some of the dances of the ideas that are working within your syntactic structures.

Q: *Do you have the poem pretty much complete inside you before you start to put it down onto the paper, or is it that you hear this* tala, *and that gets you into the poem, but then you are interacting with the paper—or do you use a paper—do you use a tape recorder or something?*

A: No, I write by hand when I write. But before I write, I do it in my mind many times—

Q: *The whole thing?*

A: Almost the whole thing. The first step is the rhythmic measure, the second step is a set of pre-verbal visual images which move to the rhythmic measure, and the third step is embodying it in words—and I have learned as a discipline over the years to avoid writing until I have to. I don't put it on the page until it's ripe —because otherwise you simply have to revise on the page. So I let it ripen until it's fully formed and then try to speak the poem out, and as a rule it falls right into place and completes itself by itself, requiring only the smallest of minor readjustments and tunings to be just right to my mind.

Q: *How long does that ripening process usually take?*

A: Anywhere from a day to a half a year. I have several things that I've been holding in mind now for five years.

Q: *Only in your mind? You don't write down even a line?*

A: Well, I must confess I have a few notes on them, but the greater part of it's in my mind.

Q: *Do you keep a notebook?*

A: I keep many notebooks—many notebooks and many useful files.

Q: *With an idea of these visual images?*

A: Visual, and also working phrases, working images as written out, even individual words, some of the words that I have since been working with. This is the way that I am working on MOUNTAINS AND RIVERS WITHOUT END, which is still in progress.

Q: *Do you think of one line of poetry, then, as the melody, another part as the accompaniment?*

A: Only metaphorically. That leads into another area which is more structural, structural in regard to imagery over syntax. In that sense metaphorically there are some idea or image lines that are equivalent to the melody line, and some idea or image lines which are like a recurrent chorus or a recurrent subtheme, or repetitions that revolve in various ways, bringing different facets to light in the unfolding of the poem.

Q: *Do you rewrite?*

A: No.

Q: *Not at all?*

A: For the reasons I've just explained—

Q: *Not at all?*

A: I tune, I make adjustments, I tamper with it just a little bit—

Q: *So that once you have the poem down and you put your name at the end of it, that's it?*

A: Well, once in a while a poem will come out half-formed, and what I'll do with that is put it aside totally for several months and then refer back to it again and then revisualize it all. I'll replay the whole experience again in my mind. I'll forget all about what's on the page and get in contact with the pre-verbal level behind it, and then by an effort of re-experiencing, recall, visualization, re-visualization, I'll live through the whole thing again and try to see it more clearly.

Q: *Well, this is a kind of information retrieval, almost—you were talking about notebooks and files before, and this is almost an index type of question—Do you keep those in some sort of order, or do you have cross-references?*

A: Yes, they're all organized, but their only function is mnemonic aids, like signals to open up the inner world. The inner world is too large to ever put down; it's a sea, it's an ocean; and guides and notes

272

and things like that just help me—they're like trail-markers. It's like finding your way back to the beginning of the right path that you were on before, then you can go into it again.

Q: *Can we talk a minute about the way you go into it—do you use meditation as a way to get into it? Is meditation a way of focusing for you?*

A: Curiously, I don't "use" meditation in this way, but it serves me well. I'm a practicing Buddhist, or Buddhist-Shamanist, perhaps; and every day I meditate. I do zazen as a daily practice. Which does not mean that my daily meditations are poetic or necessarily profound, but I do them, and in actual fact the inception of the poem generally seems to take its beginnings more while working, rather than while sitting. But the exercise, the practice, of sitting gives me unquestionably an ease of access to the territories of my mind—and a capacity for re-experience—for recalling and revisualizing things with almost living accuracy; and I attribute that to a lot of practice of meditation; although, strictly speaking, that is not the best use of meditation.

Q: *There's a book around called* ZEN AND THE ART OF ARCHERY *by Eugen Herrigel which says that through a kind of disciplined inattention the archer and the target become one. The artist and the creation become one. Do you find that meditation has worked this way for you?*

A: Well, yes, because, like I say, I never try to use meditation deliberately—for the reason that, as anyone who has done much meditation knows, what you aim at is never what you hit. What you consciously aim at is never what you get. Your conscious mind can't do it for you. So you do have to practice a kind of detached and careful but really relaxed inattention, which lets the unconscious do its own thing of rising and manifesting itself. But the moment you reach out—it's like peripheral vision, almost—the moment you reach out to grab it, it slips back. It's like hunting—it's like still hunting.

Still hunting is when you take a stand in the brush or some place and then become motionless, and then things begin to become alive, and pretty soon you begin to see the squirrels and sparrows and raccoons and rabbits that were there all the time but just, you know, duck out of the way when you look at them too closely. Meditation is like that. You sit down and shut up and don't move, and then the things in your mind begin to come out of their holes and start doing their running around and singing and so forth, and if you just let that happen, you make contact with it.

Q: *Is that something like what Buddhism calls the* "Erasure of the Self?"

A: That's one kind of erasure of the Self. That's the simplest kind, where the conscious mind temporarily relinquishes its self-importance, its sense of self-importance, of direct focus and decision-making and lets peripheral and lower and in some sense deeper aspects of the mind begin to manifest themselves.

Now of course surrealism is a *conscious* attempt at doing this in poetry in its own way, too. My feeling about surrealism is that it tries to skim too near the top; it doesn't go deep enough.

Q: *Zen, the disciplined inattention, would allow one to get much closer—*

A: Well, I wouldn't assign it just to Zen. Zen is the particular discipline, the particular tradition, and it is not of itself necessarily interested in stimulating these kinds of processes. Furthermore, what I'm describing I think is common to the creative process for all kinds of people, and all kinds of arts, and they arrive at it not necessarily by formal practice of meditation, but by practice of an intuitive capacity to open mind and to not cling to too rigid a sense of the conscious self.

Q: *Before you started to describe yourself as a Buddhist, and then you amended that to Buddhist-Shamanist, and you had also mentioned something about rattles and drums, and you're a contributing editor to* ALCHERINGA *magazine, and all this somehow ties together. Is that what you referred to once as rediscovering, reaching back to the archaic past?*

A: Yes, and it connects with a little of what I said earlier about my sense of poetry as a very ancient art which predates and does in no way ultimately depend on writing systems, belonging to the very days of the origins of language itself, perhaps—founded on cultures, functional in all cultures, with one particular focus on its (poetry, we're talking about)—on poetry as a healing act.

Q: *Healing?*

A: Healing. Song as healing magic. There are all kinds of song. The genres are: work-song, a personal power-vision song, war song, death song, courting song, hunting song—all of these are used by people for their own needs and uses. But the special genre is healing song. The Shaman was the specialist in that. He returned to his power-vision song experience many times and deepened it over and over again, whereas other people had one power-vision song and that was enough. The power of this type of song—the power that the Shaman connects with—enables him to hear and to see a certain classic song which has the capacity to heal. And I think that we could say that self-conscious, quote, "literary" poetry of the sort that has been transmitted for the last two millenium in the West—the best of it belongs to that genre: healing song.

Q: *Can you describe what you mean by* healing?

A: Integrating—

Q: *Integrating—you don't mean healing the sick, but—*

A: Sometimes.

Q: *Sometimes?*

A: Yes, but—O.K., we'll be civilized and say it means healing psychological distress, integrating people in the Jungian sense, their inner discontinuities harmonized—

Q: *Creating a harmony, soothing—*

A: Well, as it turns out, *soothing* is maybe too mild a word. Because in the dialectics of things, to be healed is to be sane, and to be sane is to be very energetic, rather than tranquilized.

Q: *Healing is kind of a magic word, too.*

A: Indeed, yes. I wrote a whole poem about healing called THE BLUE SKY, which is one of the sections of MOUNTAINS AND RIVERS WITHOUT END, in which I tried to sketch some of this out. But another level is the healing intention of myth, and the use of myth as the harmonizer of man, society and nature.

Q: *Bringing all of society together—*

A: And nature. *And* nature. In that sense Dante's PARADISIO and INFERNO is an attempt, a massive attempt, of healing song.

Q: *Is that what—*

A: Because it's culturally integrated, or its intent is to be culturally integrated. And Goethe tries it again, Blake tries it, Milton tries it, and James Joyce tried it. And Pound tried it. Now those are massive attempts in Western history to re-speak the primary and most archaic-ness of our tradition in a form that would integrate, harmonize and heal people's minds. In the nature of civilization and history, it can't be said that any of them were totally successful. But the effort is the most ancient kind of poetry, I think.

Q: *You have any number of poems—specifically, say,* SHARK MEAT, *which seem to pull everything together; in fact the very ending of* SHARK MEAT *speculates that this shark has crisscrossed and has been here before and has now come back to be with us. Is that something like that healing process? Is that what you had in mind in that poem?*

A: In that poem, yes, on not so intense a level. I find it always exciting to me, beautiful, to experience the interdependencies of things, the complex webs and networks by which everything moves, which I think are the most beautiful awarenesses that we can have of ourselves and of our planet. Let me quote something:

> The Buddha once said, Bigshoes, if you can understand
> this blade of rice, you can understand the laws of
> interdependence and origination. If you can understand
> the laws of interdependence and origination, you can
> understand the Dharma. If you understand the Dharma,
> you know the Buddha.

And again, that's one of the worlds that poetry has taken, is these networks, these laws of interdependence—which are not exactly the laws that science points out. They are—although they are related —but imagination, intuition, vision clarify them, manifest them in certain ways—and to be able to transmit that to others is to transmit a certain quality of truth about the world.

Q: *There are times when what you've been writing has been what would obviously be called* poetry, *and other times you convey that in what would ordinarily be called* prose—*would you try to explore the border between poetry and prose in your expression, or would you regard those as two separate things?*

A: You are thinking of the essays in EARTH HOUSE HOLD?

Q: EARTH HOUSE HOLD *and* BACK COUNTRY. WHY TRIBE, *for example, is something like that.*

A: Well, BACK COUNTRY, I guess, is really all poetry, to my notion, and EARTH HOUSE HOLD is all prose, to my notion. But it's a thin line sometimes. The first difference is that (this is me speaking of my own sense of my own prose) that what I call prose does not have the musical phrase or the rhythm behind it. Nor does it have the content density or the complexity, although the complexity of some of the writing in EARTH HOUSE HOLD is fairly—it is fairly complex sometimes. I don't really think of them as different so much as—I adopt whatever structure seems to be necessary to the communication in mind. And I try to keep a clear line between, say, notebook journals, journal jottings and poems—and again, the real line is in the music and the density—although again, to be fair, not all my poems are necessarily that dense in terms of content analysis, but have maybe a musical density sometimes.

What I might add to that is this: I seem to write—to myself, I seem to write very different poems that—all of the poems that are most interesting to me are different from each other, almost all of them. And I see them almost as different, each one a different form and a different strategy for dealing with a different impulse, and different communication.

Q: *What brings about some of these different impulses? Are these environmental factors, indoor or outdoor, hot, cold, whatever?*

A: Hmm. In part that. In part—the major environmental influence is the work at hand. I feel very close to the rhythms of work, and the rhythms of whatever my work is, which is sometimes—I do a lot of work with my hands. Sometimes it's carpentry, sometimes it's gardening, sometimes it's logging, sometimes it's firewood cutting, sometimes it's trucking, sometimes it's working on cars—a lot of variety—sometimes it's skinning poles, and like this summer, I got into mostly fencing. I was doing fencing most of the summer. I don't know if any poems will come from that yet.

There's another level—in the longer loop—like, we've been talking about short loops now—but in the longer loop I have some concerns that I'm continually investigating that tie together biology, mysticism, prehistory, general systems theory, and my investigations in these things cause me to hit different new centers in interrelationships, different interstices in those networks of ideas and feelings, and when I hit those interstices, sometimes a poem comes out of there, and that's a different place. Each one of them is a different face, many-faceted, of whatever it is I'm trying to work around.

Q: *The ones you've just described seem to be intellectual, as opposed to emotional concerns.*

A: Yes. Those are emotional-intellectual concerns! Again, they shade off. Like, it's the sanctity or the sacredness of all sentient beings

277

as an emotional concern. The richness and the diversity of all sentient beings and the necessity for the survival of the gene pool for this to continue to be interesting is a biological concern. They shade over into each other.

Q: *You were talking a couple of minutes ago about activities like logging and pole-skinning—well, you have come to the NYQ office by subway. You're giving a poetry reading at the 92nd Street Y tonight. How can you reconcile—how do you manage to put this all together—staying close to what presumably are the sources of your inspiration, like the back country, like these activities, with what a poet has got to do, giving readings and bothering with publishers and being interviewed like this?*

A: Well, I don't find it particularly contradictory, but then contradictions don't bother me. Giving poetry readings is part of my work, because the poem lives in the voice, and I do it not just for money, although that certainly is a consideration, but because I feel this is where I get to try my poems out and I get to share a little bit of what my sense of the music of them is with others. And I wouldn't feel right if I didn't do that. The poem has to be sung once in a while. To travel around the country is a pleasant luxury, which may not be possible much longer as the whole transportation system gets increasingly fucked up, but as long as it's possible, I'll indulge myself in it and what I gain from that is keeping in touch with the whole amazing network of American intellectual life and seeing many levels of things happening all the time, which I have no objection to seeing, you know. That's part of one's education and keeping one's level of awareness up. Living in the country for me is not a retreat, it's simply placing myself at a different point in the net, a different place in the network, which does not mean that I'm any less interested in the totality of the network, it's simply that's where I center myself.

Q: *If you lived in the city, do you think you would write very differently from the way you write?*

A: Probably not too differently, especially as I'm learning to see cities as natural objects. I'm getting better able to see what is natural and what is musical.

Q: *You're stressing finding your own voice, your own identity. Does it help? Has it helped you? Would you recommend that others study with other poets?*

A: Yes. I feel very strongly that poetry also exists as part of a tradition, and is not simply a matter of only private and personal vision. Although sometimes something very remarkable comes out of that kind of spontaneous and sort of tutored singing. There are several things that are more universal that we must tap into before personal utterances can become truly poems. One level is the very level of the language and its tradition of songs. We are immediately tied into a tradition by the very fact that we are dealing with the language, and the language is something with an enormous amount of history embedded in it—cultural history.

I feel that one should learn everything about poetry, that he should read everything that he can get his hands on, first from his own tradition and then from every other tradition that he has access to, to know *what* has been done, and to see *how* it has been done. That in a sense is true craft: that one learns by seeing what the techniques of construction were from the past and saves himself the trouble of having to repeat things that others have done that need not be done again. And then also he knows when he writes a poem that has never been written before. I feel that I have written several poems that have never been written before, to my knowledge—one on the conception of a child, another on the child of the moon, and several other things that are apparently unique.

I like to extend it out into other traditions for the very reason that we now are becoming totally cosmopolitan—we might as well do it. For me it's the Chinese tradition and the tradition of Indian vernacular poetry, and also classical Sanscrit poetry of India that I learned most from.

What parallels that is the inner level of universality which is in a sense the collective unconscious that belongs to more than your private self. When you touch on those deeply archetypal things in yourself and at the same time are in touch with what the generations before you have done with the same kind of impulses and the same depths of the mind, then you're able to steer a course with your own voice that will be a new creation, it seems to me. Without that drawing the cross between the personal unconscious to the collective unconscious and one's personal use of language into the collective use of language, you remain simply private. And poetry to be poetry has to speak from a deeper place than the private individual.

Q: *One thing you've done are translations.* Cold Mountain Poems. *Would you suggest to poets that they get into a fair amount of translating that way?*

A: I'm not sure I would. Translation is too tempting, and I think as an exercise it's good, but it takes you away from yourself finally, from

279

your own work. I think that too many poets take up translating —well, I shouldn't say this. *Some* poets take up translating because they seem to have run out of water in their own well. And maybe they should just keep digging at their own well instead of going over and borrowing it from somebody else's, which is what it seems to be.

Now the way I did the Han-shan translations was very much like what I described earlier. I stumbled on it, you know, that you could read what the Chinese said and then visualize what the Chinese, what the poem was, what the, quote, "poem" was, as Robert Duncan would say, the poem that's back there, and see that clear enough to then write down the poem in English directly, then look at the English and check it again against the Chinese and—to make sure that they really weren't too out of line.

Q: *Do you make it a practice to meet with other poets, poets who have either an affinity for the kind of content, or the kind of resource—like Jerome Rothenberg, for example—do you make it a point to meet with a lot of people that way?*

A: No, I don't make a point of it. One needs a lot of solitude, a lot of silence, to work. I met a lot of poets in the '50s, and we nourished each other in a grand way. We needed each other and we became a small, quote, "culture," warm and moist and nourishing—and we grew out of that.

That was a particularly deep culture of San Francisco for me at that time, and my contact with, first of all, Kenneth Rexroth, my teacher of Chinese poetry, Ch'en Shih-hsiang, Philip Whalen, Lou Welch, Michael McClure, Philip Lamantia, Robert Duncan, and other poets of that time—

Q: *No women?*

A: Not right then. There weren't any that were part of the, quote, "culture," that was nourishing itself—not as writers, no, that I can recollect. Diane Wakoski a little later, a year or two later. Diane was a very young barefoot girl in San Francisco then, and she began writing, and a little bit later Joanne Kyger came into that, and she's still writing poetry. She and I were married for a while.

But I'm thinking of that initial period. There was indeed a great need for each other, and I have much gratitude for that. *Now*, to the contrary, I think that poets perhaps place too much importance—and writers in general—on seeing each other, meeting each other, talking with each other, going to each other's house, going back to the other person's house, and then saying, "When shall I see you again," "Well, let's meet again Wednesday," and then doing it again on Wednesday.

Poetry is not a social life. Nor is it a career. It's a vocation. To be a careerist and to make a social life out of poetry is to waste the best of your opportunities, probably, for doing your work.

Q: *In addition to the poets that you mentioned that you've been close to and are still close to, would you say there are some others who have influenced you in some way?*

A: Well, I see a line, a very faint line or thread running through (we'll just leave it in the English language and English poetry)—that I feel intuitively I belong to, and that's a line that I will say—I will just start with Blake, although it goes back earlier than that—I find it in Yeats, I find it in a very special way in Pound, in the poetry of D. H. Lawrence, (I'm just sketching out main things now)—in another way in Whitman, and another way in Jeffers. Those are the men who have probably been most immediately important to me as a poet, outside of contemporaries.

Q: *Is there something that a poet can gain from formal education?*

A: Undoubtedly. How to use a library! And more than that —well, how to use a library, how to look up the professional journals and get the gossip about a particular field!

Furthermore, a poet need not be in English Literature. He can be in any field, obviously. There are, of course, many orders of education —but, yes, for the time being, a formal education can be and should be a transmission of the morals of the tribe, and one would hope to get that.

What people probably need is more education in how to educate themselves, how to discriminate between what is worth giving time to, reading and studying, and what is perhaps not worth the time. In that sense I think the Universities are wasteful of our energies, because they themselves have not discriminated an intelligent way for weaving through the overload of information that everyone is presented with now. This is a problem that we all recognize: the information overload.

Q: *Most of us who write poetry have to find a career doing some other kind of thing in order to stay alive. Any suggestions as to what some of these might be?*

A: Get a trade! Get two trades! Or, get a Ph.D.! You got no choice.

Q: *You don't teach?*

A: No. I have taught. I taught a year once. And I like to teach.

Q: *You did like it?*

A: Oh yes, except you have to talk too much! It's such a verbal activity, teaching at universities; it depends so much on language, just speech. Although it's getting better now. People feel forward enough to have silence in class sometimes, and undertake non-verbal or only semi-verbal ways of teaching sometimes—experiential ways of teaching. There's something very good that's happening.

Q: *Do you ever use words purely for the sound, the music, independent of the meaning of the word?*

A: No. I like to think there is a merger of the sound and the meaning in some of the poems I have written. I try to steer a middle path in that.

Q: *How about rhyme?*

A: I use internal rhyme fairly frequently.

Q: *Would you say that it just happens?*

A: It just happens, yes.

Q: *We got a note a few months ago from Charles Bukowski, who said that craft interviews remind him of people polishing mahogany. Do you have some response to that?*

A: I like to polish mahogany! I like to shorten my chainsaw. I like to keep all my knives sharp. I like to change oil in the truck.

Creativity and maintenance go hand in hand. And in a mature ego system, as much energy goes to maintenance as goes to creativity. Maturity, sanity and diversity go together, and with that goes stability. I would wish that we could in time emerge from traumatized social situations and have six or seven hundred years of relative stability and peace. Then look at the kind of poetry we could write! Creativity is not at its best when it's a by-product of turbulence.

The great Zen masters, the great Chinese poets, some of the great landscape painters, and some of the great Buddhist philosophers, were all contemporaries over just a few centuries in the T'ang Dynasty. The whole power that comes out of that is the power of men who have achieved sanity of a working sort in a society which has a working peace, and then have said, "Now where do we go from here?" When we get to the top of the hundred-foot pole, keep going!

There are some equivalent things you can see in India, although India has a more turbulent history than China, I think. And finally, I intuit it as being the case, dialectically the case, so to speak.

Q: *Would you say that a religious outlook is indispensable for the poet, for poetic creativity?*

A: Not as such. I would say more, but the religious outlook would take us into a lot of tedious definitions. Spiritual curiosity, yes. Spiritual and psychological and personal curiosity. Curiosity about the world—yes, of course. Curiosity about consciousness, primarily, which is what you begin to be able to do when you sing.

Q: *Do you think of your audience when you write?*

A: Sure, I think of it more as my friends, family, community, my face-to-face social network. I don't abstract my audience outside of what I see face to face. Now that comes to include many people around America whom I've seen face to face. I have a sense of who they are and—yes, I write to them. Sometimes at them, sometimes slightly over, but at least with them in mind.

Q: *You said at one point that you felt you needed a great deal of solitude to write—*

A: Not just to write, to live.

Q: *Are you a seasonal poet? Do you write more in the fall than in the spring?*

A: Well, the way I live right now, I guess I probably write more in the winter. Because in the spring I go out in the desert for a while, and I give a few readings, and then when I get back it's time to turn the ground over and start spring planting, and then right after that's done it's time to do the building that has to be done, and then when that's done, it's time to start cutting firewood, and then when the firewood's done, it's just about time to start picking apples and drying them, and that takes a couple of weeks to get as many apples as possible and dry them, and then at the end of the apple season—I also do some peaches then, and also begin to harvest the garden, and a lot of canning and drying is to do, and then when that season passes, I'm into chestnuts and picking up the wild grapes, and then

I've got to put the firewood in, and as soon as I get the firewood in, hunting season starts—that's about a week of work tanning hides, and that winds up about the end of October with Halloween festivities, and then I go East for a month to read. So December, January and February is my time of total isolation, writing; and I don't see anybody in those months.

Q: *When you say solitude, do you mean literally alone?*

A: Well, no, my family is with me. It's also during those months that we're most cut off, no electricity anywhere, no phone; the roads get snowed in and you can't get to my place. So the actual reading and writing is part of a seasonal process for me now. Although, of course, if you can get a poem going any time of the year, you'll do it—but to concentrate on that deeply, to get a lot of reading done, is a winter three-month thing. I like that cycle. It's very creative for me actually, and I'm always thinking—

Q: *At the time you lived in Japan, did you have a similar cycle?*

A: It was geared entirely to the cycle of the Zen monastery. They have an annual cycle, and it was not unlike the present one, except there wasn't so much agricultural and outdoor work to do. It's like a farmer's cycle, that's all.

Q: *Do you have dry periods when you do not write?*

A: I did at one time, for three years almost.

Q: *Did you worry about it?*

A: Not particularly.

Q: *Did you do something about it?*

A: No.

Q: *What happened?*

A: Well, I was doing Zen studies, and that was taking all my psychic energy.

There's something about craft that we haven't touched on—I can't throw any light on it, really; I'd just like to suggest it as something to keep in mind, and that is: How do you go about—what kind of criterion do you employ, in feeling that a poem is well-crafted? How do I feel when I feel a poem is well-crafted? It's an extremely subtle thing, but part of it can be described in no other way than *taste*. There

Gary Snyder

is an intuitive aesthetic judgement that you can make that in part
spots phoniness, spots excess, spots the overblown, or the undersaid,
the unripe, or the overripe, and feels its way out to what seems just
right, and that balance is what I work for, just the right tone, just the
right balance, for the poem to do just what I wanted it to do. Or I
shouldn't phrase it that way—for the poem to be just what *it* wanted
to be. Then it takes on a life of its own, and it loses no energy in the
process.

Q: *How is your work evolving now? Where is it going?*

A: I'm still working, as I have for the last fifteen years, on one
central long interconnected work in progress, with small poems being
written peripheral to that.

Q: Mountains and Rivers Without End?

A: Right. Which is not an endless poem, it has an intention of
being ended. But there's a lot of still relatively intractable material
that I'm wrestling with, trying to punch it all up and drive it into the
corral, and it takes time, because they keep sneaking back and I miss
one—
Freedom and discipline—that's where I start from, the manifesta-
tion of that. And when I feel that I have it, I know it. And if I don't
have it—the difference is between life and death, or between a light
bulb that's on and a light bulb that's off. When it's on, it's touching
some kind of energy source, the power within, the power that Blake
calls delight, when he says "energy is eternal delight," and that's
what I'm trying to touch with my poems, is to get that light, and that
delight.

Q: *What advice would you give to young poets?*

A: First of all I would recommend to them not to lose faith in their
childhood dreams and turn away from them. Because between six
and twelve everyone is really brilliant, very mystical and very
perceptive. Then in the turbulence of adolescence and the pains of
growing up they generally lose faith in that and become a conformist.
So keep faith in your childhood dreams and don't worry about being
like everyone else.
The thing for teachers to do is teach them the most interesting
poetry in the English language. Show them how to read seventeenth
Century poetry for its erotic content. Let them read Christopher
Smart, and tell them he was crazy! Then you can lead them into

285

trying other poetry. It's worth it, even if there are only two or three poems you can get across to them, to give them something from the past:

> "'. . . Ozymandias, king of kings:
> Look on my works, ye Mighty, and despair!'"

—or even a little bit of Chaucer.

There are plenty of things in our tradition that will touch adolescents and give them some sense of *I can do this!*

20

Robert Penn Warren

Q: *About the physical conditions, do you work at a desk, in longhand or on a typewriter; is there any fixed schedule, and do you carry notebooks with you?*

A: Well, my wife and I both have had a sort of schedule for years—we both have to have a certain amount of solitude a day, and we meet at breakfast, maybe, and maybe not; and at 2:30 we rejoin for lunch. And in that period between—except during the time when she was getting children off to school (one has finished college now and one next year—that was a long time ago!)—we both hole up for the morning. We have studios out in the barn, at different ends of the barn, and take no telephone calls, and have that amount of time for ourselves, each of us. If something isn't screaming to be said, I may be reading or writing letters. Usually I write letters in the afternoon so it will not interfere with my working.

Q: *Can you say anything about the amount of revision you do? Given a poem that you're working on, how much revision does it go through?*

A: A great deal. It never stops. It stops when it gets—I publish 'em when I *think* they're done, as in magazines. And then always when the corrections come there's a vast deal of rewriting in the long period before the book comes out, before I get the proofs and suddenly get started over again. I reinspect things. And then the

287

proofs come—that's a matter of crisis!—you're doing it then for keeps, more or less. And so I persist in rewriting, just sitting around with the stuff. I've just gotten a new batch of proofs, unopened yet—I've got a book coming out in August—and so from now on until I get the proofs finished I'll be doing nothing but revising, sitting around with it and mulling it over.

But there's a great deal of rewriting and a great deal of *not* published stuff. There are many unfinished poems. I just put them into a bin or some big folders and put them away—everything from lines, five, six, seven or eight lines, or even whole poems. And take them out now and then and look at them, just as I'm idling. A good many poems that are now published in books have lain, say, to fifteen years in an unfinished condition.

Q: *You're known both as a poet and an extraordinary prose writer. In poetry there would be a question about whether something was narrative or lyrical. Do you feel a shift when you move over from a strongly narrative novel to poetry? Does it feel different?*

A: Well, it feels different, and the way of *doing* it is different. The actual process of composition is different. If you're writing a novel, you have all those pages to fill. I mean, you go to the typewriter every morning. And I do something every day. But with a poem most of the actual composition is not at a typewriter. I may be swimming. I swim a great deal, I walk a great deal. And when we're in the country, up in Vermont, I'm in the woods a great deal, or in the water. Anything like a long walk, lonely walks, nobody's listening, and you can compose in your head and you can talk it out.

Q: *Once you've done that, do you feel a desire to commit it to paper immediately?*

A: Yes, usually within a matter of hours or a matter of days, I begin to assemble this stuff and get it onto paper. Anything like running or swimming or walking where your body is busy but not occupied, and you have a flow of awful energy and are not distracted, or between waking and sleeping—I do a lot of composing then. I practically never compose on the typewriter.

Q: *Is there any other distinction between the composition of prose and the composition of poetry that strikes you as different?*

A: Well, there's a great deal in the planning. The planning of a novel takes a long time. I don't start writing until I've had a novel in my head for several years, the longest being twenty years. And talking about it—I tell the story to a taxi driver, or anybody who'll listen, you know. And it's composed largely in my head, or in conversation, before I start writing. And only once have I ever made a complete outline, which was almost paragraph by paragraph—but as soon as I started to write, I felt entrapped. It killed the sense of improvisation, and it killed the idea to have to follow an outline. I must have the novel worked out in my head and know the basic movements or scenes of the play, say four movements, or five or six movements, or whatever, have those clear in my head and know the point of each one in my head before I sit down. Then I put it on paper, on one sheet of paper: movement one, movement two, and then a scribble to get what it is.

Q: *But with poetry—*

A: Poetry is different. There may be a lot of scribbling, but it's lines that I get in the process, lines scribbled down on impulse. I may be walking across a room and scribble a line of a poem I'll write down.

Q: *Are you saying that with poetry there's less conscious awareness of where it's going?*

A: There's less conscious awareness of where it's going, that's quite definite.

Q: *Of course you've written narrative poetry—*

A: Yes, the narrative element in my poetry is very large. Things that are relatively short sometimes—the germ is very often narrative of a poem. And I have one book which first came out in 1953, called BROTHER TO DRAGONS, which started out as a novel, fooled around, started as a play version, and I didn't finish—and then I wrote it as a poem. That's had numerous editions since 1953. But for twenty years I've been rewriting it—in fact, it's completely rewritten! And it's coming out next February. That's a narrative poem based on the very gruesome story of the killing of a slave by Jefferson's nephews. Since that time there's been an historical book about it.

Strangely enough, I met at a party in Lexington a year or so ago a nice youngish man, of forty-two or forty-three—at this party, after I'd done a reading at the University there. And he came over and said, "I want to talk to you. You changed my life my accident," he said. "I'm a farmer—" He was a Dartmouth farmer. He was from Kentucky and had gone to Dartmouth and then come back and bought a lot of land, about fifteen hundred acres along the Ohio River between Paducah and Upper Paducah, some twelve, fifteen miles. And he said, "That land is the land—"

A place I know well! Because when I was writing this poem I went to the place very often and read the court records. There was no consecutive treatment of it at all. It was just as folklore when I first heard it. And then I went to see if I could find the court records, and I found the court records of the case, and all that was associated with the case and spent a lot of time in this little town of Smithland, Kentucky, which was on the River. It was like Hannibal, Missouri—it was just a forgotten little town on the river, more like Mark Twain's boyhood town than anything else, where the Cumberland runs into the Ohio. And the house, the great house that the Lewises built—the family with Jefferson's sister, the mother, you see. And there was a maniacal streak in the family, and the mother died, and the father went away. The father had failed in Virginia, and that's why they had come out there—and it's all tangled up with a lot of *mother* business, too—and one of the slaves broke the mother's favorite pitcher, and they chopped him to pieces on the meatblock in the meat house and burned him.

—And this man had read my book some years ago, and he says, "Well, I own the land!" He had just bought it. He says, "I'm a real farmer, a book farmer—I read a lot of books and studied hard in Dartmouth and so forth—but I have to drive a tractor, too, and my wife's a pretty good farmer. I got interested in this subject from your book, and I discovered from your book that I own the land where it happened, and so I spent ten years trying to learn everything about that community of the period and the Jefferson family before they settled in Virginia."

And it's a very elaborate historical study of it, a beautiful reconstruction of a community of that period.

Q: *You do a lot of research, then.*

A: *He* did; I didn't. I read the courthouse records, and that's all I wanted. They were all falling to pieces then with age and lack of attention in a very musty cellar in this little town, this courthouse.

Oh, I must tell you one thing. The jail was out near the courthouse, on account of the green—an old brick jail. You could push your finger through it, looked like; and there was one old drunk in there locked in—a hot summer afternoon, and there was a pump out on the green, an old-fashioned iron pump. And a little seven-year-old daughter was there keeping her father company, outside the jail. And she would play and talk to him, and now and then she'd go bring him a glass—a cup—of water, a tin cup of water, you see, from the pump. This old derelict in jail there, and this little girl taking care of him—I remember that very well.

But anyway, Mr. Merritt spent ten years there doing research on this community and on the event and on the Lewis family in Virginia—which had not been done. And it was published by the Princeton Press last year and created quite a sensation. It was very widely reviewed. But my version had been dramatized and done in New York and elsewhere and finally was on tour for a while, for a year, for one summer, and wound up at Boston in the fall of 1975. I'm reading it again, and over these years the things I didn't like about it as a poem I've gradually rewritten, so it's now almost completely rewritten. It's coming out next February. It's been through six, seven or eight editions before that.

Q: *You said you have a book coming out in August, and this one in February.*

A: Yes. Well, the book coming out in February is the narrative poem. That's the work that took twenty years in revision and rewriting—and changes of organization, actually. And the other book in August is another book of poems, new poems, poems written in the last year and a half. Of course my last book before that was my SELECTED POEMS running from 1923 to 1976. That came out in January of 1977.

Q: *You use dreams a lot in writing your books—*

A: I don't use them; they use me!

Q: *Do you ever do as Auden did with his SEPTEMBER 1, 1939 —a poem he denied completely because he decided he didn't like it anymore—do you ever deny any of your earlier work?*

A: Well, a lot of times I just never publish. I put them in the bin. A lot of poems I never publish. I couldn't finish a short poem for ten years, between 1944 and 1954—I didn't finish a single short poem. I wrote some novels in that period, a couple I guess. Yes, I believe I did, a couple. But I couldn't finish a short poem. I have since gone back and drawn out fragments from that accumulation of stuff that started out to be poems, and I have turned them into poems, so the germ has survived. But for ten years I simply couldn't write —couldn't finish a poem.

Q: *What do you do about dry periods? Does it worry you? Do you do anything about it?*

A: I don't do anything about it, no. I read a book or take a walk or climb a mountain or do something. I don't take it too hard. I was very busy in that period. Then my whole life changed; I moved to Italy for a long period, and was living in an old castle, a sixteenth Century castle, with my wife and baby daughter. And as soon as I was living there, I began writing poems again almost automatically.

Q: *Do you think your origins in the South have influenced your work?*

A: It couldn't help but influence my work—and my play, and everything else, because you are what you are. This applies across the board to everybody; there's nothing special about that fact. But it's not a principle. I'll say this: all my fiction is about the South, because for fiction you have to know things at a very different level. You have to have a sort of *circumstantial* knowledge of things. And the South is full of tales, many of them ready-made for you, asking to be made into novels. And I've never written any fiction, except one story, that wasn't laid in the South. But the poetry has been—it's much more immediate and personal, so I have many poems about Vermont, with a Vermont setting, because we spend a lot of time in Vermont—my family are skiiers. (I'm not; I'm a snowshoe-er, if anything!) But I like the outdoors and we live in the woods there. The question of the poem—poems connected with places belong to Italy or even Greece, a lot of Vermont, a lot of Connecticut, as well as the South. Poems have no automatic place. I can't conceive of myself writing a piece of fiction that wasn't laid in the South.

Q: *Recently you said the difference between 1910 and 1920 was that when finally Eliot came, people in this country were reading Baudelaire and reading poets that in 1910 they had no awareness of—*

A: When I was in college in the '20s, it was just after the return of the Americans—the Army—from Europe, and many of my teachers were European-trained. Several were at Oxford. And it was a place where there was a real, almost general interest in poetry, where an old Southern fullback would be a poet (though he kept that pretty much a secret—until his brother turned him in!)—but poetry was a very active thing then, not as organized, not as taught—there were no courses in it, but it was just simply a spontaneous thing among a lot of people who were connected with each other.

That was a strange period of this widespread interest in poetry and the writing of poetry. In fact, everybody I knew had read all THE WASTELAND before it got in book form. They knew it from the magazine. Now this was not true of all the *professors*, mind you. There were some who took no interest at all. This was primarily an *undergraduate* interest. And that continued for quite a while.

Now Randall Jarrell was a student of mine at Vanderbilt. That's another generation, you see. That was my second year of teaching, and he was in his freshman year. I had him in a couple of classes there. And Randall was a most remarkable man, an extraordinary boy, and he was writing some of his best poetry by his sophomore year at Vanderbilt, some of his very best poetry then, for he never beat it. And he was, by the time he was a sophomore, in his sophomore year, he said, "Red, I don't think I'll major in English." And I said, "Well, yes?" And he said, "I've read all the English literature worth reading, I think,"—and he *had*, probably. And he said, "French, too. I don't think I'll take French, 'cause I think I've read all I want to read. I think I'll major in psychology." Which he did. But this didn't stop the flow of poetry; he kept on writing.

Q: *The book* UNDERSTANDING POETRY *is probably the most successful textbook, the most universally used during the period, and it seems to have gone hand in hand with what the average person would think of as the New Criticism.*

A: Well, there's some reason for that, and part of it is libel!

Q: *Do you mean that in some hands the text might have been misused or misdirected?*

A: Well, I wasn't thinking of that. What I was thinking of is that when the book was written, it was written by a kind of accident. That is, Cleanth Brooks and I had been friends as students at Vanderbilt, then we had been together at Oxford, and then we had been together teaching at Louisiana. It was an old friendship; it went back to early boyhood. We were both interested in poetry, though he never wrote but one poem that I know of. He lived with poetry all the time; he was crazy about it. He was also deeply interested in the theoretical side of it, more than I was. But I was also interested in that side of it. And we pooled our poetry notes on poetry courses we gave at Louisiana.

They were different kinds of courses, but they were both poetry. We were great friends, so we saw each other and talked a lot. The University asked us to do a little mimeographed booklet for use in teaching poetry to sophomores. Which we did. It was just mimeographed. That was then used—this was a big place, you see—it was used in many classes. And we kept expanding it for our own purposes, because it was only a reduction, anyway, of what we did. And then the University Press said they would publish a book which involved both prose and poetry if we would write it, chiefly from our notes, from what we did in class. And then they published this as a regular book, which was used then by all sophomores, you see, in the university, sold to the sophomores.

Now this publishing it was not our idea. But then a publisher came through, on a visit, you know, making his rounds; and he saw a copy of the book lying on the desk of our office. He looked at it for half an hour, and said, "How in God's name did this get done by a University Press?!" This was Crofts–Crofts Company, which became Appleton Century Crofts, and has now been bought by Prentice-Hall. He said, "I'll go buy it from them." And he crossed the hall, where their offices were, and came back in half an hour and said, "Well, I've bought it!" And he published several editions, and then Appleton-Century published several editions, and there was one just recently out.

There were two books, you see. One was called APPROACH TO LITERATURE, which had poetry in it, done the same way, and prose, too. That's the one he took, and just had its sixth edition out now, I think. A few weeks later another publisher came by and saw a stack of mimeographed stuff on poetry on the desk, and *he* looked at it, and he said, "Look, if you'll put this into the shape of a book, we'll take it at Holt." And so we did. And the first edition of UNDERSTANDING POETRY was published by Holt. But there's a cross between the poetry—the work it used was the same in both those books. And the fourth edition of that's just recently out.

Q: *The question is obvious. What we're talking about is the* composition *of poetry; what you're talking a great deal about is what might be called the* non-cognitive *approach to poetry—the intuition and dream-states and fever-dreams—*

A: Well, I think that once the poem exists as an artifact, then the question is *What do you make of it?* And these books are about what you make of literature when you face it.

294

Robert Penn Warren

Q: *In criticism and in teaching—in the work of some of the New Critics—Mr. Ransom and Mr. Winters and Mr. Tate, where this would sometimes seem to go over into the composition of poetry, where we would think of poetry as a very rational and conceived thing—*

A: Well, I knew them both very well; they're two of my closest friends.

Q: *That's Mr. Tate and Mr. Ransom—*

A: Ransom was my freshman English teacher, and he's the first *poet* I ever knew. He had published books of poems, you see! It was very remarkable to see a live one! He once forgot and left his toothbrush in his pocket in the morning! His was like a second home to me, really; I spent a great deal of time with that family over the years. A remarkable man. Tate and I—he was much younger, he was only six years older than I—

Q: *And Mr. Winters—*

A: I knew him, but I didn't know him well. I've been to see him quite often in California when I was at Berkeley. He was down at Stanford. But I had no great sympathy with his views of poetry.

Q: *Did you yourself take an interest in the different aesthetic, theoretical controversies that were going on during the period?*

A: I followed them, I followed them. But Winters meant nothing to me, except for the fact that I like his *poetry* very much. But Winters was a *moralist*, a strict moralist, and I didn't see that as being an essential. He would lecture me on this very frequently.

Q: *Today, is it your impression that what had been current during the New Criticism, which was a lot of aesthetic discussion and disputes sometimes—*

A: Quite often disputes!

Q: *But today there does not seem to be so much of even interest in aesthetics in contemporary poetry.*

A: Well, I wouldn't know how it would compare. But there was a sense of a whole new view of poetry which belonged to the younger generation then, which was *not* like what you found in the universities in the ordinary faculty, where poetry was taught primarily from a straight *historical* view, and a *biographical* view, and you might say a *moralistic* view—and that was the way it was taught primarily when I was a student.

Q: *Now here we're talking about the artifact, the poem that is finished —this has nothing to do with how it comes into being—*

A: Certainly. No, the poem is made. It *is* in itself. I should say that the poem is a symbolic artifact. It involves human experience, it's a symbol for human experience—but it's a symbol according to the law of its medium. It's a verbal symbol, which has verbal emotional effects because of its form. *Because* of its form. And it's related to human experience directly. And therefore in the widest sense of the word *moral*, it's moral in the way that all human activity is moral.

Q: *Winters once said, "Poetry is the rational statement of human experience."*

A: He said that, period.

Q: *That was dogmatic.*

A: He said that, period. I would say that's the starting point, not the end. Winters took this view: He found a moral equivalent between rigorous meters and moral statements. I would say that's totally wild nonsense. I agree with Delmore Schwartz, who attacked him on that, about a thousand years ago, when Delmore said, "Well, in that case, what do you make of the PSALMS?! They're not rigorously metrical!" He said, "You're talking about *English* poetry, and that's all you're talking about. You're not talking about *poetry!*"

Q: *Nor have we had any critic in the last two decades who's been interested in a definitional approach.*

A: A definitional approach, no. It was a by-product, as you say, of interest. It was not aesthetic, it was a sense of trying to see, to understand, its definition as a part of understanding its meaning and its origin. Certainly Brooks and I had no sense of belonging to a school. We belonged to a *generation*, or two generations that overlapped there—because this goes back to an older generation than we belonged to. Richards, you see, and Eliot, belonged to another generation. But also we were both soaked in Coleridge. That lies behind Richards, quite obviously. It wasn't just "pick me up some pieces." We had some soaking in the standard history of criticism. So we had some little modest background in that world, too. So we could recognize its relation to this, and saw how parochial, or how limited what we had been getting in classroom was. And this was general. We've known a lot of people of our generation who felt they had been shortchanged in literature courses—by these terrible courses, because they did not deal with the nature of literature as literature. Many people felt that.

Q: *At the height of the disputes and the theories, and so forth, of course there was the* KENYON REVIEW *and many other magazines publishing articles and essays. There don't seem to be so many magazines today devoted to the criticism of poetry.*

A: No, not as many—THE SOUTHERN REVIEW and SEWANEE—

Q: *As if there is no longer a need or desire for that sort of thing?*

A: Well, there wasn't an audience for it. Now it's become more academicised.

Q: *In what sense?*

A: Well, I mean, the people, say, at Yale—the people interested in poetry at Yale are mostly much more academic than the people were a generation back.

Q: *In an earlier edition of* UNDERSTANDING POETRY *there's a marvelously detailed analysis of the rhythm of Yeats' poem* SPEECH AFTER LONG SILENCE—*did you do that, or did Brooks do it?*

A: Well, we did that book, actually, as a collaboration. We sat side by side; we talked these poems out together—there would always be long conversations first. And then we'd sit side by side, one at the typewriter, and as we'd talk it out, we'd type something down. So it's practically impossible now for us to sort out with any certainty who said what. Because it was really a collaboration. Now later on in revision we have no doubt separated things out a little bit.

Q: *You've mentioned some of the poets you're interested in. Who are some of the other poets who have influenced you, or are there any influences?*

A: Oh, well, lots of them! There are so many—you know, people say this or say that, but they are always lying because they never make it big enough! They don't know they're lying. But I know I'd be lying if I gave two names or three names. But I can sort out people who have had a great effect on me. But you change. There's a right time for certain kinds of influences, and a wrong time for them. Now I think for a man seventy years old to be influenced by Housman,

297

there'd be something wrong with him! But when I was seventeen it was the right time for it—or eighteen. But speaking of continuity—Thomas Hardy was a great continuity, from the first time I read him until now. I read him constantly, and in many different ways—I don't try to write the same kind of poetry. I know exactly how I felt about his early poetry. He was writing about a world he knew, also a rather rural world. He was making poetry out of his observable life, and that *fact* was important.

The same thing was true when I read the first book of Ransom's when I was a freshman. He was making poetry out of a world I could look out the window and see. That brought it home to me. I never tried to imitate Ransom; I never took him as a model, except I took him as a model human being in many ways 'cause he was one of the most impressive men I ever knew. But my poetry has very little in common with his. Though I admire it greatly, but I mean it's not a direct influence anyway. But I'm sure his general influence of *thought* was very *great*, you see. I mean, he's one of the important poets of the century, I think. I think he will survive.

Q: *Have you observed any of the work of some of the Rock Poets, the work of people like Bob Dylan?*

A: I've observed it, and I never saw anything written by Bob Dylan I thought was a poem worth remembering. And I decided he's something, but I—it isn't the kind of thing I'd just sort of go out and hunt for and try to "take to the Lord in prayer!"

Q: *You introduced Mr. Eliot at the last reading that he gave in this country, in New York at the YM-YWHA Poetry Center.*

A: Yes, yes—

Q: *And you introduced him as "our age's dearest enemy," or "the dearest enemy of our age." In terms of the stance that a poet has towards his time, does the value that Eliot and some other poets have for us, come out of their stance of opposition or staying outside and writing* about *something?*

A: Perhaps. I still think I was struck by him, as I knew everybody was at that time, and I still admire him greatly. My friend Mark Strand absolutely forbids his students to read Eliot; he really just loathes him! I think Mark is crazy for it. In no sense do I feel any basic sympathy with Eliot, though I admire him enormously and still think he was a poet of the first order, too. He was one of the makers of this century, no question about it. I feel the same way about Pound. But I never felt as close to them as I felt to Blake or Hardy.

21

Karl Shapiro

Q: *Where do you write? In what atmosphere?*
   Do you write in the sun? In a sort of neutral trance?

A: I have a lot of sun poems, almost no moon.
   In my poems bombs fall from the moon.
   I've always written in the sun when possible,
   Moved to the sun, worked in it.
   I'm writing this in the sun, on an atrium
   In the far west where I dream to be and am.
   This tends to sunniness, not a popular thing.
   I started in the sticky Baltimore sun,
   Moved to the west New Guinea sun in war,
   Poems from the weak Connecticut sun,
   Greasy Chicago sun, thicker Nebraska sun,
   Eventually to this no-nonsense staring sun,
   No sun for painters. I sit with a flyswatter.
   Let's say I like to write in a sweat.
   I'm working on a "major" Milton poem,
   It's about light, his holy light
   Which when it went out his poetry blazed.
   Night was never my time, nor dreams.
   I've written only one aubade, and that
   Was when my wife and I were in hiding.

Q: *Do you write drafts in notebooks?*

A: Bits and pieces, pieces and bits,
Scraps of paper, anytime, anywhere,
Ring-binders, spring-binders,
Well-bound account books,
Mostly lost or mostly sold,
Or deposited, as we librarians say.
Your question implies that I don't compose
On the typewriter. You are right.
I'm suspicious of typewriter poets.
Typewriters are for prose.

Q: *What do you have to say about revision?*

A: I'd rather call it bungling. Beethoven
Called himself Beethoven the bungler.
No comparison intended but everybody knows
That the creative process doesn't change.
The only difference is time, pace;
Some bungle faster than others.
With me the pace is unpredictable.
I recently finished a thirty-line poem
Which has to have a thousand changes
And still isn't finished, but the end's in sight.
The sad thing about students is
They don't know how to revise,
They don't know what or where or why to revise;
They don't know the goal of the poem;
They don't know how to bungle.

Q: *You're one of the first Creative Writing teachers,*
You haven't stopped for thirty years.
How does it look to you now?

A: In the beginning Creative Writing
Was an academic stepchild.
Now it's the bully of the Humanities.
But what do you expect? Poets, like people in love,
Always behave badly, except on occasion;
And generally speaking, poets teach badly.
Creative writing classes are the pits,
Yet by some osmotic-symbiotic-

Empathetic catalysis people learn,
At least the two percent with talent learn.
The others do their spontaneous thing,
Surrealism as a rule.
The worst start all their poems with *I*
And end with *me*. And nobody reads.
How did they get this far? Who let them in?
Are these rooms holding-pens?
What made these mindless egos?
See how they jog! See how they run!
See their egos bouncing toward the cliff!

Q: *Are you going back to rules? To rhyme!*

A: Rhyme is metaphor for prosody,
Rhyme is techne, skill, the rules,
The rules of art itself. An adversary
Poetic teaches cacophony
Before melody, melody as parody.
But rules aren't in the sky,
Rules are made by masters,
Rules live in masterpieces.
Get them to read the masters, let them
Learn some humility for art;
Let them copy, let them imitate,
Memorize models, learn languages,
Above all master their own. Sounds stuffy.
Depends on whose ox is being gored;
This way—back to the drawing-board.

Q: *You've written so much criticism,*
You tackle great and small. Is this
An obligation of the poet?

A: Criticism is a bastard art,
Very seductive; it can break your heart.
I got the vice early, never gave it up;
Early I discovered most poets are chicken
And only whisper opinions. They hold their tongues
And connive for position. Maybe they're right.
I once sent T.S. Eliot, whom I knew,
A copy of my POEMS OF A JEW:

He never acknowledged it. Later,
I tackled Eliot's racial-Christian views,
Pound's nazism, Yeats' priestcraft.
But for every meat-ax essay I wrote two
To praise old masters and new.
By choice and situation I've stayed free
Of poetry lobbies, schools and gangs
To sound off and have paid the price
Sometimes, but can't really complain.

Q: *You still ride shotgun on the craft*
    And talk about the downhill speed
    Of American poetry which, as you put it,
    Plunged out of the classics,
    Out of the modern masters,
    Out of all standards, into the playpen,
    The buccal-fecal carnival, you call it,
    Alienates, nihilists, disaffiliates . . .

A: There's as much good poetry as there ever was,
    And that's never much, but there's much more bad.
    There's more bad poetry in the twentieth century
    Than in all the other nineteen combined,
    But bad will never drive out good.
    Maybe I mean the Creative Carnival,
    Officialization of the less-than-talented,
    Substitution of Life Style for art,
    Welfare Poetry by Welfare Poets,
    Refugees from the Sixties.

Q: *Is it only poetry? How about painting,*
    Psychiatry, politics, university?

A: I hate to think that those millenialists
    Were right, and it's too trashy to believe
    That poets are prophets, but look around
    At all the vulgarity we wallow in,
    Quacks, meditators, seekers of self.
    When amateurs no longer know
    They're amateurs, arrogance usurps
    Value and reputation, language itself.
    Nuance and color turn to mud.
    Pollution is in art as well as nature,

In poetry and in lakes,
In painting and in clouds and streams,
In government and in sex,
Especially in architecture and psychiatry;
The university is at mud-tide,
Creative writing in the ooze;
There are millions of rules and no rule,
Millions of laws and no law.

Q: *What's legitimate? Who's to say?*

A: Poets aren't legislators, that's for sure,
Acknowledged or unacknowledged.
Good poetry gives man pause,
Exemplifies the quest, suggests a goal;
Great art legitimizes man.
Bad poets build soapboxes.

Q: *You write that Auden had no theory;*
Do you have a theory? Do most poets?

A: When we are young we theorize,
Old we philosophize. In-between poets,
"Mature" poets as they say,
Simply don't have time for that;
There's too much work to do.
Modern poetry is a forest of theory,
Theory thick as weeds and deep as smog.
It's a fine climate for critics now.

Q: *Do you think of yourself as poet-in-exile?*
You have a recent poem about that.
Are you an Eastern Establishment dropout?

A: I've never been either in or out
Of the Establishment. You'll think it's foolish
But I still don't know what Establishment means.
My exile poem is, well, Ovid,
Ovid as metaphor of moth and flame.
A poet that close to the seat of power
Is a sitting duck or burning moth.
Princes and presidents who harbor poets
Are up to no good. Poets see too much
And what they don't see they blab,

       Poetically, of course.
       My poem said, poet, stay out of the White House!

Q: *Your poems are full of social assessment,*
      Value judgments. Don't Ovid-poets
      Perform a social function?

A: One hopes opinion won't intrude
      Or at least not dominate. At least I pray
      Stupid Opinion won't steal the show.
      Let valuation bury itself
      Deep in the loam of the poem.
      Even a poet is a sum of his opinions
      But he hopes to have the decency
      Neither to hide them or wave them like a rag.
      Poetry of politics is the lowest form,
      Lower than doggerel. Doggerel is good,
      Makes no pretences, is dog poetry
      At home in its kennel. Respect doggerel
      But call it by name. Now poetry,
      Real poetry is situational.
      The poet, part of his world, is ordinary,
      Partakes, gives thanks, is critical
      But always at home, never an alien.
      Poet is patriot,
      Immigrant, and to make matters worse
      Believes in God with a capital gee.
      The essence of the situation is
      That poet's at home. To him the world.

Q: *You hang everything on substantive,*
      Person, place and thing, you worship noun.

A: What is more glittering than abstraction,
      Why do philosophers hate poetry,
      And aren't critics philosophers,
      Both always quoting it? Psychiatrists,
      Why do they hate art and artists?
      —Poetry couldn't care less.
      Poetry isn't at home in Russia.
      The objects, the particulars are all,
      What we materialists materialize.
      This is our creativity.

22
Amiri Baraka

Q: *Would you describe the physical conditions of your work—whether it's writing in longhand, and when you're on the move, do you carry notebooks with you? How does it go through the process from first impulse through notes to final form?*

A: I work in no real absolute pattern, I type most of the time, but occasionally with poetry I do it in longhand—that's usually because there's no other choice at the time.

Q: *Can you actually compose on the typewriter?*

A: Yeah, I can write on the typewriter, poetry, without much trouble, and actually I find that the typewriter helps, because I think poetry has to take into consideration the total movement of the world, the total motion of everything, scientific advance, social advance, it's sometimes very difficult to keep up with your thoughts when you're writing in longhand.

Q: *Is it different in kind when you're working on a play?*

A: With a play, I almost have to type it—there you're talking about more sustained writing, writing over a longer period, and so that would become a real chore, for me at least, writing in longhand. Essays, plays, prose, fiction, I usually have to write on the typewriter.

305

Q: *Can you work in notebooks, when you're on the move?*

A: Yes, I have a notebook, which I use for poetry, and for whatever kinds of ideas, various lists of things I have to do, but specifically, I try to deal with notes, notes for lectures, notes for an article or a play I'm going to do, or it can be notes for an actual poem.

Q: *You teach both writing and lecture courses? Is the energy it takes to teach a lecture course different from the energy it takes to write a poem?*

A: I'm used to lecturing, and I've taught a lot. For me the problem with teaching and writing is the problem of the time it takes you to prepare for a class, and in my case, I have to travel, and that's a specific hardship. I travel back and forth to Washington, D.C., and last year to New Haven, and that's really time-consuming.

Q: *Do you ever have dry periods?*

A: Yeah, Mine are usually from being discouraged about where to publish, because I don't have to tell you how few places there are to publish any writing, and for a writer like myself who has a certain political aura that a lot of people don't want to associate with, it gets difficult. If people were asking me to write plays, we're going to perform this, write it—or if people were asking me to write novels, I would be doing it. But I still manage to produce, at some kind of rate if not the one I'd like to.

Q: *Is there anything you do, when you're in a dry period, to try to get back on the track—do you ever do exercises or word games to challenge yourself?*

A: No, not really. Usually I read. Anytime I'm not doing a lot of writing, I try to do a lot of reading, because I usually find that sort of fuels the writing impulse.

Q: *You also have to read a lot of student manuscripts.*

A: Yeah, for the writing course I do. Writing courses are okay. I'd rather teach a literature course, then you have to prepare for it with the reading, and I need that, I like that.

Q: *What do you think is the value of writing workshops, and did you ever take one when you were younger?*

306

Amiri Baraka

A: Writing workshops generally give people some general ideas about what writing actually is, as opposed to what it is not. Also it provides them with some models, bibliographies, so they can actually begin to see some practitioners. And to look at some of their work and begin to criticize it, in the state that it's in, and give them encouragement, that's about it. I use Mao Tse Tung's YENAN FORUM ON ART AND LITERATURE, as my standard text for writing. Then I've been using Bertolt Brecht's article on socialist realism, Brecht on non-objective painting, Langston Hughes' manifesto, ARTIST AND THE RACIAL MOUNTAIN, Richard Wright's BLUEPRINT FOR NEGRO WRITING.

Q: *Had you yourself taken any workshops when you were younger?*

A: I did take a creative writing course, my senior year in high school, I guess that was the closest thing to it. I was writing short stories then, I guess influenced by Edgar Allan Poe and Stephen Crane, THE RED BADGE OF COURAGE. And science fiction and horror stories, for some reason, when I was a kid.

Q: *You can't gauge the importance of the students coming up against a model, not just poems, but a person as a model—as in one of your early poems, in which you describe the importance of Robert Duncan to you, not just as a poet but as a presence for you.*

A: I think young people like to see writers, especially they like to see people whose work they admire, and find out how their brains work, what their lives are all about, they really do become models. I think the fact that I was influenced by T.S. Eliot when I was in college, when I first started writing poetry seriously, is normal enough, given the fact that I was taught that in freshman year in college. But I think that after a while those kinds of purely literary models give way to models that we can use to draw parallels to our lives as well—unless we're just hopelessly bookish, hopelessly removed from reality.

Q: *You mention Eliot as an early influence—you had written in* HOW YOU SOUND: *"And all that means that I must be completely free to do just what I want, in a poem. 'All is permitted:' Ivan's crucial concept. There cannot be anything I must fit the poem into. Everything must be made to fit into the poem. There must not be any preconceived notion or design for what the poem ought to be. 'Who knows what a poem ought to sound like? until it's thar.' Says Charles Olson . . . & I follow closely with that. I'm not interested in writing sonnets, sestinas, or anything . . . Only poems. If the poem has*

307

got to be a sonnet (unlikely though) or whatever, it'll certainly let me know. The only 'recognizable tradition' a poet need follow is himself . . ."
Is that "recognizable tradition" you refer to, Eliot's insistence on tradition?

A: Yeah. Well not only Eliot's insistence, but what I took to be a whole school of academic poetry that I, like most people, was raised on.

Q: *Probably came out of Eliot.*

A: Yeah.—and reacted to. Certainly the 1950s, when I went to college and generally came to consciousness about poetry, the 1950s was a period of deep reaction in this country, and I think not only politically—McCarthyism and the Cold War and the whole attempt by this country to eliminate the ideas that had come out in the 1930s, complete with purges and inquisitions of artists. But it seemed to me then a strait jacket was placed on American poetry—the whole rise of the Southern Agrarians, and the so-called New Critics, and textual analysis as opposed to understanding the social context out of which literature arises. That's what I was rebelling against, as a kind of whole.

I think now about tradition, it is good to know history, and to know tradition, but we should look at that tradition critically, and we should use what we can use and dismiss what's inappropriate for our particular time. I don't think we can completely dismiss tradition because that's ahistorical and one-sided, but we can't be slaves to it either.

Q: *You're saying that a poem can't be made to fit into something, but that everything has to fit into the poem. In the Donald Allen* NEW AMERICAN POETRY *book (Grove), that statement goes right along with Creeley's saying "form is content" and Ginsberg saying "mind is shapely." That's almost a new aesthetic, and almost the first new aesthetic that's come along since the New Criticism. In fact, aside from these precepts from you, Creeley, Olson, Ginsberg, Dahlberg, there has been no other interest in aesthetics, as far as contemporary poetry goes.*

A: Well, it's a little particular. See, those folks you mention, and some other folks, like Frank O'Hara, I'd say the people from the so-called New York School. O'Hara, Koch, Ashbery—and the sort of Beat school of Ginsberg, Corso—the Black Mountain School of Creeley and Olson—as a sort of figure towering over that—and then the other west coast school like Snyder and Whalen—and some other folks—I think all these people formed a kind of popular front against what we took to be dead academic poetry à la Eliot and the New Critics. Later on, it became more and more obvious that within that popular front against the academy, there were contradictions and great gaps as well. That is, there was no monolothic agreement as to what was or what wasn't anything. We had sort of banded together loosely against what we thought was a deadening influence on American poetry. But I think there were further elaborations of those particular aesthetic statements. Certainly in the 1960s the whole Black poetry movement, though it seemed primarily political, its pro-nouncements on art had a definite aesthetic view. And I think that the whole question of the Afro-American poetry of the 1960s was related to the Beats and the projective verse in this way, that it also was in reaction against the academic idea with the added weight that it also had a political difference with it.

It could also be perceived as exclusivistic, that is, largely dealing with whites, largely middle class that is, the poetry establishment. And I think the aesthetics of the best poets of the '60s took a step further and made a poetry specifically germane to what the Black poets wanted to do, based on the kind of national consciousness developed in that period. The whole poetry reading thing, the whole question of including real life in the poetry, the speech of the people, had definitely been raised by Olson and Ginsberg and the rest.

Q: *If the earlier reaction against the dead academy poetry was a commonality, and you were all united against something, and if Ginsberg's* HOWL *was a witnessing against something but without programmatic action to it, it was simply a voice. In the 1960s, you wrote An Explanation of the Work in* BLACK MAGIC:

A: Sabotage meant I had come to see the superstructure of filth Americans call their way of life, and wanted to see it fall. To sabotage it, I thought maybe by talking bad and getting high, layin' out on the whole chorus. But TARGET STUDY is trying really to study, like bomber crews do the soon to be destroyed cities. . . .

Ginsberg had titled one of his books THE FALL OF AMERICA, *but this statement of yours seems to be more programmatic in a political sense than simply a voice reaction against something.*

A: See, that's where we began to find a contradiction in our own popular front in the 1960s. Given the dynamism of the civil rights movement and the Black liberation movement and Malcolm X's emergence, and the whole international situation as far as Africa and Cuba were concerned, my own poetry then became much more political. The book, THE DEAD LECTURER, was actually a great moan about, is politics relevant to poetry, and if not why not, and if so, why? And trying to get clear in my own mind as to my own position on it. But say Allen Ginsberg and some of the rest, although Allen has been the closest thing to an activist, but generally there was a great feeling that poetry should not be related to politics. And that's where I began to depart from that whole kind of anti-academic grouping.

Q: *In* THE DEAD LECTURER *you have this poem:*

> *Duncan*
> *told of dance. His poems*
> *full of what we called*
> *so long for you to be. A*
> *dance. And all his words*
> *ran out of it. That there*
> *was some bright elegance*
> *the sad meat of the body*
> *made. Some gesture, that*
> *if we became, for one blank moment,*
> *would turn us*
> *into creatures of rhythm.*
>
> *I want to be sung, I want*
> *all my bones and meat hummed*
> *against the thick floating*
> *winter sky. I want myself*
> *as dance. As what I am*
> *given love, or time, or space*
> *to feel myself . . .*

Is this dance primarily aesthetic, or is it extendable to a dance which can be seen in active political terms? The same dance, the same feeling of the body? That poem ends wanting to create a reader who "sits now/breathing on my words/ . . . One that will love me."

In politics, that love through poetry doesn't extend into the political area,

310

one isn't looking for love so much as for change. But the dance metaphor still stays?

A: It stays because dance, in Duncan's use of the term and certainly in my perception of it, dance was act. That is, to dance one had to act, to move to the music, to become the music of moving. And dance, in that particular thing, I perceived, I interpreted that way. So in THE DEAD LECTURER, that is sort of an urging of myself and everybody else that action finally is the principal form of human life, that we must be about. The dance, the doing, the acting, rather than just the thinking.

Q: *This would be simultaneous with your going into the theatre, and the action of the actor? So it's both theatrical and political.*

A: Yeah, meaning act, meaning finally political. Between the contradiction of thinking and doing, many people are hung up on the thinking, the Hamlet complex. What I perceived in Duncan was the idea of actually dance, move, act. And that, in political terms too, corresponded with my development, feeling that the doing was principal. If I wanted to talk about politics I had to become a political activist, I had to act.

Q: *How much do you feel there was true poetic communication during that period, and how much was seized on journalistically, lines such as, "Up against the wall, mother-fuckers" And, "Will the machine gunners please step forward." And even some of the reaction to plays like DUTCHMAN, taken as alarmist without full comprehension of what your meaning was?*

A: Well, I think you have to take the context of the times themselves. Say, that poem, WILL THE MACHINE GUNNERS PLEASE STEP FORWARD, that was written in the early 1960s, and actually that was written in a period of transition of myself thinking that I was a poet and had nothing to do with politics, until I began to see that only political action would change the world. And that's what that means, WILL THE MACHINE GUNNERS PLEASE STEP FORWARD. And ironically, that was written around the time I went to Cuba, just before I went to Cuba.

As far as DUTCHMAN was concerned, now you're talking about March of 1964, in February 1964 you had the opening of BLUES FOR MISTER CHARLIE in which James Baldwin, who comes into public life criticizing Richard Wright and Wright's social protest which was what the whole spirit of the 1950s was, to criticize the social protest of the 1930s. James Baldwin then reversed his whole position, to the extent that by 1964 in BLUES FOR MISTER CHARLIE he actually questioned the value of non-violence. I think it was after that that Jimmie had to go to Europe, because I think that the reaction from the various powers that be was decidedly negative.

My own play DUTCHMAN opens the next month, which then takes it a step further, that is, not the question of violence versus nonviolence, but also now the question of when will we be violent against this violence that is being done to us? August of that year, you had the Harlem Rebellions, and July of the next year you had the Watts rebellions. So in that context the ideas in the works are coming from the context of society itself. So it would be only natural for these critics representing the side that I'm attacking, it would only be natural for them to say whatever they had to say, to try to identify the work for what they thought it was, as dangerous, opposed to their particular world view. And I think that's what they were doing.

Q: *The "decidedly negative" reaction someone like Baldwin got, you certainly weren't immune to that yourself. How did that affect your own writing?*

A: Well, what it did, it actually made me much more dependent on the people themselves. Because once it became clear to me that I was going to be attacked, by the NEW YORK TIMES, and NEWSWEEK, and TIME Magazine, as being all these terrible things—"not only a bad man but a bad playwright"—it certainly altered my perspective. Because I understood the things I was saying to be true. That never shook me, whether it was true or not. It shook me that obviously they didn't want to hear it. So it made me then much more focused on the people, because about that time we went up to Harlem and opened the Black Arts Theatre, because it was clear, or it would have been clear if we had been well educated politically, that if you're going to attack something they're not going to support you. Quite to the contrary, they're going to try to attack you.

Q: *In 1970, you helped to found the Congress of Afrikan People. On December 27, 1974 in the NEW YORK TIMES, there is an interview with you, with a four-column banner headline,*

BARAKA ABANDONS "RACISM" AS INEFFECTIVE
AND SHIFTS TO "SCIENTIFIC SOCIALISM" OF MARX

Amiri Baraka

Now, there is only one other poet in this country that we can think of, who would make headlines in the NEW YORK TIMES for a philosophical shift in his political stance. That poet is T.S. Eliot—when he came out and said he was a loyalist, a conservative, and an anglo-catholic. What other poet can you think of, that we'd give two cents if they changed from Republican to Democrat?

A: By that time, I had been a cultural nationalist, a Black nationalist, since the mid-sixties, and had not only talked cultural nationalism but had helped create several organizations, mobilized people in this time to elect all these Black elected officials that they're now cursing —and I had been personally during that period a political activist, so that was said not only about the poet, but it was said about the political activist. Because they realized that since I was a nationalist, what they were trying to do was to confuse a lot of people who would read that article. Because that article was trying to say, okay, he's a Marxist so that any talk of the national liberation of Black people he thinks is racist, which of course is a distortion and a lie.

Q: *The interview says: " 'It is a narrow nationalism that says the white man is the enemy,' says the forty-year old Mr. Baraka."*

A: Absolutely, I mean I believe that, definitely.

Q: *We sense a relief on the part of the TIMES, that Baraka has shifted from racism to something a little more abstract.*

A: Sure, what they're trying to do is confuse Black folks and say, the only thing this is, is the abandoning of Black struggle for some kind of an abstract thing. That's the way that article has been used. That's why they had that headline, they were aiming it at Black activists, and the Black liberation movement, and only secondarily at the literary aspect of it.

Q: *The question we want to pursue is about Eliot, and the tandem of his poetic work together with his social and political opinions—whatever we may feel about those opinions; you seem to have been developing your social and political point of view simultaneously with your poetic work; we can think of no other American poet who has been so concerned to define himself aesthetically and politically. Just as T.S. Eliot did both simultaneously. The tension between his artistic identity and his sociopolitical identity.*

A: Even a man like Pound, you would have to say, was more of a political activist than Eliot was, Pound who trouped off to Italy and broadcast for Mussolini, he actually did broadcasts for a fascist

313

government, and certainly that is a political activism. It is a political activism I certainly would oppose as violently as I could, but it is a political activism.

Poets, like Langston Hughes, in the 1930's, when he was at his strongest poetically, represented these two aspects, the poet and the political activist. The whole nature of his poetry was markedly activist. The question is, if you are a writer, how does one focus his concerns as art? How does one create art, from the focus of one's concerns? That's the important question, and Mao Tse Tung is very clear on that when he says there must be a unity of politics and art, what we demand is revolutionary politics and artistic power. Just because you think you have the correct social view, if you can't create a powerful art out of that, if you're just phrase mongering, as Mao said, the poster and slogan style, then that's hardly going to be convincing of your point of view.

So the whole question of a blatantly political artist like myself is always focus on the fact of creating art with those views and that focus, instead of just phrase mongering and poster and slogan style.

Q: *You had written in* BLACK MAGIC, *"I write poetry only to enlist the poetic consistently as apt description of my life." Now that could be read, "my life," as its broadest political and social concerns. Is there a break from the earlier view of one's life as a dance, as a lyrical appeal for love, as an aesthetic life?*

A: It's a transition from the earlier aesthetic method of viewing reality, to a principally political view.

Q: *Do you think there are some people who have a genius for this kind of total political view in art, like yourself, Brecht, Ginsberg—and there are some other people like Mayakovsky who have been crucified on the political view, in art, because he just wasn't by temperament disposed to write Marxist poetry?*

A: I know Mayakovsky had problems trying to bring together some of his involvements in the petty bourgeois radical poetical movements, and say the demands that were made on him by a socialist society, and apparently he wasn't strong enough to deal with it.

Q: *Or during the anti-Vietnam political protest poetry, we've seen a good number of American poets try to write political poetry and fall flat on their faces.*

A: A good deal of it is orientation, because we're brought up in this country with an aesthetic that's totally opposed to all that, we're

314

brought up thinking that poetry should not be political, we're taught that the opposite is true. So what you get is sloganizing.

Q: *Would you as a teacher of writing advise a student to try writing a political poem?*

A: The first thing I tell them is, it's all political. I begin by letting them see how in art and writing, the first thing you look for is the stance. For example, what side is the person on? For instance, I couldn't see anyone being on the side of the majority of the people in this country, who could write poems in favor of capitalism or racism or women's oppression.

Q: *What new books will you have coming out?*

A: William Morrow is bringing out the SELECTED POEMS in the fall of 1979, plus a reader. I'm selecting a lot of poems in the SELECTED POEMS from BLACK MAGIC, which is out of print. Some poetry from the DEAD LECTURER, some poetry from PREFACE TO A TWENTY PAGE SUICIDE NOTE. Poetry from volumes that came after BLACK MAGIC —SPIRIT REACH, HARD FACTS, latest book, POEMS FOR THE ADVANCE.

Q: *Would you talk about your name change?*

A: I was given the name Ameer Baraka, which is an Arab name, by this Muslim Imam, who buried Malcom X. I changed the name, swahilised it, when I became an Afrikan nationalist, to Amiri Baraka.

Q: *The French poets like Paul Eluard and St. John Perse and a few poets like H.D. are the only modern poets who have published poetry under names that are other than their given names, their primal ego names.*

A: My own name change was meant to change my own self-perception, and the way others perceived me, Afrikan consciousness, Black consciousness, where we wanted to get rid of the American names, the slave names, and take on an identity which was in tune with African liberation. And while I certainly don't feel that changing a name is going to bring revolution, I see no reason to drop it, as a lot of people might perceive that as trying to liquidate the whole revolutionary nationalist struggle that we went through in the 1960s.

Q: *We're trying to get at the persona "I," which someone like Paul Eluard would be using in a love poem—does that perception go right into the persona of the "I" in a poem?*

A: Sure, because I think the whole changing of a name does change one's whole perception, and then the perception that one does have for writing that love poem, that love poem is perceived by that changed person.

Q: *There's so much in your early poems about the need to be loved—in* THE DEAD LECTURER *and even in* BLACK MAGIC. *Is the need to change politically in order that love may be more possible in the world?*

A: Yeah, that's always my perception. Because now love is not possible. In this very negative society, which satisfies only a handful of folk, most people find themselves almost unable to love, or to love at great effort, because of the kind of dismal condition of the society. That's what I'm usually talking about. First the feeling of estrangement, and then the need for change in the society so that love can exist "freely and cleanly."

Q: *That includes self-love.*

A: Yeah, a lot of times this is the case with people who find themselves oppressed, they hate themselves worse than they hate their oppressors.

Q: *Revolution then must entail evolution, both a stance against and an openness both politically and poetically, an openness to meet new possibilities.*

A: Without that openness, one cannot see how things change, or the need for change. I feel the only constant is change. The closer we get to objective reality, the closer we get to experiencing change and understanding change. The evolution is actually a kind of quantitative thing, from one stage to another stage, there is a kind of accretion or build-up which is a quantitative amassing of elements or force, but then you reach a certain point, and there's a qualitative change which is the revolutionary leap.

Q: *So then the whole thing does go back to the dance.*

A: In the sense of action, yeah.

Q: *The difficulty of having a continuous focus on the society.*

A: It becomes more and more difficult to publish. Any poet or writer who thinks he has any real integrity and wants to take a stance against society had better get a job. Because he'll find he cannot make a living as a writer.

Then the publishers have become so commercial. For instance, a publisher like Knopf which is hooked up to Random House which is hooked up to the Yankees, which is hooked up to C.B.S.; it's like you have to measure your book against Reggie Jackson's batting average to see whether it's going to get published or not.

MacMillan, at the same time they refused to publish my last novel, were publishing a history of wallpaper, which I think is needed by fewer people than good writing is needed.

23
Charles Bukowski

Q: *How do you write? In longhand, on the typewriter? Do you revise much? What do you do with worksheets? Your poems sometimes give the impression of coming off the top of your head. Is that only an impression? How much agony and sweat of the human spirit is involved in the writing of one of your poems?*

A: I write right off the typer. I call it my "machinegun." I hit it hard, usually late at night while drinking wine and listening to classical music on the radio and smoking mangalore ganesh beedies. I revise, but not much. The next day I retype the poem and automatically make a change or two, drop out a line, or make two lines into one or one line into two, that sort of thing—to make the poem have more balls, more balance. Yes, the poems come "off the top of my head," I seldom know what I'm going to write when I sit down. There isn't much agony and sweat of the human spirit involved in doing it. The writing's easy, it's the living that is sometimes difficult.

Q: *When you're away from your place do you carry a notebook with you? Do you jot down ideas as they come to you during the day or do you store them in your head for later?*

A: I don't carry notebooks and I don't consciously store ideas. I try not to think that I am a writer and I am pretty good at doing that. I don't like writers, but then I don't like insurance salesmen either.

Charles Bukowski

Q: *Do you ever go through dry periods, no writing at all? If so how often? What do you do during these periods? Anything to get you back on the track?*

A: A dry period for me means perhaps going two or three nights without writing. I probably have dry periods but I'm not aware of them and I go on writing, only the writing probably isn't much good. But sometimes I do get aware that it isn't going too well. Then I go to the racetrack and bet more money than usual and come home and drink much more than usual and scream at and abuse my woman. And it's best that I lose at the track without trying to. I can almost always write a damn near immortal poem if I have lost somewhere between 150 and 200 dollars.

Q: *Need for isolation? Do you work best alone? Most of your poems concern your going from a state of love/sex to a state of isolation. Does that tie in with the way to have to have things in order to write?*

A: I love solitude but I don't need it to the exclusion of somebody I care for in order to get some words down. I figure if I can't write under all circumstances, then I'm just not good enough to do it. Some of my poems indicate that I am writing while living alone after a split with a woman, and I've had many splits with women. I need solitude more often when I'm not writing than when I am. I have written with children running about the room having at me with squirt guns. That often helps rather than hinders the writing: some of the laughter enters. One thing does bother me, though: to overhear somebody's loud TV, a comedy program with a laugh track.

Q: *When did you begin writing? How old? What writers did you admire?*

A: The first thing I ever remembered writing was about a German aviator with a steel hand who shot hundreds of Americans out of the sky during World War II. It was in long hand in pen and it covered every page of a huge memo ringed notebook. I was about 13 at the time and I was in bed covered with the worst case of boils the medics ever remembered seeing. There weren't any writers to admire at the time. Since then there has been John Fante, Knut Hamsun, the Celine of JOURNEY; Dostoesvsky, of course; Jeffers of the long poems only; Conrad Aiken, Catullus . . . not too many. I sucked mostly at the classical music boys. It was good to come home from the factories at

319

night, take off my clothes, climb on the bed in the dark, get drunk on beer and listen to them.

Q: *Do you think there's too much poetry being written today? How would you characterize what you think is really bad poetry? What do you think is good poetry today?*

A: There's too much bad poetry being written today. People just don't know how to write down a simple easy line. It's difficult for them; it's like trying to keep a hard-on while drowning—not many can do it. Bad poetry is caused by people who sit down and think, Now I am going to write a Poem. And it comes out the way they *think* a poem should be. Take a cat. He doesn't think, well, now I'm cat and I'm going to kill this bird. He just does it. Good poetry today? Well, it's being written by a couple of cats called Gerald Locklin and Ronald Koertge.

Q: *You've read most of the NYQ craft interviews we've published. What do you think of our approach, the interviews you've read. What interviews have told you something?*

A: I'm sorry you asked that question. I haven't learned anything from the interviews except that the poets were studious, trained, self-assured and obnoxiously self-important. I don't think that I was ever able to finish an interview; the print began to blur and the trained seals vanished below the surface. These people lack joy, madness and gamble in their answers just as they do in their work (poems).

Q: *Although you write strong voice poems, that voice rarely extends beyond the circumference of your own psychosexual concerns. Are you interested in national, international affairs, do you consciously restrict yourself as to what you will and will not write about?*

A: I photograph and record what I see and what happens to me. I am not a guru or leader of any sort. I am not a man who looks for solutions in God or politics. If somebody else wants to do the dirty work and create a better world for us and he *can* do it, I will accept it. In Europe where my work is having much luck, various groups have put a claim on me, revolutionaries, anarchists, so forth, because I have written of the common man of the streets, but in interviews over there I have had to disclaim a conscious working relationship with them because there isn't any. I have compassion for almost all the individuals of the world; at the same time, they repulse me.

Charles Bukowski

Q: *What do you think a young poet starting out today needs to learn the most?*

A: He should realize that if he writes something and it bores him it's going to bore many other people also. There is nothing wrong with a poetry that is entertaining and easy to understand. Genius could be the ability to say a profound thing in a simple way. He should stay the hell out of writing classes and find out what's happening around the corner. And bad luck for the young poet would be a rich father, an early marriage, an early success or the ability to do anything very well.

Q: *Over the last few decades California has been the residence of many of our most independent voice poets—like Jeffers, Rexroth, Patchen, even Henry Miller. Why is this? What is your attitude towards the East, towards New York?*

A: Well, there was a little more space out here, the long run up the coast, all that water, a feeling of Mexico and China and Canada, Hollywood, sunburn, starlets turned to prostitutes. I don't know, really, I guess if your ass is freezing some of the time it's harder to be a "voice poet." Being a voice poet is the big gamble because you're putting your guts up for view and you're going to get a lot more reaction than if you're writing something like your mother's soul being like a daisy field.
New York, I don't know. I landed there with seven dollars and no job and no friends and no occupation except common laborer. I suppose if I had come in from the top instead of the bottom I might have laughed a little more. I stayed three months and the buildings scared the shit out of me and the people scared the shit out of me, and I had done a lot of bumming all over the country under the same conditions but New York City was the Inferno, all the way. The way Woody Allen's intellectuals suffer in N.Y.C. is a lot different than what happens to my type of people. I never got laid in New York, in fact, the women wouldn't even speak to me. The only way I ever got laid in New York was to come back three decades later and bring my own with me, a terrible wench, we stayed at the Chelsea, of course. The NEW YORK QUARTERLY is the only good thing that has happened to me out there.

Q: *You've written short stories, novels. Do they come from the same place your poems come from?*

A: Yes, they do, there's not much difference—line and line length. The short story helped get the rent and the novel was a way of saying how many different things could happen to the same man on the way to suicide, madness, old age, natural and unnatural death.

Q: *You have a fairly distinct persona in most of your poems, and your strong voice seems to come out of that persona. It's the mask of a bored, dirty old man who's boozing it up in Li Po manner because the straight world isn't worth taking seriously. Usually there's an hysterical broad banging your door down while the poem is taking shape. First do you admit to this persona in your poems, and then to what extent do you think it reflects Bukowski the man? In other words are you the person you present to us in your poems?*

A: Things change a bit: what once was is not quite what it is now. I began writing poetry at the age of thirty-five after coming out of the death ward of the L.A. County General Hospital and not as a visitor. To get somebody to read your poems you have to be noticed, so I got my act up. I wrote vile (but interesting) stuff that made people hate me, that made them curious about this Bukowski. I threw bodies off my court porch into the night. I pissed on police cars, sneered at hippies. After my second reading down at Venice, I grabbed the money, leaped into my car, intoxicated, and drove it about on the sidewalks at sixty m.p.h. I had parties at my place which were interrupted by police raids. A professor from U.C.L.A. invited me to his place for dinner. His wife cooked a nice meal which I ate and then I went over and broke up his China closet. I was in and out of drunktanks. A lady accused me of rape, the whore. Meanwhile, I wrote about most of this, it was my persona, it was me but it wasn't me. As time went on, trouble and action arrived by itself and I didn't have to force it and I wrote about *that* and this was closer to my real persona. Actually, I am not a tough person and sexually, most of the time, I am almost a prude, but I am often a nasty drunk and many strange things happen to me when I am drunk. I'm not saying this very well and I'm taking too long. What I am trying to say is that the longer I write, the closer I am getting to what I am. I am one of those slow starters but I am all hell in the stretch run. I am ninety-three percent the person I present in my poems; the other seven percent is where art improves upon life, call it background music.

Q: *You refer to Hemingway a lot, seem to have a love/hate thing for him, what he does in his work. Any comment?*

A: I guess for me Hemingway is a lot like it is for others: he goes down well when we are young. Gertie taught him the line but I think he improved upon it. Hemingway and Saroyan had the line, the magic of it. The problem was that Hemingway didn't know how to laugh and Saroyan was filled with sugar. John Fante had the line too and he was the first who knew how to let passion enter in, emotion in, without letting it destroy the concept. I speak here of moderns who write the *simple* line; I am aware that Blake was once around. So when I write about Hemingway, it's sometimes a joke thing but I'm probably more in debt to him than I'd care to admit. His early work was screwed down tight, you couldn't get your fingers under it. But now I get more out of reading about his life and fuckups, it's almost as good as reading about D. H. Lawrence.

Q: *What do you think of this interview and what question do you wish we'd asked you? Go ahead and ask it of yourself and then answer it.*

A: I think the interview is all right. I suppose that some people will object that the answers lack polish and erudition, then they'll go out and buy my books. I can't think of any questions to ask myself. For me to get paid for writing is like going to bed with a beautiful woman and afterwards she gets up, goes to her purse and gives me a handful of money. I'll take it. Why don't we stop here?

24

Leo Connellan

Q: *I've been reading through all your poems. And, there are so many long poems which, usually, are seen by poets as a challenge. When did you start writing long poems?*

A: When I was very young I wanted to be, if possible, a short story writer like Stephen Crane and I couldn't do it. No matter how I tried, it didn't come out. So, I tried writing novels and every other thing and they didn't come out and after a long time, I began to try to see if I could write poetry. But in the beginning, in the early 1960s, it was an accomplishment if I could get off the page. It was an accomplishment. It was really—I wrote a poem called LAMENT FOR FEDERICO GARCIA LORCA that runs about two and a half pages and to me it was an achievement that I could actually write what I thought was a poem that long.

Q: *Let me ask you a question about that poem. That poem ends:*

> *Federico, Garcia, Lorca . . . some of us*
> *some of us are heartbroken . . .*
> *They do not make enough candles*
> *in all the world's churches*
> *to burn for you.*
> *Not enough Rosaries can be said*
> *or Acts of Contrition.*

324

> *Because I know*
> *it will happen again.*

You seem to have a great talent for talking directly to a subject or to the reader. Are you aware of doing this?

A: Not consciously. No. But in writing poems, one of the things that I've tried to do is read it silently to myself as if it were being read to me so I could try to understand it. And if I can't seem to understand what I thought I've gotten on paper, then I try to make what it is "clear for me;" if it's clear to me it may be clear to you . . . It's a device I've tried to perfect.

Q: *Does that get into revising endlessly?*

A: I didn't revise. For me the thing that defeats people who say they want to write is not realizing that writing is work! You have to write everything out. Everything about whatever it is you want to write. Even if doing it will fill 100 pages. Knowing you may only be able to use half a page. I seldom revise. If I get to the point where I think through that process of writing every single thing out about a poem and the poem is finished, then what I do is edit, edit, edit, cut, edit, cut again. But once I've done that, I never touch the poem again . . . for any reason. Now for instance, I wrote a poem that the NYQ published called THE MOON NOW FLUSHED and I wrote a poem called PORTRAIT OF A POET. I wouldn't touch these poems. I'm an older person now, a different person. They were written twenty years ago. But when they were delivered to the editor, or to the world, they were and are in the best shape that I would ever be able to make them. Revising them now would be breaking faith with one's development. They are what I was and what I wrote when I wrote them. Now that I might know more does not give me a right to cheat art and who I was then and am now.

Q: *You also wrote a poem* WATCHING JIM SHOULDERS. *It seems like some of the poems are searching for a hero of some kind. Are you aware of that?*

A: Interesting you ask that. I have no conscious awareness of picking athletic heroes or picking heroes at all. I've had several periods in my life as a very heavy drinker. Once I was in Colorado Springs, Colorado as the guest of the Salvation Army and they got us indigents tickets to go see a rodeo. I went along to get along

. . . Someone I had never heard of suddenly came lunging out of a corral on the back of a steer, and somebody said it was somebody called Jim Shoulders who, even though he'd seriously hurt his back, was nevertheless riding that steer to keep his North America title for the United States . . . I saw a man who had seriously injured his back come out of a corral and throw a steer in a matter of seconds while blood squirted up his back; I saw him stand erect and walk back as if nothing was hurting him; and it suddenly occurred to me that I had to wonder: when did my manhood awaken to its whatever . . . And, later, years later in New York City, I'd come down into Greenwich Village and sat in The Limelight and things like WATCHING JIM SHOULDERS would occur to me to try to make into poems.

Q: *O.K. Of the long poems,* LOBSTER CLAW, IN LOBSTER NIGHT COMING TO CUNNINGTON TO TAKE KELLY, CROSSING AMERICA—*many of these poems start with someone coming into a town or coming back to a town, or, like environment, dying, leaving the town. Exits and entrances seem to be very important in the long poems.*

A: I'm not conscious of that. I'm conscious of a feeling that everyone is searching for who they are, where they are, whether they ever leave where they are or not. I come from New England. There are people in New England who never go five miles from where they were born and they are some of the most neurotic, frustrated, resentful, upset people I've ever met in my life. And they don't know why. They need you to come to spend your money, but they resent you for the ability to earn it somewhere else and, apparently, to be able to pay your bills and have enough left over. They need you to spend in their town but resent you for being able to—and I think I get a sense of displacement and I don't think I'm unique. I think Shakespeare certainly wrote from that point of view and most writers, many writers, are disturbed by the fact that there—as Hemingway said "There is no separate peace . . ."

Q: *You keep insisting that you are not conscious of certain things that I see in your work. What the hell are you conscious of when you're working? Are you thinking about line breakage? The way the poem falls on the page?*

A: No. That never bothers me at all.

Q: *What do you think about?*

A: I think about what I want to try to do with the poem. In other words, I make a plan. For example, in the poems that you mentioned, if I could write a poem of any kind about where I came from and the people, that would be a vantage point (or practice point) for me to try to do a body of work about my origins later on. Because I think of writing as, well, let me talk about me. I have to give myself permission to fail in order to try to succeed . . . as Yeats suggested. So first, before I try for my real work, my big effort, I have to try to write about little things I notice. So if I'm crossing America, I'll try to write about what I noticed about, say, Kansas, or about hitchhiking, or if I go to New York City I'll try to write about the Staten Island Ferry and the subway hoping the day will come when I have a right to write about my New England. Then, perhaps, I have the right to try to see what I think may bother human beings . . . I think my subject matter better "move" me, "disturb" me or it's certainly not going to reach out and touch complete strangers and move them to consider what I'm writing about.

Q: *But you say you do throw away a lot?*

A: If you see a poem of mine that's twenty five pages long, you can rest assured that it was 200 pages long and the twenty-five pages, the final version, is edited, everything, everything written out about whatever it is I'm trying to write about, several times in pen and ink, all out—200 pages, finally everything thrown away but what can't be; then, maybe I've trapped my poem—maybe!

Q: *You type several drafts?*

A: No. I never type it until I'm ready to send it to a publisher. I never type it until the poem is written. The poem is written in pen and ink until it satisfies me. It may go through one draft—I carried the manuscript of CROSSING AMERICA around with me for ten years, for example . . . I didn't even think it was a finished work . . . Another example is my book MASSACHUSETTS POEMS; the CUMMINGTON POEM was written in two months in a motel room that I lived in while at the company headquarters where I worked in Pinebrook, New Jersey . . . And up in Peabody, Massachusetts and wherever I happened to be as a traveling salesman making my living. I would go out all day and make my living as a salesman and come back into my hotel room and write, work!

Q: *You talk as if you were constantly at work on something. What is the longest period of dry that you've ever gone through, that you haven't been writing?*

A: Ah, it's very funny. I was dry probably from the time I was a young man, probably from 1947 through to about 1964. In other words, I had written some poems in high school, but no matter how many times I tried to get going I just couldn't do it. I couldn't do it in New York City, I couldn't seem to write when I was in various cities of the U.S. or Canada, and I sense that a lot of it, for me, had to do with the fact that I lived my adolescence probably between age twenty and thirty rather than between age twelve and twenty. Suddenly, when I married and came back to New York City in the early 1960s, a city, mind you, that loomed large in my head as a place I'd always failed in, I wasn't thinking in terms of "books" but of individual poems. Could I write one poem!? I mean I would go out and write a poem, and the big accomplishment of the month was if I had a poem half finished. And in that way, I wrote two books at the same time, I wrote ANOTHER POET IN NEW YORK and PENOBSCOT POEMS at the same time. If I got tired of writing about the New York subway system, I'd turn around and write about a Maine lobster fisherman.

Q: *You're talking about two kinds of geography—where you come from and where you are when you are writing the poem . . .*

A: The city that I love and the state of Maine which is my origin seem to be basically what I write about or—a lot of my work when I was trying to teach myself to write was about Maine and New York.

Q: *Do you have any feelings of kinship with the other great Maine poets like Robinson, Coffin . . . and who are the other Maine poets? Millay. Edna St. Vincent Millay . . . Who else?*

A: Well, no. Millay, now you know, don't you, that Edna Millay and I both come from Rockland, Maine . . . let's see, I'll tell you something . . . When I read your own plays THE MARRIAGE, and especially a work of yours like MY NAME IS BOBBY, it did far more for me, probably triggered some of my own guts to try to write my work, than any of these poets you've mentioned . . . I don't think, I mean I think it sounds awfully nice to put yourself in a group like Robinson, Frost, even the other sea poet Jeffers . . . but I'm a loner. I'm so unrelated to them that I've never felt either involved with them or that I ever wrote anything because of them . . . I owe you, Bill, and, say, Richard Wilbur, Federico Garcia Lorca poets of the world, if I owe anyone . . . which I hope I don't . . .

Leo Connellan

Q: *I'm going to read this poem—*

THROUGH THE WORLD THE LITTLE WORM FOREVER

In blizzard at toll booth
trucks backed up like
empty egg crates, their
lights on in the snow falling linen dust
makes them look furious beetles
bright round large bulbous glazed eyes
dead or glaring, like giants
tied held prisoner, taunted,
by something that didn't occur to them possible.

All backed up the falling snow
flicked against trucks windshield glass
like feathers of cotton candy sticking
to windows like furry little hands it
takes scraping to get off. Cold sticking
and cunningly worked under their
big thick tires to skid them out of control.
through the world the little worm forever while
big species vanish, invisibility is power,
victory your opponent's ignorance.

That poem has such an extraordinary observed detail which is where in poetry
of someone's actually re-creating the way those big trucks looked when they're
backed up and the way the little snowflakes stick on the windshield. You say
you did this in a motel room?

A: Yes . . . I'll tell you something, too, and I'm not trying to
impress you . . . I just want you to see how I work. That poem is a
practice poem, was written as a practice poem.

Q: *A practice poem?*

A: I was trying to develop the ability in sharp poetic sharp lines to
describe something to help me get ready for the work I was writing at
the time, which was called COMING TO CUMMINGTON TO TAKE KELLY
and I was about to try to take on a running scene, a scene of imagined
action. So, in my room, I had the habit sometimes of writing what I
call throwaway poems. Sometimes I'd send 'em out until I—'til

somebody buys one for a magazine or even puts it in the little book that you noticed from Western Maryland Press.

Q: *Do you do these warm-up poems all the time?*

A: Constantly. When you asked me about dry periods, this is why it was hard for me to answer you literally because if I can't write what I do is practice. In the poem you read, my, THROUGH THE WORLD THE LITTLE WORM FOREVER, I was trying to work with the conclusion that sometimes one wins by being invisible and sometimes your victory is in your opponent's ignorance . . . meaning, too, that none of us are so good that we can afford enemies. If I can't write what I do is practice, practice. I try to use myself every day. I get up every morning of my life, nobody asks me to. And I'm certainly not suggesting it to anyone else. But I get up at half past four and I go out and put the coffee on and between about ten of five and about six thirty, every day, I write something. If I'm going to write a poem, that's good. If I'm not I practice. I try to—I take a truck or I take a telephone pole and I take a cat. I take something and I try to see if I can describe it . . . I'll tell you something, Bill, I used to get anxiety attacks at the idea of having to go out and throw bull to sell something to feed my family—until the idea occurred to me in this getting up early that, really, quite honestly I was doing what I wanted to do *first* every day before I had to go and do what I must for "the man" . . .

Q: *You do readings of your work from time to time. Do you find that you get anything as a creative artist from reading aloud your work or does it create any problems for you?*

A: Well, it's a very difficult thing to answer. Number one, everybody has an ego and I'm certainly no different than anybody else. You work so long alone that the idea of being asked to read your work—if you're a human being—has to interest you. I suddenly find that the most important thing to me is if a professor will say to me later, somebody will say, "You know Leo, somebody heard you read your poems and they really want to look at one of your books" . . . now that means my work has reached someone I have never met and I think that Karl Shapiro gave me the finest definition of what a poem is: "A poem is an anonymous gift to an anonymous recipient" . . . and when you are finished with it, it doesn't belong to you anymore but to whoever wants it. So the value of poetry readings to me is if I can read my work and somewhere in that room somebody is touched enough or if somebody says . . . "I thought I was the only one who knew what it was to get your fingers cut while working in a soldering factory;" or—"I thought I was the only one who ever had that thought about the Staten Island Ferry."

Q: *I understand.*

A: And if I could do that then I feel that I'm in tune with the time I write in . . . I'm talking too much and not saying much. Writers write, they don't talk!

Q: *You have also taught from time to time, poetry. Do you feel that helps or harms?*

A: Helps or harms who?

Q: *I'm talking about the process of your own writing. Does it help you get in touch with your writing or does it take away from your writing?*

A: I think the value of writing workshops is that they create a job for the writer, for me; and for a lot of lonely, lonely people, they create an opportunity to come out of themselves and meet new people and make friendships. Most of the writers I know only teach at workshops because they have to eat.

Q: *Would you describe writing workshops as a social problem?*

A: Not social. They're like somebody coming to dinner to try to have you touch your forehead, as if in doing so you can say "Now go forth and be Edna St. Vincent Millay" . . .

Q: *You're describing it like a church.*

A: I'm describing it like an invention, an invention of lonely people to play at writing and an ingenius invention of real writers to work near their trade while they earn cash to pay their bills. Neat for all!

Q: *You never attended workshops yourself?*

A: No. I have gone to hear writers I respect hoping they could say something I could hear with my middle ear, with my inside gear and use. I've gone to the 92nd Street Y to hear a great writer read, or I've gone to hear a great writer lecture or read, but I have never signed up to take any workshop.

Q: *Do you feel that the workshops that you've taught, that the work has been on any level?*

A: I find that some writing students said I ought to go to hell and that they don't know why they paid to hear me and those people I have hope for—especially the ones who could tell me I know absolutely nothing. I'd think "could Thomas Wolfe have just left my class or Hart Crane or Delmore?"

Q: *We've talked earlier about solitude—which is the loneliness of a writer. Yes? Are there certain writers who have meant a lot to you, I mean, perhaps even been a reason you've written?*

A: Yes. But writing is such a singularly tough pursuit that you have to work at it and somebody doesn't eventually take you up, make moves for you, you can't have success. I've been very lucky. I've had you, Bill and thank you very much for all the space time after time in the NEW YORK QUARTERLY. I've had Karl Shapiro who, when I was young, took the time and this man had the Pulitzer Prize—he had everything and I was nobody; he took the time to write me and give me advice and to encourage me and I've had Richard Wilbur who is a gracious gentleman as well as a great, great writer when we need him most, and I've had William Wallace Davidson, God rest his soul, who took my first poems at THE GEORGIA REVIEW, and I've had Richard Eberhart who to me is one of the most remarkable people, remarkable not only because he has genius, but he has the genius to touch and support all kinds of writing and to support it, to support even the last thing he'd ever write . . . that blessed man! Allen Ginsberg. Don't you kid yourself, Allen Ginsberg has one of the finest talents in America and has been most generous to other poets without ever letting anyone know about it. I think I've seen Allen Ginsberg maybe twice in my life. Probably at Saint Mark's Church and once in Washington Square Park walking around by the old hanging tree. Charles Bukowski, too, and Lynn Savitt . . . they're excellent and they're so good, like you are Bill, as to frighten the pompous and revitalize literature . . . I've found that real writers, the writers who write, are more than willing to try to do what they can for writing which really means you . . . Because helping you live, pay your rent, eat . . . in a way they're helping themselves . . . They're justifying themselves . . . Their work really does that but since they are human beings, helping other writers does it better for their souls.

Q: *O.K. I'm going back to the beginning of this interview. I've asked you about the long poem. Poets have tried writing it and have fallen on their faces because they couldn't sustain a lyric impulse beyond two or three pages. You*

have recently been working on a triology of poems of which the first is
COMING TO CUMMINGTON TO TAKE KELLY. *And the second is* SHATTER-
HOUSE. *You're working on the third part of the triology now. Is this
something you propose to yourself? A huge structure like an architecture, and
then you set yourself to complete it.*

A: When I was very young and drinking very heavily, and I could
say that to you because I'm, well, we all think of what wasted our
lives. And I was in Canada. Somebody asked Hemingway if Paris and
London were wonderful cities to write in and he said they were
wonderful cities but perhaps he wasn't so good when he was in
them. Well, I think that I began to say to myself in my late twenties.
"I'm going to do, as I live, the large trilogy of the condition of my
country, its people, where we're at, or where we've been, where we
may go. And before I can do it I'm going to practice. So I'm going to
make the best short points I can. And then very slowly, I'm going to
see if I can write a longer poem. But if there's a secret to the long
narrative poem—You mentioned my book SHATTERHOUSE. It's one
poem, sixty-six pages long, in six parts. It either has something to say
or it's going to fail. And if I don't have something to say and if it
wasn't something that I felt was the culmination of everything I've
ever been, or ever thought ever wanted to try to become, then it
wouldn't have a chance of holding up. I think that some people who
try long poems really have nothing at the center of the poem but
wills.

Q: *I see.*

A: There is no simple idea. There is no intent. I feel that if you
have a good intention, you've got to give it a race. You could come in
twentieth just by intending to.

Q: *Yes.*

A: But if you have no intention you run 'im in the race. But either
you drop out six miles down the road or you come in one thousandth.

Q: *When this interview is published, it will be common knowledge that
you have received the Shelley Memorial Award from* THE POETRY SOCIETY
OF AMERICA. *You have survived through your life as a salesman, as a
teacher, at odd jobs. In one of your poems you even describe crossing America
with a skillet that you kept clean as a way of insuring a day's job and some
dining. Now you are coming into recognition and awards. You must have*

*gone through years of seeing other poets getting awards that you may have felt
did not deserve them. How does this change in status make you feel?*

A: Let me answer you the only way I can: In the first place, no one
ever asked me to write. And I am on my own. A writer is on his own
or her own. I think that the help along the way and especially the
acknowledgment by complete strangers that perhaps we put something valuable down, is very healthy. I think that I've come to feel this
way about awards. It was, never will be a reason why I write or why
any real writer writes, but on the other hand, it could get me a job. It
could overcome things like a lack of sheepskin. Somebody could say,
"We can have you now because so and so has given you this." I think
other people's societies get pensions at the end of working years, and
a lot of work is so alone and so all by himself; I think prizes let you
know that someone, someone really did read and evaluate what you
tried hard to write as no one else had written it. I think that does
mean something. I don't think that having a prize is either going to
make you a writer or not make you a writer. I think what it may mean
is: That a total stranger or a group of people that you may not have
ever known existed, took the trouble to look at something that you
tried to spend your life doing and said, "Well, gee, it looks like he
tried good and well enough to get this" and what they give you might
mean that you get a job. And I don't think that anyone who's
sensible, who writes, really allows the possession of a prize in itself to
influence them one way or another.

Q: *Let me ask you now, towards the end of this interview: Is there any
question that you'd want to propose to yourself?*

A: I don't know where personal motivation is going to come from
in America. I think I mean we're getting awfully good at heart
transplants and computers; we're putting computers in front of
children to talk to them and tell them how to multiply, how to do
geometry, how to do everything for them. And I don't know, you
know, a hungry man fights to get a meal, and I think that a good
writer is hungry to write. I don't know what will motivate anyone in
the future to try to write or to act or to put themselves into
something. And I think that question is what I might be dealing with
after I finish my triology. And I ask myself what will happen when I
write for (free?) I mean, will I suddenly be ready to die?

Q: *You seem to have had very strong motivation throughout your life
always to keep writing. Do you ever have any fear about that motivation
dissipating?*

Leo Connellan

A: Well, many times. I, in fact, didn't get going until awfully late and who am I to think that I can write? I think any writer might say that you write because you can't help it.

Q: *You talked about motivation as a problem in our culture. Do you think that the proliferation of creative writing programs and the MFA degree have helped or hindered the motivation for writing really good poetry?*

A: I don't want to make people mad at me; but I will say this to you: I think that in order for the college process to succeed, if you turn someone over to a master of fine arts degree the next logical thing is: A job has to be found for them. And I think that perhaps the stress on that degree is stronger than on the ability and quality of the writing of the person who has that degree.

Q: *You keep talking about jobs, jobs, jobs. Does it occur to you that you would not perhaps have written the extraordinary poetry that you have written, if you had been a tenured English professor in some small college for forty years? But that because of the diversity of your experience that you draw from in your writing—*

A: I think that you're hitting on something that's very important. And I'm certainly not trying to correct you. I'd just like to bring something out: The reason I kept saying jobs, jobs, jobs. I have a wife, as you know, and a daughter. And I think that I made the decision to be responsible for my child and try to be responsible to contribute to my marriage and to our income. Now when I didn't have this feeling of responsibility, I wasn't being worried about a job. I didn't care where I was and I never thought about it. And if I was washing dishes in Seattle tonight and on a bus tomorrow or hitchhiking to Omaha, Nebraska tomorrow, I really didn't think about what would happen in Omaha. Suddenly, in my middle fifties, I'm wondering how I can educate my daughter or even how can I have an old age and if this job thing becomes an obsession. Because without one I don't know where I'll be. Or what will happen to me.

Q: *And yet the poetry still keeps getting written.*

A: Because it's all I want to do and it's all I've ever wanted to do, and I'm not very good at it. But, I certainly wasn't a novelist and I certainly was not a playwright. And I certainly wasn't an essayist. So the only thing left to me was to try to do this, and dammit I'm trying because I can't help myself.

335

25

Michael Moriarty

Q: *This is the first of some craft interviews we want to do with people who have vocations that are close to poetry but may be known for other things. We're interested in the relation between the performing arts and the creative art of poetry. As we do this interview, you are appearing in* THE CAINE MUTINY COURT MARTIAL *at Circle in the Square. Do you find, in performance, that your poetic mind works better than when you're not performing?*

A: The basic common denominator I have through writing poetry, prose, or acting is music. And that's my own approach, my only aesthetic now. With each breath either of prose or of poetry there are certain principles of balance to music. Then, no matter what's in it, I never question its integrity or its authenticity. And, the more I look at the world through musical terms, the more I shed outworn modalities, outworn paradigms. And, an example: the diatonic system in Bach's time reached its highest level—then it had to be re-examined, and so the Romantics and the twelve tone series came along, and their creators said: "I don't care what people say; certain notes *can* live together and ought to live together." And they've proven that point well. And the same thing exists in plays and exists in life, like living in New York City. New York is a perfect example where not only certain notes can live together, but certain people can live together brushing elbows every day. People who are antithetical to one another can somehow live in relative peace and harmony. So I think of words, pauses, gestures, and communication generally in terms of music.

Q: *You have a line in your play,* A COMEDY, *about Shakespeare—there is a line about* pause. *You say, a pause was the discovery of the modern playwright.*

A: No no, not exactly—"The modern playwright discovered the pause! The dear young fool was terrified—and so he shot it through with sex! If sex is what's required—do not fear to give poor words their little romps! They have so few!" And I was speaking mainly of Pinter. I'm not a big fan of his. I much prefer Beckett because when my Shakespeare describes the meaning of a pause he says, "But there upon the stage—a pause is only true—when players see nothing! Huge voids within the vast and airless regions of our minds! A place where new—(pause)—worlds may appear! A clean and starless region—clear of all illusions which our words reduce us to!"

And then Shakespeare says:

Words come to me because I treat them well! They're free
to play without responsibilities!
What far-
fetched meanings we have filled them with—have left them
knee-deep in the mire of meaning-full-ness! Lives are started and then ended cruelly—for Man has trea-
ted words—as if they were the things they mar!

In the beginning was the Word—for someone in
the *World*—had asked for some lame explanations set
in words! Words, words! The thousand visions set within
my mind—required a million words to free—and yet
I did not convey half their grace—nor half their sin-
fulness. When you see God—and then are left to fret

with words—My only consolation is that God
saw Man! He heard the fool cry—"What is happening?!"
—and God was also left with words—to tell this odd
and frightened animal—that all his rich and king-
ly words—will bring him to himself—and to his wad-

dling nature—to the maddeningly cherished ring
of pride! (Pause) But not an inch-closer to God.

Q: *This is an example of retentive memory—you have just recited lines
which you wrote some time ago. We want to ask about retentive memory in
performing as in writing—would you be able to remember word for word
from a role you played, say, five years ago, from a part in Shakespeare that
you played?*

A: No.

Q: *That's interesting.*

A: No, but words come to me easily, just the same. When they
don't then I know it's bad writing. There is something about great
writing that is already written inside all human beings and it just has
to be drawn out. The reason I couldn't remember five years ago is that
the same problem exists between me and the memory . . . Time is a
corrosive or barnacle. When we read great words we learn them
quickly. When I have trouble, then I realize that the writing is very
bad.

Q: *When you say words, are you talking about a word as if it were a
spoken word in the mind?*

A: I'm talking about it as melody. As an example: I loathe the
national anthem we have. It's a terrible song. I forget the words and I
don't want to sing them. But then I heard the HATIKVAH which is this
melody that's existed in the heart of man—(*sings tune of the Hatikvah*)
—or like GREEN SLEEVES—(*sings tune of* GREEN SLEEVES)—those are
primal melodies that have been unearthed by man, and learning
them is a process of really rediscovering them in ourselves.

Q: *Then if words are music, there's no qualitative distinction between the
act of writing and the spoken performance?*

A: Well said! And I'm sure that's why Shakespeare found writing
so easy.

Q: *Is there any difference in your mind between the craft of acting and the
craft of writing?*

A: I don't know. Probably in great writing or great acting there's
not, but in terms of calculated acting or calculated writing there's

338

probably a difference. I don't know. I do know—how do I say this? You know, right now I wait until the ghosts of my characters sit down beside my typewriter and begin to talk to me. And like some sections of the Shakespeare play, I guess he just sat down and typed them. And I just got out of the way. And so I believe in ghosts, and no ghost frightens me anymore. I have long conversations with them.

Q: *Would that be similar to the process of getting into a character?*

A: Yes. Yes.

Q: *The practical difference of course in acting is that you don't have time. You have to get up and deliver, as opposed to writing where you can pace yourself.*

A: Well, the unfortunate thing about it is the Broadway system of eight times a week. It's a tragedy that they continue this and that the city doesn't have a major Rep company like the Royal Shakespeare Company or the National Theatre or the Comèdie-Francaise, where actors are treated the way dancers are treated in terms of rep, or opera stars or symphony orchestras. They don't have them sawing away at the same symphony eight times a week. It's ridiculous. They might as well be playing for Lester Lanin. I don't care how great the piece of music. You play it eight times a week, it's going to get a little sad or tired. You're going to ask for some kind of other fare. So to that extent, the unnecessarily hard part of acting is repeating the same performance eight times a week.

Q: *In relation to the music of the words in Shakespeare, in Racine, and Chekhov, do you feel a difference in the kind of music and a difference in adaptation in acting?*

A: Well, I discovered in Racine the highest, most ideal and purest form not only of theatre structure but of language and of morality. He placed all his characters in a vice, a hugely demanding moral vice that is exciting to attempt and one can never totally succeed at achieving it. There's a reason that the actors don't move much in Racine. The reason is their spiritual beauty. They must be in a state of grace to do the work because the ideal of all Racine's major characters is grace, the ideal is an absolute pure state of grace. It is a spiritual heavenly pursuit much like Dante's and the actor must embody it as a pursuit and one knows going in that one cannot be human and still maintain the extraordinary point of view. When Phedre is talking about her

339

passions, the passions are only frightening if they are hurdled inside an angel, if they tear at the tendrils of a very high, high consciousness. And the same goes for Theseus. And to maintain that it's very hard, whereas with Shakespeare his people are so human and they have such a wonderful bawdy outlook, when they do address sexuality they address it with humor for the most part. Even the lofty characters take a black comedy view on it and they're not torn apart on a moral level. Except Hamlet. I would say he is Shakespeare's most Racinean figure insofar as he's so upset by his mother's sexuality on such a high level, tormented by it. I think his tragedy is destined because his ideals are inhuman. I find the most repugnant character in HAMLET is the ghost. He is in a self-imposed hell. He can think of nothing but his wife with his brother. It's purely self-imposed. And as long as he continues to, one, want revenge, and two, think about his wife in bed with his brother, he will continue to stay in hell. I mean it's a clear decision on the part of his own spirit whether he wants to, and then to drag his son into his inability to forgive. The universe is a larger space in which his soul can roam and he doesn't have to sit and mire and muck about in the frailties of his wife and brother. So I have a totally opposite view of the normal view of that play. The villain is the ghost. He drives his son to madness. "And Christ said call no man your father." Hamlet's obsessed with fulfilling his earthly father's calling. Hamlet's real father is in heaven.

Q: *Chekhov's language, in his plays, is not written as poetry.*

A: Well, to me Chekhov was the greatest of the twentieth century playwrights. Tennessee comes close. But I see more god in Chekhov. A secular mind whose vision of god and understanding is so supreme and full and complete that—oh, he's just awesome. Awesome.

Q: *There must be a difference in the relation of the language to the subtext action in Racine, Shakespeare, Chekhov. Chekhov somehow writes counter to the subtext.*

A: Oh absolutely. Dances on top.

Q: *With Shakespeare it's simultaneous, language with action. In Racine it's declamation. From an acting point of view, that must be quite an adjustment. Different attitude, the way language seeks action.*

A: Well, I discovered last night a rule I knew a while ago and forgot. That theatre is a lie. And it's the secret lie that people pay money to come to see so that they can see other human beings lie with absolute total commitment and passion. And I realized walking on stage as I watched the people in the audience and the other actors. I just looked at the whole not in terms of a naturalistic truth or truth in a literal sense or any kind of truth on a worldly point of view. The event is to see how deeply and passionately all these gentlemen onstage can lie. And the interesting thing is its metaphor for life: no one in the end knows the truth and we all know that despite our best intentions, we lie every day. We take a breath and say, "Why did I say that. It just makes no sense." But it's the depth and passion to which the song is sung. It has nothing to do with, "Well I recognize that person." "Boy, I can really identify with that guy." No. That's movies, and naturalism. No, the theatre is a live experience of actors getting on stage and lying through their teeth and having the best time.

Q: *That's like Plato saying that in the act of life we get ourselves into a state of mind where we believe a lie, we suspend disbelief.*

A: Beyond the lie. It has to be beyond good and evil.

Q: *Yes.*

A: I remember someone described my Queeg as touching the morality that lies within all, all human beings. And my point of view is that the actor must go on stage from an amoral, not an immoral or moral point of view, but an amoral point of view. I approach it from the point of view that moral paradoxes are no more inconsistent than Schoenberg's twelve tone system, that a minor second is a very acceptable tension in the scheme of the universe. And once you do that you start to see that they must be played with as much passion as you would play the balanced elements of Mozart. And when you do, then, then all these petty ideologies that are running around the world killing people, are erased. And, the only thing I know that instantly erases any form of contradiction is music. It will automatically take the contradictory and make it harmonious.

Q: *With your intelligence, is it difficult sometimes to get into a character that is not as intelligent as you are?*

A: In many ways, no. See, in many ways it's much more pleasurable because what's made up for a refined mind is passion, the ability to be passionate. And Queeg, he's a good ole boy. He's got roots that sit in a really earthy relationship to what's right and what's wrong. And he is on many levels, amoral. For his own survival. And as a result of that, I could dig down more deeply into my guts for tones that I wouldn't ordinarily get because the intellect of your educated man or Greenwald who is the educated one, sits above man and manipulates the dumb but envies them at the same time. For their simplicity.

Q: *We're interested in the rate of your writing when you're working on a character or when you're not too involved in a production. You were talking about a repertory company in this country. And you've worked in classics. Do you have any feeling of whether this culture through its poets has given something that you could use? Do you read much contemporary poetry?*

A: I read the poetry of poets I know. I'm not that acquainted with the present scene. But I've discovered that I don't read much fiction. I read biographies. And I look around the world. Because I'd rather use that as a substance from which I draw rather than to go to fiction itself. As an example, my writing structure has more to do with the structures of music, the sonata form, and the symphonic forms than it has to do with what might be considered the structure of a poem or play. I'm not drawn to fiction. Because fiction, if I'm influenced by fiction, it becomes an imitation of an imitation. It's like understudying is hard because you don't begin fresh, you begin with an imitation of an imitation. So I'd rather make an imitation of a reality. Not reality; reality is a stupid word. Of a worldliness I guess. Of a worldliness, than of fiction.

Q: *We wonder about the relation between the isolation of the artist as opposed to performance, whether it's music or acting, working with other people in concert.*

A: While observing my creative cycles, I realize they are just like childbirth. Some pieces take six weeks to roll out because that's their gestation period. The action of actually putting these down on the page is a little like scrubbing the floor. The work is being done on a level that I don't even, can't . . . I mean, can a mother watch her baby develop in her belly? She just knows it's growing. She has to have the faith. She has a nightmare that the baby will be deformed or that the baby will be this. But, the work goes on, it goes on whether you're waiting tables or whether you're acting. Like I notice with my piano. I

342

have to thrash around. I'm working on a, I'm learning a new piece. I really have to make the ugliest kinds of sounds and make wrong notes in order to set the underlying structure. Whether I'm in a solo for two courses in the piece, whether it's a stanza, or I can only do it once, or whether I can play the melody can go for eight or nine choruses. To do that I just have to get down there and just bang at the piano, anything that comes to me. And it's just noise at first. All my friends say, "What are you playing, the wrong notes?" Well, I'm finding the structure of it before I can play its external beauty.

Q: *More than any art form, acting is affected when the reviews come out which will be written responses to the performance. But the performance must still continue and grow. Will reviews affect the birth or growth process?*

A: In a timid soul, in a tender young actor the performance can die. A tree can die in its first year because the winter may get too cold. Now if the critics come in and blast him that performance is going to die. But, Queeg's an old barnacle. Ain't nothing they can say about Queeg that is going to stop him. And he'll grow in his own way. And as Stravinsky said, "Grow straight. Life will bend you. You don't have to worry about accommodating anyone. Life will bend you." I always tell my actors, "Perform up. Don't perform at an audience. Perform up. Always go up." They'll take what they want to get. When I played Queeg in Stamford, one review said I wasn't insane enough and for the same performance, one review said I was too insane. So that really made the absurdity clear. I mean it was sitting right there.

Q: *There will be a shaping in your own process of what's taking place?*

A: Last night Queeg became an oak, a big oak. At the matinee he was on the edge of an oak; he started out an elm. But now he's an oak. Big wonderful oak.

Q: *This would be like the process of revision in writing, of taking a piece and endlessly revising?*

A: From my point of view of writing, I think of the creativity pushing out from me. And the more I feel like an observer to it, and watching it happen, the better work I can do. I don't get as exhausted. And I know that it will out willy nilly. There's nothing I can do about it. And when I do that, I'm much more relaxed when it comes out and I'm not harsh about what I see; what looks like a mistake turns out,

343

later on, in another part of the piece, to be exactly what was needed.
But it has to keep pushing out and pushing out until it's all out. And
once it's all out then it can restructure itself.

Q: *All of these metaphors for you have ground in music?*

A: Yes.

Q: *What kind of music do you like?*

A: The old kind. "Give me excess of it!"

Q: *Is there any kind of memory that is less sharp and specific and is
accessible? I'm thinking of artists who have the experience of being nebulous
and not quite remembering something.*

A: I did that all the time. I got into such a neurotic pattern that I
finally had to accept that I didn't remember, and I also had to accept a
mystical belief in the universe: That I will remember what I will have
to remember, and if I didn't remember it was more appropriate that I
didn't remember than had I remembered. The pause I took was more
meaningful than opening my mouth in memory. I'm firmly convinced of that. The more I trust it, the more I remember what I have
to remember and the more I don't worry about what I forgot.
Although I am embarrassed when I forget names and I . . . But I'm
starting to get more courageous and I say, "I'm sorry, I forgot your
name." You know.

Q: *Do you feel a separation in the arts today, that the poet is over on one
side and the actor is over on another side? And do you see any way out of
that?*

A: I see it as a disease of the whole society. Specialization. I
consider the Renaissance man not exceptional. I consider him normal. That's what we all should be. We all should have our fingers in
music and writing and economics and history. That's the normal state
of man. But, I went to one doctor, he ended up sending me to three
others. What I ended up with in terms of information could have
been done by one man in one visit. And I was infuriated. They had
set up the situation where they only do one thing and I get so bored
with it. So with my images of Shakespeare and with the Renaissance
as the complete fruition of a sensibility where you have an actor
who's also a manager and he's also a playwright and he probably
played music, and I'm sure he knew the political scene and he was a
rather good observing wit on the situation. He probably was a bit of

an inventor like Benjamin Franklin. I bet you know at home he could do this or do that. And that to me is a human being.

Q: *We wonder where Shakespeare would fit in Dante's world?*

A: Oh he'd of, Shakespeare would have been in one of the circles of hell. Oh, no doubt about it. Dante'd of put him right into hell! The point of my play is . . . Heaven is now. Hell is now. Purgatory is now. Now, now, now. This second. There's no future. The point of view is that hell is living in the past, purgatory is living in the future, and heaven is living in the present moment. Obviously when you live in the present moment, the only way to do it, there has to be this joyous synthesis of both the past and the future. And, redemption is an individual decision. It has nothing to do with forces outside yourself. It's an individual decision. Camus' end of THE STRANGER where he says: "I will be hung and I will look forward to the howls of execration." The man is redeeming himself despite his sins. That moment in his heart, he's in heaven. The man's in heaven. The world would say he's in hell but he's not. His psyche and his inner spirit—He has found redemption through a decision to accept who he was and to accept the arc of life and the cycles of the seasons, and so it's a decision, it's a bursting inside. The seed bursts. And the recognition of heaven is not tomorrow. It's now.

Q: *You imply that in the process of creativity, one has to surrender.*

A: Absolutely. There is no other alternative. There's no new news. Life is surrender. Nothing but surrender.

Q: *You also imply there is a period of accomplishment, that one has to be protected. The critics and the blows of the world, and so forth, the wild wings, being nurtured and learning how to like it.*

A: Yes. I learned that the hard way. I exposed quite a few to a world. And, they died. It was too young a company to undergo the harshness of the winters of this critical discontent.

Q: *But in a larger context, in terms of where our culture is, and whether we can ever unite language and heroic action, you're still hopeful?*

A: No, it's not just hopeful. It's inevitable. I mean, we're a young country. The realization Europe has made—they realized how they have to treat their performers: one, they can't overpraise them. They cannot be too harsh in their criticism. And second of all, the audiences know that they can't listen to critics too much. Although

345

America has turned around and infected Europe with a star system that is ridiculous and ludicrous. The American system destroyed England's new crop of actors from the beginning of Albert Finney and Peter O'Toole. They came in and swept 'em away—there could have been a crop of actors that were like Olivier, Gielgud, Richardson, and Scofield. But the minute Hollywood moved into the English theatre on a grand scale, it took away Richard Burton. Destroyed him. It took away Peter O'Toole. Destroyed him. Took away Albert Finney and almost destroyed him. These are babies who were killed by success interestingly enough. And our diseased attitude about looking for a hero is: this country is still a baby looking for a hero. Ronald Reagan thinks that he is the hero. I only think of Brecht's statement in GALILEO. One says, "Unhappy is the country that has no hero," and Galileo comes back and says, "Unhappy is the country that *needs* a hero."

Q: *It seems like you've come to the classics as a way of protecting the creative spirit.*

A: Oh, no doubt. I always go to what's lasted up over time. Time is the only test so I go back to reread ULYSSES which is the monumental novel of the Twentieth Century. I keep coming back to it. I go back, even though I don't like his point of view, to Dante. I go back to Shakespeare, Chekhov because they have lasted through time. And the lessons I learn from them are: if I learn them, my work will last through time.

Q: *What do you hope for in terms of poetry and the theatre eventually coming together in some kind of classical form?*

A: Well, a time when the critics finally wake up and realize that theatre is not a place for movies, is not a place even necessarily for plot. It is a place for the word. It is the last haven the word has, the spoken, regardless of character. Regardless of plot structure. One of the best evenings I had was FOR COLORED GIRLS WHO HAVE CONSIDERED SUICIDE WHEN THE RAINBOW IS ENOUGH, an entire evening of poetry. The actors came out and sang it with passion. They sang it right out to the audience. It was a live experience. You knew you were in the theatre. The entire structure of plays that want to lead you to believe that you're not in the theatre. What really pathological concept of theatre! I want to be reminded that these are actors and not the real people! I mean when I go to the opera I don't assume that that's really Pinkerton up there. It's not. It's an artist singing a universal tale of lost love. And, I want to know I'm in the theatre. But the influence of so called "realism" which has not only afflicted America but has afflicted the Soviet Union. They call it Socialist Realism? They were stepping all over Brecht saying, "Shape up. You're not well." There is an insidious attitude that somehow the theatre has to be like the movies. Well, we can't do what the movies do. And the thing about the movies is that they are not realistic, they're surreal. These faces on that screen are bigger than life. They think they're so real up there. They're not. They're gigantic. They're big giants. If you want to be a giant in the theatre you have to say, "I'm in the theatre and I'm not real. I'm an actor singing my heart out."

Q: *So you don't make the distinction between the dramatic on the one side, and the literary on the other?*

A: No. It's the levels of humanity. You have rationalists like Dante and Racine; you have a whole different point of view of the world. If you have humanists, spunky, funky humanists like Shakespeare and Joyce, then you say, "yes," as Molly Bloom says at the end. "Yes," to everything. "Yes, yes, yes."

Q: *Why were you attracted to Dante's structure in writing the play on Shakespeare?*

A: Well, I wanted to take all the classic forms as a set of rules. I made my lines hexameter instead of pentameter (Dante is in pentameter). I made them hexameter because I wanted to play out Racine's Alexandrine. The terza rima was a nod to Dante. The figure of Shakespeare himself was a nod to Shakespeare. So I'm going to take these huge, vast, how you say, archetypes of human achievement and set them up as a standard for myself. I would rather fail at trying the hardest than succeed at the banal. I need that. I find the more creative I am, the more I need discipline for my own sanity. Plus, I find it's more entertaining. It's just much more entertaining. Plus, I didn't know I knew as many words as I did until I gave myself a rhyme scheme. I didn't know I knew that many words and the only way I knew it was there was a rhyme. So the discipline has taught me more about myself; that I do know more than I think I know. My dream is to see it filmed. It requires as vast an imagination, as vast a volubility cinematically as it has in terms of the language. I'm writing a Twentieth Century response to Dante's DIVINE COMEDY and saying, "as much as I love you, Alighieri, I couldn't disagree with you more."

Index

Index

Index

Index

Index

Index